The History of
MAIDSTONE

The Making of a Modern County Town

D1262122

THE HISTORY OF
MAIDSTONE

THE MAKING OF A MODERN COUNTY TOWN

Peter Clark &
Lyn Murfin

ALAN SUTTON PUBLISHING LIMITED

First published in the United Kingdom in 1995
Alan Sutton Publishing Limited
Phoenix Mill · Far Thrupp · Stroud · Gloucestershire
in association with Maidstone Borough Council

Reprinted 1996

British Library Cataloguing in Publication Data

ISBN 0-7509-1103-4

*Cover illustrations: top: a First World War food queue (photograph supplied by Kent
Messenger Group Newspapers); bottom: a view of the Medway (Maidstone Museum and
Art Gallery)*

Typeset in 10/13 Plantin Light.
Typesetting and origination by
Alan Sutton Publishing Limited.
Printed in Great Britain by
Hartnolls, Bodmin, Cornwall.

CONTENTS

FOREWORD

Maidstone, the county town of Kent, has a colourful history, reflecting the changing political, social and economic conditions over the centuries. The knowledgeable observer can still see many clues to the past in the town of today.

As Mayor, I was conscious of the list of office holders dating back to the first charter of 1549, and beyond, representing the tradition of municipal government. Despite too many losses, Maidstone also retains a wealth of old buildings such as the Town Hall, many of them little known to modern citizens.

Given the interesting history it is surprising that Maidstone has not attracted more historians since *The History of Maidstone* by J.M. Russell (1881). Advances in historical studies have not been made widely available to the local reader. As a knowledge of history can stimulate civic pride, as well as shaping future development of communities, the historical perspective needed strengthening locally.

In 1991, Maidstone Borough Council resolved to commission a history of the town. The Centre for Urban History of Leicester University was chosen to undertake the project due to its reputation for excellence in urban studies and because Professor Peter Clark, the distinguished historian at the head of the Centre, brought to the project the necessary blend of knowledge, interest and sensitivity as a Maidstonian.

Let this History stimulate further study and interest in the past of Maidstone, as well as contribute to discussions about developing a vision for the future of the town.

Paul E. Oldham
Mayor of Maidstone 1993/4

PREFACE

One of the earliest references to Maidstone as a county town was in William Newton's *History and Antiquities of Maidstone, The County-Town of Kent*, which was published in London in 1741. Newton was a clergyman and scion of a local trading family and his book, with its useful sections on the corporation, ecclesiastical history and trade, exemplifies the important growth of antiquarian histories in the early Georgian period, written mainly for the genteel classes. By the start of the nineteenth century public interest in the study of towns was spreading to the educated middle classes and in 1809 Walter Rowles, a London ironmonger's clerk, wrote for this audience a rather anodyne *General History of Maidstone*. More controversial was W.R. James' *Charters and Other Documents relating to the King's Town and Parish of Maidstone* (London, 1825) which as well as printing a number of the town's key municipal documents attacked the endemic political corruption of the town's leaders before municipal reform in 1835. Other summary accounts subsequently appeared by Baverstock, Gilbert and Lamprey but the most important of the Victorian histories was J.M. Russell's *History of Maidstone* (Maidstone, 1881). Apparently a journalist by profession, Russell sought in his work to provide 'a full and consecutive history [of the town] . . . exhibiting a picture of its rise and progress, its past and present condition'. The book was a classic example of late nineteenth-century antiquarianism at its best. Russell scoured not only the town records but the British Library and Public Record Office and the volume is replete with information, insights, moral judgements and civic pride. Though it has less to say about the Victorian age than earlier centuries, the book remains an invaluable work of reference.

Another important source book for the study of the town is the edition of *The Records of Maidstone*, published by the corporation in 1926 using material collected by K.S. Martin from the borough and other records then at Maidstone Museum. But, in general terms, post-Russell studies have been rather less original and more photogenic, tending to rely on earlier studies and other secondary literature. None the less, books such as Hilary Watson's *The Book of Maidstone* (Buckingham, 1981) offer attractive, well illustrated guides to the history of the community.

Yet if there has been only limited local research on Maidstone since Russell, the general study of British urban history has been increasingly lively and wide-ranging during the late twentieth century. Since the 1960s there has been an extraordinary upsurge of academic research on British urban development. Although the initial wave of interest, led by Prof. H.J. Dyos, focussed on the Victorian city, in recent years there has been a spate of interest in the medieval and early modern periods, and increasingly on the twentieth century as well. The University of Leicester has been an active centre of this new research.

Our new history of Maidstone, which has been commissioned by Maidstone Borough Council, is intended as a detailed account of the town from early times to the mid-twentieth century. We hope that the volume will be of major value to local people interested in the complex evolution of their present-day community. But we also believe that the study of this important county town will have a wide general appeal. In writing it we have sought to combine the insights and interests of a local community study with the current research approaches and methods of urban historians. Implicit is a concern to describe and understand Maidstone's history as a county centre in a wider comparative framework, comparing the community's experience with that of other British cities and towns, with the aim of trying to comprehend what was special about the making of this modern county town. The volume explores the principal changes in the population, economy, social organisation, politics and government as well as the cultural life of the community during the main phases of its development.

The book owes its origin to the proposal of Maidstone Borough Council for an authoritative history of the town and the council must be applauded for its imaginative support of this major project. Funding from the council has enabled the employment of a research officer, Dr Lyn Murfin, on the project for three years from 1991. We are particularly indebted to the encouragement and help provided on numerous occasions by Councillor Paul Oldham (mayor 1993/4). Other people have also made important contributions to the successful completion of this project. We are grateful to: Brian Weddell, Henry Middleton and Richard Stutely at Maidstone Museum for help with illustrations, sources and much else; Kath Topping and her colleagues at the Kent Archives Office for access to the borough records and other materials; Janice Cordwell, Christel Pobgee and Lesley Spencer at the Maidstone Reference Library; the vicar of All Saints, Maidstone, Christopher Morgan-Jones, for access to the parish registers; the Kent Archaeological Society for access to their library; Mr Barry Langston and former students at Maidstone Grammar School for work on the parish registers. For the pre-Norman period we are grateful to: Dr Harold Fox of Leicester University and Claire Mason of Maidstone Museum for advice; Dr David Mattingley, Dr Neil Christie and Dr Richard Pollard of Leicester University and Dr John Williams and Liz Dyson of Heritage Conservation, Kent County Council, for helpful comments on the draft text; Richard Cross of the Canterbury Archaeological Trust and Sally Howard and the staff of the Planning Department, Kent County Council for providing Sites and Monuments Record listings; Mark Houliston of Canterbury Archaeological Trust for information about the Mount Roman Villa excavations in 1994; Sally Jones for preparing the map of Roman sites and finds. For the map of the medieval town in Chapter Two and advice on the early development of the town we are heavily indebted to Dr Terry Slater of the University of Birmingham. For Chapters Nine and Ten, we are indebted to Mr George Blake, Miss Funnell, Mrs Vera Nicholson, Mrs Peggy Smith, Mrs R. Waters, Mr P.C. Webb, Mr Douglas Elphee, Mrs K. McLoughlin and others who preferred to remain anonymous, for their oral testimony about twentieth-century Maidstone; Miss Joyce Brett and Mrs P. Whale for kindly sending their written reminiscences; Mr H.R. Bristow, Mr M.J. Fuller and other members of the Maidstone Industrial Archaeology Group for access to their unpublished work; the Kent County Council and the *Kent Messenger* for permission to use photographs and other material in its collections; Alistair Milne, John Welshman, Kate Crispin at the Centre for Urban History, Leicester University for their assistance; Peter Clifford at Alan Sutton for his support for the book; and to David Elphee, Louise Clark, Mrs M. Stutely, Mrs V. Stutely, Dr Anne Hardy, Dr R. Borthwick and Jatinder Sohal for a large miscellany of kindnesses.

The book has been planned, revised and drawn together by Peter Clark. Most of the research on the period after 1700 was carried out by Dr Lyn Murfin of Leicester University who also drafted Chapters Six to Nine; Dr David Reeder (Leicester University) has taken an active part in revising and editing the chapters on the nineteenth and twentieth centuries as well as researching and writing sections on education and public health. Part of Chapter One (on the pre-Norman period) was written by Crispin Flower, formerly of Leicester University; Chapter Two has been contributed by Dr Richard Holt of Birmingham University. The remainder has been researched and written by Peter Clark. In order to ensure that the book is accessible to general readers, detailed source references in the footnotes have been kept to the minimum, but each chapter has a bibliographical note outlining the principal records and materials used in the study to help future research. For this study is not intended as a historical tombstone. Rather we hope that it will stimulate more studies and work by local and academic historians, enlarging, revising and extending our analysis.

Chapter One

INTRODUCTION

The first known description of Maidstone was written by the topographer John Leland in Henry VIII's reign who referred to it briefly as 'a market town of one long street well builded and full of inns'. The Elizabethan William Lambarde in his *Perambulation of Kent* in 1576 was also fairly summary in his account, but over the next century descriptions of the town were increasingly frequent and fulsome, reflecting Maidstone's growing importance in the shire. In the 1650s Richard Kilburne praised it as 'a sweet, large and populous town' and these views were echoed a decade later by that inveterate diarist Samuel Pepys who found it 'very pretty as most towns I ever saw', though not big. During the expansive Georgian era observers like Daniel Defoe, William Newton and Richard Pococke were even more enthusiastic in their comments, lauding Maidstone for its trade, prosperity and sociable entertainments. Under Queen Victoria, however, there were less enthusiastic reviews, as the town faced new economic and social challenges. H.S. Vaughan in the 1890s averred that despite its antiquity Maidstone 'is not keenly interesting . . . [due to] its intensely commercial and vulgar qualities' with the town suffering from the malign influence of the metropolis. Another report soon after was no more flattering, dismissing it as 'fairly picturesque but not really beautiful . . . an old county-town atmosphere pervades it'. After the First World War, however, visitors turned more favourable again, as economic vitality returned. One writer in 1936 described it as 'the great centre-point of Kent . . . the finest town on the Medway, a twentieth century hive of life . . . Maidstone draws all Kent to it'. A few years later we hear how the town is 'crammed to bursting point with traffic, reflect[ing] the prosperity of the "Garden of England".'

Maidstone was an important focus of settlement from pre-Roman times, but, as these contemporary accounts show, the town's development did not follow a simple inexorable pathway to prosperity; rather there were distinctive phases in its evolution associated with changes in the community's economic, political and cultural position in the local area, county and nation. As we shall see, our evidence suggests that Maidstone did not become a real town until the start of the thirteenth century, but even in pre-historic times there was considerable activity in the fertile Medway valley. By the first century BC, during the Belgic period, a major hill fort with defensive earthworks was located near the site of the modern town, along with coins and wheel-made pottery. During the Roman occupation from AD 43 Maidstone, standing at the juncture of the Medway with the important Roman road from Rochester to the South Coast (Stone Street), seems to have been the hub of extensive but diffuse rural settlement, with numerous villas and masonry buildings. After the Romans withdrew in the fifth century the picture is darker with little evidence of any continuity of settlement. But from the seventh century Maidstone was the centre of a major estate of the Archbishop of Canterbury and had the important minster church of St Mary's (later All Saints), promoting and sustaining the Christian faith in the area.

Though the size and functions of Anglo-Saxon Maidstone are still open to discussion, by the time of Domesday Book in 1086 the place was clearly a bustling centre of craft and religious activity on the Medway. As we shall find in Chapter Two, with one of the wealthiest parish churches in Kent, Maidstone probably had an informal Sunday market as well as regular manorial courts. Over the next two centuries England's population grew markedly, generating a rising volume of trade, linked with a sharp increase in the number of English towns. Maidstone emerges as a recognised town soon after 1200, receiving charters for its market and fair a few decades later. The regular layout of the town suggests that it may have been planned by the Archbishop of Canterbury, the manorial lord. In the late Middle Ages the town consolidated its importance, with the foundation of a large collegiate church (All Saints) in the 1390s and the establishment before 1445 of the important religious and social fraternity of Corpus Christi, drawing its membership from the better-off classes of town and countryside. By the fifteenth century the town had a range of small-scale industries (including stone quarries) and busy markets and fairs. But its population remained small and the community could hardly compare with the bigger chartered and walled towns of Kent such as Rochester, Canterbury and the Cinque Ports. Though the ancient meeting place was at nearby Penenden Heath from the eleventh century (if not before) the town had yet to assume any major county role.

The transformation of this small manorial market town into a buoyant county town and borough began in the sixteenth century. The Reformation ended the Archbishop's dominance over the town and in 1549 a charter of incorporation, giving it municipal status, was granted by Edward VI. Chapter Three argues that the town's population grew steadily during the decades before the English Civil War and its economic world was increasingly diversified. In the 1560s the arrival of Protestant refugees from the Low Countries boosted the textile industry, while paper-making and wholesale brewing appeared after 1600 – two of the town's leading manufactures into the twentieth century. Though municipal government got off to a shaky start (with the loss of the charter under Queen Mary), by the reign of James I the corporation was pursuing an active policy of civic and religious improvement. The town's grammar school was founded in 1549 and under the early Stuart kings Maidstone became a prominent Puritan centre. Despite the damage and destruction caused by the Battle of Maidstone in 1648, as royalist and parliamentary armies fought over the town during the second Civil War, Maidstone was firmly established by the 1650s as the leading administrative town in West Kent.

None the less, as we shall discover in Chapters Four and Five, it was the Georgian age which marked the town's heyday before the twentieth century. Its markets and shops prospered from rising living standards for many better-off people and skilled workers, its specialist industries, notably brewing and paper-making, flourished. Its inns and public houses, lawyers, doctors and teachers, printers and booksellers served a multitude of customers from town and countryside. In the eighteenth century Maidstone was increasingly regarded as the county town of Kent with a kaleidoscope of administrative, political and fashionable social activities – from balls and assemblies to concerts, clubs and cockfights; there was also an extensive repertoire of more popular leisure activity for the lower orders. Although civic and parliamentary politics were pervaded by party conflict and corruption, (leading to the forfeiture of the charter between 1742 and 1747) the Georgian town witnessed impressive civic improvements, not least the erection of the neo-classical town hall in 1764. By the end of the century urban growth was generating new social problems and exacerbating old ones; from the 1790s one sees waves of social distress and lower-class protest. By the early nineteenth century, however, Maidstone had replaced Canterbury as the biggest and most important town in the county.

Up to this time the topographical heartland of the town remained much as it had been in the Middle Ages, focused around the old Roman road (Week Street and Stone Street), the main streets down to the river (Earl Street and High Street), and near to the church (Knightrider Street). The nineteenth century saw accelerating expansion in the built up area of the town, reaching out in all directions, but most strikingly across the river to the hitherto less populated West Borough, where there was large-scale suburban development. This physical growth was paralleled by a surge in the town's population from about 8,027 in 1801 to 20,740 in 1851 and 33,516 in 1901; just before the First World War the figure had reached 35,475 people. The making of Victorian and Edwardian Maidstone is discussed in Chapters Six to Eight.

While the rate of population increase was lower than in the great manufacturing cities, the town's demographic advance produced many social, environmental and other problems for the community. These problems were aggravated by the inability of the local economy to sustain all the momentum and prosperity so notable in the Georgian era. Staple industries such as paper-making and brewing saw continued progress and the period was marked by the emergence of the engineering sector and, later on, the food processing trades. The town's shops multiplied in number and size, but for the wealthy classes in town and countryside there were the powerful competing attractions of the brilliantly lit emporia on Oxford Street and Regent Street. Other difficulties appeared. As the countryside became increasingly civilised the landed classes spent less time in the town. The recession in British agriculture from the 1870s did not affect the mid-Kent area as badly as other regions, with a good deal of diversification into hop and fruit growing; but the town market may have suffered from the decline in grain and sheep raising in its hinterland. More positive for future growth was the establishment of the Kent County Council in Maidstone in 1889, which after a small start had nearly 200 employees by 1914, amplifying Maidstone's importance as the county town.

Victorian Maidstone became a predominantly middle-class, even a bourgeois town. The response to the town's many and growing problems and needs – as for instance schooling – often relied heavily on a wide variety of voluntary, philanthropic and private action. It was only towards the end of the century that municipal intervention was increasingly crucial in ensuring a wide range of public services for the population, though without any pretence to the grand civic style of the great provincial cities. Self-help also played an important part in other spheres of town life with Maidstone's Victorian image designed and decorated by an efflorescence of churches, religious bodies and voluntary associations.

The First World War inaugurated a new phase in the town's development, as will be evident from Chapter Nine. The inter-war years witnessed a significant boost to the urban economy as the old manufacturing towns of the North went into decline and there was a shift of industrial output towards the smaller urban centres of southern England. In Maidstone established industries such as engineering diversified and were complemented by the advance of retailing and service trades, and the growth of the house-building industry. Urban employment was also stimulated by a further expansion of the county council and borough council. All this helped the town to weather the inter-war recessions without acute unemployment or deprivation. And yet as the town's prosperity burgeoned, its older sense of urban identity was challenged. Staple industries such as paper-manufacture started to move further down the Medway; a growing proportion of the population lived in new council and private housing estates on the urban outskirts; and the town's churches and voluntary societies, pillars of the Victorian community, experienced a loss of support, with mounting competition from new leisure activities particularly the cinema and motor car. In all these ways Maidstone was becoming integrated into a wider economic, social and cultural world. At the same time, the town responded positively to these challenges and through a combination of revived prosperity, municipal action and new forms of cultural attraction retained much of its traditional communal coherence and civic identity as a county town – an identity in some ways strengthened by the Second World War. After the war the pressures accelerated with major changes in the urban economy, the rise of commuting, the growing impact of central government and the county council on municipal administration. However, in several policy areas particularly housing, the borough council maintained its authority up to and beyond local government reorganisation in 1974 and was able to influence the town's prosperous image in a rapidly changing and generally dynamic regional economy.

Yet while there were important and distinct stages in the town's advance from a medieval market town to an increasingly suburbanised county and commuter town in the late twentieth century, major continuities are evident as well. Of these the most obvious was the physical site in the fertile Medway valley at one of the major river crossing places near to Stone Street. In early times settlement was dispersed around this strategic nexus and Anglo-Saxon Maidstone probably had several separate centres of activity – a quite common phenomenon in embryonic communities. But the planned town of the thirteenth century gave an essential topographical unity to the core of the town which has survived into the twentieth century.

Other less tangible continuities have also been influential in shaping and forming the town. Even before it became a recognised urban centre, Maidstone with its archiepiscopal manor and minster church served a wider area of peasant communities in the Medway valley and beyond. This relationship was given an explicit economic dimension with the development by the twelfth century of the town market, at which rural producers exchanged surplus goods for urban wares and services. With the growing exploitation of the Weald in the later Middle Ages this marketing hinterland expanded and by the Georgian era Maidstone was well-established as the principal commercial entrepôt in West Kent, supplying villages and market towns as far as Sussex.

Part of the explanation for Maidstone's commercial success was the river. Though the upper Medway did not become navigable until the mid-eighteenth century, the lower reaches were always accessible to small ships and ensured a transport lifeline to the North Kent towns, London, East Anglia and the continent. The Medway enabled shipments of stone from Roman and medieval times; in later centuries it facilitated the timber, paper and brewing trades. Only with the arrival of the railway in the 1840s did the river's importance start to ebb.

Not all of Maidstone's relations with the wider world were harmonious. As the town expanded it came into competition with other urban centres – with neighbouring market towns and bigger cities such as Rochester and Canterbury. The rise of Maidstone in the eighteenth century was paralleled by the economic and social stagnation of Canterbury – a stagnation which continued until after the Second World War. However, with one city – London – there could be no effective competition – at least from the seventeenth century. The fifteen-fold increase in the capital's population from the sixteenth to the late eighteenth century, reaching nearly a million in 1801, offered a constellation of economic opportunities to Maidstone – as a local market for metropolitan food supplies and as a supplier of specialist consumer wares. But metropolitan economic power posed many challenges. It overwhelmed the town's cloth market before 1600, while the grain market was crowded with merchants squeezing out local buyers. Yet for much of the period into the nineteenth century the relationship was mutually beneficial. In the Georgian era, for instance, though great county grandees resorted to the costly social pleasures of the West End, their lesser landed cousins contented themselves with more modest (and cheaper) London-style entertainments by the Medway. In the modern period the relationship with the capital became more unbalanced as the national economy and cultural world, mediated through London, steadily invaded the local community. By the 1890s national chain stores were competing hard with local retailers. In the early twentieth century growing numbers of middle-class residents went on shopping excursions to London by train. During the Second World War and after, working men and their wives took the train or coach to the capital to see popular 'shows' by Ivor Novello as well as American musicals. Since the Second World War the metropolitan impact in Maidstone as elsewhere in the Home Counties has become highly pervasive.

As will be obvious, Maidstone's relationship with the county community has also had a powerful influence on its development. Already in the Middle Ages county courts and other meetings, including those for the election of the knights of the shire (county MPs), were held at nearby Penenden Heath. From Elizabeth's reign meetings of county sessions and assizes were increasingly held at Maidstone, bringing county justices, lawyers and litigants to town, and by the eighteenth century the town's administrative pre-eminence as the county town was buttressed by Maidstone's fashionability as a gathering place for the county's upper classes. While this latter function declined after 1800, Maidstone's administrative importance steadily grew in the nineteenth century and was confirmed by the arrival of the county council. As in other county towns, relations with the shire authorities were not always harmonious. In James I's reign the county justices threatened to move county meetings to Rochester after a clash with the corporation, though the dispute was quickly patched up.

Another vital relationship highlighted in this study is that between the town and the central government. In 1549 the Crown endowed the community with a royal charter and all the paraphernalia of municipal institutions, setting it apart from the rest of the small market towns in the area. In the 1560s the government established a community of foreign refugees in the town which helped to boost the town's economy. But during Charles I's reign, as we shall see in Chapter Three, there was mounting conflict between Maidstone's Puritan magistrates and the state and ecclesiastical authorities. In 1649 Andrew Broughton, then mayor, signed the king's death warrant. After the Restoration, despite sporadic interference by Charles II and his brother James II, the town experienced only minimal intervention by the central government. But in 1835 the town's charter and unreformed corporation were swept away by the Municipal Reform Act and in the later nineteenth century state intervention began to have a significant impact on municipal policy. This increased dramatically during the twentieth century, especially after the Second World War.

As this book makes clear, Maidstone's historical development has been wrought and affected by the interaction of many pressures – forces both for continuity and change. Such a study of the town's history raises many issues. For some questions, for instance concerning the way that ordinary townspeople viewed their community, whether in times of prosperity or crisis, how they regarded the town council or outsiders, we can often only guess at the answers. Too often there is a lack of documentation about the popular and private experience of town life in the past, though for the twentieth century we have tried to overcome this deficiency through detailed interviews with older inhabitants. For other topics and questions, however, the documentation for Maidstone is fortunately very extensive. In this study we have sought to deploy a wide range of archival, printed and other material from local and national sources to provide a systematic analysis of the town's demographic, economic, social, political, physical and cultural development in the main periods of its history up to the Second World War.

But there is no attempt here to provide a comprehensive encyclopaedia of the town's past, even if that were possible. Rather we have endeavoured to address two broad underlying questions. Firstly, how during this extended period of urban development from the twelfth century to the twentieth century the town's inhabitants sought to create and define, against a backcloth of economic, social, spatial and other changes, their own communal image and collective identities, both for themselves and the outside world. Understanding the process by which communities make and re-make their urban image is important not only for the light it sheds on a particular urban world, but because it helps us to see that community in the wider, comparative context of British towns as a whole. For from the seventeenth century if not earlier Maidstone was part of a more and more integrated system of urban communities, embracing the enormous metropolis of London, regional capitals like Bristol and Norwich and later Manchester and Birmingham, traditional middle-rank shire towns, burgeoning manufacturing and resort centres, and diminutive market towns. One of our main interests, as we have already said, is in the competing and complementary relations with other towns in local and regional networks. But we must also ask, and this is the second fundamental question of the study, how Maidstone's experience compares with that of other English towns in general, and in particular with the hundred or so other middle-rank county towns up and down the country. As a class, England's county towns have not received the attention they deserve, especially for the modern period, and this work may therefore help illuminate the resilience and strength of those important communities which have acted as the backbone of the traditional English urban system up to recent times. But at this point we must go back to the beginning.

The pre-history

A wealth of archaeological finds, most of them made by chance through quarrying, building and even digging the garden, show that humans have lived in the Maidstone area for up to 400,000 years. Handaxes and other Palaeolithic flint implements have been found in profusion in the Medway gravels, particularly at Aylesford, where the remains of mammoth, woolly rhinoceros, elephant, lion and red deer give some idea of contemporary fauna. Modern humans (*Homo Sapiens Sapiens*) first appeared in Europe in the Upper Palaeolithic period (from *c.* 40,000 BC), but there is no evidence for their presence in West Kent until the Mesolithic, when the glacial ice had retreated for the last time.[1] The presence of Mesolithic hunter-gatherers in the Medway valley is demonstrated by finds of their characteristic tools, including flint picks, tranchet axes/adzes, hammer stones, flakes, blades and scrapers.

The transition to a sedentary agricultural way of life began in the late fifth millenium BC, with the introduction of domesticated animals and the cultivation of crops in small forest clearings. This radical change in subsistence methods and social organisation was accompanied by changes in material culture, notably the introduction of pottery and implements of polished stone, and by the construction of impressive enclosures and funerary monuments. The Medway valley was an ideal location for these early farmers, due to the good arable soils and plentiful water sources, and numerous polished stone axes and flint implements have been discovered in Maidstone and the surrounding parishes. More dramatic testimony to the achievements of the Neolithic period are the Medway megaliths. About 3 miles north of Maidstone are the Countless Stones, Kit's Coty House, the Coffin Stone, Smythe's Megalith and the Upper White Horse Stone, while 5 miles to the west of these are the Addington Long Barrow, the Chestnuts, and the barrow at Coldrum. Very little is known about the precise dating and function of these megalithic structures but Kit's Coty House, Addington, Coldrum and Chestnuts were all tombs of a form apparently unique in Britain, with a stone chamber in the east end and a covering mound. The Medway megaliths were not simply tombs, however; their construction, requiring enormous investments of communal labour, and their ceremonial use and reuse over many hundreds of years must have played a central role in expressing the ideologies and beliefs of the local farming communities.

The later third millenium BC saw the appearance of a new and distinctive type of drinking vessel in the archaeological record, examples of which have been found at Upper Fant Road, Hermitage Farm and Beaconsfield Road, Tovil. These 'beakers', which were often placed in graves, and may originally have held mead and other alcoholic drinks, are found in varying styles over most of Europe. It is likely that their arrival in Britain and the Medway area reflected a general increase in long-distance cultural contact and trade with the continent in this period.

Metal-working techniques, initially using copper but later adding tin to make the harder metal bronze, reached Britain by the late third millenium BC. A bronze flat axe and two daggers from a grave at Aylesford represent the earliest metal implements in the Maidstone area; they were produced by pouring the molten metal into simple one-piece open stone moulds. The widespread use of flint continued for nearly a thousand years, but from around 1400 BC bronze was used for the majority of tools and weapons. Bronze Age finds in Kent are concentrated in river valleys, particularly the Medway. Two palstaves have been found in Maidstone, while socketed and flanged axes, a sword, and two spearheads have been discovered in Aylesford and Bearsted. In addition, nine gold torcs and an armlet, most of which seem to have been deliberately broken, and four gold armlets in a box, were found in the Medway in 1861; these remarkable finds, which were almost certainly cast into the river as votive offerings, testify to the wealth of the local Bronze Age elite, and also to the increasing social differentiation and competition which characterised the period. Although British smiths began using iron from around 650 BC, the Maidstone area has produced little evidence for Iron Age occupation until the first century BC, when dramatic changes in material culture, society and economy occurred with the advent of the 'Belgic' culture.

The Belgic cremation urns found in the extensive cemetery at Aylesford, and at sites such as Allington and Hermitage Chapel, Maidstone, represent the first wheel-made pottery in Britain, and show marked similarities with forms produced in parts of Roman Gaul. Explanations for this important development in ceramic technology, and for the appearance of Gallo-Belgic coins in Kent in the early first century BC, have traditionally referred to the famous passage in Caesar's *De Bello Gallico*, in which he spoke of 'Belgic immigrants who came to plunder and make war . . . and later settled down to till the soil'. There can be little doubt that a migration of some sort occurred in the early first century, but much of the archaeological evidence may also be due to indigenous development and contact with the Roman world. Thus it has been suggested that many of the early Gallo-Belgic coins were brought into the south-east by British mercenaries, known to have assisted the Gaulish tribes in their resistance to Caesar. As well as the many urned cremation burials, several 'potin' coins,[2] Gallo-Belgic imports, and locally produced silver and gold copies have been found in Maidstone and the surrounding parishes; particularly notable is the concentration in Boxley parish, where no less than thirty-four coins, including a hoard of twenty potin coins, have been unearthed, mainly on the escarpment of the Downs near the pre-historic Pilgrims' Way and North Downs Way.

After the invasions of 55 and 54 BC, Caesar wrote that he had encountered four kings in Kent, whose forces had opposed him throughout the campaign. Beyond this, however, very little is known of the inhabitants and political organisation of Kent, except to suggest that both Belgic and indigenous elements were present. The hostility of the Kentish tribes to Caesar appears to have turned the area into something of a commercial backwater in comparison to areas north of the Thames, where the aristocracy accumulated wealth through treaties and trading relationships with the Roman empire. Kent produced few luxury imported goods from this period; the obvious exceptions coming from three Belgic burials at Aylesford containing fine bronze tableware and a wood and bronze bucket.

In terms of settlement, the most important development of the pre-Roman period in Kent was the construction of three fortified camps, or *oppida*, including one at Quarry Wood, 2 miles south of Maidstone (see Figure 1; site 23). This important fortified site, which was probably constructed in the early 1st century AD, is likely to have served as a defensive retreat in times of war or perceived threat, and may also have been a focus for craft and production industries. The amphora handle found on the site, and the two amphorae found nearby in a possible grave, confirm that the *oppidum* was involved in trade with the Roman world, and illustrate the Celtic liking for wine so well attested by Classical writers. Perhaps the most interesting feature of the Quarry Wood Camp is the series of defensive earthworks which appear to have delimited a substantial territory around it. Traces have been found to the north and east, but the most impressive remains lie around a half mile to the south of the settlement, where the bank and ditch run along the escarpment for a distance of nearly three miles, from Linton Park to Chart Corner. From the limited dating evidence it seems that Quarry Wood Camp was only occupied for a short time, and it has been suggested that its abandonment was associated with a shift in power to Rochester, where the discovery of coin-moulds implies a centre of some importance in the pre-Roman period.

During the hundred years following Caesar's invasions, Kent became embroiled in a series of dynastic upheavals and power struggles between philo- and anti-Roman factions. The reigns and territories of the various kings can be tentatively traced by the distribution of their coins, and examples dedicated to Tasciovanus and Dubnovellaunus, who ruled over parts of Kent at around the turn of the millenium, have been found at Aylesford and Boughton Monchelsea respectively. A gold 'stater' found at Coxheath was dedicated to Cunobelinus, king of Essex and Kent, whose reign from *c.* AD 10 marked a period of relative stability in the region. However, on his death in AD 40, the anti-Roman faction, led by Togodumnus and Caratacus, returned to power; the subsequent flight from Britain, first of Cunobelinus's son and then of the pro-Roman king Verica to seek protection and assistance from Rome provided the new Emperor Claudius with the diplomatic pretext to invade.

The Roman period

In AD 43 four legions led by Aulus Plautius landed in Kent, quickly overcoming local opposition after a two-day battle by the River Medway. Resistance in the south-east was short-lived, and the Romans imposed their authority by creating the unified civitas of the *Cantiaci*, with its capital at Canterbury (*Durovernum*), and a second important administrative town at Rochester (*Durobrivae*). Following the invasion, the Roman army constructed Watling Street, which ran from Richborough fort through Canterbury and Rochester, and ultimately to the provincial capital at London. The road running southwards from Rochester to Maidstone and the Hastings area (Stone Street), which provided access to the iron-producing areas of the Weald, was probably added shortly after.

Romano-British buildings, burials and artefacts found in the vicinity of Maidstone are plotted in Figure 1. The status of Maidstone in the Roman period has been the subject of much debate. Early arguments that it was a small town, or *vicus*, were inspired by the discoveries of Roman buildings at the Mount, Allington and Little Buckland, and by the belief that present-day 'Week' Street is a corruption of Anglo-Saxon *wyke*, deriving from the Latin *vicus*. The apparent clustering of coins and other finds in the area of the modern town has also been used to support this interpretation, but this pattern may simply reflect the level of modern building development, quarrying and resulting chance finds, rather than any underlying archaeological reality. As can be seen in Figure 1, the distribution of known villas and masonry buildings actually reveals a more diffuse spread of settlement, focusing in particular along the River Medway and the Roman road. It is of course still possible that Roman buildings, such as a *mansio*, remain to be discovered beneath the streets and buildings of the modern town but on present evidence we can only say that Maidstone was probably the focal point of a dispersed and wealthy agricultural community, and that, by merit of its location on both river and road, it may have fulfilled some function as a central place within the broader settlement pattern.

Of the many known villas and masonry buildings in the Maidstone area, particular mention must be made of the Mount villa (Figure 1; site 1), which occupies a commanding position on the eastern side of the Medway, about 200 yards north-west of the East Station. The south wing was excavated in 1843, after part of the river bank had collapsed to reveal masonry, and in the 1970s proposed development led to further excavations, which helped to elucidate the overall plan and chronology of the villa.[3] Further major excavations were carried out in the first quarter of 1994,[4] ahead of improvements to the Maidstone northern approach road, and, while the results of this project have not at this time been fully analysed, they have already shed new light on the history of this important site. Built of local ragstone, the main villa structure was probably constructed in the later second century, and was around 67 metres long by 27 metres wide. Aligned roughly parallel to the river, the building consisted of two wings linked by a double range of rooms, and probably also had a portico on the eastern side. Several rooms had floors of *opus signinum*[5] or of red tile embedded in black cement in a crude mosaic effect, and two rooms in the north wing were equipped with hypocaust heating systems. After various alterations, the villa seems to have been demolished by the end of the third century, though some signs of occupation in the immediate vicinity continue into the fourth century. Finds from the excavations revealed evidence for cloth-making and the manufacture of pins from red deer antler, and also included a pair of copper alloy tweezers, an iron hammer, a bracelet, and an iron candle-holder.

The 1994 excavations, as well as revising earlier interpretations of the villa's layout, made clear that this was not the first major building to occupy the site. At least three phases of early Roman timber structures were uncovered, the second including four bays of a substantial aisled building. The evidence is not yet conclusive, but it is possible that this was the first 'villa' on the site, later replaced in grander style by the ragstone 'winged corridor' construction.

Unlike the Eccles villa near Aylesford, which was constructed on a palatial scale soon after the invasion and may have belonged to a philo-Roman aristocrat or Roman official, villa-estates such as the Mount were usually the property of native landowners. From the second century onwards, the *pax Romana* and the expanding military and urban markets allowed many of the native elite to accumulate wealth through farming, and to demonstrate their status by erecting large residences in the

Roman style. The clustering of villas along the Medway and on the Roman road reflects the degree to which the livelihood and wealth of these villa-estates depended on easy access to external markets, such as Canterbury, Rochester and London. As well as its rich arable soil, another important resource in the Maidstone area was ragstone, which was used to construct the villas at the Mount and Barton Road (site 3) in Maidstone, and the bath-house at Boughton Monchelsea (site 11). Ragstone from local quarries was also employed in the defensive wall of London in the late second or early third century, transported by barge via the Medway and Thames.

The many villas and masonry buildings in the Maidstone area represent only the top of the settlement hierarchy; the landscape around these high-status sites would have contained many 'peasant' houses and agricultural buildings, traces of which

KEY to FIGURE 1 – Roman Finds in the Maidstone area

Site Number	Description
1	The Mount villa – see text for description.
2	Possible Roman building discovered during building at the corner of Week Street and High Street.
3	Barton Road villa: foundations of substantial Roman villa excavated in 1870, featuring hypocausts, an octagonal tower, and a long room with an apsidal end and a floor of red and white *tesserae* in herring bone pattern.
4	Foundations of Roman building, found while cutting drain in 1893.
5	West Borough Roman cemetery: see text for description.
6	Walled cemetery, East Barming: see text for description.
7	Roman villa: foundations, pottery, bricks, tiles and three coins found in 1797, about 100 yards east-south-east of East Barming church.
8	Roman building, possibly a villa, with substantial foundations and a cistern, partially excavated in 1879.
9	Foundations of Roman villa, with third-century copper coin, found in 1838.
10	Probable Roman building found near Pimp's Court.
11	Roman bath-house, partially excavated in 1841, with Samian pottery, fibulae, glass, coins (first- to fourth-century Roman) and animal bones. British and Gaulish coins also found.
12	Roman foundations found 1933, visible in 1960 as concentration of ragstone fragments, brick, tile and pottery in ploughsoil.
13	Walled cemetery, Boughton Monchelsea: see text for description.
14	Roman foundations found 1840.
15	Foundations of an apparently extensive Roman villa found while planting an orchard in *c.* 1835.
16	Probable site of Roman building: four large hypocaust tiles, found 1844.
17	Probable Roman building at Boxley Abbey: Roman roofing-tiles, box-tiles and *opus signinum* incorporated in foundations of church.
18	Bronze figure of Mercury and two brass coins found *c.* 1826.
19	Bronze statuette of Sylvanus, 2 inches long, found buried with Roman lamp in *c.* 1820.
20	Hoard of twenty-two coins of Tetricus in third-century urn, with 'Castor ware' beaker, found 1907.
21	Hoard of 58 *sestertiae* of Emperors Domitian (AD 81–96) to Commodus (AD 177–192), found in 1935 beneath the pavement on the north side of Church Street.
22	Earthwork enclosure (about 10 ha.), at Mangravet (now largely lost to development). Excavations in 1927 failed to produce dating evidence, but probably Roman (based on alignment with Roman road); function unknown, but possibly a pasture ranch or enclosed settlement site.
23	Quarry Wood Camp – Belgic *oppidum*. See text for description.

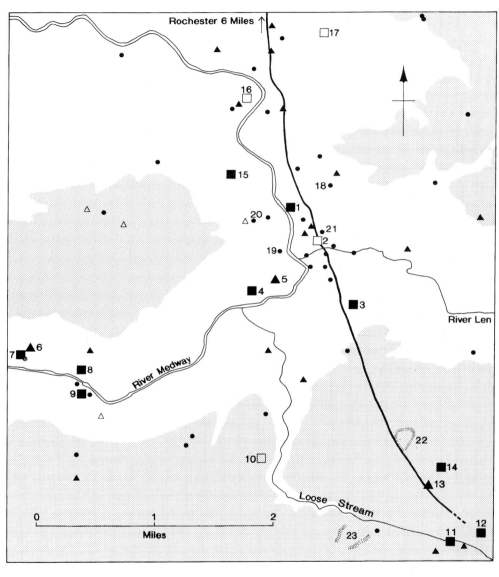

Rochester 6 Miles ↑

River Len

River Medway

Loose Stream

0   1   2
Miles

■ Villa/masonry building.
□ Probable villa/masonry building.
▲ Cemetery.
▲ Burials.
△ Probable burials.
● Other finds.

＼ Roman road.
⸫⸫ Earthworks.
░ Land over 200 ft.

Fig. 1   Roman sites in the Maidstone area.

have yet to be discovered. Romano-British burials, on the other hand, have often survived and been discovered in great numbers in the area (see Figure 1). Of particular importance are three sites: the walled cemeteries near East Barming church (site 6) and on the Roman road near Boughton Monchelsea (site 13), and the cemetery in West Borough, between the old boys' grammar school and the West Station (site 5). Walled cemeteries are comparatively rare in Britain, the majority occurring in Kent, and they seem to have been high-status sites, restricted to use by one or more neighbouring villas. That at East Barming, almost certainly associated with the adjacent villa (site 7), was discovered in 1797 and was found to contain cremation urns and fragments of a late Roman sarcophagus. The walled cemetery on the Roman road in Boughton Monchelsea was also located near a Roman villa (site 14), and contained two large ragstone tombs decorated with painted plaster. Excavations in 1842 also revealed seven cremation burials, along with pottery, glass and bronze vessels, iron lamps, two amphorae, and the charcoal remains of funeral pyres. The West Borough cemetery was found in 1859–60, and excavations in the eastern part produced about 150 cremation burials and 25–30 inhumations; no dating evidence is available, but in general the practice of cremating the dead was dominant until the late third and fourth centuries, when inhumation gradually became the norm. Many of the burials included coins, possibly as payments to Charon, who was believed to ferry the souls of the dead across the River Styx. Religion in Roman Britain was highly eclectic, including and often combining indigenous, Roman and other imported cults. No temple sites are known in the Maidstone area, but evidence for the private worship of classical deities is provided by the bronze figurines of Mercury and Sylvanus (sites 18 and 19), the latter found buried with a lamp in a garden beside St Peter's Hospital in around 1820.

The later fourth century witnessed a gradual decline in the economy and administration of Roman Kent. The reasons for this process are not entirely clear, though the abandonment of many villas in the south east seems to have been linked to the increase in Saxon and Frankish raiding. More important perhaps was the state of political and military upheaval in Rome and the empire as a whole, since increasing numbers of troops were withdrawn from Britain to support rival 'Emperors' and to counter the barbarian invasions on the continent. Certain aspects of Roman culture persisted into the fifth century, but by the time the last Roman legions were withdrawn by the newly elected British Emperor Constantine III in AD 407, the market economy, the coinage system, the centralised industries, and many other trappings of Roman civilisation had effectively disappeared.

The Anglo-Saxon period

By the fifth century AD the Medway valley and Maidstone area had been settled and farmed for around 4,000 years. However, this was more than just a convenient and fertile area for settlement. The remarkable clustering of the Medway megaliths, the Iron Age fort at Quarry Wood, and the importance of Penenden Heath as an

ancient meeting place, suggests that from a very early period the area had become
the focal point of a wider region. The proximity of the Pilgrim's Way, providing
access to long-distance trade routes and cultural contacts, must have contributed in
this respect, but equally important was the dual role played by the River Medway
itself. Cutting through the line of the Downs, the river not only provided a means of
transport and trade, but also probably represented a physical and symbolic
boundary. As we shall see below, the Medway formed the western limit of the Jutish
kingdom, and it is possible that the social and cognitive division between 'Men of
Kent' and 'Kentish Men' originated in this period or even earlier.

Many factors contributed to the continued importance of this fertile valley
beneath the Downs, but what prompted the rise of the settlement of Maidstone
itself? The villa estates of the Roman period brought wealth and the trappings of
Roman civilisation to the area, but they were essentially dispersed, and there is little
to indicate that they constituted the 'origins' of the later settlement, even less the
medieval town. Yet Maidstone certainly existed by the time of the Norman
Conquest, its name recorded in King William's great Domesday survey of 1086.
The evidence for the intervening Anglo-Saxon period, traditionally known as the
'Dark Ages', is elusive and frequently ambiguous, but within this complex web lie
the origins of the modern county town.

Legend claims that in the political and economic upheaval which followed the
withdrawal of Roman troops and authority, Hengist, a Jute with royal connections,
came to Britain as an exile with his followers and settled in Thanet, later assuming
control of Kent and causing the Britons to flee the kingdom.[6] There is considerable
archaeological evidence to support this tradition with the Jutish origins of the
settlers in Kent attested by characteristic cremation burials and Scandinavian
brooches and gold bracteates dating from the mid-fifth century onwards. During
the sixth century, the establishment of alliances and monopolistic trading contacts
with the Merovingian Frankish kingdoms allowed Kent to emerge as the most
powerful and prosperous kingdom in England. This culminated in the rise of King
Ethelbert to the position of overlord or *'Bretwalda'* of all kingdoms south of the
Humber in *c.* 593–7, and the foundation of the first English see at Canterbury in
597. This Jutish kingdom seems to have been bounded to the west by the River
Medway, and to the south west by the thickly wooded country of the Chart and
Weald; evidence from early cemeteries to the west of the Medway show that this was
Saxon territory, belonging to the kingdom of Surrey.

In most of East Kent there is persuasive evidence for continuity of land use and
estate structures between the Romano-British and Anglo-Saxon periods. Population
levels may have declined substantially in the post-Roman period, but the early Jutish
settlers seem to have lived in and farmed the same areas as their Romano-British
predecessors. The Medway valley, on the other hand, appears on archaeological
grounds to contradict this pattern of continuity. Only the important crossing point
at Rochester has yielded evidence for occupation in the fifth century, and the
absence of any finds from the fifth or earlier sixth century in the Maidstone area

may arguably reflect a period of abandonment; perhaps this frontier zone was dangerous or disputed territory in the early phase of Jutish control, and so undesirable for settlement. On the other hand, different forms of evidence have been put forward to argue that Maidstone presents a particularly strong case for continuity.

To understand this problem, we must first look at the existing archaeological evidence for the Maidstone area in the early Anglo-Saxon period. The first tangible data for the presence of some form of settlement and population in Maidstone itself probably dates to the earlier seventh century: in 1823 and 1836 inhumation burials were found on Wheeler Street, containing weapons, a bronze wheel ornament, a bracelet, pottery urns, and a garnet brooch dating to *c*. 590–620. At Eccles villa near Aylesford, excavations in the 1960s and 1970s showed that the old Roman site was re-used by the Anglo-Saxons. Large numbers of burials, dating from the mid-seventh century onwards, were found in and around the ruined villa, and were associated with a small timber structure which may have been a chapel. Unfortunately this cemetery is the only Anglo-Saxon site in the Maidstone area to have been properly excavated; no settlement sites are known, and other finds have generally been unearthed by accident without evidence for related structures or stratigraphy.[7]

What about other evidence? Domesday Book records that by the time of the Norman Conquest the manor of Maidstone belonged to the Archbishop of Canterbury. Archiepiscopal manors in Kent generally came into the ecclesiastical possession by royal bequest, usually before AD 762 when Kent came fully under the rule of the kings of Mercia. It is likely therefore that the Maidstone area comprised some form of royal estate before this time. In addition, the Domesday Monachorum of Christ Church, Canterbury, also compiled about 1086, notes that Maidstone was the site of an important minster, with seventeen daughter churches.[8] Minster churches in Kent were always located on royal or archiepiscopal estates, and seem to have been founded in the seventh century, soon after the establishment of the sees at Canterbury and Rochester in AD 597 and 604. In his seminal study of the Kentish landscape, Professor Alan Everitt used this pattern of minster and daughter churches, along with topographical evidence such as place-names and the routes of parish boundaries, to reconstruct early Jutish estates.[9] According to Everitt, the Maidstone estate incorporated the parishes of Boxley and Detling to the north, Thurnham, Bearsted and Otham to the east, and Loose, Linton and Boughton Monchelsea to the south – a territory of some 22,000 acres. Originally the estate may have extended southwards into the Weald, probably reaching as far as Goudhurst on the Sussex border. With over 40,000 acres this was probably the largest Jutish estate in Kent.

Once it came under archiepiscopal control this estate was clearly centred on Maidstone, but the situation in the earlier period is far less clear-cut. Was there a settlement here in the early Jutish period, as Everitt argued, and, if so, was it the *villa regalis* or royal estate centre? The scanty archaeological evidence does not support this contention. Indeed there is some speculation that the administrative centre and *villa regalis* of the western district of the early Jutish kingdom was elsewhere, at Wester near Linton. This would emphasise the importance of the foundation of the minster church at Maidstone for the development of the settlement. No doubt many factors contributed to this move, not least the convenient and fertile location, the river crossing and proximity of the Roman and pre-historic roads. Another possible reason may lie in Maidstone's name. First encountered in the Domesday entry as 'Meddestane', the name is Anglo-Saxon for 'the maiden's stone', and perhaps originally referred to a neolithic standing stone or megalithic structure in the area. On the advice of Pope Gregory, the early Christian missions in England often founded churches close to such pagan cult sites, and it is therefore possible Maidstone owes its later importance, as well as its name, to this maiden's stone. Though the picture is very uncertain and tenuous, taken together these various strands of evidence point to the likely emergence of Maidstone as a settlement in its own right during the seventh century.

J.M. Russell writing in 1881 portrayed Anglo-Saxon Maidstone as a 'little rude village, scattered . . . along the eastern bank of the Medway'.[10] In fact, Maidstone at the time would have focused on the wealthy minster church of St Mary's, on the raised ground south of the Len where All Saints Church stands today. There is unfortunately no evidence for the physical structure of St Mary's since the church was completely rebuilt in the fourteenth century and the early foundations remain buried. The early church was almost certainly stone-built, possibly using ragstone from old Roman buildings, but it would have been a small and simple structure in comparison with the later church of All Saints. Associated with the church would have been the living quarters and outbuildings of the minster priests. Living off the dues from the estate, these priests played an important role in spreading Christianity, travelling the surrounding countryside to preach to and convert the rural population.

How far this complex was associated with a larger settlement is hard to say. The minster probably supported a substantial number of slaves, servants and craftsmen, whose dwellings may have clustered around the religious complex, or perhaps have formed a separate focus north of the Len – multi-centred settlements are common in the early medieval period. The agricultural population would not have lived in a nucleated settlement but close to their fields in the surrounding landscape. However, as the centre of a large estate, Maidstone had a significant administrative and probably judicial role, and may also have served as a meeting place and informal centre for redistribution and trade. The old Roman road to Rochester doubtless continued in use, probably now becoming known as 'Stone Street' because of its superior construction, and wharves may have been built in Maidstone to serve river trade. The date of the first bridge at Maidstone is not known, but the fact that the parish includes land west of the Medway implies that a reliable crossing point must have existed in the Anglo-Saxon period. This would point to a significant clustering of population and settlement functions by the ninth century. But we are not speaking of a large population. The landscape around Maidstone was sparsely inhabited. Even by the time of the Domesday survey, when the population had risen substantially, Kent contained only around 40–50,000 people, compared to over one million in the early twentieth century.[11] Most settlement was dispersed, consisting of isolated farmsteads and small hamlets; their inhabitants paid dues to the estate centre, but would otherwise have been highly self-sufficient and independent. Pastoralism seems to have played an essential role in the Anglo-Saxon economy of this area. Sheep and swine were driven into the woodlands of the Chart and the Weald to feed in the summer and autumn, returning in winter to areas of permanent settlement and arable agriculture in the Holmesdale region around Maidstone. The legacy of this practice is visible in the modern landscape, particularly in the place-names: for example, the remarkable presence of names ending in -den (Old English for 'swine pasture') in the Weald indicates that these settlements probably originated as temporary dwellings in summer pasturelands. Furthermore the fact that most of the ancient roads and tracks east of the Medway run generally north-east to south-west betrays their origins as early drove roads. South of Maidstone, the place-name Loose (Old English 'pigsty') again testifies to the importance of swine in the local economy, and Marden (Old English 'pasture for mares') may also have fulfilled some specialist role in the estate. Maidstone's important links with the Weald were well established long before it became a town.

From around the eighth century onwards the old archiepiscopal estate began to break up. New territories were carved out of the old estates through grants to various lay lords, who frequently founded churches or chapels as expressions of their new status. The settlements at Loose, Otham, Linton, Loddington, Bearsted and Boughton Monchelsea may all be seen in this context, and as the boundaries and land-rights of these new estates gelled, probably in the tenth or eleventh centuries, so they became the parishes of the medieval period. One result of this was a limitation of the power of the manor and minster church, a process which was compounded by the repeated Viking raids of the ninth and late tenth centuries. In AD 999 a Danish force sailed up the Medway and laid waste a large part of western Kent. The minster church at Maidstone would have been a prime target; the Viking bearded axe found in Sandling Lane testifies to their presence in the area and was perhaps lost in that raid. On the other hand, the long-term growth of population and trade in the late Anglo-Saxon period may well have contributed to the steady economic consolidation of the settlement at Maidstone. Already by the eleventh century, if not before, nearby Penenden Heath was recognised as an important county meeting place and, as we shall see, Domesday Book records the wealth and economic activity of the community. By comparison with East Kent ports such as Sandwich, Hythe and Romney which had emerged by this time as embryonic towns, along with the major urban and ecclesiastical centres at Rochester and Canterbury, Maidstone appears less developed, probably held back by the slower development of the West Kent and Wealden economies. None the less, by the time of the Norman Conquest the settlement was already well established and of growing significance.

Notes

1. Archaeological evidence for the Upper Palaeolithic in Kent is likely to be buried beneath thick alluvial deposits due to subsequent rises in sea level.
2. Potin coins were locally produced, and were made in strips by forming a two-piece clay mould over papyrus blanks, then etching the design in the clay before casting.
3. D.B. Kelly, 'The Mount Roman Villa, Maidstone', *Archaeologia Cantiana*, vol. 110 (1992), 177–235.
4. The excavations were carried out by Canterbury Archaeological Trust on behalf of Kent County Council Highways Department. Mark Houliston kindly provided a pre-publication copy of the interim report on the excavations, which is to appear in the 1994 CAT Annual Report.
5. Crushed brick and/or tile in plaster.
6. Historical accounts of this period are given in four main sources: Gildas's *De Excidio et Conquestu Britanniae* (probably AD 545–549), Bede's *Historia Ecclesiastica* of AD 731, the ninth-century *Historia Brittonum*, and Anglo-Saxon Chronicle. For detailed discussion see N. Brooks, 'The creation and early structure of the kingdom of Kent', in S. Bassett, ed., *The Origins of Anglo-Saxon Kingdoms* (Leicester, 1989), pp. 55–74.
7. Other chance finds in Maidstone include a gold sword mount, a knife and a spearhead.
8. This church, St Mary's, was re-dedicated to All Saints when it was refounded and rebuilt as a collegiate church by Archbishop Courtenay in AD 1395.
9. A. Everitt, *Continuity and Colonization: the Evolution of Kentish Settlement* (Leicester, 1986).
10. J.M. Russell, *The History of Maidstone* (London, 1981), p. 10.
11. F.W. Jessup, *A History of Kent* (London, 1974), p. 45.

Bibliographical Note

Information concerning sites and finds in the Maidstone area is largely derived from the Sites and Monuments Record (SMR), held in the Planning Department of Kent County Council, Springfield, Maidstone. For references to other sites see the foot-notes.

There is also an extensive printed literature on the region and area. Work used here includes: E.W. Black, *The Roman Villas of South-East England* (Oxford, 1987); J. Blair, 'Introduction: from Minster to Parish Church', in J. Blair, ed., *Minsters and Parish Churches* (Oxford University Committee for Archaeology, Monograph No.17, 1988); J. Blair, 'Minster Churches in the Landscape', in D. Hooke, ed., *Anglo-Saxon Settlements* (Oxford, 1988) pp. 35–58; N. Brooks, *The Early History of the Church of Canterbury: Christ Church from 597–1066* (Leicester, 1984); N. Brooks, 'The creation and early structure of the kingdom of Kent', in S. Bassett, ed., *The Origins of Anglo-Saxon Kingdoms* (Leicester, 1984), pp. 55–74; T. Darvill, *Prehistoric Britain*, (London, 1987); A. Detsicas, *The Cantiaci* (Gloucester, 1983); P. Drewett, D. Rudling and M. Gardiner, *The South-East to AD 1000* (London, 1988); A. Everitt, *Continuity and Colonization: the Evolution of Kentish Settlement* (Leicester, 1986); S.C. Hawkes, 'Anglo-Saxon Kent: c. 425–725' in P.E. Leach, ed., *Archaeology in Kent to AD 1500: in memory of Stuart Eborall Rigold* (CBA Research Report No.48, 1982); R. Holgate, 'The Medway Megaliths and Neolithic Kent', *Archaeologia Cantiana*, vol. 97 (1981), pp. 221–34; F.W. Jessup, *A History of Kent* (London, 1974); D.B. Kelly, 'Quarry Wood Camp, Loose: a Belgic oppidum', *Archaeologia Cantiana*, vol. 86 (1971), pp. 55–84; D. B. Kelly, 'The Mount Roman Villa, Maidstone', *Archaeologia Cantiana* vol. 110 (1992), pp. 177–235; R.J. Pollard, *The Roman Pottery of Kent* (Kent Archaeological Society Monograph, vol. 5, Maidstone, 1988); C. Roach Smith, 'On a Roman villa near Maidstone', *Archaeologia Cantiana*, vol. 10 (1876), pp. 163–72; J.M. Russell, *The History of Maidstone* (London, 1881); Canon Scott Robertson, 'Traces of Roman Occupation in and near Maidstone', *Archaeologia Cantiana* vol. 15 (1881) pp. 68–80; G. Webster, 'Small towns without defences', in W. Rodwell, and T. Rowley, eds, *Small Towns of Roman Britain* (Oxford, 1975).

Chapter Two

THE MEDIEVAL MARKET TOWN

After a long period of growing significance as an ecclesiastical and administrative centre, Maidstone became a town, a truly urban community, during the high Middle Ages following the pattern of many other small English towns across the country. Though most of the major Roman cities had revived by 1066, buttressed by a considerable number of middle-sized ports and inland towns, it was during the centuries following the Norman Conquest that England saw the emergence of up to 500 lesser towns, often established by local lords, to meet the demand for markets and other specialist services from a growing population of peasant farmers. By the later Middle Ages Maidstone had developed a small but diversified economy and a number of important political, social and cultural institutions including the portmote court and fraternity of Corpus Christi. At the same time, the Church continued to mould the special character of Maidstone in the period before the Reformation. Not only were the archbishops of Canterbury, the manorial lords, probably involved in endowing the twelfth- and thirteenth-century town with a regular ground plan, but they established an important palace near the river. Under Archbishop Courtenay the parish church was lavishly rebuilt and renamed in Richard II's reign as the setting for a wealthy new college and it may be about this time that the town's first bridge was built.

Maidstone at the time of Domesday Book

Domesday Book, the great survey made in 1086 of William the Conqueror's new English kingdom, supplies the earliest survey of Maidstone. It has to be emphasised how incomplete this is; the intention was simply to identify and evaluate the sources of the estate's profitability. The archbishop's manor was assessed as being some 10 sulungs – notionally around 2,000 acres – of which 4 sulungs had been granted out as four sub-manors held by tenants owing military service. In all, the manor was said to be worth the considerable sum of £35 10s, of which the archbishop's part amounted to £20. There were 25 *villani* or tenant farmers each ploughing their own land, and a further 21 smallholders; in addition to these 46 households there were probably sub-tenants and landless men working for wages. The archbishop's military tenants in turn had a further 32 *villani* and 10 smallholders. Domesday

Book has nothing to say about where all these people lived, although for the most part their houses are likely to have been scattered throughout the agricultural land of this extensive manor. There is no indication that Maidstone had any urban characteristics in 1086, no sign of any part of the population living by commerce or manufacturing rather than by agriculture.

Yet as we know, the settlement which was to become the town of Maidstone had already for a long time served as the central place for the people of the locality. Most important, it held their centuries-old church of St Mary's which the Domesday Monachorum about 1070 recorded as one of the most important and wealthiest churches in Kent. Standing on its vantage point above the river, the ancient church was the focus of its own extensive parish as well as continuing to be the superior church of a much wider area. This was where the people of all the parish of Maidstone came to worship, and to pay their dues to the Church. Not only were they baptised and buried at St Mary's, but here they probably came to sell their surplus crops and buy simple necessities, for the church provided the setting for an informal Sunday market. Such markets were common, particularly in large parishes, and Maidstone's Sunday market survived into the fifteenth century. There was a permanent population too, for as a wealthy minster or superior church St Mary's was doubtless served from the early Middle Ages by a group of resident priests, forming with their households an influential little community dwelling in the church's shadow.

It was not just the church that brought people from all over the manor of Maidstone to this site by the river. In 1086 the archbishop's manor had five water-mills, the whole complex worth the considerable sum of £1 16s 8d per annum, while another mill worth five shillings belonged to the sub-manors. Domesday Book gives no clue to their location but in later centuries the archbishop's mills were on the River Len adjacent to the church, and it may well be that this was where the people of the eleventh-century manor came to mill the corn for their bread.

The demesne, the lands of the manor directly under the archbishop's control, was in part cultivated with his own three plough-teams – doubtless by the ten slaves that Domesday Book also records. Just as important was the contribution made by the tenants of the manor, performing ploughing services with their own ploughs and oxen. They also provided much of the labour needed to tend and harvest the lord's crops, as well as paying rents in cash and in kind. At the heart of the economic life of the manor, therefore, was a complex of estate buildings: barns, granaries, byres, stables, with accommodation for slaves and hired servants, as well as a hall and private rooms to shelter the lord and his retinue whenever they chose to visit Maidstone. We cannot be sure that this complex was originally situated within the area of the later town. The archbishop's palace on the north side of the parish church was built only after Archbishop Stephen Langton acquired the existing rectory of the church early in the thirteenth century. But that acquisition of land probably represented only an extension to land already in archiepiscopal hands, as indicated by the great size of the palace complex.

The manorial complex, probably on the site of the later palace, would have been the customary location for regular sessions of the manorial court. In later centuries courts were held every three or more weeks, with separate courts for the people of the town and the people of the rest of the manor, but before the development of the town there would have been a single court for the whole manor. By the eleventh century, Maidstone was also the centre of a hundred, an important administrative division of the shire, and so would have provided the venue for courts dealing with criminal cases for an extended region encompassing the manors of the nine Domesday Book vills of Boxley, Penenden, West Barming, East Barming, East Farleigh, Loose, Hunton, *Burgericstune* as well as Maidstone itself. As already noted, the courts for the whole of Kent were held by the sheriff at nearby Penenden Heath, which, according to Domesday Book, was the traditional meeting place for the county. This role continued throughout the Middle Ages with sessions of the monthly county court and less frequently sessions before royal justices. Felons condemned at the assizes were hanged on the heath by the archbishop's people, since Penenden lay within his Liberty. In the fifteenth century a hangman was employed for 11s 8d a year, but at other times the task was performed by the estate ploughmen.[1]

Urban origins

It is not surprising then that a town grew up at Maidstone. In addition to the factors already mentioned which brought people to the settlement, it was the site of an established river crossing, making it an obvious place for a market serving more than just the immediate locality. There is no direct evidence for when the town of Maidstone originated, although it is quite clear how it took shape – not in a haphazard way, but as a planned enterprise. The provision of a separate town court indicates a formal act of foundation by one of the archbishops. At the same time a simple town plan with regular house-plots would have been laid out within the existing topography of roads and settlement. This is certainly what happened at other, better documented, towns. In many such cases the act of foundation can be dated by a surviving charter of liberties granted to the townspeople by their lord, or more often by the lord's purchase of a royal charter allowing him to hold a market and collect tolls. The only record of a market charter for Maidstone is dated 1261, and it allowed Archbishop Boniface and his successors to hold a weekly market on Thursdays at Petrisfeld in Maidstone. But this cannot have been Maidstone's first legally-held market, as there is evidence – however scanty – of an already established town. A shop in Maidstone was sold in 1248, a sure sign of the commercial character of the place. Thus the town of Maidstone, which had not yet been founded in 1086, certainly existed soon after 1200.

Paradoxically, the very absence of a market charter for the town before the thirteenth century points to commercial life having been established in the decades following 1086, and certainly well before the middle years of the twelfth century. By

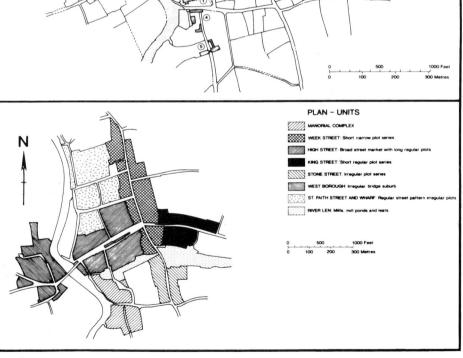

1. All Saints Collegiate Church
2. Archbishop's Palace
3. Stables
4. The College
5. College Farm
6. Corpus Christi Guild Hall
7. St Faith's Church
8. Chillingstone House
9. Hospital of St Peter & Paul
10. Butter Market
11. Court Houses and Cross
M. Mill
W. Well

PLAN – UNITS

MANORIAL COMPLEX

WEEK STREET: Short narrow plot series

HIGH STREET: Broad street market with long regular plots

KING STREET: Short regular plot series

STONE STREET: Irregular plot series

WEST BOROUGH: Irregular bridge suburb

ST. FAITH STREET AND WHARF: Regular street pattern irregular plots

RIVER LEN: Mills, mill ponds and leats

Fig. 2   Medieval Maidstone.

that time new markets could only be founded with the permission of the Crown, and some record of a royal grant would almost certainly survive. Further confirmation that Maidstone was already an established well populated town in the thirteenth century is given by the provision of a second place of worship, in addition to the parish church. St Faith's, a dependent church of St Mary's, was first recorded in 1268 as the location of an annual fair to be held every 13 October. But it was certainly not a new church in the 1260s, its possession of burial rights suggesting that it was probably founded before 1200, before such rights came to be jealously preserved by existing churches. Moreover, the location of St Faith's within the planned street-grid to the north of the High Street also provides a date for those streets, suggesting that they likewise were no later than 1200.

However tenuous the evidence for Maidstone's urban origins, we can postulate with some degree of confidence the chronology and extent of each phase of development. The pre-urban nucleus of Maidstone lay to the south of the River Len, and consisted of the parish church, the archbishops' watermills, and presumably the other buildings of the manorial complex. The houses of the priests serving the church and of any secular retainers would also have been in the vicinity, perhaps on the site occupied by the later college buildings or along Knightrider Street – although that street and its name are not recorded before 1600. Nearby to the east the ancient Roman road represented by the later Stone Street and Week Street carried north–south traffic and Maidstone's first merchants and craftsmen probably settled along this road. The first real phase of urban development was initiated by one of the archbishops of the late eleventh or the early twelfth century, and entailed the laying-out of the broad High Street as a market place, along which traffic passed to and from the river crossing. House-plots along either side of the High Street would have been marked out at this time, and let on attractive terms to tradesmen coming to settle in the new town. Perhaps at the same time, but more probably as a second phase of development later in the twelfth century, and definitely before 1200, the streets to the north of the High Street were laid out, and new house-plots made available along both sides of the present-day Earl Street and St Faith's Street. After this, there were no substantial additions to the basic form of the medieval town; though at some point house-plots were laid out along the east side of Week Street and along both sides of Stone Street. But a possible attempt during the 1260s to develop land on the west bank of the river met with only limited success.

The impact of the Church

In about 1207 Archbishop Stephen Langton acquired Maidstone rectory as a residence, but it is likely the archbishops of Canterbury had a residence at Maidstone from early in the Middle Ages. A major archiepiscopal estate-centre for centuries, the acquisition of the rectory probably signified no more than the intention to enlarge and improve the archbishop's quarters. The palace was extended and rebuilt by successive archbishops, so that by the time of Archbishop Courteney (1381–96) it was grand enough to become a principal archiepiscopal residence. There was further expansion and embellishment notably by Archbishop Morton in 1486.

A hospital – often referred to as 'le Newerk', or in Latin as *novi operis*, the New Work – was founded about 1260 by Archbishop Boniface and remained firmly under the control of his successors. It was dedicated to Saints Peter and Paul, although on occasions it was also called the hospital of St Philip and St James.[2] Situated on the west side of the Medway, in the West Borough, its location at the edge of the town followed the usual contemporary practice in founding hospitals and minor religious houses. However, the acquisition of a charter in 1261 enabling the archbishop to hold a market at the new hospital was a novel feature, and suggests that the foundation was the occasion for a further attempted phase of urban expansion, though as we have said nothing seems to have come of the scheme, judging by the subsequent lack of medieval development on the west side of the river.

Despite the frequent claim that the hospital was built to accommodate pilgrims on the road to Canterbury, an inquiry in 1375 reported that its purpose was to maintain a chaplain and ten poor men. Under the terms of the foundation, each of the men was to receive his bed, and every day a dish of food, a loaf of bread, and six pints of ale; the chaplain was to be the resident master of the house, and had to celebrate mass daily for the souls of the king and his predecessors, and of the founder and his archiepiscopal successors. But the inquiry in 1375 also noted that some of these provisions had lapsed in recent decades. Only five men were now maintained at the hospital and recent archbishops had given places in the hospital to their servants; in other words, the hospital was used to pension-off loyal servants who had become too old or frail to work. The upkeep of each man cost 1s 2d a week, making a total of over £15 for the five men annually. In addition, the master received a stipend, which is unlikely to have been less than £10 and may have been more. But the hospital's income probably more than exceeded its needs, for it enjoyed the profits of the churches of Sutton by Dover, Linton and East Farleigh which had been appropriated to it; on top of this we find income from land and other temporal sources assessed at £5 10s 5d in 1384. It is hardly surprising that Archbishop William Courtenay felt this revenue could be put to better use when towards the end of the fourteenth century he decided to create a new religious institution in the town. Combining the income of the hospital with that of the parish church was sufficient to enable the foundation of a secular college – an institution rather similar to a monastery, but served not by monks but by men in priests' orders who shared only a semi-communal life and could be active in the world.

On 25 June 1395 Pope Boniface IX empowered Courtenay to convert the parish church into a college consisting of a master, and twenty-four chaplains and clerks. On 2 August Richard II gave his permission, and authorised the incorporation of the hospital with all its property into the new college. Six months later, on 10 February 1396, he granted a licence allowing the master and college of All Saints, Maidstone, to acquire further lands and rents up to the value of £40 a year. In September 1396 the king gave the college the advowson of the church of Crundale, and the reversion of the manors of Tremworth and Fannes when their current tenant – the famous architect Henry Yevele – died. The foundation was an ambitious one, and was to have a fitting new church. Courtenay was ready to start building in June 1396 when he received royal permission to conscript forty-eight local masons; St Mary's was swiftly demolished, and the new church of All Saints was said to be already finished by 1398. It is possible that the new stone bridge to the West Borough was also built at this time, although there is no hard evidence either documentary or archaeological.

John Wotton was appointed master of Courtenay's college, and along with the four clerks who had previously served St Mary's a further number were recruited to bring the number up to the prescribed twenty-four. The college continued to prosper, and in 1407 it acquired the manor of Wittersham together with numerous pieces of land in and around Maidstone, bringing its income in a short time up to £40 a year. The advowson of the college was retained by the medieval archbishops, who saw the value of their patronage over such a wealthy institution. They could reward and provide for officials and other servants, who as clerks prayed for their patrons' souls. There may have been a progressive reduction in the number of clerks during the fifteenth century. Roger Heron, who had been the archbishop's treasurer and held office as master between 1419 and his death in 1441, bequeathed to the brethren and his successor as master a dozen dishes, a dozen plates, and a dozen salt cellars, which suggests that by then the college numbered twelve in total rather than the original twenty-five members. At the Archbishop's visitation in 1511 the college had only a master, a sub-master, and five other fellows.

Of those serving the college, the most distinguished was undoubtedly William Grocyn, master from 1506 until his death at the age of about seventy-three in 1519. Grocyn was a major figure in the late medieval Church, a respected scholar who may have been the first teacher of Greek at Oxford during the 1480s, and who was certainly teaching the language there in the 1490s after returning from an extended period of study in Italy. He was known as the friend of the great Dutch scholar Erasmus, who held Grocyn's learning in the highest esteem although apparently regretting his continued interest in the scholastic writers, his conservatism in preferring the philosophy of Aristotle to that of Plato, and his conservative religious views. By 1500 Grocyn had left Oxford, and was living in London off a succession of wealthy livings; his appointment to Maidstone was a favour from Archbishop William Warham, who thirty years previously had been his pupil at New College, Oxford. The mastership of All Saints was one of the most valuable gifts at Warham's disposal.

Population

Maidstone's relationship with successive archiepiscopal households, though influential for the long-term development of the town, tells us little about its importance or otherwise as an urban community. By contrast, the brief association of the Franciscan friars with Maidstone is much more indicative of the community's urban status, suggesting that it was well established but below the first rank of towns. As friars lived on charity, they founded their houses in major centres with populations large and prosperous enough to support them. Thus it is significant that in 1331 preparations were made to found a Franciscan friary in Maidstone, and just as significant that the project failed. One John atte Water purchased the Crown's permission to give property to the Franciscans: two messuages or houses in Maidstone, together with six acres of land, on which they intended to build a church and living accommodation. But the friars seem to have failed to obtain further support and nothing more is heard of their projected house in the town.

The town's population in the early fourteenth century may have been in the region of 2,000, though the figure is only tentative. More certain, fifty years later, after the appalling attrition of the Black Death of 1349 and subsequent outbreaks of plague, Maidstone had at least 1,700 inhabitants. In 1377 there were 844 Maidstone people who paid the poll-tax, charged at a flat rate tax of 4d on every adult person over the age of fourteen.[3] Making adjustments to take account of poverty and evasion, and also for the large number of children in the community, historians have computed that the poll-tax payers in any town constituted rather less than half the total urban population. By comparison, Canterbury's poll-tax payers totalled 2,574, indicating a population of over 5,000 and suggesting that the city was three times the size of Maidstone. As we have said, the population was doubtless greater before the pandemic of the 1340s. In 1327 Maidstone had 102 people prosperous enough to pay the property tax, presumably heads of wealthier households; evidence from elsewhere suggests that around one in twenty of the urban population might have paid the tax. Thus Canterbury with 339 taxpayers may have had upwards of 7,000 inhabitants in 1327; Rochester, with 94 taxpayers, had perhaps a population of around 2,000 – like that at Maidstone.[4]

What does the population level tell us about the physical extent of the town? Though some Maidstone people may have escaped the poll-tax of 1377, established households probably found avoidance much more difficult. The 844 taxpayers doubtless included all the householders and their wives, together with a small number of single householders, as well as resident servants who were adults. There can have been no more than 400 households in Maidstone in 1377, even as few as 300. This would point to the town having no more than 300 houses – probably scattered in clusters across the extensive site of the planned town with few inhabitants across the river in the West Borough. These estimates of the size of the town in the late fourteenth century are similar to those reported by contemporaries two centuries later in the mid-sixteenth century. This would seem to confirm that Maidstone, like other English towns, either declined in size or remained static during the agricultural recession of the fifteenth century. In conclusion, Maidstone experienced marked variations in its demographic fortunes during the centuries after its foundation. Initially, the population grew rapidly to reach its greatest size sometime around 1300. But it then experienced periods of decline and population stagnation, until growth re-commenced probably sometime after 1500.

The economy: markets and industries

Even at its medieval peak Maidstone was a small community, and its economy remained rather basic and unspecialised in the period before the Reformation. Like other small towns, its essential living was derived from providing the predominantly rural population of its hinterland with a place to sell their surplus produce – grain, livestock, poultry – and supplying in return simple manufactures made in the town and a modest array of services. The best evidence for the scale of Maidstone's economy is the number and diversity of recorded occupations of its inhabitants. Eighty-one townspeople are described by their occupation in a range of documents between 1273 and 1479 – although most of these are from the later years of the period, and, as a sample, the list is inevitably incomplete and selective. It undeniably ignores other aspects of economic life for which no record survives, but which are sometimes highlighted by other evidence, as for instance the fourteenth-century pottery kiln discovered on the south-west side of 125 Week Street in 1922. But whatever the list's limitations, it does draw a picture of the daily business of medieval Maidstone mainly from the close of the fourteenth to the late fifteenth century.[5]

Twenty-seven different recorded occupations in a limited sample is a large number, and indicates a thriving economy; the broad pattern of the different trades is very informative. The largest group, totalling 23 men in all, comprised the craftsmen producing clothing and footwear. There were 11 tailors – the most prominent single group in the whole sample – as well as 6 cordwainers or shoemakers, 3 skinners or furriers, 2 doubletmakers and a glover. Of those involved directly in industrial or raw-material production, the number of named masons – 10 – reflects the importance of ragstone production in the local economy. As in other towns the leather-trade was also important with 5 tanners listed. But it was rare for a single specialist activity to dominate the economy of any medieval town, for strength lay in diversity, in serving the varied needs of the people of its hinterland. Among the other traders, we find clothmakers including dyers; smiths, carpenters, waxchandlers, butchers, bakers, and various dealers in better quality goods, such as mercers, vintners and spicers. The presence of 5 barbers in our sample underlines the fact that in an ordinary market town something as basic as a shave or tooth extraction was much more in demand than the expensive goods and services offered by luxury traders. When the Corpus Christi guild bought the wine for their annual feast they often chose not to purchase it from a local vintner, but instead sent a man to buy it in London, where presumably there was better choice and prices were more competitive.[6]

The only significant local specialism was the production and working of Kentish ragstone, which was put to a range of uses. The wars in France and the needs of the garrison at Calais ensured a demand from the Maidstone quarries for stone missiles for siege engines and guns; for instance, in 1418 John Benet of Maidstone, mason, was commissioned to supply 7,000 gunstones of various sizes from the quarries of

Maidstone and elsewhere. Two years later Simon Lewes, another Maidstone mason, was one of the men in charge of transporting the king's great cannons, which he was also to furnish with 400 of the largest stones. But ragstone was mainly in demand for building, and had a high reputation: a contract made in 1384 to enlarge a wharf in London specified the work would be 'only of Maidstone stone'. Men of Maidstone were constantly called upon to supply from the king's quarries building stone for castles and other royal buildings such as the Palace of Westminster. The industry employed many local men: not only skilled builders such as Laurence atte Wode, Geoffrey Dune and John Westcote, stone-cutters of Maidstone who were employed in the 1390s to build a section of the Rochester town wall, but also the labourers, the *hardehewers*, who excavated and presumably dressed the stone. For particularly urgent work, stone-masons might be conscripted, but this was undoubtedly unpopular and in the 1360s – and possibly other times – it met with stiff resistance. The king's serjeants in charge of building works at Leeds castle were given powers to conscript local workers in 1362, but two years later complained that they had been assaulted by John Capell of Maidstone and others. Sometime later they protested that when visiting the town they had been assaulted by a large gang of people, so that they no longer dared leave the castle. Although the king had first call on the masons' services, this privilege could be granted to others; in 1396 the Archbishop of Canterbury was allowed to conscript 24 *fremaceons* and 24 *ligiers* for the work on Maidstone's new church of All Saints.

There was clearly a hierarchy among the men who worked as masons, with those at the top of the profession being in fact skilled civil engineers or building contractors, and important local employers. Socially, they would have been on a level with the mercers and other retailers of luxury goods. As elsewhere, at the pinnacle of Maidstone society was a small number of merchants, men such as William de Vallibus or Vaus, who purchased a licence to export large quantities of wool in 1273. Exporting wool was a profitable business, and it is noteworthy that in 1327 Maidstone was selected as one of the towns ordered to send representatives to a wool-merchants' assembly at York where they could be briefed on the king's commercial policies. A factor in this trade must have been the navigability of the lower Medway which made the town an important inland port. During the long French wars of the fourteenth century, Maidstone was always on the list of ports where vessels of more than 40 or 50 tons capacity could be commandeered, and local people were engaged in the coastal shipping trade, not least with London. Typical perhaps was Thomas Kyng of Maidstone who in 1367 brought a shipload of hides from London to Maidstone to be tanned. But the lower Medway was not always the best route for traders. In 1441 Thomas Carter of Maidstone and other wool-merchants from Rochester and Billericay chose to take their wool overland to Higham, on the Thames estuary towards Gravesend, whence they shipped it to Tilbury, to deliver it to merchants supplying the cloth town of Colchester.

The transportation of large quantities of hides from London to Maidstone to be tanned sheds interesting light on the leather industry. Cattle were butchered at the point of sale, and hence a great meat-consuming centre such as London produced vast numbers of hides. London was also a massive consumer of leather. But tanning itself was an unpleasant polluting industry, which also needed ready access to timber and water; it was thus not ideal as a metropolitan industry. This may have encouraged Maidstone tanners to enter the trade, undercutting their London counterparts. Numerous fifteenth-century credit agreements recorded in the Close Rolls show connections between Maidstone men and Londoners, and in several cases the Londoners were workers in leather. All the signs are that in the fourteenth and fifteenth centuries – and perhaps earlier – Maidstone men were heavily involved in tanning London's leather, fetching the raw hides from the capital and returning the tanned leather to the city's craftsmen.

Yet there can be little doubt that the heart of Maidstone's economic life was the local trade that passed through the market. Thursday was the official market day and the town was filled with country people buying and selling. Furthermore there was still a Sunday market in the fifteenth century which was attended by people coming from villages in the adjoining countryside. Thus we know that at six in the evening on Sunday 21 December 1408 Thomas Lord – having travelled some miles on his way home from Maidstone – was robbed of twenty shillings and murdered at Mereworth. In addition, four annual fairs were held, probably as in the sixteenth century on 2 February, 1 May, 9 June and 6 October. These were primarily for trade in the region's agricultural surplus, but they also brought unusual throngs of country customers to the town and its craftsmen and traders.

Also of obvious benefit to the local economy was the long-established role of Maidstone as the location for sessions of manorial, hundred and county courts, with litigants, petitioners, jurors and others coming in from the region and the shire. As well as benefiting the craft and trade sectors, it also stimulated the urban service sector. One sign of this was the number of inns which had emerged by the end of the Middle Ages, mainly victualling and accommodating the wealthier classes. John Leland – passing through in the 1530s – saw Maidstone with the eye of the seasoned traveller and observed that the town had one long street, well built and full of inns. One of them would have been the Hart, which Thomas Croft, a tailor, sold to his fellow-tailor Thomas Toby in 1509.[7] Leland may also have seen the Ship on the east side of Gabriel's Hill, and both the George and the Bull a little further to the north. The Chequers was located at the corner of the hill and on the High Street stood the Queen's Arms and the Swan. From the later sixteenth century the town's principal inn was the Star, also in the High Street and this was also probably of some antiquity. There is no direct evidence linking these Tudor inns with the late medieval town, but such a cluster mostly around the top of the High Street must have perpetuated a long-standing pattern.

It was not just the more affluent inns which profited. The fairs, markets and courts generated work for women as well as men particularly in the ale trade. The large number of brewers in Maidstone, almost invariably women, undoubtedly reflected the great demand for ale from visitors to the town. At each session of the portmote numerous women were fined for brewing against the assize – a technical offence that constituted in effect a system of licensing. The numbers varied but 106 women were named as brewers at one court held in 1386.[8] This figure compares with that of 844 adult taxpayers (or between 300 and 400 households) recorded for Maidstone nine years earlier in 1377. In other words, a quarter – and perhaps as many as a third – of Maidstone's housewives were brewing for sale at that time. For any woman able to buy or borrow the necessary brewing vessels, malt and spices, brewing, whether for a few days at a time or longer, presented an important commercial opportunity.

It is only because brewing was controlled by the portmote that we can identify its importance. Other commercial activities, also part-time or irregular, and also attracting mainly female labour, in many cases probably went unrecorded. Evidence from other towns shows that most small-scale retailing, particularly of bread, dairy products, vegetables and fruit, was done by women street-traders. There is no evidence of the activities of these hucksters in Maidstone, but there may have been considerable numbers of them. As far as one can tell, career opportunities for women were limited. They were not known by their own occupational surnames, nor were they defined in legal documents by their occupations. There is only one exception in the Maidstone records: Margery Midwife was sued for debt in the portmote in 1397. Evidently she had no husband to provide her with a surname, or to be sued alongside her, and she maintained herself by a traditional female trade. She also turned to brewing on occasion. Of course, the fact that many women would have helped their husbands at their trades is another reason for their work going largely unrecorded. One of the rare exceptions relates to John Elmer who was employed by the Corpus Christi guild in 1474–5 to work on the garden at the guild hall. Elmer drew wages for himself and his wife, both of them also being fed at the guild's expense. Most ordinary women, we may assume, followed some profitable activity or other. Even Thomas de Horsseleye's wife Alice, who was blind, had to work: she hawked old clothes to passers-by, and in June 1285 sold a tunic for 5½d to a woman on the road near Maidstone. We only know about this because she gave her husband the money; when four of the pennies proved counterfeit he was arrested on suspicion of forgery.

It is not just the role of women in the town's economy which is hidden in shadow. Other activities, particularly in the service sector are poorly documented. Thus lawyers have left no trace of their presence, though they must have done a growing amount of business in and out of the town's courts. Here there is a suggestion that bigger lawyers though practising in towns often lived outside them in the countryside before the seventeenth century. Again, in the Tudor period, as we shall see in Chapter Three, Maidstone became well-known for its surgeons and physicians; but there is little sign of them in the late Middle Ages, probably due to inadequate sources. Certainly there are many unresolved questions about Maidstone's medieval economy, but our overall picture of limited localised activity is persuasive.

Politics and dissent

Ignoring the practice followed in many other rising towns of the twelfth and thirteenth centuries, none of the archbishops gave Maidstone a foundation charter · of liberties. Possibly they felt it was undesirable and unnecessary to enshrine the rights of their tenants in law; alternatively the townspeople were insufficiently wealthy to pay for such a charter. It is significant that there is no medieval reference to burgages in Maidstone or to burgage tenure – the free tenure that was specifically granted to the tenants of new, chartered boroughs, and which conveyed extensive rights including privileged access to the market. The inhabitants of Maidstone were never described in the court rolls as burgesses – that is, as free men – but always as customary tenants, who were unfree; in property conveyances their houses were described not as free burgages but always as messuages, a neutral term that carried no legal connotations. In everyday practice, however, the inhabitants probably had all the commercial privileges enjoyed by the burgesses of chartered boroughs. They also held their houses on terms indistinguishable from burgage tenure, enabling them to sell or dispose of their land as they wished without paying for their lord's permission. But by insisting on the preservation of traditional legal distinctions, successive archbishops were able to retain control of their town and the revenues it generated. The situation tended to be similar in other towns founded by ecclesiastical lords, the Church being more tenacious than secular lords in defending their rights and profits.

On the face of it, the town community controlled its day-to-day affairs through its own elected officials, principally the portreeve. In 1597 an official memorandum, looking back at the way the town had been governed before the incorporation of 1549, recorded that the portreeves had been assisted by twelve of the leading men of the town, and on occasion by a further twenty-four. The royal letters patent of 1549 granting incorporation to a mayor and twelve jurats were less specific, saying only that previously the government of the town had formerly been in the hands of certain of the inhabitants, commonly called the portreeve and brethren. But a set of regulations issued by the portmote in 1474 confirms that the medieval town administration, in its latter phase, had been in the hands of a portreeve, twelve brethren and twenty-four commoners elected on St Clement's day (23 November). The town's officials were elected by all the suitors to the portmote who were the archbishop's tenants in the manor; in the later years of the fifteenth century they elected two men to the office of portreeve (of whom only one would serve), four ale-tasters, two bedells, and four constables. A century before, it appears to have been customary for the archbishop's tenants to have chosen only the portreeves and two ale-tasters.

In theory, the portreeves were the servants of the archbishop, although it is impossible to tell quite how that theoretical relationship translated into practice. The method of election provided a mechanism for compromise because, as we have said, the archbishop's tenants assembled at the portmote had to name not one man but two – with the final choice of the portreeve presumably left to the archbishop's steward. Whether he ever felt able to reject both men and impose his own candidate is unknown, but tensions could become acute from time to time. Thus at the court held on 4 November 1385 both of the nominated candidates for portreeve, Bartholomew Carewey and Simon Poslynge, refused to accept the office. This was no isolated, personal protest because the two men elected as ale-tasters likewise refused to accept office. Without their cooperation little business could be brought to the court, and the official response was to resort to coercion, to distrain their goods until they relented and submitted. But they clearly resisted as long as they could, for another court was not held for a further seven weeks – an unusually long interval; only then were Carewey and the ale-tasters duly sworn to office. We catch a glimpse of the administration of the town from a set of regulations formally agreed by the portreeve Robert Reve, twelve brethren and twenty-four commoners in November 1474. In publishing the regulations – which were probably a restatement of existing rules – the concern of the town's officials was, they said, to maintain the good government and reputation of Maidstone. They forbade unauthorised assemblies and gatherings, and disorderly games; they laid down rules to govern terms of employment and apprenticeship. They enjoined attendance at church services, and they attempted to control likely criminals, dubious newcomers to Maidstone, and suspicious characters such as nightwalkers roaming the streets. By this time one has a sense of an increasingly well organised and self-conscious town administration.

How far then did the rule of an ecclesiastical lord provoke the same sort of resentment in late medieval Maidstone that we know it did in larger towns – such as Cirencester, St Albans, or Bury St Edmunds? The evidence, unfortunately, is sparse and it is debatable whether the dispute in 1385 was an isolated incident or if there were regular disagreements with the archbishop and his officials. Nor is it clear how far it was linked with other, but different, expressions of social hostility or public disorder. Disturbances occurred in 1297, for instance, when Archbishop Winchelsey and his household claimed to have been besieged at Maidstone by a large number of armed tenants, who would not let him leave the rectory where he was staying. Since he was embroiled at this time in a dispute with Edward I over clerical taxation, part of the archbishop's problems may have been caused by the sheriff of Kent whipping up trouble out of loyalty to the king. The local people involved, however, almost certainly acted out of hostility to their lord. It is a measure of the sense of solidarity in the town that despite threats of excommunication against all involved, Winchelsey could not find anyone willing to come forward and identify the culprits.

The wide social divisions in medieval society ensured that whatever its origins, any particular expression of discontent might soon turn to unrest and open violence. Of the medieval disturbances that affected Maidstone, the Peasants' Revolt of 1381 was the most serious because it was the most widespread, and because it was the only occasion during the Middle Ages when a substantial body of the common people seriously challenged the established social order. The revolt began in late May, almost simultaneously in both Essex and Kent. After a period of widespread disturbances throughout central Kent, a band of rebels from Dartford, Erith, Bexley and a number of smaller places came together and on 6 June they attacked and took Rochester castle. Now numbering thousands, the rebels swept on to Maidstone, the ancient county centre, where they beheaded John Southalle, described by one chronicler as 'one of the best men of the town'. Why the rebels bore a grudge against him is not known. His house was looted, and the rebels moved on to loot and destroy William Topclyve's manor house at the Mote.

It was at Maidstone that the two most important and charismatic rebel leaders emerged from obscurity: Wat Tyler and John Ball. Tyler may have come from Essex to join the revolt in Kent, although one of the best-informed commentators believed that he was a Maidstone man. Resourceful and intelligent, he was chosen as the rebels' leader at Maidstone on 7 June, and in the days that followed he showed an extraordinary capacity for decisive and effective action, leading his army first in an attack on Canterbury and then in a lightning march on London, reaching the outskirts on the night of the 12th. It is perhaps surprising that while the king's gaol at Maidstone was opened on the 7th and the prisoners released it was not until the 11th, on a second visit to the town, that the rebels opened the archbishop's gaol and freed the dissident priest John Ball. During their brief period of triumph, until the resolve of the Kentish rebels collapsed with Tyler's murder at Smithfield on the 15th, Ball was the ideologue of the revolt. His earlier history is uncertain but, according to the chronicler Henry Knighton, he had been a preacher of radical doctrines and a thorn in the side of a corrupt Church for many years. He had been sentenced to life imprisonment shortly before the revolt – hence his presence in the archbishop's gaol. On 15 July Ball was hanged, drawn and quartered at St Albans, and the revolt was effectively over; but still local pockets of popular agitation persisted. As late as 1 July, John Gybonn of Maidstone – presumably with others – was at the town hall of Canterbury, forcing the city bailiffs to levy a tax on the community to finance resistance against royal officials in Kent. Two months later it was the Maidstone district that saw a significant if doomed attempt to rekindle the flames of revolt. John Cote, a mason from Loose, admitted that on 30 September a large number of people from Maidstone and several villages to the south, such as Loose and Hunton, had been called together at night on Boughton Heath by another mason, Thomas Hardyng. Their aim was to regain the concessions Richard II had made before the revolt's collapse, and which had been subsequently revoked. They were encouraged in their actions by reports received from pilgrims travelling to Canterbury from the north that John of Gaunt, the king's uncle and the second man of the kingdom, had freed all his serfs. Optimistically, they planned to discover if the story were true, and if so, to make him king.

Maidstone's involvement in Cade's rebellion seventy years later was more limited. The rising was a reaction to incompetent and corrupt government which had culminated in the loss of England's remaining possessions in northern France during the winter of 1449/50. Unrest spread across much of southern England with Kent, as in 1381, a principal seat of the rebellion which lasted from May until the death of the Kentish leader Jack Cade in July. But there is no evidence that Maidstone was a centre of the revolt. Forty-three Maidstone men took advantage of the royal pardon offered to the rebels on 6 and 7 July but it is not clear how active they were in the rising, nor what their precise grievances had been. An important issue in Kent was widespread dissatisfaction with government officials, who were seen as abusing the privileges of office. Prominent in this respect was Robert Est of Maidstone who had used his high connections to put himself above the law. Among the many allegations against him, he had reportedly acted as an accomplice in an armed raid on the house of Edward Neville, Lord Abergavenny at Singlewell in 1449. In Maidstone during the 1440s he had secured property by fraudulent means, and had extorted money by false pretences. His unpopularity was compounded by his activity as a rent-collector for the archbishop of Canterbury, while he had abused his powers as keeper of Maidstone gaol – on several occasions imprisoning people illegally until they paid to be released. He also served the government in the lucrative office of escheator for the counties of Kent and Middlesex. Corruption and influence ensured that Est and others like him could escape the due process of justice, probably fuelling general dissatisfaction with members of the local elite.

The guild or fraternity of Corpus Christi

Est's unscrupulous dealings and flagrant abuse of power form a fascinating counterpoint to his public display of piety. For it was Est who in 1445 was one of the two Maidstone men granted a licence to set on a new footing the town's fraternity or guild of Corpus Christi. His action may appear more in character if we understand that – in the absence of more formal institutions – the Corpus Christi guild played a central role in fifteenth-century Maidstone. Guilds such as this were ubiquitous in medieval Europe, and all acted as associations to support the religious observances of their members. But they also had important secular and communal functions; social or commercial affinities drew their members together, and in every guild drinking, feasting and solidarity were given a high priority. At the same time, different guilds might fulfil very different roles, depending on the identity and interests of their members. In the smaller English towns of the later Middle Ages it was common for the wealthier burgesses to establish a single, prestigious guild through which they might consolidate their position as leaders of the community, especially when it remained legally dependent on an ecclesiastical or secular lord. At Birmingham the master of the guild was regarded as the leading man of the town, above the bailiffs who were formally the de Birmingham family's representatives; at Stratford-upon-Avon the guild members utilised their meetings to settle the affairs of the town, and only then took matters to the borough court to be ratified in the presence of the officials of the bishop of Worcester.[9] Everything points to the Maidstone guild having been important enough within the town to perform a similar role.

The specific purpose of the guild was to celebrate the feast of Corpus Christi, the greatest of late medieval urban festivals. Held on the Thursday after Trinity Sunday, it commemorated the body of Christ in the form of the sacramental bread, and was celebrated with a grand procession of the sacrament through the streets. The occasion became an important early summer holiday for townspeople across Europe. Its popularity made it a favourite dedication for guilds, which generally took charge of organising the festivities. There is no record of when the Maidstone guild was founded, beyond the meagre information conveyed by the letters patent granted by the Crown in 1445 which made clear that the guild already existed before that date. The point of the grant to Robert Est and Richard Barbour was to enable the guild to acquire and hold landed property worth up to £20 a year. It legalised the guild's existence, and provides us with a little information about the guild's activities. The brothers and sisters of the guild (most guilds were mixed) were to elect, every year, two wardens or masters to govern their affairs, and a chaplain was employed to celebrate mass daily in All Saints church for the welfare of the members and their souls after death. The guild's altar was in the north chancel of the church; the guild hall, a substantial building at the lower end of Earl Street, had apparently been acquired in 1422. There is no record of the guild in the national survey of guilds ordered by the government of Richard II in 1389,[10] but since the surviving returns are very incomplete – only one guild is recorded for the whole of Kent – we cannot be certain that the guild did not exist then.

Financial accounts for the guild provide more information on its activities.[11] A source of this nature cannot convey the full flavour of everything that the guild signified to its members, yet the details of income and expenditure identify the material concerns the brethren and sisters shared. Covering most years between 1474 and 1498 the accounts give the impression of a flourishing, confident organisation with a healthy income. In the year after 24 June 1476, for example, 138 men and 14 women paid a subscription; these women were clearly widows, the men's wives presumably acquiring privileges of membership through their husbands. The amount each guild member paid varied according to their circumstances: the largest subscriptions, of 3s 4d, were paid by the abbot of Boxley and the prior of Leeds – local grandees making a gesture of friendship towards the town and its religious life. Of lesser standing, although still important enough to be listed separately before the remaining members, were men like Richard Colpeper, esquire, who paid 2s, and John Brunston, esquire, who gave rather more in the form of four bushels of wheat. The ordinary members paid 2s or less, and for the most part sums between 1s and 3d – though even the lowest figure was a considerable sum, and effectively excluded poorer people from joining the guild. These probably were not the only costs that members had to bear: the accounts do not include payments made in connection with the religious celebrations on Corpus Christi day and which would have imposed a considerable additional burden on the membership.

In the year 1476–7 the accounts show that the income from the members totalled £11 7s 11d. In addition, there were small miscellaneous sums including a bequest of

A view of the Medway showing the medieval complex of All Saints Church, the College and Palace, with the medieval bridge. Photograph: Maidstone Museum.

The fifteenth-century house known as Mill Farmhouse in Knightrider Street.
Photograph: Maidstone Museum.

Corpus Christi Fraternity Hall, which dates to the late fifteenth century, was later the town
grammar school.
Photograph: Maidstone Museum.

Market and courthouse buildings in the Upper High Street about 1623.
Photograph: Maidstone Museum.

John Halle, surgeon and leading Protestant in
the mid-sixteenth century.
Photograph: Maidstone Museum.

Digons, Knightrider Street. Home of the Washington family, 1602–19.
Photograph: Maidstone Museum.

Astley House, a fine pargetted house in the High Street, was demolished in 1871.
Photograph: Maidstone Museum.

5s from William Bele, one of the two wardens, who died during the year, and 11s raised from the hire of the guild's large cooking or brewing utensils. But almost half of the guild's income came from rents from its properties – six houses in Maidstone, a parcel of land, and a mill called the Apple Mill, which together brought in £9 13s 2d. So the guild's total income was £21 17s 11d; expenditure apparently was slightly less, amounting to £21 8s. Property repairs came to £4 6s 5d, and the salary of the guild priest or chaplain, William Downe, was £6 13s 4d. Payments to priests, clerks and the sexton for the funerals of brothers and sisters of the guild summed to a surprisingly low 6s 8d, although the guild chaplain had the main task of saying mass for the souls of deceased members throughout the year. An inventory of the guild's property, entered on the back of the account roll, shows that Downe had in his keeping a mass book, two chalices and other altar fittings, with an assortment of new and old altar cloths, and three vestments – one of them purple, and another decorated with moons and stars. But there had been no lavish expenditure on elaborate furnishings: only one of the chalices was of silver, most of the metalwork including the candlesticks being of pewter, brass alloy or lead.

From the evidence of the accounts, the principal interest of the members of this fraternity was the annual guild feast, held on Corpus Christi day. In 1477 the feast fell on 5 June and £9 6s 6d was spent on it, or almost half the guild's income – a pattern repeated in other years. In line with this, much of the guild's property recorded in the inventory consisted of the fittings at the Guild Hall, which included a fully-equipped kitchen and bakehouse: 16 tables and 30 trestles, a cauldron and great pans and brass pots, 360 pewter dishes, and numerous jugs, basins and pots and other equipment necessary for preparing and serving great quantities of food and drink – for members and their wives. Every year, the main dish was goose but there was much else to eat as well; in 1477 123 geese were consumed along with 70 chickens and 41 pigeons, 14 pigs, 2 sheep, 5 lambs, 3 calves, and a large amount of beef. To drink there was a hogshead of wine (probably about 50 gallons) and upwards of 45 gallons of ale. In 1478 and 1479 the guild paid 20d for 18 gallons of beer – brewed with hops in the continental fashion, and something of a rarity in fifteenth-century England.

By the late fifteenth century there are indications that the Corpus Christi fraternity dominated the religious and cultural life of the town. Certainly it is one of the better documented areas of urban activity, but as in other smaller centres it is likely that townspeople were engaged in a range of communal and ceremonial activities. As far as education is concerned, the community lacked the endowed grammar school established at Sevenoaks in 1432.

The Reformation

The doctrinal and ecclesiastical changes inaugurated by Henry VIII in the 1530s and 1540s encompassing the break with Rome, the dissolution of the monasteries and chantries, and the adoption of a Protestant theology had profound consequences for Maidstone. There were a few signs of Lollardy in the Maidstone area in the early years of the sixteenth century and in 1530 Thomas Hitton, who was a former curate of Maidstone and a regular visitor to the continent, was arrested and subsequently burnt for spreading continental heresy. But there is little evidence of the precocious Protestantism on the ground that one finds at Canterbury or Sandwich in the 1530s; in terms of major shifts in religious belief at Maidstone these probably did not come until the second half of the 1540s. The first impact of the Reformation came in the way the town was governed. For as part of the Crown's policy of stripping away much of the Church's wealth, the archbishopric of Canterbury was forced to relinquish many valuable lands including all its property in the manor of Maidstone. This took the form of an exchange of lands between Archbishop Cranmer and the king in 1537, in which predictably the archbishopric fared worse. The town of Maidstone was surrendered to the Crown along with all the valuable demesne lands, the advowson of the college of All Saints, and the archbishops' gaol in the centre row of the High Street (later to become the corporation's own gaol). Even the archiepiscopal palace had to be given up. The town remained the property of the Crown until 1549 when (as we shall see in Chapter Three) the latter granted the community a charter of incorporation establishing a civic magistracy with a mayor, twelve jurats and commonalty, a magistracy at last emancipated from seigneurial control.

About 1537 part of the shrine at Boxley Abbey was exposed at Maidstone as a fraud. In 1541 several townspeople were making complaints to the government against the traditionalist master of the college and two years later there was a proposal to establish a Protestant preacher at Maidstone – as in other market towns of the county. With the growth of Protestant opinion in the town the dissolution of the college of All Saints in 1547 and the confiscation of its property provoked no apparent opposition. Indeed leading townspeople probably used the opportunity to seize some of the plate, ornaments and other liturgical items in the church for communal purposes. The dissolution of the Corpus Christi guild after 1547 may have induced more mixed feelings. Though its religious function had been largely negated by the Protestant rejection of Purgatory and the efficacy of prayers for the souls of the dead, the fraternity, as we have seen, had played a major social and cultural role in the town. In the event, what happened was that the old fraternity was subsumed into the new civic regime after 1549. Leading townsmen used money raised from the sale of church goods in All Saints to purchase the fraternity lands which became corporation property, while the Guild Hall was recycled to house the new town grammar school,

Overall, Maidstone from the twelfth and thirteenth centuries steadily consolidated its position as an established urban community on the Medway. Even during the national population decline of the late fourteenth and fifteenth centuries when numerous small towns fade back into villages, Maidstone maintained its urban identity, helped by its flourishing market and courts, by a number of successful trades and crafts such as tanning and stone-masonry, as well as its development of the political institution of the portmote and the social and cultural role of its Corpus Christi fraternity. As well as the large fraternity building on Earl Street, the stone bridge over the Medway, and the extensive complex of collegiate and archiepiscopal buildings around All Saints by the fifteenth century, there may have been a small number of significant domestic houses at the top of High Street and in Lower Stone Street. But about 1500 Maidstone remained a small country town, compared to the large cathedral cities of Canterbury and Rochester with their fortifications, castles and numerous churches, or in contrast to many of the Cinque Ports such as Sandwich or Dover with their civic corporations and complex of ecclesiastical and civic buildings. The transformation of the town began in the sixteenth century.

Notes

1. F.R.H. du Boulay, *The Lordship of Canterbury* (London, 1966), p. 311.
2. *Registrum Roberti Winchelsey*, vols. I and II, ed. R. Graham, Canterbury and York Society, vol. 51 (Oxford, 1952, 1956), p. 491.
3. Public Record Office (PRO): E179/123/32.
4. PRO, E179/123/10, m.55; mm.1–2d; 63–63d.
5. The sources are the patent and close rolls; the rolls of the portmote; the small number of deeds relating to Maidstone at the Centre for Kentish Studies [Kent Archives Office], or published in various volumes of *Archaeologia Cantiana*; final concords, published in the volumes of *Archaeologia Cantiana*.
6. Centre for Kentish Studies: Maidstone Borough Records, Md/G5, 6.
7. S.T. Aveling, 'Rochester Inns', *Archaeologia Cantiana*, vol. 21 (1895), p. 319.
8. Lambeth Palace Library, ED 621, m.5d.
9. R. Holt and G. Rosser, eds, *The English Medieval Town 1200–1540* (London, 1990), p. 12.
10. H.F. Westlake, *The Parish Gilds of Mediaeval England* (London, 1919), pp. 36–48, 137–238).
11. Centre for Kentish Studies: U1823/1/02–013; Maidstone Borough Records, Md /G1–7.

Bibliographical Note

The principal repositories of unpublished documents relating to medieval Maidstone are Lambeth Palace Library, which contains the archives of the archbishopric of Canterbury, and the Centre for Kentish Studies at Maidstone. Neither archive, however, contains extensive material relating to the medieval town. The estate documentation of the archbishopric has little to say about life in Maidstone, and even the small but useful number of surviving rolls of the portmote or borough court are of only limited usefulness. For the history and operation of the estate see F.R.H. du Boulay, *The Lordship of Canterbury* (London, 1966). Of the small amount of material relating to medieval Maidstone held at the Centre for Kentish Studies [Kent Archives Office], the most important is the series of accounts of the Corpus Christi guild. Published materials for Maidstone are quite extensive: the volumes of *Archaeologia Cantiana* are a particularly fruitful source of information for the town, although articles published by the society in its earlier years often lack accuracy and balance. In addition to those specifically cited, a number are especially useful: note by L.R.A. Grove on the Week Street pottery in vol. 82 (1967), pp. 294–6; W.K. Jordan, *Social Institutions in Kent 1480–1660*, vol. 75 (1961); G. Ward, 'The lists of Saxon churches in the Domesday Monachorum and White Book of St Augustine', vol. 45 (1933), pp. 60–89; R. Graham, 'The siege of Maidstone rectory in 1297', vol. 38 (1926), pp. 1–3; C.E. Woodruff, 'The Chronicle of Wm Glastynbury, monk of the priory of Christ Church, Canterbury, 1419–1448', vol. 37 (1925), pp. 121–51; A. Hussey, 'Testamenta Cantiana: East Kent', extra vol. (1907); C.E. Woodruff, 'Inventory of the church goods of Maidstone', vol. 22 (1897), pp. 29–33). Of the antiquarian works on the town, J.M. Russell's *History of Maidstone* (Maidstone, 1881) provides a useful quantity of information on the medieval centuries, although it is not always reliable. Edward Hasted's 4-volume *History of Kent* (1797–1801) contains useful information that needs to be approached with caution. Lesser works on the town include W.B. Gilbert, *The Accounts of the Corpus Christi Fraternity* (Maidstone, 1865), which contains unfortunately very incomplete transcripts of some of the guild's accounts, and J. Cave-Browne, *The History of the Parish Church of All Saints, Maidstone* (not dated). K.S. Martin, *Records of Maidstone*

(Maidstone, 1926), presents the town's records of the post-incorporation period. Volume II of the unfortunately incomplete *Victoria County History of Kent* (London, 1926) provides a still authoritative account of Maidstone's major ecclesiastical institutions. A large quantity of miscellaneous evidence for Maidstone is to be found in the Public Record Office, much of it enrolled in the patent rolls, close rolls and charter rolls, and all published in calendar form. Most of the references to individuals and events in this chapter come from those sources. Quantities of property transactions are recorded in the several transcripts of final concords published in *Archaeologia Cantiana*, and in I.J. Churchill, R. Griffin, F.W. Hardman, eds, *Calendar of Kent Feet of Fines*, Kent Archaeological Society Records Branch, vol. 15 (1956). The events of 1381 in Maidstone are described in E. Powell and G.M. Trevelyan, *The Peasants' Rising and the Lollards* (1899), and W.E. Flaherty, 'The Great Rebellion in Kent of 1381 Illustrated from the Public Records', *Archaeologia Cantiana*, vol. 3 (1860); the chroniclers' accounts of the revolt are to be found in R.B. Dobson, *The Peasants' Revolt of 1381* (London, 1970). The most useful book on Cade's rebellion is I.M.W. Harvey, *Jack Cade's Rebellion of 1450* (Oxford, 1991).

Chapter Three

THE TUDOR AND EARLY STUART
BOROUGH: 1549–1660

The incorporation of Maidstone in July 1549 proved a decisive turning point in the town's development. After the changes wrought by the Reformation and discussed in Chapter Two, Edward VI's charter created a new political regime for the town with a civic magistracy of mayor, jurats and commonalty, courts and other paraphernalia of municipal government, which was to last more or less up to the Municipal Reform Act of 1835.[1] When William Lambarde wrote his *Perambulation of Kent* in the 1570s his account of the town began with its Edwardian charter but during the following century or so the town grew substantially. William Camden in Elizabeth's reign called Maidstone large and populous, while in the 1640s John Taylor lauded it as 'a fair, sweet, pleasant, rich and populous market town'. Maidstone's growth reflected renewed general urban expansion across the kingdom after the stagnation of the late Middle Ages. During the Tudor and early Stuart period national population increase boosted trade and the fortunes of the wealthier classes. Some cities like London advanced in a spectacular fashion, reaching over 400,000 inhabitants by the 1640s, many provincial towns grew more slowly. But the decades after the Reformation witnessed the emergence of a new urban framework in England, with the chartering of many boroughs, the development of markets and fairs, moves towards the development of county towns as administrative and service centres, and the formation of a new-style civic identity associated with Puritanism. As we shall see, a number of these trends can be observed in Maidstone.

But Maidstone's progress in the Tudor and early Stuart period was by no means inevitable or painless. As with many middle-rank English towns at this time the community faced considerable problems. Economically the town suffered competition from other urban centres in the region as it sought to diversify. Demographic expansion was accompanied by rising poverty, while civic government suffered repeated set-backs and challenges including: the loss of the charter in 1554 following the town's involvement in Wyatt's Revolt (the charter was not restored until 1559); protracted legal disputes with landowners in the 1620s; and conflict with the Crown in the 1630s. In the next decade Maidstone was affected by the political and military upheavals of the Civil War. However, in the long term, the town's important communications position astride the Medway counted increasingly in its favour, with the industrial and agricultural development of the Weald and the growth of London demand for food and other supplies boosting the town's commercial role. At the same time, the presence of a considerable number of prosperous gentry in the area encouraged the town's new-found importance as an adminstrative focus for the shire.

Population

The earliest estimate for Maidstone's population comes from the chantry returns for 1548 which give 1,440 communicants for the town; this would suggest a total figure of just over 1,900 people. In 1557 Archdeacon Harpsfield's visitation recorded 1,600 communicants in the town (1,776 in the wider parish) indicating an increased population of about 2,100 in the town (2,330 in the parish). However, the late 1550s witnessed a major influenza epidemic sweeping the country, followed by a terrible outbreak of plague in 1563. The diocesan survey in the latter year gives two sets of figures with 300–352 households in the town or about 1,425–1,672 inhabitants – suggesting a marked decline of population. But recovery was probably rapid: a return in 1565 gave 420 households or nearly 2,000 people, though another the following year numbered only 294 houses. Later figures are in short supply but in 1642 the townspeople claimed the parish population was about 6,000 – almost certainly a great exaggeration. By the time of the Compton Census in the 1670s the population of the town possibly numbered about 3,000.[2]

These rather shaky estimates suggest that the town may have nearly doubled in size between the accession of Queen Elizabeth and the Restoration of Charles II. This pattern of substantial growth is broadly confirmed by the parish registers for All Saints over the same period – see Figure 2.[3] Baptisms rose steadily in the first half of Elizabeth's reign followed by a plateau during the last critical years of the century (affected by disease and harvest failure), then renewed increase up to the 1640s (apart from the distressed 1620s). For much of this time baptisms ran substantially ahead of burials – typical of smaller urban centres. Though the 1560s and late 1640s saw particularly high mortality, other burial crises were limited in number and severity.

Epidemic disease was a recurrent menace. Outbreaks of plague occurred in 1563–4, 1575–6, 1595, 1604, 1609 and 1626 with the infection spread from the capital in almost all cases and in some instances (as in the 1590s) enhanced by harvest failure. The magistrates tried to prevent or restrict the spread of disease with elementary precautions. In May 1563 householders were ordered to sluice down the streets every day, while later that year the October fair was cancelled – to stop an influx of Londoners. The following year one of the town's almspersons was appointed to look after those afflicted by plague. But plague was not the only problem. As well as influenza in the late 1550s, we hear in 1578–9 of 'the sickness time for the poor' and in 1602 there was a smallpox attack.

Though Maidstone did not suffer the heavy demographic deficits of bigger cities – where burials often ran far ahead of baptisms – it was none the less dependent on immigration for a significant proportion of its population growth before the Civil War. Early modern England was a highly mobile society with a great deal of migration from the countryside to towns. According to church court records, it is likely that among male inhabitants of Maidstone during the later sixteenth and early seventeenth centuries only a quarter had resided there since their birth; over four in ten had been born elsewhere in the county and nearly a fifth had moved to Maidstone from outside Kent, including the South West and the North. The picture was similar for townswomen. Among the newcomers were apprentices (mostly teenage boys), coming to town to work in the expanding economy, serving their masters for seven or more years and aspiring to become respectable freemen and traders in their own right. Most of these had moved short distances, from up to ten miles, like Nathaniel Salmon from Yalding, the grandson of a yeoman farmer who was apprenticed in 1591 to Richard Shepherd a Maidstone mercer. But during the late sixteenth and early seventeenth centuries English towns suffered an influx of poor immigrants, forced from the countryside by poverty and housing shortages, sometimes tramping long distances in search of work or relief. In 1608 the Maidstone magistrates protested how 'many of the poorer folk either of their own desire or being for their idle and disordered life driven out of other places do come to inhabit and settle themselves here.' A number tried to work as servants or set up in trade without having been apprenticed, and others drifted into petty crime.[4]

The corporation tried hard to exclude these poorer migrants. In 1566 owners of small tenements were ordered to remove recent tenants unless they were willing to give surety that these newcomers would not need poor relief. Eight years later there was a prohibition on non-free traders retailing in the town. Further attempts at settlement controls followed in later years. In 1632, for instance, landlords of poor tenants 'coming out of any other town or parish' were fined a swingeing 5s a week as long as any outsider stayed there. These measures had only a marginal effect. The problem of poor outsiders only abated when general living standards began to improve later in the seventeenth century.

More beneficial to the town was the arrival in the 1560s of a small group of religious refugees fleeing civil war in the Low Countries. Dutch and Walloon migrants settled in a number of English towns including London, Canterbury, Colchester, Norwich, Sandwich, Southampton and Maidstone. The Maidstone community of Dutch refugees seems to have been established in response to the town's petition to the Crown in 1567 asking for sixty families able to make a variety of cloths, as well as pots, paving tiles and other wares. The foreigners were granted the right to have their own church – in the old chapel of St Faith's – and other privileges similar to their brethren at Sandwich. The number was never large. In 1576 we hear there were 200 in the town (women excepted). Some tried to return to the Netherlands to join the war against the Spanish; others sought to keep up their trading links with Antwerp. There were additional sources of friction with the authorities. In 1568 the Maidstone magistrates endeavoured to force the newcomers to sell their cloth to local retailers; soon after official searchers were appointed (both Dutch and English) to inspect the quality of the cloth being manufactured. In 1572 the foreign congregation and corporation suffered the joint embarrassment of being tricked by a young Dutchman claiming to be possessed by the Devil.

During the 1580s, as the Dutch revolt against Spain reached its climax, there may have been a further influx of continental refugees to the town. But the early seventeenth century saw the Dutch community fade away, partly through inter-marriage with local people, and partly through migration to London and elsewhere. In 1622 just over twenty members of the Dutch community were left, the great majority English born. Now the main industry was thread-making, for which, it was said, 'the poor both of the town and country adjoining are employed by spinning'. The Dutch church under its minister John Miller survived until Archbishop Laud's attack on the stranger churches in 1634 when it was swept away (see below). By then Maidstone's ethnic community which had played a significant role in the rise of the town's industries had become increasingly marginal to its economic development.

Markets and fairs

The medieval Thursday market and four annual fairs remained at the heart of Maidstone's economy well into the seventeenth century. The 1549 charter specifically confirmed the fairs at Maytime (30 April–2 May), Midsummer (19–21 June), St Faith's (5–7 October) and Candlemas (1–3 February). As we noted earlier, during the period before the English Revolution, population growth and the expansion of agricultural and inland trade boosted the marketing role of many towns including Maidstone. As a rough indicator, the town's total fair and market income rose from about £12 per annum in the mid-1590s to about £15 in 1610–11; by the 1620s the profits were being leased for £18 a year. Before the Civil War one visitor asserted that Maidstone 'is now the principal market town in the county'.

Magistrates endeavoured to promote the town's market and fairs by improving facilities. In Elizabeth's reign the main market place at the top of the High Street had a corn-cross for the grain trade, while fish were sold nearby in the old shambles and cloth at the school-house; dairy products, animals and fruit were traded at the corner of Mill Lane. From 1608 the new court-house was also used, at least initially, as a corn-market while the old corn-cross was converted into a fish-market, and the old shambles into a place for the sale of vegetables. In 1570 the corporation decreed that the May, Midsummer and Autumn fairs should be held in the Fairmeadow or Queen's Mead by the river, but the Candlemas fair was kept in the High Street, stretching from the corn-cross down to the Great Bridge. Initially the management of the fairs was delegated to the wardens of the town companies or guilds, but it was later taken over by civic officials, and then from the 1620s leased out in order to pay off some of the town's debts.

However, if marketing activity was generally expanding in the period up to the English Civil War, there were notable shifts in trading patterns. In 1567–8 nearly 26,000 broadcloths (probably local as well as Wealden cloths) were sold at the Candlemas and May fairs, with a smaller number in October. But there was growing competition from the London markets. In the 1571 Parliament a bill was proposed requiring that Kentish cloths be sold only at Blackwell Hall in London and not at the Maidstone fair. Despite the defeat of this bill, Londoners tried again in the same session with another proposed measure giving the mayor of London power to regulate all the cloth fairs in Kent and Sussex. Again it was unsuccessful, but in the long run Blackwell Hall won out and by 1603–4 the cloth trade at Maidstone had disappeared, though we do find cheaper kersey cloths being sold in Maidstone, mainly outside the traditional open market. As far as the fairs are concerned, the main item being traded by the early seventeenth century was livestock, with Welsh cattle bought to be fattened on Romney Marsh and in the Weald and subsequently sold for London consumption. The October fair was particularly important for livestock sales. In 1641 Sir Roger Twisden of East Peckham acquired animals at Cranbrook, Tonbridge and Malling fairs, but his most important purchase by far was of Welsh cattle at Maidstone's October fair.

By the late sixteenth century Maidstone had an important grain market – the second biggest in West Kent (after Gravesend). Sales were made increasingly to London dealers with supplies coming by coastal shipping from a growing area of eastern England. During the seventeenth century the town also became a flourishing fruit and hop market. Even so, up to the Civil War Maidstone's marketing activity was not particularly specialised – with a wide range of wares and agricultural goods on sale. By 1640 the town's fairs and market also faced growing competition from commercial outlets outside the open market – from inns and other drinking houses and the growing number of retail shops.

Potentially the town's marketing hinterland stretched up and down the river valley, along the scarpland and into the Weald. In 1574, for instance, we find two women walking from Marden via Loose 'to sell butter and buy certain wares' at Maidstone market. Trade was also growing with the capital. At the same time, the town faced considerable difficulties in taking full advantage of its central position in mid-Kent. Roads to the town were often in poor condition. Even the old Roman road from Maidstone to Rochester was overgrown with trees and bushes and in some places nigh impassable. The Medway was navigable below the town and free of tolls but the upper reaches were obstructed by weirs and mills restricting navigation and so commercial access to the Weald. From the 1580s small boats were able to pass intermittently for six or so miles to Yalding, but attempts to open up the river for regular traffic were resisted by neighbouring landowners. In 1600 there was a determined attempt by leading West Kent gentry, several with links to Maidstone, to push through a navigation scheme for the upper Medway, but this was defeated. In the late 1620s another attempt was made, strongly supported by the Crown which hoped to speed up the shipment of ordnance from the Wealden iron industry to London and the royal dockyards; but again it ran into fierce local opposition on the upper Medway and failed. Despite renewed efforts after the Restoration, it was not, as we shall see in Chapter Four, until the 18th century that the upper Medway became fully navigable, giving a major stimulus to the town's Georgian advance as a commercial entrepot.[5]

None the less, failure on the upper Medway should not detract from the town's growing importance in the sixteenth and early seventeenth centuries as a river port. Already in the Middle Ages the town had a considerable number of ships, while the increase of stone quarrying in the parish relied on shipments down the Medway. In the 1540s hard stone was shipped from Maidstone to repair the royal fortifications at Calais, while stone transported from quarries at Barming, Boxley, and Boughton Monchelsea was used extensively for private and public construction in southern England with masons from the town undertaking the work. In 1617 three horse-drawn wagons carted stone from Boughton to Maidstone where it was laded on to a boat and transported to the Isle of Sheppey to erect a tombstone for an Eastchurch man. The depth of water at Maidstone could however cause problems: one report in the 1560s counselled that shipments of stone cannot be made 'but in the spring streams and if it happen then to blow much wind they cannot carry from the foresaid places'.

As well as the town quay there were minor havens nearby at Millhall and Newhithe, where the river may have been deeper. The corporation took some steps to improve the port facilities. In the 1560s a new stone wall was built at the Fairmeadow; the river was dredged near the bridge; and a new quay was made in the early seventeenth century. In 1566 a return to the Crown listed the town as having four ships of between 30 and 50 tons, but there were doubtless many smaller ones as well. Certainly by the end of the sixteenth century it is evident that Maidstone's port was engaged in a wide variety of trades. As already noted, the grain trade with London was increasingly large-scale, with some reshipment of cereals brought from East Kent and East Anglia. In the 1590s it was said that Maidstone and other places on the Medway 'convey away much barley and malt'. When harvests failed in the 1620s, grain was imported from France and Poland for local consumption. The transport of cloth was also important. John Collier, for instance, was said to carry the goods of Robert King, a Cranbrook clothier and those of Maidstone clothiers to London in his boat, bringing back to the town wool, oil, madder and other wares from the capital. Small boats carried quantities of consumer wares from London. A ship wrecked in the river in the 1620s was laden with oil, earthenware, Spanish and French wine, bacon, Cheshire cheese, two kegs of sturgeon, a box of tobacco pipes (tobacco was increasingly popular), ironware and cottons – all destined for sale in the town's markets, shops and inns. This consumer traffic with London was to become particularly valuable after the Restoration.

However, other major trades also need to be noted. One was traffic in timber, principally for the expanding dockyards at Rochester and Chatham. Already in

1540 large amounts of timber were being supplied for the king's works at Rochester. After 1588 oak and other wood for Elizabeth's navy came from Maidstone and there were further supplies in the early seventeenth century. Despite the problems on the upper river, some Wealden cannon and ordnance was also moved down river to the dockyards, London and abroad.

In the early Stuart era we discover growing shipments of fuller's earth, used in textile production and mainly extracted at Boxley. Already in the 1590s local people complained that the river was 'continually frequented with hoys, lighters and other boats for the shipping away of fuller's earth'. In Charles I's reign Richard Roodes from Maidstone had a warehouse by the river for shipping the product. The government was concerned that exports abroad would assist foreign cloth industries at the expense of domestic clothiers. In 1623 there was a proposal for licensing shipments to Suffolk and Essex with the mayor of Maidstone in charge of regulation. In this and other trades there are signs that some Maidstone ships were engaged in overseas commerce, but the most important business by far was river and coastal traffic, increasingly with the capital.

Industries and the service sector

The markets, fairs and port were clearly fundamental to the growing economy of Maidstone in the period up to the Civil War, but there was also a great deal of employment in the wider industrial and service sectors. Lists of townsmen admitted as freemen of the town between 1600 and 1617 indicate that clothing and textiles (20.9 per cent), together with distribution (19.6 per cent) and the food and drink trades (12.4 per cent), were the three most important occupational groupings in early Stuart Maidstone, though with a range of other crafts and service trades.[6] As in the medieval period, clothing workers such as tailors were a staple urban group, supplying local and rural customers on a regular basis. But it is clear that textile production, relatively unimportant in the earlier period, was of increasing importance in Maidstone in the decades after the Reformation. Fulling mills multiplied on the Len during the sixteenth century, converted from earlier corn-mills – Lambarde noted thirteen fulling mills in the area by the 1570s, encouraged no doubt by the good supplies of fuller's earth. Most of the early output may have taken the form of traditional broadcloths, though there are also reports of Suffolk-type short cloths called manikins being made in the town. The Dutch incomers also added to the variety of cloths manufactured in the town with the introduction of the so-called new draperies including grograms, mockados and sackcloth. In 1604 the corporation appointed searchers to inspect the cloths of both Dutch and English masters making new draperies; these now included fustians, diaper and mixed cloths such as linsey woolsey, as well as older products. Cheaper kerseys were also being sold and possibly manufactured in the town in the early seventeenth century. The freemen lists for 1610–17 even include a small cluster of silk-weavers. By the 1630s, however, the Maidstone cloth industry like that elsewhere in the county was probably starting to decline, adversely affected by the disruption of European markets due to the Thirty Years War and by competition from textile manufacture in other regions. Increasingly Maidstone's textile activity was confined to the specialist trade of thread-making – pioneered by the Dutch. In 1604 it was said there was 'much flax dressed within this town more than of former times has been used'. Poorer townspeople were employed in harvesting the flax and spinning thread. In 1625 we hear of fields of flax being harvested in the town fields and at nearby Loddington. A few years later Roger Cherson declared that his trade was 'the beating and dressing of flax and for the following of that calling he is constrained to live and abide at Maidstone among the thread-makers.' During the 1640s Maidstone was probably the principal thread-making town outside London.

The leather trades, significant in Maidstone during the late Middle Ages, may have had a reduced role, with only 11.1 per cent of freemen in this category under James I. During the 1630s Wealden and scarpland tanners were selling hides in the town to the numerous shoemakers, glovers and allied craftsmen. But competition was increasingly tough. During James I's reign collarmakers at Maidstone, Canterbury and Faversham complained of outsiders setting up in the trade and undermining their business. In 1639 James Betts, a shoemaker, was effectively denied the freedom 'in regard there already many of that trade' in the town. More important for the future were two new trades: paper-making and commercial brewing, both well established by the mid-seventeenth century. Early paper-making in Kent was based at Dartford but by Charles I's reign there was at least one substantial paper-maker in the town – Thomas Taylor – and others quickly followed – taking over the old fulling mills of the declining cloth industry. Commercial brewing advanced equally fast. Traditionally, most brewing was done either in the home (for domestic consumption) or by innkeepers and alehousekeepers. From the fifteenth century, London and the major provincial cities saw the rise of commercial brewers accompanied by the spread of hopped beer, cheaper and more palatable than the old-style unhopped ale. At Maidstone wholesale brewers emerge during James I's reign, benefiting from local supplies of grain, clean stream water and the growing cultivation of hops in the vicinity. A number of beer-brewers are listed in the freemen lists 1600–17. About 1612 Mark Short set up a brewhouse in the town with its own manager and a decade later we hear of five brewers in the community. By the 1630s one of the leading townsmen was the brewer Thomas Stanley (mayor in 1641) who owned brewhouses at Rochester and Gravesend. The first major brewery premises appeared about 1650 with the Lower Brewery in Lower Stone Street and the Upper Brewery in Brewer Street.

These large-scale breweries supplied drink to growing numbers of victualling houses in the town. In 1577 the Hundred of Maidstone (including neighbouring villages) had 10 inns, 2 taverns and 27 alehouses. By 1610 a survey of licensed premises in the town listed 6 inns and 24 alehouses – the largest number of premises in High Street and Middle Row;[7] in addition there was a crowd of illicit boozing dens. By the reign of James I the most important of the inns was the Star on High

Street, close to the market area, which had acquired a complex of rooms, stables and yards stretching over 400 ft back to Earl's Street. As well as offering wine, beer, meals and accommodation for gentlemen, merchants and other better-off customers, inns started to develop commercial functions – as places for farmers and traders to buy and sell and settle their bills. From the late sixteenth century they also became meeting places for gentry and justices of the peace. The Star, for instance, had a great county room called the justice chamber where the county JPs met during sessions and assizes for political debate. In 1614 an acrimonious discussion occurred there about the Crown's demand for additional fiscal levies, and in 1642 the Kentish petition was organised at the Star, one of the crucial steps in the quick march to the English Civil War.

By contrast to the inns, most alehouses were smaller, more basic establishments kept in ordinary houses, often in a backroom, offering mainly beer and food to lesser townspeople and the poor. Inventories of the town's alehousekeepers who died between 1560 and 1640 show that four out of five had less than £40 in personal wealth. Despite the introduction of licensing laws in 1552 the number of premises multiplied in most English towns during this period with growing numbers of poor people setting up illicit tippling houses, frequently supplied by the new commercial brewers. In 1588 the town council or Burghmote decreed that unlicensed victuallers should be fined a draconian 20s. Other attempts to regulate the trade included heavy fines on brewers for serving unlicensed houses, but such measures had limited effect. There was growing popular demand for alehouses – as a place for cheap refreshments, as a stop-over point for poor migrants, and as a neighbourhood and communal centre for small craftsmen and labourers.

Victuallers and brewers were joined by butchers and bakers to form an important group of food and drink traders in the early Stuart freemen lists. As we saw above, another important occupational cluster in those lists covered distribution. By the early Stuart era the town had a growing number of specialist shopkeepers – mercers, haberdashers, drapers and others. These comprised one of the wealthiest occupational groups in Maidstone. Shopkeepers like this benefited from the general expansion of inland trade during the Tudor and early Stuart period, the rising affluence of the better-off classes in the countryside and a general drift of business away from the crowded markets and fairs. In Maidstone they also benefited from the town's growing population and its increased significance after 1600 as a county town, with the growing influx of gentry from the shire. Not all of Maidstone's distributive traders, however, were wealthy; there were considerable numbers of petty chapmen and the like, doubtless supplying small farmers and others in the area.

The growing diversity and strength of the town's economy was also marked by an increased presence of professional men, though their modest number in the early Stuart freemen lists confirms that their major impact on the urban economy was after the Restoration. In the mid-sixteenth century two eminent surgeons were associated with the town: Thomas Vicary, the king's surgeon, and John Halle. Vicary (d. 1561) was reportedly a minor practitioner in the town until he treated

Henry VIII's leg in 1525; he subsequently became serjeant of the king's surgeons and master of the new London company of Barbers and Surgeons. He owned a house at Boxley though he eventually died in London. Halle (?1529–1566) was a leading figure in mid-Tudor Maidstone. Closely linked to the Edwardian reformers in the town, he was imprisoned for his part in Wyatt's revolt, and denounced Catholics in the town after the accession of Elizabeth. He corresponded with London physicians about venereal disease, translated medical texts into English and published a vitriolic attack on quacks, soothsayers and other unqualified practitioners. One of his *bêtes noires* was Thomas Lufkin who came to Maidstone in 1558 and combined the activities of physician, surgeon, astrologer, palm-reader and fortune teller. By the 1630s Maidstone had at least seven licensed physicians and surgeons, along with various other unlicensed practitioners of the Lufkin variety – all providing medical care, almost equally ineffectual, to the town and its hinterland. When Lady Anne Twisden became ill at East Peckham in 1638 her son Sir Roger sent for Dr Ramsey to come from Maidstone who stayed overnight and advised she would recover, but, true to form, she died soon after.

Lawyers emerge as an increasingly influential professional group before the English Revolution. In 1600 Maidstone may have had half a dozen attorneys (our modern solicitors) operating in the town, pleading in the town courts, writing wills and conveyances, giving legal advice. In addition there were several leading attorneys resident in the area such as John Webbe, the clerk of the peace for the county, who maintained his chamber at Clifford's Inn in London as well as serving as town clerk of Gravesend and legal adviser to a number of landed families. In 1608 the corporation imposed a limit of eight attorneys appearing in the court of pleas, suggesting legal business was expanding. From the 1630s the town attorney Andrew Broughton rose quickly to prominence, building up a large local practice, becoming a senior official in county administration, and after 1640 clerk of the peace for Kent. In 1648 he was elected mayor of Maidstone and the following year read the Parliamentary death sentence on Charles I.

There was also a small but significant group of barristers in the town. In Elizabeth's reign the post of town clerk was combined with that of recorder which was held by a succession of barristers. One of the most eminent of these was Nicholas Barham (d.1577) who became a bencher of Gray's Inn and later one of the serjeants-at-law. Barham owned Chillington House and the Digons in Knightrider Street and sat as MP for the town in 1563. Chillington House was later occupied by another barrister (and bencher of Middle Temple), Henry Halle. Halle was a prominent Puritan who left extensive bequests to the town's poor. Another leading lawyer resident in the town was Lawrence Washington, also a bencher of the Middle Temple and Registrar of the High Court of Chancery, who lived in Knightrider Street. Though one of the advantages of Maidstone for these lawyers was its relative proximity to London and the Westminster courts, they may also have exploited the town's burgeoning importance as an official and legal centre with its growing influx of gentry by Charles I's reign.

Pivotal here was the meeting of county quarter sessions and assizes in the town. During the century before the Civil War both courts dealt with a growing volume of litigation and administrative business and attracted throngs of landowners, lawyers and countrypeople. Quarter sessions records indicate that Maidstone was well established as the sessions town for West Kent by the last part of Elizabeth's reign, while East Kent sessions was held at Canterbury castle. In 1588 William Lambarde observed at Maidstone sessions how 'often and ordinarily do we repair to this place and for this service, good friends and neighbours'. Eight years later there was a move, perhaps initiated by the clerk of the peace, John Webbe, to transfer the Canterbury sessions to Maidstone; but the East Kent gentry doubtless protested and the Privy Council had to intervene to stop the move. In James I's reign a dispute blew up between the town and some of the county justices over the town's judicial privileges under its 1619 charter, and there was a proposal to shift county sessions to Rochester, but the dispute was quickly settled and Maidstone retained its control over West Kent sessions.

Becoming the county assize town proved more difficult. While nearly half of all assize sessions were held at Maidstone in the 1560s, during the next decades Rochester was the preferred venue. Only after 1600 did the assize judges increasingly travel to Maidstone, so that from the 1620s virtually all meetings were held there. Court facilities may have been decisive. When the assize court moved from Penenden Heath to the town it is unclear, but by the later sixteenth century a court-house had been built at the upper end of the High Street – by the town and West Kent justices – to house the sessions, assizes and civic meetings. But temporary buildings also had to be put up at assize times to accommodate the courts. This unsatisfactory arrangement ended in 1608 when a new court-house was erected by the town close by the old one. As well as improving court facilities the corporation spent lavishly on gifts, entertainment and other *douceurs* to attract the assize judges, paid for in part by a special tax on victuallers. By the early seventeenth century the town boasted the county gaol and new House of Correction for West Kent and increasingly all kinds of other judicial and administrative gatherings took place in the town, while the county court and county elections continued to be held at nearby Penenden Heath. Little wonder Richard Kilburne declared in the 1650s that Maidstone was now 'accounted the shire town [for Kent] . . . the fittest place for public meetings of the county'.

As well as benefiting from gentry visitors to sessions and assizes, the town's shops, markets and crafts were encouraged by the growing numbers of gentry who resided in and around the town for at least part of the year. Under Edward VI Lord Cobham and Sir Thomas Wyatt received grants of the College and the Archiepiscopal Palace; after 1581 Sir John Astley, the Master of the Queen's Jewel House, lived at the Palace, and was probably responsible for its new Elizabethan frontage; he in turn was succeeded by his son Sir John junior, Master of the Revels. Other important landowners lived nearby like Thomas Hendley at Otham who had important business ties with the Elizabethan town. By the 1620s, however, there was a sizeable cluster of gentry resident in Maidstone, mostly in the area of the Palace and Knightrider Street, among them Sir Humphry Tufton, Richard Duke, Edward Filmer, Lady Walsingham and later Sir Robert Filmer. Relations were not entirely amicable – as we shall see, there were several clashes between the corporation and local gentry before the Civil Wars. But there can be little question that gentry demand was good for the town's economy. In 1642 we find the town laying out a bowling green in the King's Meadow – the first of the new urbane leisure activities which were to make the town so attractive to the genteel classes in the Georgian period.

The expansion of new industries and service activities were clearly important for long-term economic development, but it is essential to remember that in this period as in earlier centuries the town retained close links with agriculture. Admittedly, the number of freemen with agricultural trades was small, confirming the basic 'urbanness' of early Stuart Maidstone compared with smaller market towns. But, outside the built-up town, in the wider parish many inhabitants were farmers or agricultural labourers and numerous townsmen may have worked smallholdings in conjunction with their trades. Here increasing agricultural specialisation was having an impact with the spread of hop cultivation in the area. As early as 1604 we find fifty or more men, women and children going out of the town hop-picking at Chart Sutton – a seasonal activity which continued for many poorer townspeople up to the 1950s.

The corporation tried to regulate the town's economy through trade companies or guilds which admitted inhabitants as freemen and excluded non-freemen from trading. From 1551 we find four general trade companies for artificers, victuallers, drapers and mercers operating in the town. But these new creations lacked the social function of the ancient guilds found in other Kent towns and were probably never very effective. In 1605 the corporation agreed to re-establish them but their revival was short-lived and in 1613 Burghmote ordered they should be dissolved, though there were further sporadic attempts to revive them in 1621–2, 1625 and 1637. By the end of our period such protectionist or interventionist measures were increasingly unnecessary in an expanding urban economy.

In conclusion, Maidstone's economy suffered from a number of problems and constraints in the century after incorporation: inadequate communications, particularly on the upper Medway but also overland; competition from other towns in West Kent; and the heavy influx of poor outsiders without much capital or expertise which undermined the position of established tradesmen. But generally speaking, by the mid-seventeenth century a number of the economic foundations had been laid – including the emergence of specialist industries, an expanded service sector and gentry residence – which were to underpin the town's Georgian prosperity.

Social change

The growing presence of gentry underlined mounting social polarisation in the community. Among the top quarter of the town's inhabitants one can discern a significant improvement in living standards with enlarged housing together with the spread of fashionable consumer wares, particularly household furnishings. Lower down the social order, the wealth levels and living conditions of small craftsmen and traders stagnated, while the bottom third of the urban population experienced declining real incomes as a result of price inflation and sluggish wage increases.

Probate inventories shed some light on the personal assets and lifestyle of the better-off classes in early Stuart Maidstone.[8] Though evidence of this kind is patchy and selective, inventories taken between 1600 and 1640 confirm, as one might expect, that those townspeople with the greatest personal wealth were gentlemen – having on average over £350 at their deaths. A number were minor landowners of the type already mentioned – taking up residence to enjoy the growing social attractions of town. Thus Richard Duke who was engaged in various battles over civic jurisdiction in the early 1620s had total personal wealth of nearly £650 at his death in 1626; another gentleman George Fenner who died a few years before had £415 in personal goods. Both owned considerable quantities of comfortable bedding and other fashionable furniture, as well as books and extensive silver plate. Thomas Reve, who died in 1617 was worth almost £900 and occupied a house with twelve main rooms, fitted out with carpets, tapestries, drawing tables, books, pictures, a clock and plate.

After gentlemen, shopkeepers and other distributive traders had the greatest personal wealth – on average about £327 in the early Stuart era. Among them we find a number of affluent mercers such as Alexander Beale who died in 1618 worth about £860 in personal assets. His house had eight or nine main rooms, including the shop, while the inventory listed a variety of furnishings, plate and books, miscellaneous shop goods worth over £200, and a lot of outstanding debts. As well as trading in the town Beale was engaged in farming, owning cattle in Sheppey. Robert Wood was a town jurat who died in 1635 worth over £1,060. His goods included a large shop stock worth more than £700 including spices, hops, and great quantities of cloth. As well as mercers, this affluent group also included drapers, ironmongers and merchants. One of the wealthiest men to die in the town before 1640 was Joos van de Bush, a foreign merchant, probably linked to the Dutch community, whose total assets were valued at about £1,700 at his death in 1624. As we have already noted, innkeepers were increasingly important figures in the community. Thomas Davies who died in 1639 had an estate of about £818. His inn, possibly the Bell, had about twenty rooms with about a dozen chambers, a great quantity of featherbeds, plate and wine.

In contrast, the professional classes as a group were somewhat less prosperous: their average inventory valuation in early Stuart Maidstone was about £120. Barristers tended to be the most affluent: for instance, Henry Halle who died in 1622 occupied a large house with good furnishings, books and the like worth about £376. Attorneys and physicians had a more modest social standing, as did most of the town's surgeons. Nicholas Bennett who died in 1640 had 'glasses [and] waters and medicine in them', as well as a saw and other instruments of surgery in a house with five main rooms: his total personal wealth was just under £40. The golden period for the professional classes was to come in the 18th century.

Manufacturers belonged more to the middling and lesser ranks of urban society. Those in the textile trades had an average of about £99 in personal goods, though one does find a few wealthier clothiers like John Basden whose estate was valued at about £575 in 1626. But fullers and thread-makers were smaller men – like William Swinhog with his twisting mill, flax and yarn worth only £49. Leather-workers – glovers, shoemakers and so on – were generally of moderate standing, with an average wealth of about £97. In contrast some of those working in the new specialist industries were much better off. In 1640 the jurat and paper-maker Thomas Taylor died worth £689 in personal estate including a papermill and a considerable stock of paper. Among the commercial brewers John Sanders, another magistrate, left goods and debts assessed at £2,349 in 1612 – putting him among the higher ranks of provincial townsmen in early Stuart England. He had a large house and brewhouse, malt worth over £500, and a quantity of household furniture. Another brewer Thomas Rassell left almost £1,000 in goods in 1638.

The growing affluence of these higher social classes was reflected in urban building. Though only a fraction of the town's Tudor and early Stuart houses survive, we find clusters of substantial new or rebuilt houses in the centre of town – in King Street [East Lane], at the top of High Street, and down Earl Street and Bank Street (multi-storeyed houses with ornamented frontages). Among other large new or remodelled houses were Chillington House and Digons, both occupied by lawyers. However, many town inhabitants were much less well off. Henry Broad a shoemaker who died in 1618 left personal property valued at just over £12 including leather, tools and shoes worth 31s, a simple joined bed priced at £1, clothes and ready money worth 20s 2d and two psalm books, among various other odds and ends. A bricklayer Gabriel Steddall died in 1620 worth £7 6 8d, but of this £4 3s was owed him by various people. George Gosling who was described as a labourer at his death in 1623 left a similar amount, mainly comprised of his apparel, a bed, and a cupboard. But most labourers like the majority of adult townsmen were much too poor to have inventories made of their goods.

For the lower ranks of urban society the late sixteenth and early seventeenth centuries were a time of growing difficulty, with many townspeople suffering from rising prices, unemployment and housing shortages, exacerbated by pauper immigration from the countryside. Some ordinary townsmen managed to get by except in the worst harvest years, but others, particularly small craftsmen and labourers with families, were reduced to the poverty line. Unfortunately there are no detailed listings of the poor for Maidstone as there are for several other English towns at this time, but it is likely that the long-term increase of urban poverty was badly aggravated by recurrent harvest failures and plague outbreaks. In 1596, after a sequence of bad harvests, the town magistrates proclaimed that the 'number of poor people inhabiting within this town and parish (by means of the long time of scarcity and dearth as well of all kinds of grain and corn as also of all manner of victuals) is now grown and come to be very great'. About the same time, a Maidstone merchant noted 'the exceeding number of very aged, lame and poor people who through their great wants have not wherewithall to set them nor their children in work'. In addition to the local poor – widows, orphans, labouring families and others – there were numerous vagrants from the county and beyond.

This growing phalanx of poor not only needed relief: they threatened public order. Thus Tabitha Taylor, a poor woman, came from Ashford in the 1590s hoping to work for her kinsman a shoemaker in Week Street, 'but at her coming she found that he was otherwise provided'; after a few days she went off to Sittingbourne and was charged with stealing clothes. Poor vagrants, lodging in alehouses or sleeping rough in barns, hung around the town robbing countrymen visiting the market. Though Maidstone apparently escaped the food riots which affected other Kent towns in this period, social unrest bubbled close to the surface. In 1603 a Maidstone labourer denounced the accession of King James and threatened 'he will be in danger to be killed before Michaelmas day next . . . with an arrow or a gun [and] . . . after his death . . . there shall be no king in England'.

The town council attempted to deal with the poverty issue in a variety of ways. As we saw earlier, there was a growing wave of settlement regulations against poor newcomers trying to live in the town. From the 1570s if not before vagrants and rogues were regularly whipped out of the town. In 1593 the town was divided into thirteen wards each under a magistrate in order to take speedy action against poor incomers, vagrants and the disorderly poor. The practice of warding was revived in 1618, 1622 (in conjunction with the trade companies), 1637, 1650, 1656 and 1659. Unlicensed alehouses, the common resort of the poor, were a prime target: in 1624 the town reported they had suppressed many such establishments.

As well as these police measures, there was growing expenditure on poor relief. Statutes from the 1530s placed growing administrative responsibility for relief on parish officials, but in Maidstone it is evident by the 1580s that the town magistrates had taken effective charge of provision for the poor. Relief took the form of weekly payments or pensions to the local indigent (mostly widows and labouring families), and casual payments to the itinerant poor and those suffering seasonal or short-term deprivation. The level of expenditure rose from about £9–10 a year in the early 1580s to £14 in 1594–5 to nearly £23 in 1606. In the terrible plague year 1604–5 the cost of relief soared to £46 with heavy payments for the aid of infected households in Pudding Lane, 'the sick houses by the wharf' and elsewhere. It would seem that the town organised a common poor stock or fund with income raised not only by the poor rates, but from freedom fines and other sources, including charitable bequests. In the late sixteenth and early seventeenth centuries the town received a number of donations for the poor from townspeople and others, worth in all about £300. Money from the poor fund was used to establish a grain stock to supply the poor in time of dearth. In 1631 the mayor reported that to assist 'poor day labourers and [the] poorest inhabitants . . . the town has provided 2d loaves of bread' at a discount. Likewise, attempts were made to set the unemployed and paupers on work. In 1594 a weaver George Langley left a house in East Lane to be sold 'to make a stock to set the poor people of the parish . . . on work'. Two years later the town gave £100 to a weaver from Wye to put the town's poor on work, though this scheme proved abortive. In 1631 the town employed poor women and children in spinning, making buttons and twisting thread. Not all the poor stock went to the needy. In 1608 £68 was diverted to the erection of the new court-house, causing a wave of protest and hasty repayment.

The town also had various almshouses to house the local needy. Among those which came to the town with the fraternity lands in 1549 were three almshouses in Pudding Lane, two more in Stone Street, another on the bridge and more in Week Street. Those in Pudding Lane were in such decay by the end of Elizabeth's reign that the town council ordered them to be demolished and new ones erected. Further help to the poor came from casual donations when gentry and others visited the town.

How far urban relief in its various forms made any significant contribution to ameliorating the distress of the town's lower orders is questionable. At best it provided a minimal safety network for a minority of the poor; many others fell through the net and were harassed by settlement and other controls. What is clear is that the problem of poverty and the need for expanded relief provided a good opportunity for the town corporation to extend and consolidate its power and authority in the community.

Civic politics and administration

Edward VI's charter of 1549 established a rather basic civic polity consisting of a mayor, a bench of twelve jurats and commonalty (the freeholders). The mayor was chosen by the freeholders from two members of the bench nominated by the jurats; the jurats were in turn co-opted from the inhabitants. There was no specified common council as in many older corporations. The Edwardian charter also sanctioned arrangements for the courts, markets and fairs, and, most important, confirmed the purchase of the extensive property of the Corpus Christi fraternity and institution of the grammar school. Incorporation clarified the new political order in the town after the Reformation and surrender to the Crown of the archiepiscopal manor in 1537. Charters were granted to a number of other middle-rank towns in the mid-Tudor period for similar reasons. At Maidstone, however, there are signs that the leading advocates of incorporation were committed Protestants who wanted the new charter and the grammar school to entrench their position in the town. Thus John Denley and Peter Maplesden, strong reformers, were prominent in the petition for purchasing the fraternity in 1548 and became jurats under the new charter. The first grammar school master Thomas Cole was a radical Protestant.

Relatively little is known about the working of the Edwardian corporation, apart from the establishment of trade companies. In 1553 the town exceeded its charter privileges and attempted to elect MPs to Parliament – two outsiders William Wotton and John Salveyn; but it was duly rebuffed by the House of Commons. Other set-backs followed. After the accession of Mary several inhabitants were arrested for opposing the restoration of the Catholic religion and in January 1554 a number of prominent townsmen including Peter Maplesden, John Halle the surgeon, Clement Lutwick, William Smythe, and Alexander Fisher became involved in Wyatt's revolt. As we know, Wyatt owned considerable property in the town and directed preparations for the rising from nearby Allington castle. One of his key agents in recruiting support in the area was the Edwardian jurat William Tilden, a draper, who had a considerable trade with Wealden clothiers; William Smythe was one of Wyatt's tenants and had led the town opposition to Rome the previous autumn. Though a coalition of gentry, rural and urban groups participated in the revolt for a variety of reasons, there is firm evidence that Maidstone's involvement owed much to a concern to preserve the Protestant religious order in the town.[9]

The defeat of Wyatt's forces by Mary's army at Ludgate Hill, London on 7 February 1554 proved a disaster for the town. A score of townsmen were arrested and charged with treason, though almost all were later released on payment of heavy fines. Worse, the town's charter was apparently forfeited and the corporation dissolved. It is possible that leading townsmen maintained informal rule in the town, several of them for instance (including William Smythe) serving as churchwardens. But the revival of the corporation had to await the succession of Elizabeth in 1558. Within a few weeks of Mary's death the Privy Council was writing to the 'mayor of Maidstone', though a new charter was not granted until 1559. This nominated William Tilden, Clement Lutwick, and William Smythe among the first jurats. As well as recovering its Edwardian privileges the town gained new rights: for its mayor to act as a justice of the peace; for an extended jurisdiction over the Medway from East Farleigh to Hawkswood (in Burham) and most important the power to elect MPs to Parliament.

The revival of the corporation in 1559 after the Marian interregnum was aided by the continuity of some personnel from the Edwardian council. In May 1560 the first new freemen were admitted and in September the following year the corporation demonstrated its new-won jurisdiction over the Medway by reading the new charter at East Farleigh bridge. A few months later the corporation at its Burghmote meeting issued a series of constitutions or orders for the government of the town. Though the first two charters made no reference to a distinct body of common councillors, there may have been a *de facto* one in existence by 1563 – possibly continuing the late medieval tradition of the twenty-four commoners of the portmote. There remained some confusion however and it is likely that the early Elizabethan Burghmote was also attended by ordinary freemen and other townsfolk, though an order of December 1566 specifically excluded those who were not freeholders in the town.

Despite this, the magisterial bench exercised growing power. Burghmote meetings of the whole council were erratic with an order in 1563 limiting sessions to three times a year. From 1565 one of the two chamberlains was chosen by the mayor, the other by the jurats and freeholders. The ward system introduced in 1593 to deal with poor migrants and disorder was controlled by the bench. Three years later the mayor and two to four jurats were given authority to hold their own courts every fortnight to enforce the town's ordinances.

The consolidation of power in the hands of a small group of magistrates was typical of sixteenth-century English towns and reflected the social polarisation in urban communities, a general Crown preference for oligarchic government, and the growing pressures of town administration. The Burghmote minutes reveal a town government increasingly active in dealing with public hygiene, plague, water supply (provided now by conduits from Rocky Hill), and the threat of fire. There was also the essential work of regulating the town's fairs and markets, repairing the medieval stone bridge, supervising the crafts, and maintaining good relations with local gentry to ensure quarter sessions and assizes met in the town. But a pressing concern by the end of the sixteenth century was dealing with poverty and poor relief, which required constant attention from the bench rather than the sporadic intervention of the Burghmote.

In 1604 the town obtained a new charter from James I in order to clarify 'certain doubts questions and ambiguities' in previous charters. One result was that the election of jurats was restricted to freeholders, another that the town's control over the parish church was confirmed. But uncertainty remained over the position of the common council and in January 1605 the Burghmote agreed that while the new charter gave the power of election of justices and jurats to the bench, such elections should only take place with the approval of twenty freemen until a common council was formally established to give consent. Later that year because of the 'confusion and disorder at Burghmotes in regard of the multitude of that assembly not altogether of the sufficientest . . . but many times of the meanest and unfittest', a common council was set up with between 24 and 40 members chosen by the mayor, 6 jurats and 6 freemen. This was linked with the revival of the town companies and tough measures against non-freemen. There seems to have been a concerted effort to consolidate the authority of the urban elite. The same year the common meadow of the town was enclosed – at the expense of ordinary freemen. In 1613 the admission of freemen was delegated to the mayor, jurats and some of the freemen which seems to have caused tension with the common council as a whole. The mayor's authority was enhanced by new regulations in 1618 over civic ceremonies on court days, fair days and Sundays.

Friction with local gentry led to the town obtaining a new charter in 1619 which enlarged the authority of the town's rulers. The mayor, recorder and two senior jurats were now empowered to act as JPs; the Burghmote might now choose non-freemen and non-freeholders including gentry as jurats; taxes could be levied on all inhabitants of the town; the jurisdiction of the court of pleas was extended to include East Farleigh, Barming, Loose, Boxley, Linton and Otham; and county justices were not to exercise their jurisdiction in the town. This caused mounting conflict with the county gentry. Threats by some West Kent landowners to move the county sessions to Rochester led to recognition of the county's rights in a supplementary charter of 1621. But the town's power to elect gentry as jurats proved more contentious and was a recurrent motif in the conflict between the town and local landowners for a decade or more. At the same time, the 1619 charter confirmed the position of the common council in civic administration, though the issue was to resurface as a source of contention in the early 18th century.

The period after 1559 saw the corporation steadily extending its authority and control over the town. As well as the medieval manorial court, the old portmote, which dealt with maintenance of pavements and other minor administrative matters, charters provided for a court of pleas to hear civil suits, a market court and a court of sessions. These courts were presided over by the recorder and town steward. In the critical period of the town's administrative formation during the first part of Elizabeth's reign the recorder was the important lawyer Nicholas Barham who also acted as town clerk. From James I's reign the post of recorder was increasingly separated from that of town clerk which was occupied by a series of local attorneys. Courts were important not only for the administration of justice, but also for generating civic revenue.

The town estate was another major preoccupation of the town's rulers. The purchase of the fraternity lands in 1549 endowed the corporation with numerous properties and the town had made a number of further acquisitions by the 1630s. In 1563–4 the town's estate generated income of about £13 12s and by 1640–1 this had risen to over £68, well ahead of general price inflation. Town revenues also relied heavily on the dues from the markets and fairs and increasingly on local taxes or assessments (with a separate levy on the small Dutch community).

Civic finances were controlled by the two elected chamberlains. As in other towns at this time, they faced considerable financial difficulty with rising deficits. In the early seventeenth century this was caused in part by the refusal of a number of freemen and other inhabitants to pay the town rates. In 1615 defaulting freemen were disenfranchised and their names published at the court-hall. Attempts to levy rates on gentry led to growing opposition. At the same time, the town faced growing expenditure from a widening range of administrative activities. As well as the rising cost of poor relief there was the recurrent burden of obtaining the assize sessions, while the new charters of 1604 and 1619 together with subsequent litigation likewise proved expensive.

Alongside the mayor, recorder, town clerk and chamberlains, the town had only a small number of officers. These included the wardens of the four trade companies (intermittently), the beadle of the markets and the serjeants at mace. In addition various parish officers such as the overseers of the poor and surveyors of the highways were effectively under corporation control. The corporation also appointed the master and usher of the grammar school and supervised the running of the school. This limited bureaucratic machinery with only a handful of salaried officers imposed heavy administrative burdens on the town magistrates, usually leading townsmen. In the late sixteenth century the jurats were frequently distributive traders, though other occupations including brewers and paper-makers appear in the early seventeenth century. Magistrates might expect some recompense for their service in the form of grants of town lands, contracts and general patronage. A number of provincial towns at this time saw widespread allegations of corruption and abuse, fuelling conflict between the magistracy and ordinary inhabitants. But in the years before the Civil War internal conflict was not apparently a serious problem at Maidstone.

One reason for political harmony may have been the relative newness of the corporation and the small size of the civic honeypot available for abuse. Another may have been the strong Puritan influence established in the town by the end of Elizabeth's reign, enhancing standards of civic behaviour. Communal solidarity may also have been boosted by pressure on civic autonomy from outside – from the county and landed classes and later the Crown.

In the late sixteenth century there seems to have been little conflict with outside bodies. Here the town's Protestant reputation during Wyatt's revolt and the patronage of leading county figures like Thomas Wotton and Sir John Leveson were probably beneficial. Although relatively little is known about the town's parliamentary elections for much of our period, those elected MPs under Elizabeth were mostly prominent local landowners maintaining the town's connection with the Court. In the early Stuart period the picture was similar; we see the return of sympathetic county magistrates like the moderate Puritan Sir Francis Barnham of Hollingbourne, who represented the borough in every Parliament bar one between 1614 and 1640, frequently sitting with a member of the important Fane family, strong supporters of the town.

In Maidstone's parliamentary elections before 1640 there seems to have been little of the Court interference or internal conflict which afflicted other boroughs, but in other political directions there was mounting friction. After 1600, as we have seen, the corporation made an increasingly successful effort to consolidate Maidstone's county importance as the sessions and assize town. This in turn caused a growing influx of landowners and, paradoxically, increasing political tension with the county. Attempts by the corporation after 1615 to overcome its financial difficulties by levying double taxes on outsiders caused long-term discontent, while the election of three gentlemen including Richard Duke as jurats in January 1619 provoked a *quo warranto* action in the Westminster courts against the town. As we have seen, the corporation's new charter in 1619 only aggravated the situation. It caused a short-term crisis with the West Kent justices and, more serious, a decade of disputes with local landowners.

Conflict with the local gentry focused not only on their election as jurats and the issue of taxation, but on a jurisdictional dispute with Sir John Astley junior over the Old Palace.[10] In 1620 the mayor and jurats (acting on their own) tried to defuse the first issue by discharging Duke and the other gentlemen as jurats, but this was opposed by the common council. After consulting legal counsel, the town asked two sympathetic gentry, Sir Francis Fane and Sir Francis Barnham, to mediate, who urged the gentlemen should be released from office. Unfortunately the situation was now inflamed by the refusal of numerous landowners in the town, led by Sir John Astley, Lady Sackville and Sir Humphrey Tufton, to pay the taxes levied by the Burghmote to pay off the costs of the litigation. In 1623 the corporation re-elected Duke as a jurat (and also as a justice of the peace) with further elections of gentlemen the following year.

In 1624 the Privy Council attempted unsuccessfully to end the dispute over the civic elections, first supporting the town but then backing down. Next year the town itself endeavoured to resolve the dispute with Astley over his property claims and other issues by declaring its willingness to live in amity with the town's gentry and by making a series of concessions. But unfortunately this compromise proposal seems to have failed and Astley and Tufton brought another *quo warranto* suit against the town. Despite further attempts at settlement the gentry persisted with their litigation, seeking to get the Old Palace and Mote exempted from the town's jurisdiction and issuing a writ of seizure against the town's privileges. Legal action seems to have finished in stalemate but about 1630 Astley and Tufton were still refusing to pay civic taxes.

By then conflict with the local gentry was increasingly overshadowed by another serious confrontation – with the Crown. Up to the early 1620s relations with the government seem to have been amicable. The town was dependent on the Crown for its corporate privileges, as events in 1554 had made plain, and it had also clearly profited from the Crown's location of a Dutch community there in the 1560s. In 1614 the corporation supported the government's forced loan despite opposition from some of the Kentish gentry and five years later the town's loyalty was rewarded with extended privileges under the new charter.

Relations with the Crown soured over two issues: firstly, fiscal levies and, secondly, Charles I's religious policies. In 1626 one of the leading Puritan townsmen, Ambrose Beale, was hauled before the Privy Council for his opposition to militia levies (though opposition was more widespread in other Kent towns). Four years later Charles's attempts to raise extra revenue by imposing knighthood fines on the county affluent ran into resistance at Maidstone with all kinds of dubious excuses being made to the king's commissioners by prominent townsmen. But it was the levying of ship money after 1633 which caused most difficulty. In 1635 there were complaints that the town was attempting to evade the tax by compelling neighbouring villages such as Boxley and Linton to share the cost. As one irate landowner declared from Boxley 'the town . . . ceases not in very insolent manner daily to terrify my neighbours with the fear of being doubly charged'. The Privy Council was forced to intervene to stop such illegal levies and was then subject to petitioning from the town for a reduction of the tax. By 1638 the town owed considerable arrears of ship-money. None the less, it was the Crown's religious policies which proved especially explosive at Maidstone in the 1630s and we need to consider these in the next section.

Religious and cultural life

As we saw in Chapter Two, Maidstone appears to develop as a Protestant centre rather later than some of the East Kent towns – perhaps due to the conservative influence of the College before its suppression. In Edward VI's reign, however, committed Protestants took a prominent part in the purchase of the Corpus Christi lands, the town's incorporation, and the establishment of the grammar school. Thomas Cole, the first schoolmaster, was a Protestant radical who participated in sectary meetings at Bocking in 1551 and was forced to renounce his beliefs in a sermon before Archbishop Cranmer in 1553.

With the suppression of the College the rectory of All Saints eventually passed to Sir Thomas Wyatt but control of the church came to the town. Church goods were sold to pay for the purchase of the fraternity lands and in 1550 the altar was taken down. After the accession of Mary a number of townsmen were arrested, with William Smythe charged with 'the framing of a supplication for the retaining still of their new [Protestant] religion' against the restoration of Catholicism. As we have seen, in 1554 some leading townsmen participated in Wyatt's revolt; others fled into foreign exile.

Maidstone was adversely affected by the Marian reaction. In 1554 on Wyatt's attainder the rectory was forfeited; the advowson was granted to Cardinal Pole and the tithes went to the Catholic landowner Christopher Roper. Under Mary the incumbent was John Day who in June 1557 preached in the King's Meadow at the burning of Protestant heretics including the wife of a townsman. After Canterbury Maidstone witnessed the greatest number of executions of Protestants in the county. In addition, a number of other townspeople including the Edwardian magistrate John Denley were burnt elsewhere. Day claimed subsequently that those executed at Maidstone were sectaries who 'denied the humanity of Christ and the equality of the Trinity'.

Despite the restoration of the Catholic mass and altar, former Protestants retained their important position in the parish: in 1557 the churchwardens included William Smythe. Later the following year Elizabeth's accession led to the release of Protestant prisoners from the gaol while Catholics like Day came under attack. From the 1560s the restored corporation intervened increasingly in the running of the parish church. In 1562 the Burghmote ordered fines against anyone disputing the allocation of pews by the churchwardens. Patronised by strongly Protestant county landowners such as Thomas Wotton and Thomas Randolph, both foreign exiles under Mary, the town became a committed supporter of the godly reformed church. A growing number of measures were enacted to establish religious and social discipline, including the removal of the maypole (in 1567–8), regulations for the public humiliation of unmarried mothers, and the denunciation of gluttony and drunkenness. In 1575 the corporation took charge of the payment of the minister Richard Storer who (like his predecessor) was made a freeman. By the 1580s considerable numbers of nonconformists appear in the town, some Catholics, others probably Protestant. Nonconformity was encouraged by the large extent of the parish. In 1586 the churchwardens complained that the number of parishioners was so great that they could not recognise everyone attending church and by 1590 or so there are indications of religious tension in the town.

At the end of Elizabeth's reign Maidstone and its vicinity seems to have become a focus for Puritan critics of the Church. The lawyer Henry Halle, who denied the authority of High Commission (the main disciplinary court of the Church) lived at Chillington Manor, while the leading East Kent minister Josias Nicholls, deprived of his living at Eastwell in 1602 for Puritan polemics, moved to the area, buying property at Loose and taking up teaching there. One of Nicholls' close associates was the radical Puritan landowner Thomas Whetenhall of East Peckham, brother-in-law to the Jacobean recorder of Maidstone, William Gull.

By the start of the seventeenth century the magistrates seem to have largely suppressed traditional ceremonies and ritual in the town, limiting civic celebrations to the mayoral election and the mayor's 'fishing', when the corporation went on the river to assert its jurisdictional rights under the charter. At this time the town magistracy appears to have been led by conformist Puritans who supported visiting preachers, but also made payments to companies of itinerant players performing in the town, no doubt entertaining genteel as well as local audiences. In 1613, however, the corporation asserted its authority over the town church by setting up a board or table of church fees at All Saints, overturning higher charges introduced by the incumbent Robert Carr. In 1618 Carr was succeeded by Robert Barrell. Initially a moderate, Barrell drifted towards religious conservatism as High Church policies became fashionable at Charles I's Court. During the 1620s the town's relations with Barrell steadily deteriorated. In 1622 the Burghmote sought power from the church authorities to regulate the seating at All Saints without reference to the minister. Three years later the Burghmote made an order that those too poor to pay the poor rate should be buried at St Faith's and not at the parish church. Next year battle was joined with the minister over his attempts to levy higher church fees and the town offered to pay the legal costs of anyone opposing him. In the meantime Barrell was appointing and removing the parish clerk without the sanction of the mayor, jurats and parishioners, leading in 1629 to threats of further litigation.

Already in the 1620s two leading townsmen, Robert Swinnock and John Crompe were reportedly giving support to a nonconformist preacher in the Weald. About 1630 Swinnock, one of the town jurats, secured the presentation to Otham rectory and obtained the services of the young Cumbrian minister Thomas Wilson. Wilson attracted to his congregation large numbers of townspeople. In 1634 it was alleged that 'hundreds . . . of Maidstone have gone often to Otham in the afternoon on Sabbath days' to hear him preach. The religious situation in the town became increasingly difficult. Townsmen serving as churchwardens agreed not to make any changes in church seating without the consent of the corporation. In 1632 Barrell tried to restore his credibility in the town by proposing the revival of a combination lectureship at All Saints paid for by a voluntary tax on parishioners. The preachers were to include Wilson and John Swinnock, another Puritan minister, as well as Barrell, and the Burghmote happily endorsed the proposal. However, the election of the conservative William Laud as Archbishop of Canterbury in 1633 ended all hope of compromise. The issue of the Book of Sports which repudiated Puritan controls on traditional socialising and games, at the alehouse and elsewhere, led to open conflict between leading townsmen and the authorities. Like several other Kentish ministers Thomas Wilson refused to read the Book in church and was suspended. Supported by his patron Robert Swinnock, Wilson moved to Maidstone where he doubtless encouraged Puritan leaders to resist the measure. A number of young people were arrested by magistrates for organising popular games in the town after Sunday service; the magistrates were summoned before the Privy Council and forced to give way. The following year, during Archbishop Laud's visitation of Canterbury diocese, action was taken against the foreign churches at Canterbury, Sandwich and Maidstone, despite their privileges of religious immunity. In December 1634 Laud's vicar-general Sir Nathaniel Brent visited Maidstone and ordered the small Dutch congregation to conform to the Anglican liturgy and attend the parish church; the minister John Miller soon after departed for London and the Dutch church disappeared. Probably about this time, Barrell turned the communion table back into an altar at the east end of the church.

Early in 1635 there was a further attack on the town's Puritan magistrates, probably encouraged by Barrell. The mayor Caleb Bankes and Ambrose Beale (the nonconformist patron of the 1620s), and other leading townsmen were called before High Commission in London and charged with usurping ecclesiastical authority over the fixing of church fees, the nomination of the parish clerk, stopping church bells being rung on Sundays, and conniving at the failure of the churchwardens to prosecute those flocking to Wilson's sermons. The town faced the humiliation of having its Burghmote books examined by the Commission. In May 1636 Bankes and Beale were fined a swingeing £50 each and were ordered to make a public submission at Canterbury; the tables of fees were burnt and the offending ordinances in the Burghmote books ordered to be cancelled and defaced.

As in other provincial towns, official harassment of Puritan magistrates only polarised the situation. About 1638 the Maidstone magistrates retaliated against Barrell by petitioning Archbishop Laud that the vicar had overturned the parish custom of electing churchwardens and collecting tithes. The aim seems to have been to entangle Barrell in yet more costly lawsuits. As the political pendulum swung against the Crown in the later 1630s, mainly due to the escalating crisis over Scotland, Thomas Wilson was allowed to return to his living at Otham. But in 1640 with the outbreak of the second war against the Scots trouble erupted once again. Ordered by the government to preach against the Scots, Barrell obeyed but Wilson refused. There was an attempt to arrest him but he fled to the safety of the Maidstone house of George Halle (the son of the Puritan lawyer Henry Halle), and later to London. Within a few months, however, opponents of the Crown were increasingly in the ascendant in both town and kingdom.[11]

The growth of committed Protestantism and later Puritanism owed much not only to urban activists but also to the support of local gentry and the importance of commercial links with the Weald and London, both important centres of Puritan godliness. But religious developments were also linked with educational changes. As we have seen already, the establishment of the town grammar school in 1549 was a cornerstone of the Edwardian reformation in the town. What happened to the school during the Marian reaction is unclear, but with the new charter of 1559 the corporation quickly issued detailed regulations for the management of the school. As in grammar schools elsewhere, teaching was traditional, preoccupied with Latin grammar, poetry, rhetoric and Greek grammar. Admission was selective. Though formally open to the children of all freemen paying taxes, new boys had to be able to read and write their own name before entry. After 1566 the schoolmaster received (in addition to his salary of £10 per annum) an additional 4s a year from the parents of each pupil he taught; further fees were introduced in 1575. Poorer families had little real opportunity of sending their children to such a school. None the less, the school prospered under magisterial patronage, and in 1567 provision was made for an usher or deputy to assist the master. In the 1570s William Lambe from Sutton Valence enlarged the school endowment enabling higher salaries to be paid to both teachers.

Throughout the period after 1559 the school remained firmly under civic control. In 1598 the Burghmote ordered that the mayor and jurats should visit the school annually to enforce civic regulations and to hold a competition for the best scholars. Thomas Simonson was schoolmaster more or less continuously from 1582 until 1628 and was an active member of the corporation. There were other links with the borough. In the early years of Elizabeth's reign the school-house served as the town court-house (and as a venue for fairs), while town elections were held there until the 1620s. The grammar school remained primarily a town school throughout this period. Although it taught at least some of the sons of local gentry (who paid higher fees), it never attracted a large number of gentle pupils from across the region like Tonbridge school which became an embryonic public school.

As well as the grammar school, there were numerous other schools operating on an informal basis in the town, mostly petty or primary schools teaching basic literacy. In the late sixteenth century the town had about six licensed teachers rising to nearly thirty in the decades after 1600. As well as licensed teachers, we find unlicensed ones as well. Thus in 1634 we hear of Mr Peters, James Balsar and Nicholas Segars without licences; Balsar was said to be a 'very poor old and lame man' who instructs 'a few little children'. Though the majority of pupils in the town's schools were boys, girls also attended the petty schools. In 1585 for instance we hear of Mary and Elizabeth Kennett, servants, sent by their master to school with goodwife Hames and Leeds' wife 'to learn to sow, read and make buttons'.

With the expansion of schooling and rising prosperity at least among the better off, one can discern a marked advance in literacy in Kentish towns. At Maidstone 86 per cent of those townsmen giving evidence in the church courts between 1628 and 1640 could sign their own name, with distributive traders and clothiers well represented; the proportion was substantially lower among women. Literacy was necessary not only to trade more efficiently but also to read the Bible and other books. In the 1590s Thomas Ayhurst left money for a copy of Calvin's Institutes to be kept at All Saints and by the 1650s there may have been a small parish library in the church. But private book-ownership was increasingly widespread. During the 1560s about one in five townsmen whose goods were inventoried at their deaths, owned books; by the 1610s the figure had increased to over a third in a much bigger sample; and in the next two decades the proportion was as high as 45 per cent. Among Maidstone women too there was an increase in book-ownership though the overall rate was lower than for men. In the early Stuart era we discover a growing number of people owning and presumably reading not only the Bible but a variety of religious works, pamphlets, some of which were bought from town shopkeepers. In the 1630s it was said that the grammar school master was teaching from the works of the nonconformist Puritan Thomas Wilson. Within a few years the English Civil War had broken out.

The English Revolution

In 1640 the county was broadly united in its opposition to the king, his ministers and their disastrous religious and other policies.[12] In the elections to the Short Parliament in the spring there were only two candidates: Sir Francis Barnham, the town's long-standing MP, and Sir Humphrey Tufton, another Puritan landowner who was likewise returned, despite his conflict with the town in the 1620s. By the autumn, however, growing political tension spilled over into a more acrimonious election. The local landowner Sir John Sedley was refused the freedom by the mayor to stop him standing as a candidate; Sedley complained that this was part of a scheme by Barnham to keep the second seat for Sir Henry Vane (Fane) junior, the future parliamentary radical who had recently returned from New England. When the elections were held on 28 October the three candidates included Barnham, Tufton and a Mr Beale, probably Ambrose Beale the Puritan mayor in 1637. In the event Barnham and Tufton were returned, suggesting that the town was trying to maintain its strong links with the county's moderate gentry, though personal rivalry led to a brawl between Barnham and Tufton before the return was declared. Barnham was nearly expelled from Parliament in 1643, due to his poor attendance possibly because of unhappiness over the war, though he held on to his seat until 1646; after his death he was replaced by the recorder Thomas Twisden. Tufton continued to sit until he (and Twisden) were purged by the army radicals in December 1648.

In 1640 prominent townsmen were also involved in the county elections at Penenden Heath with the Puritan Swinnock for instance supporting Sir Edward Dering, the successful anti-Court candidate. After 1640 the town's defeats of the 1630s were speedily reversed. Godly controls on social behaviour were reinstated, and those who had defended the town in High Commission were recompensed for their losses. In May 1641 numerous townsmen petitioned the House of Commons against Robert Barrell presenting a catalogue of charges. Four months later the corporation restored the Burghmote ordinances obliterated at the behest of High Commission. However, as the Long Parliament and the country became increasingly divided over the terms of a political settlement with the king there was growing political tension within the town. Local Puritan leaders were increasingly at odds with those influenced by more moderate and royalist tendencies in the county. The election of the brewer and landowner Thomas Stanley as mayor in late 1641 provoked dissension and in February 1642 the prominent Puritan John Wall was dismissed from the Burghmote for opposition to the mayor. The following month a large number of moderate and loyalist gentry gathered in the town for the assizes and drew up the Kentish petition calling for the maintenance of the Church of England and an agreement between king and Parliament. The gentry leaders were arrested and impeached by Parliament. Shortly after, royalists clashed with parliamentarians at the West Kent sessions at Maidstone, exacerbating divisions in the shire. Town politics were riven by uncertainty: in April Thomas Twisden was made recorder but a few weeks later there was further action against the radical John Wall. When the summer assizes opened in July Robert Barrell, still minister, launched a fierce attack on Parliament at the assize sermons in All Saints. But the county's moderate gentry were racked by indecision and in the late summer an armed force led by Colonel Sandys secured the county, including 'the malignant town of Maidstone', for the Long Parliament.

The following months saw the Puritan group slowly but steadily establish control over the town. In May 1643 Barrell was forced to appear before the House of Commons and was sequestered from his living. Thomas Wilson eventually succeeded him as minister. In addition to his official duties, Wilson held prayer meetings at Robert Swinnock's house and preached a weekly market day sermon. He also took a vigorous part in promoting a strict Presbyterian regime on the Sabbath. He urged inhabitants 'to forbear vain walking, idling at their doors, also to draw their water on Saturday night' so that the streets were empty after the Sunday sermon. In late 1643 Swinnock was elected as mayor and a few weeks later John Wall was restored to his place on the Burghmote. In February 1644 Stanley and eight of his supporters on the corporation were expelled. Later that year Andrew Broughton, common councillor and clerk of the peace for the shire, was appointed the town's agent in the London courts; in late 1647 he was chosen a jurat.

By that time, however, the end of the first Civil War in 1645 and the failure of Parliament to agree a lasting settlement with the king caused renewed political uncertainty in the county and the town. In August 1647 the minister Thomas Wilson's house was attacked and in October a group of town conservatives, including some councillors, protested at the actions of the Burghmote, but their complaints were rejected and several of the councillors fined. Two months later the Kentish rising began with disturbances at Canterbury. Royalist agitation spread across the county to Maidstone. Unfortunately, the borough records are incomplete at this critical time and shed no light on what was happening in the town. In May Parliament sent a large army under General Fairfax against the royalist forces encamped around Maidstone and the decisive battle took place in the barricaded town on 1 June. The parliamentary army attacked from the south with every street and house contested by royalist troops. How far townsmen took part in the defence is unclear, though it is possible that some conservative Presbyterians gave their support to the royalist cause.

The destruction of the royalist army in the second Civil War was followed that autumn by the election of Andrew Broughton as mayor. Two months later Broughton assisted in the trial of Charles I and read the sentence against the king. According to an eighteenth-century account, after the king's death Wilson preached against the execution at All Saints and Broughton left the church in anger never to return, but there is no independent confirmation of this story. Wilson died in 1653 but Presbyterian influence in the town remained strong, with apparently little sectarian activity apart from a small Baptist congregation. Though Augustine Garland, a regicide and member of the county committee, was elected an MP for the town in 1654, John Banks, a moderate (and future London tycoon), was returned for all three Protectorate Parliaments. There were repeated Sabbatarian orders against social disorder, though not without opposition. In 1656 and 1657 we find large crowds playing traditional sports at Shrovetide. Next year the arrival of Quakers, John Stubbs and William Caton, to preach in the town led to brutal action against them by the authorities. In 1659 Broughton was elected mayor once again (and also MP), but by then the Puritan cause was disintegrating.

Despite the political uncertainties of the period there is no evidence of an economic or social crisis in the town. The parish registers indicate a sharp rise in mortality in the late 1640s, in part due to epidemics, though about two hundred people were killed in the battle of Maidstone. More surprising is the sharp decline in baptisms at this time, which may be due to parents withdrawing their children for baptism elsewhere. On the economic front, metropolitan demand for food and other supplies probably continued unabated, indeed may have expanded because of the provisioning needs of the army and the disruption of supplies from the Midlands and the West due to the war. The assize courts ceased to be held in the town from late 1642 until 1646, and quarter sessions may have met more erratically during this period, but other important gatherings did take place there, including various parliamentary committees for the shire, and after January 1646 the general county committee for Kent rented offices in the town. In 1648, according to one report, 'the town was much plundered' during the battle of Maidstone, but in the 1650s the town was boosted by the return of the greater gentry to county meetings and the demand for naval supplies for the expanding Medway dockyards. As we saw above, major commercial breweries were established in the town at this time.

On the eve of Charles II's restoration in 1660 Maidstone had established itself as the leading town in West Kent. Though the enlarged population was still concentrated in the old core town, there was a growing number of large, well furnished houses for the better-off along the main streets. The community had gained important new industries, complementing its ancient role as a market town. It was also starting to become a gentry town. Politically the corporation was firmly in charge, despite conflict with the gentry in the 1620s and the Crown in the 1630s, and despite the problems caused by the Civil War. The next century and a half was to see mounting prosperity, but also recurrent social and political problems.

Notes

1.   For the town's charters see K.S. Martin, *Records of Maidstone* (Maidstone, 1926), pp. 8–11; also in more detail W.R. James, *The Charters and Other Documents relating to the King's Town and Parish* (London, 1825).
2.   For sixteenth-century population estimates for Maidstone see J.S. Moore, 'Canterbury Visitations and the Demography of Mid-Tudor Kent', *Southern History*, vol. 15 (1993), pp. 36–85; for the Compton Census figures see A. Whiteman, *The Compton Census of 1676: a critical edition* (London, 1986).
3.   The parish registers of All Saints remain (1995) in the parish church. The aggregation of the registers from the sixteenth to the early nineteenth centuries was carried out by a group of Maidstone Grammar School boys under the supervision of Mr B. Langston; we are grateful to them for their work. The raw data was processed, refined and analysed by Alistair Milne at the Centre for Urban History, Leicester University.
4.   Cf. P. Clark, 'The Migrant in Kentish Towns 1560–1640' in P. Clark and P. Slack, eds, *Crisis and Order in English Towns 1500–1700* (London, 1972), pp. 122–32.
5.   See P. Clark, *English Provincial Society from the Reformation to the Revolution: Religion, Politics and Society in Kent 1500–1640* (Hassocks, 1976), p. 263; also C.W. Chalklin, 'Navigation Schemes on the Upper Medway 1600–1665', *Journal of Transport History*, vol. 5 (1961).
6.   Centre for Kentish Studies [Kent Archives Office], Md, Rf 2/1. Occupations are specified for 153 freemen, with 32 unspecified.
7.   Centre for Kentish Studies [Kent Archives Office], U47/16, 03
8.   The probate inventories used in this section are in PRC 10/1–72, 11/1–7, 27/1–8, 28/1–20, now kept at the Cathedral Library and Archives, Canterbury.
9.   For a detailed account of Wyatt's revolt and the names of Maidstone participants see D.M. Loades, *Two Tudor Conspiracies* (Cambridge, 1965); also Clark, *English Provincial Society*, pp. 87–97.
10. For much of the documentation for these disputes in the 1620s see Centre for Kentish Studies [Kent Archives Office], Md currently uncatalogued.
11. Clark, *English Provincial Society*, p. 365 ff; also the tracts by Bulteel and Swinnock listed in the Bibliographical Note (below).
12. For an account of county politics during the English Revolution see Alan Everitt, *The Community of Kent and the Great Rebellion 1640–60* (Leicester, 1966).

Bibliographical Note

For a general overview of English towns in this period see P. Clark and P. Slack, *English Towns in Transition 1500–1700* (London, 1976), esp. chapter 2 (on country towns). For county developments in general see P. Clark, *English Provincial Society from the Reformation to the Revolution: Religion, Politics and Society in Kent 1500–1640* (Hassocks, 1976).

A large part of the research for this chapter was based on the Maidstone Borough manuscripts (Md) in the Centre for Kentish Studies [Kent Archives Office]. Particularly valuable were the Burghmote minute books and chamberlain accounts as well as miscellaneous court papers. Extracts from some of these were printed in K.S. Martin, *Records of Maidstone* (Maidstone, 1926). The Centre for Kentish Studies also has various other items relating to the town in the county sessions records (especially QM/SB), and private collections (eg U522, U1044). Wills (PRC 17, 32) are kept at the Centre for Kentish Studies but the Cathedral Library and Archives, Canterbury has the important probate inventories (PRC 11, 27), and church court records (visitation and deposition books). A small amount of other documentation can be found in the Public Record Office, principally in the State Papers Domestic (SP), but also to a minor extent in Privy Council Registers and Chancery, Star Chamber and Requests records.

In terms of printed material *Archaeologia Cantiana* is rather disappointing for this period with only a limited number of articles directly of relevance, such as various pieces by R.H. Goodsall on the watermills of the Len (vol. 71, 1957) and the Astleys of Maidstone (vol. 72–3, 1958–9). On the town grammar school F. Streatfield, *The History of Maidstone Grammar School* (Oxford, 1915) has some useful material. Important primary texts include John Foxe, *The Acts and Monuments*, eds J. Pratt and J. Stoughton, London, 1877, esp. vol. 6, on the Maidstone martyrs under Mary; J. Bulteel, *A Relation of the Troubles of the Three Foreign Churches in Kent* (London, 1645), on the Dutch community; and G. Swinnock, *The Life and Death of Mr Thomas Wilson* (London, 1672) on Wilson's activities in and about the town in the 1630s and 1640s.

Chapter Four

THE LATE STUART AND GEORGIAN COUNTY TOWN: ECONOMY AND SOCIETY 1660–1835

The Georgian age was a time of relative prosperity for many English provincial towns. Urban populations increased, slowly at first and then more rapidly, economies diversified and flourished. Towns were physically transformed with the appearance of new classical style public buildings, wider streets and public walks, and the appearance of fashionable villas on the outskirts. Improvement and expansion occurred before the onset of the Industrial Revolution and was not confined to the new industrialising regions such as the West Midlands or the North but spread across southern England. The foundations of urban prosperity were three-fold. Firstly there was the growth of inland trade – boosted by population increase and a general rise in living standards and domestic demand, along with transport improvements and advances in distribution. Here traditional town markets and fairs were increasingly complemented by the burgeoning importance of inns and alehouses as trading entrepots, and by the tremendous proliferation of retail shops. The second pillar of urban prosperity was the spread of specialist industries, again closely linked with the advance in real incomes from the late seventeenth century. Georgian England experienced a powerful consumer revolution which created many new manufactures of consumer items in country towns including butchers' hats at Luton, furniture at High Wycombe, clocks at Colchester, blankets at Witney, ceramics at Worcester, and, as we shall see, paper-making and brewing at Maidstone. Linked with this was the emergence of many county towns as social and cultural emporia, as provincial beacons of European enlightenment. Provincial towns welcomed congeries of county gentry and other rural notables, who showered money on urban goods, services and a growing array of fashionable entertainments – from concerts to cock-fights, from clubs to cricket matches and coffee-houses. For the genteel classes rural life was increasingly seen as dirty, tedious and benighted. As one Kentish gentleman declared 'living in the country was like sleeping with one's eyes open' – a living cultural death – compared to the smart conversation and coffee-houses in town.[1]

After the Restoration it is evident that Maidstone enjoyed a period of sustained prosperity, which was noted by many visitors. Celia Fiennes, who toured much of the kingdom in the 1690s, praised Maidstone as 'a very neat market town [as good as] you shall see in the country' with many pretty [i.e. well built] houses and good markets', adding succinctly 'I believe it's a wealthy place'. The journalist and pamphleteer Daniel Defoe visiting the town in George II's reign was equally fulsome, calling it 'a considerable town, very populous and the inhabitants generally wealthy'. It combined industry with fashionability to make a community of 'very great business and trade and yet full of gentry [and so] of mirth and good company'. Another visitor Dr Pococke observed at mid-century that Maidstone was 'a town of considerable trade on account of its navigation [the Medway], together with good shops'. In the 1790s the acerbic John Byng was less generous, calling it 'a large, ill-built old town', but at the close of our period we hear that 'the town is in a very prosperous state; there is no want of employment'. This contemporary vision of the Hanoverian town is confirmed in large part, as we shall see below, by detailed evidence for the town's population and economy. But it was not entirely an urban bowl of cherries. During the eighteenth century the town also experienced renewed and growing social problems – including poverty and deteriorating industrial relations – particularly towards the close of the period. Moreover, Chapter Five will show how town politics throughout our period were difficult and acrimonious, fraught with 'a virulent and bitter party spirit' – for several years the town suffered the embarrassment of losing its charter of incorporation and borough status. None the less, the achievements of the town by the early decades of the nineteenth century were impressive, as it gained the leading position among Kentish towns.

Population

The town's rising importance after the Restoration is illustrated by the evidence we have for its expanding population. The population size in the early part of Charles II's reign was probably somewhat over 3,000 people. As in previous centuries, most of these inhabitants lived in houses around Week Street, High Street, East Lane [King Street] and Stone Street – with little development across the river. In 1695 a local enumeration put the population at nearly 3,700 inhabitants and by 1781 it may have been just over 5,700. In 1811 the first reliable national census records 9,400 people, shooting up to 16,000 in 1831.[2]

As before the Civil War, the parish registers of All Saints enable us to examine in detail the processes of demographic change in the town (see Figure 2). From the registers we can see that compared with the years before 1640 when baptisms in most years exceeded burials, the decades after the Restoration saw persistently high burial rates, quite often exceeding the baptismal rate. After the terrible intensity of the last plague outbreak in 1666–8 when a sixth of the inhabitants may have died, there were severe smallpox crises in 1709–10, 1719–20, 1733–4, 1740–1, 1753, 1760 (when nearly half of all deaths were due to the disease), and 1766; other

Figure 2

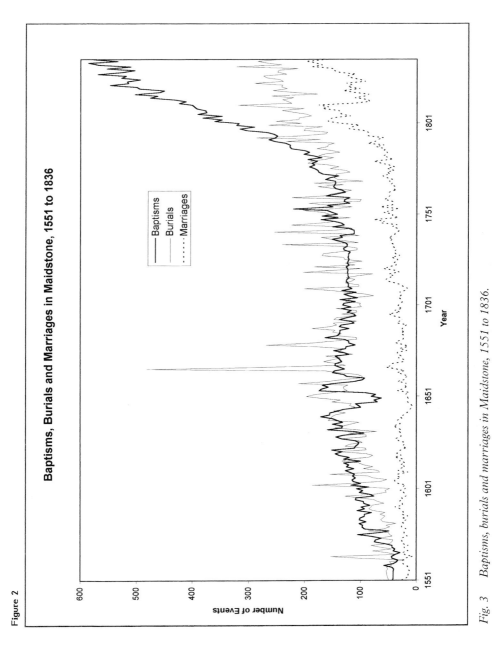

Fig. 3   Baptisms, burials and marriages in Maidstone, 1551 to 1836.

outbreaks occurred in 1772, 1781, 1796, 1818–19, and 1825–6. The 1740–1 outbreak was probably aggravated by food shortages (it was a famine year throughout Europe).[3] The parish register evidence is by no means perfect because of the number of nonconformists in the town, not attending the parish church, but the evidence is indicative. Thus compared with the period before the Civil War, the later Stuart and early Georgian town suffered much higher mortality and a lower rate of baptisms. In Maidstone, as in other southern towns, rising urban mortality may well be associated with mounting commercial contact with London which had catastrophically high infant mortality in the early eighteenth century – the worst probably in the western world. Only from the early 1770s do we start to see baptisms forging ahead of burials, which began to turn down significantly in real terms towards the end of the century. As well as improvements in housing and water supply, another factor affecting mortality was the introduction of smallpox inoculation. In 1766 the parish vestry employed Daniel Sutton from Essex to provide inoculation 'to prevent . . . the loss of many lives, which might be expected from its natural progress and effects, and that it may in great measure be eradicated from the town for a long space of time.' Six years later it was announced that 'such of the poor persons belonging to this parish who like to be inoculated with the smallpox may be inoculated at the expense of this parish, not exceeding five shillings and three pence each person.' There was also a good deal of private inoculation in the later period, with the spread of cowpox vaccination after 1804. Even with the decline of smallpox, epidemic disease remained a major threat. In the summer of 1832 there was a limited cholera outbreak despite the efforts of the recently formed local board of health (under the 1831 Act for the Prevention of Cholera).

In consequence of high mortality for much of the Georgian period, only a proportion of the town's population growth came from natural increase – the surplus of baptisms over burials. As was the case in most larger English towns at this time, Maidstone had to rely heavily on immigration to renew and enlarge its population. At the end of the seventeenth century the overall level of immigration was broadly similar to the trend before 1640 with about three-quarters of male residents having been immigrants; but a higher proportion of newcomers now were born in the district, coming to the town from the settlements of the Medway valley, the Downlands and the northern Weald. Among poorer migrants to the town between 1691 and 1740 over half had travelled less than ten miles, incomers like widow Sumers and her five children from Farleigh lodging in Mill Lane and making up tape.[4]

As we know from Chapter Three, before the Civil War immigration was in large measure due to worsening conditions in the villages – falling wages, rising unemployment, and food shortages. Up to the later eighteenth century push factors like this were much less crucial than the economic pull of the town with higher wages and a growing diversity of employment opportunities. The town was forced to take repeated action against outsiders setting up as traders, and later there were reports of large numbers of young female servants coming to the town from the countryside, presumably to work in gentle households, retailing and paper-making. After 1800 the town was increasingly swamped by large numbers of rural poor, coming in search of work and relief.

Markets, fairs and shops

The lynchpin of Maidstone's economic importance remained its role as a marketing centre with a local hinterland stretching into the North Weald and scarpland and up the Medway valley. The ancient Thursday market for corn and other general commodities was increasingly busy in the late seventeenth century, boosted by the town's growing population and the general expansion of consumer demand and inland trade. Celia Fiennes found the market 'well furnished with all sorts of commodities', including corn, fruit and 'great quantities of leather'. 'It seemed', she said, like 'a little fair for the variety of wares'. The pre-eminence of Maidstone's market was clearly recognised by the 1720s when Daniel Defoe declared that Maidstone had 'the best market in the county, not Rochester, no not Canterbury excepted'. Soon after, William Newton reported that the market was 'esteemed one of the best for cheapness and variety in the whole county', and in 1782, another writer described it as 'the most frequented in the county . . . plentifully supplied with all sorts of provisions of the best kind.' By the end of the seventeenth century the market tolls were leased by the corporation for £45 a year; by 1739 the figure had risen to £80 a year, and in 1755 to over £90.

Though the town was granted a monthly cattle market in 1682 it was not probably until a further grant in 1751 (for the second Tuesday in the month) that the livestock market developed into a sizeable affair. According to Marshall, by the 1790s the autumn market in Maidstone typically consisted of around 1,000 head of sheep and about 150 head of cattle, 'chiefly from Romney Marsh, some from the Weald'. The buyers were 'mostly butchers, from the towns and parts of this populous county; with some from the metropolis.' In May 1822 the market witnessed the sale of 200 cattle, 1,000 sheep, 600 lambs, and 300 pigs.

As Marshall indicated, the town's markets had an important wholesale trade, particularly with London. Defoe claimed that Maidstone supplied London with more commodities than 'any other market town in England', and Seymour echoed his words in 1782. Aided by the steady improvement in communications, Maidstone's markets were closely connected with those of the capital, and prices in Maidstone were largely determined by those in Mark Lane, Smithfield, Southwark and the other metropolitan markets. The weekly market was extended by the grant of a hop market in 1766. This grew only slowly, although within thirty years the town was a noted place of sale for West Kent hops, with many better-off townsmen having hop-gardens in the vicinity. By then a growing proportion of the crop was being sold outside the market to hop factors or merchants directly from the growers' own warehouses, or on a contract basis. In the 1820s several hop factors were resident in the town taking an active part in the flourishing hop market. About this time we learn that it benefited 'from the great facility and low freightage [by which] the hops from Sussex and the Weald . . . are brought to this town', so that it will soon become the depot for hops grown in those areas. In the long run, however, competition from London markets may have had an adverse impact.

The town's markets continued to be complemented for most of the period by the traditional fairs at Candlemas, Maytime, June and autumn. In 1682 Charles II's charter moved the June fair to September, but this was soon reversed. The fairs were primarily occasions for the buying and selling of horses, fatstock, and Welsh and other cattle for fattening. But they also traded in general agricultural produce and local manufactures like thread. As in the past, the main venue for the fairs was the Common or Fair Meadow, but there were also stalls in the High Street. In 1683 the Burghmote papers record that the cloisters of the grammar school were used for the sale of hops, while thread and cattle were sold in Bullock Lane [Earl Street]. This, together with the High Street, continued to be the cattle sale area until the corporation's improvement policies removed livestock from Maidstone's streets after 1824. By October 1830 sheep and cattle were being sold on Penenden Heath, while horses were shown in the Fair Meadow.

In general terms, however, the volume of fair business was experiencing a long-term contraction by the start of the nineteenth century. The May fair in 1818, for instance, was reported to be 'not up to expectation', and the following year was 'attended by few visitors'. The June fair in 1822 was well supplied with cattle and horses, but trade was generally dull. In May 1830 the *Maidstone Journal* lamented that 'we never on any previous May fair observed so dispiriting an appearance in point of business' with horse sales at a stand-still and many cattle left unsold. The October fair experienced the smallest decline. According to Hasted, it was, 'by far the greatest' of the fairs in the late eighteenth century, 'being resorted to by the country for many miles around'. It was both a livestock and hop fair and continued into the nineteenth century to attract buyers and sellers of horses and cattle. In October 1830 the fair was said to have been 'remarkably numerously attended' with 'an excellent supply of stock of all kinds' and a busy hop market. By contrast, the Candlemas fair faded and those in May and June were diminished in scale.

The fortunes of the fairs and market were not helped by the poor facilities for traders. There were repeated demands for improvements to the traditional arrangements under which the sale of different commodities was dispersed through the town. In 1771 it was decided that a new fish and vegetable market was needed, as the existing fish cross at the top of High Street was 'ruinous and very much out of repair'; but only in 1780 was the new market built. However, the corn market continued to be held in the old Upper Court House which was 'exposed [to the elements] and much complained [of] by the farmers and corn-dealers attending it as very dangerous to their healths in the winter season.' In 1818 numerous farmers, butchers and others attending the monthly cattle market protested that 'our cattle frequently suffer serious injury from unavoidable accidents in so great a thoroughfare as the High Street . . . besides being . . . a great nuisance to the inhabitants' of the town, and suggested its transfer to the Fair Meadow, but nothing was done until 1823. Following a public meeting which condemned 'the present markets [as] . . . insufficient and inconvenient', an Act of Parliament was obtained enabling the corporation to raise £10,000 on mortgage to build a new market-house. A number of buildings opposite the town hall were bought and demolished and a new gas-lit market for corn and provisions was built. The cattle market meanwhile was removed to the Fair Meadow, although pigs continued to be sold in High Street until 1829. The total cost of the new markets reached £14,550. The relocation of the cattle market was a major advance, not least for the urban environment in the central part of town, but the new provisions markets were less of a success. On the opening day in 1826 they were thronged with customers, among them 'groups of elegantly dressed ladies' all eager to be among the first to make a purchase, but in the long run many stalls remained unoccupied. There were also complaints about the coldness and darkness of the corn market. In 1834 a scheme was put forward to establish a company to build a new corn market on the same site, and this plan went ahead in 1835, when a large new exchange was opened – reportedly the most commodious in the county.

The fairs and to a lesser extent the markets suffered not only from inadequate sites but also from growing competition from private trading and shops. Fish factors or dealers had invaded the fish market by the 1730s, pushing up prices, and as well as hop factors trading outside the market, there was an army of other itinerant middlemen by the eighteenth century. Higglers travelled the surrounding countryside negotiating the purchase of crops, particularly fruit, from farmers before the harvest. By the beginning of the nineteenth century, they were particularly active in buying cherries, but they also bought apples 'on the tree', and fewer passed through the market in consequence. Some filberts were also sold to higglers, but the majority were sent directly to London by water, and bought by factors there. Consequently, few any longer passed through Maidstone market, which by the early nineteenth century was starting to lose its importance in the wholesaling system.

In addition to middlemen, there was the mounting problem of more modern systems of retailing and distribution. As we saw in Chapter Three, by the start of the seventeenth century inns, taverns and alehouses were starting to function as commercial premises where deals were struck, goods bought and sold. In the later Stuart period inns often had great warehouses in their yards where merchants stored commodities for sale, while their elaborately furnished halls and parlours were thronged with auctioneers selling books and property, itinerant traders purveying cloths and other wares, even professional men giving legal and medical advice and dentists offering to pull one's teeth. The growing general importance of these drinking houses will be discussed below.

However, in the long run markets, fairs, inns and public houses all faced their main competition from retail shops. As we know, specialist mercers, haberdashers and drapers had already started to appear in Maidstone by Elizabeth's reign and about the Restoration a spate of trade tokens were issued by the town's shopkeepers, mostly grocers. The number of shops probably multiplied in subsequent decades. During the early eighteenth century the corporation tried to regulate the number of shops through orders against non-freemen trading there. In 1724, for instance, it was ordered that 'foreigners' should be fined a draconian 3s 4d a day for as long as they traded in the town. By the 1760s there are indications of informal licensing of outside traders and thereafter the controls evidently lapsed. At the time of the shop tax in 1785–9 Maidstone's shops were assessed on a par with those of Canterbury, the Medway towns and Greenwich (increasingly linked to the capital); this was more than three or more times the rate for most other West Kent towns. According to the tax returns, many of the town's shops were in High Street, with others clustered on Gabriel's Hill and Week Street, and a small number near the Old Palace.[5] The importance of the town's shops is confirmed by the trade directories for the 1780s and 1790s which indicate that retailing was one of the most important occupational categories. Grocers were particularly numerous (with twenty-two listed in 1794) but we also find stationers, ironmongers, tobacconists, silversmiths, linen drapers, brandy merchants and china-sellers. A wide variety of consumer goods were now readily available. Thus John Blake, the printer of the *Maidstone Journal*, also ran a stationery and book shop, and in 1787 was selling playing cards, musical instruments, fireworks, backgammon tables, artists' materials and perfume. In 1782 one writer said that Maidstone had 'the best shops in the county', and another after 1800 mentioned many shops in Week Street, Stone Street, and Middle Row, with the latter especially 'elegant'. By the late 1830s trade directories suggest the number of grocers had more than doubled to 50, while haberdashers and drapers had increased from 17 to 29. The luxury trades had also expanded markedly: there were now 18 jewellers, watchmakers and silversmiths (compared to 3 in 1794).

Before the time of the French Revolution many of the town's larger shopkeepers were acting as wholesalers to smaller shops in the town's hinterland. In 1786, Wathurst and Co. of Middle Row advertised discounts to country shopkeepers, in competition with Hazell and Co. who ran a 'real cheap warehouse' for linen drapery, mercery and hosiery in Queen Street. In 1802 another of the town's firms offered ready-made shoes to shops at a shilling a pair less than any other supplier; some of these wholesalers were originally Londoners. Other London traders came to Maidstone in the early nineteenth century, bringing with them London prices and London practices, trading as cheaply as possible to undercut rivals and selling only for ready money. Because of improving communication with the capital, Maidstone's shops increasingly had to compete with London retailers, and the *Maidstone Journal* and other newspapers frequently carried advertisements from shopkeepers drawing attention to the fashionability, range and competitiveness of their stock – on a par with the capital. In sum, by the early nineteenth century Maidstone's shops like its markets and fairs were heavily influenced by the commercial pressures of the metropolis.

In the first part of this period overland traffic to the capital still relied heavily on the old Roman roads: Stone Street to Rochester and the Watling Street. By 1750 this route was turnpiked and within twenty years the mid-Kent road was also upgraded. During the 1790s seventeen coaches a week ran between the county town and the metropolis; this had expanded to nine coaches a day by the 1830s, with an extensive network of secondary services to the Medway towns as well as to other West Kent and Wealden centres.[6] But throughout the eighteenth century it was the river rather than roads which served as the most important economic artery for Maidstone. As in the past, large hoys or sailing boats carried hops, corn, and other goods to London via the lower Medway and Thames. While Maidstone's long-established role as a shipment centre for ragstone probably disappeared in this period, great quantities of timber and other provisions were shipped downstream to the great royal dockyards at Rochester and Chatham. After the Restoration a number of leading townsmen became major suppliers of timber to the Navy Board. There were, however, repeated complaints of late payment and in 1693 ten timber merchants in the town refused to deliver further quantities. In the 1750s we hear of 'a large timber-yard here for the supply of Chatham dock', (as well as corn-mills on the river producing meal and flour for the royal navy), but thereafter the town's importance in the trade may have diminished.

Nevertheless, in the Hanoverian era the river was increasingly vital for opening up the town's southern hinterland into the Weald and the Kent and Sussex border – blighted by bad roads. As we noted in Chapter Three, plans for making the upper river navigable had been debated as early as 1600 and in 1664 a group of gentlemen obtained an Act of Parliament authorising improvements on the river, but little or nothing was done until legislation in 1739.[7] This created the Medway Navigation Company, with capital of £30,000 to make navigable the upper reaches of the Medway as far as Forest Row in Sussex, some 15 miles above Tonbridge. In the event the river was only made accessible to barges of 40 tons as far as Tonbridge, but even so this was a great advantage to Maidstone's manufacturers and traders. From the second half of the eighteenth century, the company's ledgers record shipments upstream of a great variety of commodities, notably groceries originating from London, and the town increasingly became the entrepot in this trade. In the late eighteenth century it was said that the whole of the Weald, as well as much of Sussex, received their groceries via Maidstone, and the total trade was valued at £100,000 per annum. In 1780, for instance, Samuel Mills a Tonbridge shopkeeper, obtained 10 cwt of unspecified groceries by barge from Maidstone in July with almost two tons in November. In 1807 the company advertised that 'they have fitted up a barge to carry shop goods, ironmongery and goods in general from Maidstone to Tonbridge and places in between, which will load at Maidstone every Monday.' This service continued until the 1830s.

There were also attempts to improve the river downstream. A survey of the river was embarked on by the corporation in 1787 and in 1792 legislation was obtained to undertake the improvement of the river between Maidstone and Aylesford. Improvements seem to have been fairly limited in scope, although construction was started on the tidal lock at Allington, to allow vessels to reach Maidstone at all states of the tide. A further Act in 1802 established the Lower Medway Navigation Company which completed the work at Allington but not much else. The lack of progress was causing concern to Maidstone's trading community by 1823, when the Thames and Medway canal was nearing completion, with an expected increase in river traffic. There were demands for greater action by the Lower Medway Company. The result was a further Act in 1824 which enabled the company to raise additional capital of £12,000 to carry out further work on the river. Many of the new shareholders were Maidstone gentlemen and tradesmen. During the course of the next few years the river was straightened and deepened for the passage of larger vessels, Aylesford bridge was rebuilt, and a new horse tow path made. The Thames and Medway canal was opened in 1824, but it was not until 1826, when the Canal Company set up Henry Drury as a carrier of hops and general goods at Maidstone, that any vessels from the town used the canal. In 1827 Drury was advertising a weekly service to London, via the canal, 'thereby saving about 50 miles of an uncertain, tedious and dangerous navigation'. 1830 saw the first experiment with steam navigation on the Medway when a 60 ton barge was towed between London and Maidstone through the canal by a twelve horse-power steam boat; use of the canal steadily increased during the 1830s.

Even before the 1824 Act large seagoing vessels were sailing from Maidstone. In 1822 the hoyman and merchant George Poolley was advertising a 130 ton schooner working in the coal and general trades with the north of England, France and Holland. But transport advances were no longer invariably to Maidstone's advantage. With the growth of barge traffic of 40 to 60 tons on the canal, numbers of Maidstone's seagoing hoys of 100 tons or more became obsolete. In addition, vessels of 40 tons were able to complete the whole journey between London and Tonbridge without the need to trans-ship goods at Maidstone. In 1831 there were complaints that 'the improvement of the navigation of the Medway has been prejudicial to the prosperity of the town; because the increased facility of communication with London has injured the wholesale trade of which Maidstone was formerly the centre for the surrounding country.' Three years earlier one of the Upper Medway Company's barges had begun a weekly through-journey from London to Tonbridge, provisioning many Tonbridge shopkeepers directly.

Through navigation to and from London was probably not the only reason for the decline in Maidstone's trade upstream from the town. By the late 1820s the Upper Medway Company's high tolls and virtual monopoly of trade, as well as its limited work on river navigation, were causing widespread resentment in the town. In 1834 the *Maidstone Gazette* declared: 'There is perhaps no greater abuse in the county than this company'; and there was a public petition demanding a reduction in tolls and open trade on the river. The same year an attempt was made in Parliament to amend the Upper Medway Navigation Acts and, although this was defeated, the company was warned to put its house in order. Subsequently, there were reductions in some tolls, the river was widened, and a horse towing path provided.

The number of townsmen and ships employed in the river trade during this period is difficult to determine. The *Universal British Directory* for 1794 lists only two companies of hoymen, with two vessels each, but this was certainly an underestimate. In 1809 Walter Rowles listed eight Maidstone companies or individuals working as hoymen or bargees, owning between them twenty-five vessels, in addition to coal barges. Pigot's 1828 directory lists seven barge companies and Russell claimed that in 1834 there were 'upwards of fifty vessels of from twenty to ninety tons belonging to the town'.

Thus the period from the Restoration to the early nineteenth century witnessed both major changes and expansion in Maidstone's role as a distributive and commercial centre. But this was only one of the pillars of Maidstone's prosperity – albeit probably the most stable. In the trade directories of the 1780s and 1790s marketing comprised up to a half of listed occupations (almost certainly an overstatement of the true picture) compared to nearly a third for manufacturing; for the 1820s the directories show a broadly similar pattern with only a minor increase for manufacturing. None the less, there can be no question that industrial growth and specialisation played a vital part in the economic development of the Hanoverian town.

Industries

From the late seventeenth century the nature of the town's industrial base began to change. There was a decline of the earlier cloth industry and though thread-making continued to be important into the middle decades of the next century it subsequently decayed. This was not surprising. Throughout the Home Counties and East Anglia textile industries of all sorts suffered fatally from the rivalry of the industrialising regions of the Midlands and North. But as we shall see, Maidstone's industrial sector fought back, developing two major industries – drink production and paper-making.

The run down of the woollen cloth industry, already visible by 1640, accelerated rapidly after the Restoration, though some vestiges remained into the late eighteenth century. Seymour in 1782 observed that of the eleven fulling mills once on Loose stream only one continued to be used for that purpose, though this one was a large concern, which kept 'several hundred men and women constantly employed'; two years later one baize manufacturer was listed in the trade directory. The manufacture of linen thread suffered more gradual contraction. In 1664 Maidstone's thread-makers claimed to employ 8,000 workers (doubtless an exaggeration), but they also protested against the threat from imported Dutch thread. A few years later Josias Child declared Maidstone thread was carried all over the world. In 1741 William Newton, though recognizing that the manufacture was 'less considerable than in the past', still considered it to be, with hops, the 'chief trade of the town'. Much of the thread was used to make hop-bagging, but it began to be superceded for this purpose during the eighteenth century by canvas or hessian cloth, and by a type of bagging produced in Lincolnshire, which was considered superior. By the start of the nineteenth century only two small hop-bagging manufacturers survived in the town, one of which, Cliffords, has continued into the late twentieth century. According to the 1831 census, eighty-eight townsmen were employed in making hop-bags, ropes and blankets.

Wholesale brewing had already emerged in the early Stuart town, but during the eighteenth century it became a major employer.[8] The success of commercial brewing in the town owed much to the local availability of hops and grain for malting, good supplies of clean water from the Downs, and easy transport via the Medway to London and beyond. In the Georgian period the town had three major breweries at any one time, together with various smaller establishments. The Lower Brewery in Lower Stone Street, established in 1650 or earlier, changed hands several times in subsequent decades, its owners including Thomas Bliss, mayor of Maidstone in 1682 and MP for the town between 1698–1708, and William Horsmonden Turner, who was elected MP in 1734 and 1747. Between 1713 and 1762 it was run by Joseph Smalvell, and in 1764 passed into the hands of the Brenchley family, who in partnership with the Stacey and Wise families, retained an interest in the business for over a century. The Upper Brewery, in the later named Brewer Street, was owned in the mid-seventeenth century by the Cripps family who retained a financial interest until 1737. During the late eighteenth century it was run by John Seager with partners, but the business became insolvent; in 1821 it was bought and closed down by Stacey and Brenchley of the Lower Brewery. A third brewery was also in existence at the Restoration, on a site near St Faith's Green. In 1668 it was bought by John Cripps of the Upper Brewery, and the family kept a financial interest in it until 1700, although in 1679–80 it was run by Thomas Bliss, later involved in the Lower Brewery. Between 1700 and 1715 it was a relatively large concern run by James Sherborne; Samuel Hollister took control in 1715, and continued in business there until 1746, but by 1751 the brewery had closed.

Four other small breweries are known to have existed in Maidstone in the late seventeenth century. Towards the end of the next century another major brewery was opened in Earl Street by Robert Heathorn, and the 1794 trade directory also lists a Thomas Burgess, brewer. In 1815 the Medway Brewery was begun in the West Borough by William Baldwin, and four years later a new brewery was opened on St Faith's Green, but this ceased production about 1825. After 1820 yet another brewery was apparently operating in Pudding Lane, although again lasting for only a short time. Competition in the industry was fierce by the early years of the nineteenth century as high taxation depressed demand and many small brewers found it difficult to survive.

The Earl Street firm was known as the Pale Ale Brewery, and much of its produce was probably destined for India and other colonies. The Lower Brewery by the end of the eighteenth century was primarily a porter brewery, producing heavy dark beer to quench London as well as local thirsts. Commercial breweries increasingly dominated the local drink trade. Though some Maidstone public houses may have continued to brew their own beer as in the past, the great majority (as in other southern towns) increasingly bought their supplies from the main breweries. To consolidate their position in the trade, brewers after the end of the seventeenth century started to buy up and 'tie' public houses. Maidstone was in the forefront of this trend. Already we hear in 1701 that the Tory brewer Thomas Bliss had won the parliamentary election because 'the public houses belong to him'; his properties included the Anchor and Dolphin in Week Street, the Row Barge, and the Seven Stars in Knightrider Street. William Gill who was both a paper-maker and brewer owned six public houses in Maidstone in 1736. During the 1780s the Bests, Chatham brewers, owned or leased a clutch of premises in the town and by the 1830s three-quarters of Maidstone's fifty-two public houses were owned by Brenchley and Stacey at the Lower Brewery. As well as having their own workers, the breweries gave employment to a variety of other trades including coopers, cork-cutters, and draymen and horsekeepers. With their many-sided links to the countryside they served to consolidate the town's regional importance in mid-Kent.

Alongside the breweries other drink industries grew up – cider-making and the distilling of spirits. Cider was made commercially in Maidstone in the early years of the 18th century and again at the end of the century when we hear of Mr Stone a 'cider maker of great repute, in a very extensive line of business'. Distilling – at premises on Stone Street – dates from the mid-seventeenth century and this distillery was still active in the 1730s; by the 1780s we know of two distillers at Maidstone, Strain Stephenson, a brandy merchant, and George Bishop, who distilled geneva or hollands gin. A native of Maidstone, Bishop learnt his trade in the Netherlands and returned to start distilling at premises in Bank Street. He obtained a special Act of Parliament in 1789 to distil gin, and quickly built up a prosperous business as well as manufacturing spirits for apothecaries. According to Rowles in 1809, Bishop's distillery was the largest manufactory in the town and ten years later it was capable of producing 5,000 gallons of spirit a week. After Bishop's death in 1818 the licence for the Bank Street distillery was withdrawn and the manufacture of one of Maidstone's most noted products came to an end.

Paper-making was the town's second and probably most important specialist industry in the Hanoverian period.[9] Despite the arrival of foreign refugees with the necessary skills in the sixteenth century, the English industry developed only slowly, as demand for paper was fairly limited, and the market dominated by continental producers. With rising demand the industry became concentrated in the Home Counties, since London was the principal market and also the biggest source of rags, the main raw material. Paper mills came to Kent in Elizabeth's reign and were first established in the Maidstone area in the early Stuart period, taking over old corn or fulling mills. Forstal Mill, on Cossington stream near Aylesford, was producing paper by 1665, and there is known to have been a paper mill at Sandling in 1671. Millhall Mill at Ditton was operating by 1677, while Turkey Mill, on the Len (run by George Gill and later his son William), and Upper Tovil Mill, on the Loose were in use as paper mills by 1680, with three more mills in operation on the

Loose stream by the end of the decade. A second mill at Sandling, probably the one which was later known as Cobtree Mill, may have been producing paper by 1700. The industry's development in the Maidstone area was due not just to the availability of redundant mills, but also good communication with London, and the supply of clear spring water free from discolouring minerals, which enabled fine white paper to be made. Prohibitions on imports of French paper between 1678 to 1685 and 1689 to 1697 boosted domestic output of white paper, with four mills in the Maidstone area producing it by 1700. Other mills manufactured brown wrapping papers and pasteboard. Only the pounding of the rags was carried out by the mill machinery; the rest of the manufacturing processes were carried out by hand.

The total labour force needed in 1700 when there were about nine paper mills and perhaps 12 vats in the Maidstone area, may have been in the region of 150. By 1733 when there were 14 mills with up to 19 vats the number of workers was probably about 230. The English paper industry prospered in the eighteenth century, encouraged by rising demand, the adoption of the Hollander beating engine which improved output efficiency, and preferential duties on home produced paper. The number of mills proliferated in and around Maidstone. Admittedly, many mills changed hands a number of times, and bankruptcies seem not to have been unusual, but this had more to do with the nature of business and finance in the eighteenth century, and perhaps with the business abilities of individuals, than with the state of the paper industry, which was increasingly buoyant. The number of mills within a few miles of Maidstone doubled to nineteen by 1800. There was also some increase in the size of mills in the vicinity of the town, but the use of water power limited the number of vats which could be operated in one place, and manufacturers wishing to expand production usually took on additional premises. A typical eighteenth-century mill had one or two vats, and Turkey and Upper Tovil Mills, which each had five vats in the late eighteenth century, were quite exceptional and reputed to be the largest mills in the country. Padsole Mill, which was opened by James Smythe and Finch Hollingworth in 1793 was another large concern with four vats.

James Whatman and his son of the same name, who succeeded him at Turkey Mill in 1762, established it as probably the foremost producer of fine quality papers in England. Although good quality white paper was already being made at the mill under William Gill, the elder James Whatman was responsible for a number of innovations, most notably the development of wove paper which was eagerly sought by printers and artists. His son improved the whiteness of the paper by adding blue dye to the rags, and also designed a paper frame capable of making larger sized paper. In the late eighteenth century the younger Whatman was operating three other mills, in addition to Turkey Mill, giving him a total of ten vats. In 1771 he claimed to make more paper than any other manufacturer in England and in the following decade he was producing 8 per cent of the national output of high quality papers. Exports went to America and also continental Europe. In 1794 Whatman sold his mills to the Hollingworth brothers who until 1805 operated them in partnership with William Balston, an ex-apprentice and employee of Whatman. Balston then withdrew from the partnership and had the ten-vat, steam-powered Springfield Mill built on the northern edge of the town, where he continued to make high quality papers. Upper Tovil Mill, which in the later eighteenth century was operated by Clement Taylor and his son, was likewise a noted producer of fine quality papers.[10] The Taylor family was involved in a number of mills in the Maidstone area during the eighteenth century, and they too had a reputation for innovation, particularly with the use of chlorine bleach. One indirect beneficiary of the growth of paper-making was the Medway barge trade which profited not only from the carriage of paper to the main market in London, but also from the import of rags from the metropolis.

Though the industry was mostly located on the outskirts of town, paper-makers were leading figures in Maidstone society in the Georgian era. Clement Taylor was elected MP for the town from 1780 to 1796; others became mayors and magistrates. The mills employed a mixture of skilled and semi-skilled men for the manufacturing process together with children and women to carry out the dusty and unhealthy task of preparing the rags and to finish and pack the paper. Overall, the number employed in the industry in the Maidstone area in George III's reign probably did not exceed 500 but wages for skilled workers were good, those at Kent mills higher than in other parts of the country. Wages at Turkey Mill rose by about 27 per cent between 1766 and 1787. In the 1790s as trade fluctuated the masters demanded, and sometimes obtained, wage cuts, while the men resisted these or agitated for increases; but significant advances in wage rates occurred during the early years of the nineteenth century. Women and children were paid on a piecework basis, but their wages though low were above those in other parts of the country.

Relations between the Maidstone paper manufacturers and their skilled men were often tense, and there were frequent strikes and lock-outs. The employers had probably formed a trade association to regulate the industry by 1765. In the 1780s James Whatman took an active role in its organisation and William Balston chaired the Committee of Master Papermakers in the following decade. This body lobbied government over the excise duty on paper, agreed wage-rates for workers, set prices for rags and paper, and coordinated action during industrial disputes. There were attempts to introduce cheaper Scottish and Irish labour during the 1780s, and on occasions the Committee agreed to close the mills for weeks at a time in order to force down the price of rags.

In response to this coordinated action the skilled men formed their own organisation. The Original Society of Papermakers may have existed by 1784, when the men successfully resisted a wage reduction. In 1795 the Society secured a wage increase of 3s–4s a week from some employers, but the demand for a 5s increase in 1796 led to a major strike, which started in Kent and spread to the other paper-making areas of the Home Counties. Eventually the dispute became a lock-out, and some of the Kentish masters brought in cheap labour from Scotland. As a result of this strike, the masters called for government action and legislation was passed in May 1796, making it illegal for paperworkers to combine for the purpose of increasing wages. Two further general Acts, outlawing all trade unions, were enacted in 1799 and 1801, but these measures were virtually a dead letter in the Maidstone area. Despite resolutions by the masters to blacklist union members and the inauguration of a fund to finance the prosecution of Society men, the Original Society continued to operate with some success, fighting wage reductions and even winning increases. Maidstone was the head of one of five 'Grand Divisions' of the Society, and in 1801 a delegate from Sussex spoke at a Society meeting in Maidstone attended by forty-four men. In most local mills the men were able to impose a closed shop, although 'uncarded' or non-union mills did exist, including Upper Tovil.

Confrontation between masters and men continued to be typical of the industry until the changes wrought by the introduction of paper-making machinery. A machine capable of making a continuous web of paper arrived in England in 1806, and this was subsequently improved and developed by the Fourdrinier brothers, dramatically reducing production costs. It was claimed that a hundredweight of paper which cost 16s to make by hand cost only 3s 9d to produce by machine. Moreover the skills needed to operate the new machines were quickly learned and few workers employed, with many tasks carried out by children. The new Fourdrinier machines were only slowly introduced into the Maidstone area, however. The first was installed at Lower Tovil Mill in 1822 but there were no more until 1834 when the Hollingsworths set up one at Otham Mill. As makers of fine quality paper they were cautious about the change-over and they continued to manufacture by hand at their bigger Turkey Mill. Probably because the hand-made trade remained dominant in the Maidstone area, the headquarters of the Original Society moved to the town in 1815, and the union continued to be powerful in the district, though it saw its influence elsewhere steadily diminish. In 1816 Maidstone paper-makers petitioned Parliament, attacking the new machines, though initially at least unemployment in the industry was mainly caused by the general depression following the Napoleonic wars, and by the resumption of foreign imports. By 1830, however, skilled men were increasingly made redundant and town paper-makers were having to make heavy contributions to support unemployed members of the Society. In November that year there was a one day strike when Society men met on Penenden Heath to 'consider the best legal means of obtaining redress of their grievances in regard to machinery'. But their economic demands were increasingly caught up in the campaign for parliamentary reform (see below, p. 103).

As well as paper-making and the other industries already mentioned, Hanoverian Maidstone had a miscellany of other trades. A small barge building industry developed on the Medway during the eighteenth century to serve the needs of the local merchants and freight carriers on the river. The port also encouraged the development of other industry, including after 1782 a water powered seed-crushing mill which imported linseed from Archangel in Russia. Some of the oil was probably destined for the large leather dressing manufactory of Messrs Gentile, building on the long-established tanning trade in Maidstone. By the early nineteenth century, other commodities, such as cement, were also being produced at sites alongside the Medway. None the less, these trades were relatively unimportant compared to brewing and paper-making and other key sectors of the economy.

Service trades

Certainly marketing and distribution together with new industries were vital pillars of the town's prosperity in the Georgian era but they were not a complete explanation of Maidstone's economic success at this time. As Defoe stressed, it was a place of mirth and good company because it was full of gentry. As we saw in Chapter Three, Maidstone had close links with local landowners from the sixteenth century and already by the 1620s a number of gentlemen had taken up residence in the town. With West Kent quarter sessions, assizes and other official bodies meeting at Maidstone before 1640, the town benefited from a growing influx of genteel and country visitors. Once the upheavals of the Civil War had subsided, the town rapidly recovered its administrative position in the county. From the late seventeenth century Maidstone was increasingly regarded as the county town of Kent, with most of the important county meetings held there.

County meetings not only brought official business to the town. By the late seventeenth century, assizes had turned into a major social occasion in the provincial calendar, attended by numerous gentry and their families and accompanied by a variety of social entertainments. But if the summer assize week often marked the high point in the urban and county social calendar, increasingly there was a more sustained 'season' for fashionable socialising on the metropolitan model, lasting from March to May. Some gentry took up residence on the south side of the town, with a number of grand new or remodelled brick houses in the neo-classical style in Knightrider Street and Lower Stone Street such as William Shipley's Knightrider House, the splendid Stone House and Romney House. But in the eighteenth century many landowners, their wives and children travelled in from the large number of country houses in the vicinity to enjoy the social entertainments and services of the town.

As we shall see in Chapter Five, the corporation played some part in attracting the gentry with various public improvements, but other factors were also influential including better roads and the growing oxygen of publicity provided by town newspapers, town histories and other publications. No less crucial in promoting the gentrification of Georgian county towns was the growing cultural impact of the metropolis on provincial society, with centres such as Maidstone offering fashionable London-style services for middling and lesser gentry, unable to afford the high expense of a sojourn in the capital.

More will be said later about the growing range of social entertainments available in Georgian Maidstone, but here we need to stress the development of other services. Though drinking establishments were well founded in the town by the Civil War, the late seventeenth and early eighteenth centuries witnessed their growing incidence and importance. The number of licensed premises rose steadily in the decades after the Restoration – from about 50 in the 1680s to about 65 in the 1730s (about one for every 40 adult inhabitants). Most were concentrated near the markets in the High Street, down Week Street, Gabriel's Hill and Stone Street, with a small number in East Lane [King Street].

As well as becoming significant marketing centres, the town's four great inns expanded their social facilities. From the 1660s they had billiard tables and in the eighteenth century we find them hosting assemblies, balls, and society meetings – in the 1790s the Star Inn was described as 'the rendezvous of [the] aristocracy', and some years later the town's inns were praised for their 'excellent accommodation'. In addition, coffeehouses which originated in the capital in the 1650s, arrived in Maidstone about 1700; there were four such premises by the 1720s where the gentility could converse and read the London newspapers. Even lower-classes' victualling houses, the old alehouses, became more respectable, frequently called public houses by the eighteenth century and with more spacious accommodation. From probate inventories for this period we can see that most public premises had six to eight principal rooms, including special games rooms and rooms for billeting troops, and their landlords had a sizeable personal estate of about £98 on average. As well as supplying drink, food and accommodation to small traders, artisans and respectable people visiting town from the countryside, public houses like the inns played a significant part in the burgeoning recreational life of the town.[11]

The town's victualling houses also provided another significant service. From the Restoration period Maidstone was an important army centre in time of war, with extensive billeting of troops on inns and alehouses. In 1686 an official survey recorded that the town's premises had 197 beds available and stabling for over 500 horses (both Canterbury and the Medway towns had somewhat more beds but fewer stables).[12] This military function steadily expanded. During the second half of the eighteenth century the town was home to the West Kent Militia and in 1797 a cavalry barracks was built at the end of Week Street. From then until the end of the Napoleonic Wars the Maidstone area was alive with military activity, with a large camp of militia on Coxheath. The cavalry officers were prominent in Maidstone society, taking a leading role in assemblies and other elite social events. The major military presence also generated a good deal of demand for town services, alcoholic, sexual and the like. By 1813, the barracks was the army's training centre for young horses, and twenty years later the Army Riding School was transferred to Maidstone barracks, which was also used as a depot for cavalry regiments in India.

As elsewhere in the country, from the 1780s town magistrates steadily reduced the number of licensed premises; when the town's rising population is taken into account, there was an increase in the number of inhabitants per licensed house from 126 in 1780 to 265 in 1821. This reduction in licensed victualling encouraged the multiplication of small illicit houses selling smuggled spirits in the Maidstone vicinity. In 1830 the Beer Act sought to combat the problem of unlicensed premises by setting up a special category of beerhouses for the retail sale of beer. When the Act came into force in October nearly 30 houses were licensed in Maidstone, as well as many others in nearby villages, and on the first day about 1,000 barrels of beer, laden on 53 drays drawn by 200 horses, were said to have been despatched by Brenchley, Stacey and Wise's brewery. About 1839 there were 59 fully licensed houses in the community, together with 93 beersellers.

As well as its expanding victualling trade, Maidstone offered a growing number of professional services, responding to a growing shire as a well as local demand. With the town's new role as the county administrative centre, it is hardly surprising that lawyers comprised the leading professional contingent and by the 1780s we find upwards of five attorneys or solicitors practising there. A number of the town's attorneys not only held civic office but acted as county officials. From 1702 to 1753 the county clerk of the peace was David Fuller, a Maidstone attorney, and other Maidstone lawyers also served as county treasurers and such like. These attorneys also operated as surveyors, estate agents and money-lenders in the town and its hinterland. The rise of solicitors continued into the nineteenth century: in 1839 there were twenty-two firms in the town. The medical profession similarly consolidated their position during the period: by the 1780s we know of ten physicians, surgeons and apothecaries in the town; in the 1830s the figure had risen to sixteen surgeons and physicians with an unknown number of apothecaries. At the same time, the eighteenth-century town never acquired an infirmary like various other middle-rank towns (including Canterbury in 1793) – perhaps because of Maidstone's proximity to the numerous London hospitals established by this period. The first general dispensary was not opened until 1824 with the associated West Kent Infirmary soon after; nearly 1,200 patients a year were being treated by 1833, albeit only a small number as in-patients. Other professional men practising in the community at the close of our period included accountants, architects, dentists and bankers. During the 1790s the town had two banking firms and by the 1830s the number of banks had increased to three (including a savings bank). The Kent Insurance Company opened its offices at Maidstone in 1802 and twenty-two years later this was joined by the associated United Kent Life Annuity Institution, both highly profitable. Overall, however, the professional and public sector remained stable as a component of an expanding economy, comprising about 15 per cent of listed occupations in the late eighteenth and early nineteenth centuries.

In the early years of the nineteenth century the town's development as a service centre was boosted by the expansion of the county administration with the construction of the new West Kent gaol in 1811–19 (built at a cost of nearly £200,000 and with 350 inmates) and the impressive county sessions house designed by Sir Robert Smirke in the 1820s; as well as by military expenditure on the barracks on the Chatham Road. All this, along with the prosperous marketing and industrial sectors, clearly established Maidstone not only as the county town but as the leading urban centre in Kent outside the orbit of the sprawling metropolis. The social consequences of urban growth were, however, increasingly mixed.

Social conditions

There can be no doubt that the expansion and diversification of the town's economy generated considerable affluence in the upper and middling ranks of the community. Even ordinary townspeople may have benefited in the earlier part of the period from rising wages and living standards. But many lesser inhabitants remained close to the poverty line and in the last decades of the period there was a resurgence of social deprivation in the town which required large-scale relief.

Probate inventories for the late seventeenth and early eighteenth centuries show the superior classes – gentlemen, professional men, manufacturers and traders – enjoyed considerably greater wealth than their predecessors before the Civil War. One of the wealthiest townsmen after the Restoration was the grocer Matthew Chandler whose personal estate was valued at over £7,700 in 1717. He owned an extensive trade stock of tobacco, spirits and other consumer and grocery wares (worth over £1,400), together with investments in government stock and a hop-garden. His house had about ten main rooms and was smartly furnished with clocks, pictures and chinaware. Chandler was probably rather exceptional, but there were numerous other distributive traders in the later Stuart period with personal property worth between £500 and £1,000. A good example was Walter Weekes, a haberdasher, who died in 1700 and whose inventory listed goods totalling £908. The town's gentlemen (who may have included some professional folk) had a broadly similar range of personal wealth. At the top end was Robert Salmon, who left over £2,200 at his death in 1728 and who had extensive rented property, farmland, hop-grounds, and woodland; he sold timber to Chatham dockyard and had shares in several Medway ships, in order presumably to transport it. Salmon's house contained about ten main rooms which were elaborately decked out with maps and pictures, mirrors and birdcages, china tea cups and coffee ware, and valuable silver plate.

Manufacturers tended to be somewhat less wealthy in general, though John Oare, a fuller, who died in 1716, had a personal estate valued at over £900, while the thread-maker Thomas Wall was worth over £500 at his death in 1704, with £322 owed him by Londoners for thread. With rising urban affluence, housing and improvement work undoubtedly increased to the advantage of building craftsmen: one glazier and plumber who died in 1719 had personal goods worth over £2,500, though a good part of this was tied up in outstanding debts. But along with the affluent, there was a sizeable number of middle-rank townsmen – masters and shopkeepers with average wealth of between £100 and £500. Their houses were comfortably furbished with books, mirrors and furniture. Below them were various small masters and artisans and the like, but by George II's reign even their houses had a quota of consumer wares.[13]

For the late eighteenth century and after the evidence is more impressionistic, but the town's prosperous manufacturers and tradesmen seem to have enjoyed a high standard of living, buying a wider range of non-essential and luxury consumer items. The latest London fashions in dress and furnishings were increasingly in demand. By 1790 the residence of a town grocer might boast carpets, gilt mirrors, mahogany dining and tea tables as well as a bureau, beech, cherry-tree and ash chairs, a fine clock, and a great variety of quilts and other bedding. About 1800 one can detect the emergence of a distinct middle-class world among these better-off townsmen. A growing number of fashionable villas and the occasional terrace appeared on the western outskirts of Maidstone, particularly on Rocky Hill and the Tonbridge Road, to house wealthier families as they moved away from the centre of town, with its growing problems of heavy traffic and pollution. Their leisure time was increasingly devoted to a variety of political, philanthropic and other societies and associations which served as a major focus for social contact and class definition.

Over the long term, skilled and other workers did less well. In the 1720s a bricklayer and carpenter in the town was earning about 2s a day and this rose to 2s 4d in 1774 and 2s 5d two years later, reaching 3s a day before the end of the century. But whereas food prices were falling in the earlier part of this period, by the late eighteenth century they were rising markedly, leading to a significant reduction in real incomes. Though evidence for the wages of paper-workers is missing for the earlier period, by the later eighteenth century skilled men in the trade were receiving just under the rate for building workers. For the semi-skilled and unskilled the early Georgian period was similarly a time of improved living standards reversing the deterioration which had occurred before 1640. But during the late eighteenth century rising food prices imposed growing pressure on family budgets, unless supplemented by the earnings of wives and children in the paper mills or in seasonal work in the hop-gardens. Other women resorted to such strategies as taking in washing in order to make ends meet, and there is some evidence of small corner shops being kept by women. After the end of the French wars there may have been some improvement in wage rates, particularly for skilled workers, but by the 1830s even skilled workers in the paper-making industry were suffering, due to the onset of mechanisation. To protect their families from poverty, skilled workers established benefit societies to help them and trade unions might also offer assistance. In 1830, for instance, working paper-makers belonging to the Original Society claimed to be paying 8s–10s a month each to support unemployed union members. But most benefit societies limited their support to payments during sickness, old age or at death, though they also served as an important mechanism for social and cultural contact and solidarity among the artisan classes (see below, p. 110).

Lower-class friendly societies were slower to develop in southern country towns than the bigger industrialising cities, but by 1803–4 Maidstone had at least two clubs with nearly 200 members and ten years later membership had reached nearly 500; in 1818 the town had seven societies, two of which were reported to have paid out £836 in sickness and death benefits that year. The insolvency problems of individual friendly societies led to the rise of the so-called affiliated societies and by 1834 a branch of the Kent Union of Oddfellows had been established in the town, with some 150 members.

But for many poorer townspeople membership of a benefit society was beyond their means: in times of hardship they were forced to rely on parish relief. We need to consider the problems of poverty and poor relief: firstly, during the period from the Restoration to the opening of the town's workhouse in 1720; secondly, during the decades between 1720 and 1780 when trustees of the poor were appointed by a local Act of Parliament; and, finally, in the years 1780 to 1835, during which poverty returned as a massive social problem in the town.

By comparison with the situation before the Civil War, the later Stuart period may have seen a diminution in the level of poverty in the town. True, in the 1660s about half the inhabitants were exempted from paying the Hearth tax on grounds of indigence and in 1670 the corporation 'complained of the numerous increase of the poor . . . within this town and parish which we conceive has not happened amongst the ancient inhabitants only, but by reason of foreigners [i.e. local migrants] from several places creeping into this parish and settling of themselves undiscovered.' But the Settlement Act of 1662 (amended in the 1690s) and the general rise in living standards linked with falling food prices and expanded economic activity may well have reduced the influx of long-distance pauper migrants to the town by the start of the eighteenth century. Those who came now included a few exotics like the Catalonians and Turks who passed through in 1716 on their way from the coast, but most were young men and women from the neighbouring rural area looking for work as servants or in the town's shops. The ranks of local poor were increasingly confined to a core group of widows, orphans and the sick, except in times of bad harvest, trade disruption or epidemics. The parish poor received weekly pensions and other allowances for rent, clothes, shoes and medicine. They also benefited from the various charities for the poor.

The parish overseers continued to run the old town almshouses in Week Street and elsewhere, though these were increasingly ruinous and were eventually sold off at the start of the nineteenth century to build new almshouses in the Stone Street area. In addition, there was a growing number of new almshouses erected by private benefactors and separately controlled. The Maidstone-born London tycoon Sir John Banks left money in 1697 for six almshouses near Week Street; Edward Hunter provided for another six in 1736; Mary Duke about 1727 gave three houses for Presbyterian women; and rather later in the 1780s John Brenchley arranged for four poor men and women to be accommodated in East Lane. We also find a number of money charities, old and new.[14]

However, in the Restoration period, as later, the main burden of relief fell on the parish, with the overseers aiding not only the local poor but also the visiting indigent.[15] In 1668–9 parish payments totalled £450: 43 persons or families received regular weekly payments for the whole year, and a further 38 for part of the

The elder James Whatman, paper-maker.
Photograph: Maidstone Museum.

The Kent Fire and Life Insurance Office, built at the start of the nineteenth century.
Photograph: Maidstone Museum.

Cottages on St Faith Street.
Photograph: Maidstone Museum.

The early eighteenth-century Romney House, in Romney Place.
Photograph: Mr Q. Lloyd.

Mote House pictured in 1783, prior to the rebuilding in 1793–1801.
Photograph: Maidstone Museum.

The market and corn exchange, after the rebuilding in 1835.
Photograph: Kent Messenger Group Newspapers.

The Great Conduit in the High Street, which
supplied many townspeople with their water.
Photograph: Maidstone Museum.

W. Hincks fecit.

William Shipley, founder of the Society of Arts, and the Maidstone Society for Promoting Useful Knowledge.
Photograph: Maidstone Museum.

Mrs Sarah Baker's Theatre in High Street, rebuilt in 1798.
Photograph: Maidstone Museum.

A handbill for a concert at the Bull Inn.
Photograph: Maidstone Museum.

An eighteenth-century cricket match.
Photograph: Maidstone Museum.

year. During the 1690s, when war and harvest failures caused disruption to the economy, expenditure jumped, reaching £621 in 1696, but in general the system seems to have worked quite effectively in aiding the needy. By the 1710s, however, costs were soaring with a growing influx of outsiders requiring relief – probably attracted by the town's busy economy. In 1719 payments were made to 116 outsiders; this was on top of weekly payments for varying periods to 144 parishioners and regular pensions to 40 more parish poor; a further 191 Maidstone residents received single payments (due to the smallpox outbreak at this time). In consequence the cost of parish relief soared to £1,062.

At this juncture the brewer Thomas Bliss offered to provide a workhouse for the town. Since the 1690s a number of provincial cities led by Bristol had established workhouses in order to control relief expenditure. At Maidstone land was bought in Knightrider Street; the parish overseers visited workhouses in Chelsea and Chelmsford to learn about their organisation, and in 1720 the workhouse was opened. Over the door was the legend: 'To subject the poor to a better discipline of life; to promote industry rather than encourage sloth; to exonerate the parish from an expense scarcely to be borne and yet unequal to the number requiring relief' (this was later changed to the more succinct but menacing – 'Who will not work, let him not eat bread'). Under the new regime all applicants for relief were required to enter the workhouse and the number of claimants reportedly fell by half. Certainly the cost of relief was reduced. Although many of the poor went into the workhouse, out-relief continued to be paid, and in 1725 there were still some thirty-seven parish pensioners receiving regular weekly payments. That year the cost of weekly payments was £169, while the expenses of the workhouse amounted to £312. Including payments of £155 to strangers, total expenditure was about £636.

Workhouse inmates were forced to labour in return for their keep. In the 1730s they worked on cloth and linen manufacture; they also went hop-picking in the season. In 1766 sheds were erected on land adjoining the workhouse and the poor were set to work making hop-bags. But none of this was profitable and by George III's reign poor expenditure was rising sharply once more. This reflected the general increase of the town population, the decline of real wage rates for the unskilled, and mounting poverty in the countryside which was starting to spill over into Kentish towns.

In 1766, a difficult year of dearth and smallpox, the cost of poor relief reached £1,512; the following year it was £1,261; and by 1779 it had soared to £2,613, with £1,724 spent on the workhouse. These spiralling costs and the heavy burden of administration associated with them drove the town to obtain a private Act in 1780 'for the better government and regulation of the poor in the town' (20 Geo III c 22). This measure established as trustees of the poor, the mayor and three other members of the corporation along with the churchwardens and overseers and twenty-four elected men, who took over the work of collecting the poor rates and administering relief. Despite all the trustees' efforts, the number of poor and relief expenditure remained high. In the crisis years of the mid-1790s charitable subscriptions had to be organised to provide bread, flour and coal for the enormous numbers of poor, which now included unskilled men in work. At the beginning of 1795 it was reported that 900 families (or about 3,000 persons) had accepted tickets from a charitable committee entitling them to buy flour at subsidised prices. In 1796 there was an attempt to augment income from the poor rates by revising the rateable value of property in the town, but this was abandoned due to ratepayer opposition. In 1805 a second Act of Parliament was obtained extending the powers granted to the trustees under the 1780 Act, particularly their power to levy rates.

In 1802–3 poor law expenditure in the town reached £4,520. But though serious the position needs to be put into comparative perspective. At Canterbury with only 1,500 more inhabitants the cost was nearly 40 per cent higher at over £7,300; at Sandwich with only a third of Maidstone's population expenditure ran at £3,740. Nevertheless, if the underlying strength of Maidstone's economy may have ameliorated the strain, the long-term situation continued to deteriorate with major difficulties in the collection of rates, particularly during the economic depression after the Napoleonic Wars. At this time the level of distress in the town reached crisis point, with local unemployment and underemployment compounded by a large influx of poor families from an increasingly destitute countryside. Despite the actions of the parish trustees, extensive charity was needed to supplement the rates. In April 1816 the vestry resolved that sixteen acres of land on Barming Heath should be enclosed in order 'to employ the poor of this parish to bring the same into cultivation'. In December a public meeting called by the mayor 'resolved that the present distressed state of the poor, in this parish, arising from want of employment, low wages, high price of bread, and excessive rents &c loudly calls for the active exertions of the benevolent and humane, towards the alleviation of their sufferings.' Lord Romney gave the parish further land on Barming and Penenden heaths for cultivation by the poor, while a subscription fund collected nearly £1,000. This money was spent on basic foodstuffs which were sold at a discount to those living below subsistence level, the receipts being used to buy more food. The land on the two heaths was enclosed and put under cultivation by the unemployed and occupants of the workhouse. In 1818 the work gave employment for up to eighty men, women and children for much of the year, but the enterprise was never profitable.

The workhouse was full to capacity at this time with over 200 inmates. Many other poor received outdoor relief, some £3,400 being paid out in 1817–18. Of the recipients by far the greatest number were labourers, but workers in most of Maidstone's trades and industries were listed, including shopkeepers. Of the 548 listed as needing relief, forty were clearly marked as having some work, or having family members who were working, and it is evident that in Maidstone, as in the countryside, poor rates were used to supplement inadequate wages. The rates were also used to finance the emigration of a number of respectable poor to America and Canada.

The plight of the poor steadily deteriorated before 1830. The parish overseers tightened up eligibility for relief, while conditions in the workhouse were deplorable. An investigating committee in 1822 reported to the trustees 'very great mismanagement'. The committee recommended that greater attention should be given to the feeding and care of the workhouse children, and that the undeserving should receive an inferior diet to 'persons having good characters for honesty and industry'. In 1824 it was decided to build a new workhouse on Barming Heath, but a meeting of the parishioners overwhelmingly voted against moving the poor so far from the town. As a result the situation at the workhouse in Knightrider Street worsened – a rabbit warren of small crowded rooms, overwhelmed with inmates.

The years 1830 to 1832, racked by harvest difficulty and commercial slump, saw widespread distress among the town poor, and large-scale charity was needed to supplement parish relief. In the winter of 1830–1 discontent in the villages all around Maidstone fuelled the Captain Swing riots (discussed pp. 103). Many of the inmates of the workhouse at this time were unemployed, including young men unable to find work in winter and forced through desperation to remain there from November to April. By now outdoor relief supported a large segment of the town's population, including 160 widows, with 21 children, 258 families, totalling some 1,032 persons, and 173 illegitimate children. In all a total of 1,386 persons were in receipt of regular payments; a further 850 families totalling some 4,250 persons received relief on a casual basis. Thus around 9 per cent of the population was on permanent relief in the early 1830s with a further 27 per cent on temporary support. The situation was almost out of control. It was reported to London in 1834 that at Maidstone, 'the management of the poor is beyond the power of parish officers, and requires the superintendance of government'. In 1834 the Poor Law Amendment Act introduced sweeping changes in the administration of poor relief which will be discussed in Chapter Seven.

The surge of poverty in the town particularly in the early nineteenth century imposed major administrative and financial burdens on the town. As we shall see in Chapter Five, they may also have had political implications in the community. But one must not exaggerate the scale of the social difficulty. During the Georgian era at least the town as a whole became much stronger economically and also in terms of the breadth of its social structure and institutional organisation and so proved in large measure able to contain such pressures.

Notes

1.   For these general urban developments see P.J. Corfield, *The Impact of English Towns 1700–1800* (Oxford, 1982); P. Borsay, *English Urban Renaissance: Culture and Society in the Provincial Town, 1660–1770* (Oxford, 1989), esp. ch.1; P. Clark, ed., *Country Towns in Pre-industrial England* (Leicester, 1981), pp. 16–31, 170–84 (on Winchester).
2.   *Observations on the Increased Population, Healthiness etc. of the Town of Maidstone* (Maidstone, 1782), p. 3; *Population Abstract 1811* (London, 1812); *Census of Great Britain 1831* (London, 1832).
3.   See Chapter Three, note 3.
4.   The general migration figures are based on an analysis of ecclesiastical court deposition statements 1660–1720 (Cathedral Library and Archives, Canterbury, PRC 38/1–3, 39/51–5). The data for poorer migrants are taken from Centre for Kentish Studies [Kent Archives Office], P241/13/1.
5.   Public Record Office, Exchequer Tax Accounts, Land and Assessed Taxes, subsidiary documents, E182/447.

6. *Universal British Directory* (London, 1792–8); T.P. Smith, 'The Geographical Pattern of Coaching Services in Kent in 1836', *Archaeologia Cantiana*, vol. 98 (1992), 197 ff.
7. For this and the following account see C.W. Chalklin, 'Navigation Schemes on the Upper Medway 1600–1665', *Journal of Transport History*, vol. 5 (1961); Centre for Kentish Studies, S/MN records of the Medway Navigation Company, especially S/MN FLf1, S/MNA, AM2,3; S/MN, FZ1, FLZ7; records of the Lower Medway Navigation Company, especially S/MN, AM 17.
8. For the brewing industry in the town see Maidstone Industrial Archaeology Group's unpublished 'Brewing Report'.
9. For the industry in general see D.C. Coleman, *The British Paper Industry* (Oxford, 1958); A.H. Shorter, *Paper Making in the British Isles* (Newton Abbot, 1971) and *Water Paper Mills in England* (London, 1966); R.L. Hills, ed., *Studies in the History of Papermaking in Britain* (Aldershot, 1993); M.J. Fuller, *The Watermills of the East Malling and Wateringbury Streams* (London, 1980). *Parliamentary Papers*, 1837, XX, *Committee of Enquiry into Fourdrinier's Patent*.
10. For Whatman and Balston see: T. Balston, *James Whatman, Father and Son* (London, 1957); J.N. Balston, *The Elder James Whatman, England's Greatest Papermaker (1702–1759)* (W. Farleigh, 1992); T. Balston, *William Balston, Paper Maker 1759–1849* (London, 1954).
11. Surprisingly little evidence has survived about the physical layout of Maidstone's major inns but the Bell Inn on Week Street in 1921 had a 44-ft frontage, 32 rooms, an area of 16,650 square feet, and a horse sale yard at the back (Centre for Kentish Studies, U1431 E5). For probate inventories used here see Cathedral Library and Archives, Canterbury, PRC 27/22–43, 11/49–83.
12. Public Record Office, WO/48.
13. Cathedral Library and Archives, Canterbury, PRC 27/22–43, 11/49–83.
14. *Parliamentary Papers*, 1837, XXIII, *Report of the Commissioners . . . concerning Charities in England*, vol. 30, p. 360 ff.
15. For poor relief payments here and below see Centre for Kentish Studies, P241/11; also Sir F. Eden, *The State of the Poor* (London, 1797, new ed. 1966), vol. 1, p. 273.

Bibliographical Note

For general background reading on Georgian towns see note 1. There is currently no good general account of Kent or Kentish towns in this period.

The Maidstone Borough Records (Centre for Kentish Studies [Kent Archives Office], Md) are less useful for this period than before the Restoration, but the Burghmote minute books and sessions papers have some items of value (Md/ ACm 1/3–6, ACp1–17, JQr). Other manuscript sources of value in the Centre for Kentish Studies include the parish poor law records (P241/5, 8, 11, 12, 15, 18, 19, 25) and Medway Navigation Company records (see footnote 7). The important probate inventories are now at Canterbury Cathedral Library and Archives (PRC 27/22–43, 11/49–83).

Among printed primary sources, the most valuable are the local newspapers – the *Maidstone Journal* (1786–) and the *Maidstone Gazette* (1815–); these have been heavily used for research on this chapter. Also useful on the economy are the various national and local trade directories such as, *Bailey's British Directory* (London, 1784); the *Universal British Directory* (London, 1792–8), and *Pigot's London and Provincial Directory 1828–9*. Various *Parliamentary Papers* have material on poverty and trade including: 1777, IV, *Committee on the Maintenance of the Poor, Overseers Returns*; 1825, XXXI, *Report of the Select Committee on the Combination Laws*; 1833, VI, *Report of Select Committee on Manufactures, Commerce and Shipping*; 1834, XXXV, XXXVI, *Royal Commission on the Poor Laws, Town Queries*; 1834, XXVI, *Report from Assistant Commissioners*.

The descriptions of Maidstone by Celia Fiennes, Daniel Defoe and Richard Pococke are in (respectively): C. Morris, ed., *The Journeys of Celia Fiennes* (London, 1947), pp. 129–30; D. Defoe, *A Tour Through the Whole Island of Great Britain* (London, 1962), vol. 1, pp. 113–16; J.J. Cartwright, ed., *The Travels through England of Dr Richard Pococke, vol. 2* (Camden Society, new series, vol. 44, 1889), p. 77. Some details about markets appear in the charters reprinted in W.R. James, *The Charters and Other Documents relating to the King's Town and Parish* (London, 1825). Other town and county histories contain information on different economic and social aspects of the town: for example, S.C. Lampreys, *A Brief Historical and Descriptive Account of Maidstone and its Environs* (Maidstone, 1834); C. Seymour, *Survey of Kent* (Canterbury, 1782).

In the case of secondary material the *Victoria County History*, Kent, vol. 3 (London, 1932) has some good detail on specific industries including textiles, and paper-making. *Archaeologia Cantiana* has only a small number of articles of value for this chapter.

Chapter Five

THE LATE STUART AND GEORGIAN COUNTY TOWN: POLITICAL AND CULTURAL LIFE

Town government and politics up to the 1780s

The late seventeenth and early eighteenth centuries saw many English provincial towns buffeted by political disputes and upheavals.[1] This was partly the result of increased government interference in civic politics, as Charles II and his brother James II sought to remodel town corporations to ensure sympathetic Parliaments. But civic dissension was also due to growing gentry interest and residence in towns, as well as to internal pressure caused by civic oligarchy and religious divisions. In the case of Maidstone there were waves of political upheaval in the 1660s, 1680s and again after 1700, leading to the suspension of the town charter in 1742. Borough status was not restored until 1747 and even then civic bickering and disputes persisted. There was serious political conflict towards the end of the 18th century and again in the years before municipal reform in 1835.

The Restoration of Charles II in 1660 led to a major purge of parliamentarian supporters from the magistracy. Already that summer the regicide Andrew Broughton had abandoned the mayoralty and left town (he later fled to Geneva), and in the autumn Thomas Stanley and other royalist magistrates removed in the 1640s were restored to office. In August 1662 Sir Roger Twisden and several other royalist gentry visited the town as commissioners under the 1660 Corporations Act; six jurats and sixteen common councillors were removed from office, while a number of freemen were also deprived. There was some opposition: the common council refused to recognise the election of the loyalist John Cripps to the bench and there was litigation in King's Bench and a threat of a *quo warranto* against the corporation in 1666. But the town eventually saw the writing on the wall and accepted Cripps – he became mayor in 1671.

After the Restoration the formal civic constitution remained the same as before the Civil War, with a mayor, and twelve jurats, together with a common council and wider body of freeman commoners indistinctly defined.[2] As before the Civil War, power was more and more concentrated in the hands of the ruling bench which also acted as the town magistracy. These men were recruited from the ranks of wealthy shopkeepers, professional men and increasingly manufacturers, although unlike in some other towns there were no gentry mayors in the period. State governed authority was celebrated in traditional ways by civic processions and (before the 1730s) the annual excursion on the river to proclaim the town's jurisdiction, known as the 'mayor's fishing'; and by a growing amount of elite feasting. But oligarchic power was also demonstrated through open manipulation of civic government and elections, and in the Georgian period by a notable decline in the number of Burghmote meetings.

The new royal charter of 1682, imposed by the Crown, tended to consolidate oligarchic power in the town. The charter for the first time called the jurats aldermen and specified a common council of twenty-four, giving formal recognition to established practise. Nominations to the common council were put in the hands of the bench, while the Crown reserved the right to dismiss members of the corporation at will. The charter also narrowed the parliamentary franchise for the town. Traditionally all freemen had the right to vote for the town's two MPs and in 1681 there were some 400 electors. The new charter sought to confine the electorate to members of the corporation and those freemen who were also freeholders with lands and tenements, excluding many lesser inhabitants.

Under James II new purges of the corporation occurred as the Crown sought to force local elites to support religious toleration. In Maidstone this involved bringing well known dissenters on to the magistracy. In 1687 the king ordered the town to elect the Baptist Joseph Wright as mayor and in early January 1688 seven aldermen and twelve common councillors appointed under the 1682 charter were ejected by royal command with their replacements also being nominated. A further letter from the king later the same month removed another four aldermen, eleven councillors, the recorder and town clerk from civic office. In May the drastically remodelled corporation, including a number of dissenters, made a sycophantic address of support to the king. But their ascendancy was brief. The town records note: 'October 20 1688. Exit Tyrannus'. With the flight of James II after the invasion of William of Orange, the corporation repudiated the 1682 charter and restored to office many of the old members of the Burghmote.[3]

However in the long run it proved difficult to restore municipal harmony. During Queen Anne's reign there was growing conflict between the oligarchic ruling bench and the commoners over rights of civic election, inflamed by party strife at the national level between Whigs and Tories. The bench generally bribed their way to success, but in 1715 many of the commoners refused to be swayed by bribes and outvoted the bench in the town elections. The mayor and jurats then produced and read the third royal charter of 1604, claiming to hold the right of election by themselves alone. Subsequently, for over twenty years the common council and commonalty were excluded from elections to the corporation, and the bench was able to ensure that all persons elected were of their own party. In 1726 there were complaints that town lands had been sold without the full consent of the Burghmote.

Parliamentary elections during the late seventeenth and early eighteenth centuries were equally contentious, encouraged by these internal civic divisions, religious tensions (Maidstone was an important nonconformist centre), and the large freeman franchise. The number of electors increased rapidly in this period, more than doubling in the fifty years after 1681; in 1734 979 men were polled, though as we shall see numbers subsequently diminished. Like elections to the corporation, parliamentary contests were increasingly decided by bribery and corruption.

In the late seventeenth century most of the MPs returned for Maidstone were gentry living in or near the town, like Sir John Tufton elected in 1679, 1681 and 1685, or Thomas Fane the son of Sir George Fane, the early Stuart MP. No one interest prevailed in this period, though the Whigs had established a strong position in the town by the time of the Exclusion Crisis in 1679. After the Revolution of 1688 the borough's two seats were frequently divided between Whigs and Tories. Thus in 1698 and 1700 the Whig Sir Robert Marsham (later Lord Romney) was chosen along with the wealthy Tory brewer Thomas Bliss. After the second election Bliss, a reputed Jacobite, was charged with widespread fraud and abuse, showering the freemen with guineas, giving away free drink to voters at his tied public houses, parading the town 'in a tumultuous manner with trumpets and horsemen', and stoning the houses of opponents. More than one side was to blame: Bliss counter-charged his opponents with abuse and there were fresh allegations against candidates in the 1710 elections as well.

During the early Georgian period Maidstone was the cockpit of fierce electoral contests with the seat increasingly divided – as in 1716, 1722, 1727 and 1734 – between the Tory Finches, Earls of Aylesford, and the Whig Romney interest. In broad terms the Tories tended to ally with the oligarchic group on the corporation, while their opponents had the support of the commonalty and dissenters. In 1741 the Whigs seized both the parliamentary seats reflecting the increasingly precarious position of the oligarchic corporation party in the town.[4]

During the 1730s the bench's control over borough elections was finally challenged in the courts. In 1736–38 judgement was given in favour of the commonalty and two jurats who had been chosen by the bench alone were expelled. Five others who had been elected in the same way thereupon resigned, and since there were unfilled vacancies on the bench, only three jurats (chosen by the full council before 1715) remained in office. A Burghmote meeting was held early the next year to elect replacement jurats, but shortly afterwards the ousted jurats challenged the authority of the three remaining pre-1715 jurats. It was claimed that they had been elected by the mayor, jurats and common council, and not by the commonalty as a whole, as required by the 1619 charter. As a result, the three jurats were disqualified from office by the courts, having been improperly elected, and since they had taken part in the election of the replacement jurats, the election of the latter was also declared invalid. In 1742 this decision was challenged but upheld by the courts. Having lost all its jurats the corporation was defunct, and the town's charter forfeit. Civic embarrassment was not confined to Maidstone, however: a number of other boroughs lost their charters in the early eighteenth century because of similar political strife.[5]

Maidstone remained without a mayor or corporation until 1747. During this time some of the essential decisions concerning town administration were taken at parish vestry meetings, including the election of the new grammar school master in 1746. But it is clear that much of the work of municipal government was in suspense. Apprenticeship indentures were no longer enrolled, town rents went uncollected, and civic finances fell into disarray, not least because large sums were expended on petitioning for a new charter. Contending parties lobbied the Solicitor-General for a charter to suit their own interests. The old oligarchic party called for a common council limited to twenty-four, with elections to the magisterial bench decided by the mayor and jurats only; the other faction wanted elections to be decided by the whole corporation with the common council consisting of all the freemen of the town. The first of the civic parties was supported by the Tory interests of the Earl of Aylesford, while the other was associated with William Horsemonden Turner, Whig MP for the town in 1734–41 and 1747–53. But at this time members of the two groups on the corporation did not always vote in parliamentary elections on national party lines, and before the 1770s the two factions are better seen as a Corporation party and an anti-Corporation or Independent party

The sixth and final royal charter which was eventually granted to the town in 1747 pleased nobody.[6] It appointed a mayor and twelve jurats as before and a common council of forty men. Members of the common council were to be elected by the whole of the commonalty, that is, the common council and other 'principal inhabitants', while the mayor and jurats were elected by the bench and common council. The charter nominated William Horsemonden Turner as recorder and initially seems to have given the balance of power to the anti-Corporation party – both Turner and another Whig were elected MPs that year. But the Corporation party soon reasserted their influence over the bench and common council. As one indication, after 1753 parliamentary elections were once again divided between Tories and Whigs.

The Corporation party continued to hold sway in the town until 1764, when the votes of the commonalty secured the election to the common council of four men opposed to the civic junto. To stop this happening in future, a by-law was passed restricting the election of common councillors to members of the corporation and those of the commonality who had held public office. This by-law was challenged in the courts, and ruled invalid. Two years later the Corporation party tried again, and passed a further by-law which attempted to restrict the commonalty to the forty senior freemen. When that too was overruled by the courts, they endeavoured to keep the number to sixty, claiming that any larger number was unwieldy. But when an election occurred soon after, only seven of the sixty senior freemen attended the court to vote, and they were said to have been wheeled out from the workhouse and almshouses to back the Corporation party. The latest by-law was in due course overturned by King's Bench, which declared that the Corporation party 'would overturn the constitution itself if it were in their power'. The freemen had spent £900 in defending their rights, whilst the Corporation party had wasted a great deal of the borough's funds on litigation.

After this there were no more such blatant efforts to subvert the provisions of the 1747 charter, although attempts were made by the bench to reduce the numbers of freemen, in order to increase magisterial control. In the 1780s the Corporation party came close to losing command of the Burghmote and the election process. Vacancies on the bench were left unfilled for long periods, and the mayor allegedly ceased to announce the business at forthcoming Burghmotes, to keep the freemen in the dark over elections. At the same time, the Corporation party increasingly organised its supporters, sponsoring the Commonalty Society to win freeman votes. The society had an annual fishing excursion down the Medway sailing in a decorated barge with a band playing to Newhithe where they feasted and frolicked. The event, which seems to have superceded the traditional civic festivity of the 'mayor's fishing', was a major celebration of political solidarity and social importance; en route the expedition was saluted by cannon fire from the river bank, and returned to a fireworks display in the town. Their Whig opponents established the rival Keppel Society, which also lavished hospitality on their supporters with a river excursion. By the 1770s the parties on the corporation had become more clearly identified with Tory and Whig national politics, the Corporation party (the Reds or Purples) supporting the North and later Pitt ministries, while their opponents usually called the Blues, voted for Whig candidates for Parliament.

Party conflict and pressure for reform

In this political environment, outside landed influence in the town's parliamentary elections was of declining importance. In 1780 the Earl of Aylesford's candidate was decisively beaten and thereafter a considerable number of those representing the town belonged to the urban elite, including paper-makers, bankers and brewers, sometimes with London connections. Corruption and abuse now became endemic in both civic and parliamentary elections. In 1786 the Independent party won eight out of the nine contested seats on the Burghmote, and this so frightened their opponents that at the next election two years later the Corporation party mustered two hundred non-resident freemen to vote for their candidates, who were duly returned. In the same way at parliamentary polls great numbers of these freemen were ferried to the town from London, the Medway towns and further afield to vote predominantly for Tory MPs. The cost of bribing the freemen soared. By 1801 Sir Mathew Bloxham had spent £15,000 on treating at four recent elections.

As in other towns, party hostility permeated the community during the 1780s and early 1790s. Factionalism extended to refusing to trade with persons of the opposing party, and a townsman going into a public house frequented by the other faction risked being insulted if not thrown out. Even young ladies at dances were liable to reject partners not of their own party. Meanwhile, there was growing political discontent and pressure for political reform in the town. This was fanned by civic corruption and the unfairness of the freeman franchise which increasingly excluded many respectable ratepayers (due to corporation controls on new freemen). In addition, external developments – the American war, the national movement for parliamentary reform, and later the outbreak of the French Revolution – had an impact. Clement Taylor, the paper manufacturer and MP for Maidstone in 1780, 1784 and 1790, strongly supported parliamentary reform, and in the early 1790s we find growing radical activity in the town, with at least some support coming from the town's paper-workers and other artisans. As the French upheavals became more violent, Maidstone's Whig party was careful to disassociate itself from any perceived threat to the established order and in December 1792 the Blues joined with the Tories to form a loyalist association to defend 'our most excellent Constitution'. Shortly afterwards a wheelwright and a carpenter were arrested and indicted at quarter sessions for sedition for proclaiming: 'success to Tom Paine [the radical author] and his Rights of Man . . . and damn the West Kent [militia] and all your officers, and damn your King and constitution, your constitution is not worth a damn.' They received heavy prison sentences.[7]

Nevertheless, at least some of the town's respectable classes, radical Whigs, continued to support parliamentary reform and, following the acquittal of London radicals tried for treason in late 1794, there was a celebration dinner in Maidstone at which over a hundred people drank anti-government and radical toasts. In late 1795 Clement Taylor voted against the government anti-sedition laws and the next year John Gale Jones, a delegate from the London Corresponding Society, visited Maidstone. He stayed with the leading paper-maker James Smythe, met Clement Taylor, whom he pronounced to be 'a worthy and sensible man and a strenuous friend to reform', and addressed a number of meetings at the Castle Inn, then the meeting place of radical reformers. It was resolved to form or re-form the Maidstone Corresponding Society, which soon had sixty members.[8] The same year the radical Christopher Hull stood as a candidate in the parliamentary elections, espousing 'peace, reform, civil liberty and religious toleration'; having spent £3,000 on the poll he was only narrowly defeated.

In 1797 another delegate from London was arrested in the town for inciting soldiers to mutiny but was bailed by two of the town's grocers and disappears from view. However, the following year, the arrest at Margate and subsequent trial at Maidstone of four Irish radicals seeking to aid a French invasion caused a sensation and radical activity in the town evaporated – deterred by government repression, the threat of invasion from France, and the massive military presence in the area (the cavalry barracks was established at Maidstone in 1797). War with France also led to the diminution of party acrimony and division in the town with the Commonalty

Society ending in 1796, although parliamentary elections remained warmly contested, as for example in 1806.

But with the return of peace after 1815 there was a rapid revival of partisan rivalry. This was fuelled by the Whig Blues holding sway in parliamentary elections while the Tories controlled the corporation. The Commonalty Society was revived and in 1819 a more explicitly Tory freeman association, the Invincibles, was established, while the Whigs set up their own freeman society, the Inflexibles. All three clubs now had annual excursions, usually but not always on the river; the Tory societies basked in the patronage of the mayor and magistrates, whereas the Inflexibles decked their barge in light blue and enjoyed the company of Whig leaders and MPs. The clubs also paraded the town, and celebrated with fireworks, music and cannon fire. Civic and parliamentary elections were once again bitterly fought. In 1822 the election of three common councilmen continued for seven days, with freemen brought in to vote from up to sixty miles away and one side reportedly lavishing £1,600 on the contest. As a result, the Tories hung on to power.

In 1825 William Robert James published *The Charters and Other Documents Relating to the King's Town and Parish of Maidstone*, which was a detailed historical exposé of civic conflict and corruption in the town, and a denunciation of the exclusion of many respectable inhabitants from the franchise. The question of parliamentary reform rapidly became a live political issue in the town once more. In 1830 some of the Maidstone radicals joined forces with farm labourers and other poor increasingly reduced to destitution. There were outbreaks of arson, attacks on farm machinery and demands for money by gangs of semi-starving men. Intimidatory letters circulated, frequently signed by the labourers' mythical leader Captain Swing; one threatened to set the town of Maidstone on fire. The radicals linked the poverty of the labourers with the unreformed political system. In October some 500 labourers set out to march from Boughton to Maidstone. Alarmed, the magistrates called out the cavalry from Maidstone barracks, rode out to meet the men on the road, and arrested one of the leaders – a town shoemaker. Soon after over 500 people gathered on Penenden Heath, among them Maidstone paper-makers and impoverished labourers, and demanded 'Reform of the Commons House; Right of Vote for all men of 21 years of age; vote by ballot, annual or two years parliaments; these rights and privileges or nothing.'

The Swing Riots, which spread over much of southern England, gave important impetus to the campaign for parliamentary reform. A majority of Maidstone freemen were caught up in the tide of reforming zeal. Prior to the parliamentary elections in May 1831 a Burghmote was held to make free all those qualified to vote. Men reportedly came from as far away as Liverpool and Hull, at their own expense, to claim their freedom and vote for the Whig candidates, whose Reform Bill would deprive them of the franchise. In October a pro-reform petition containing 2,000 names was presented to the House of Lords on the town's behalf by Lord Romney, but when the Lords rejected the Reform Bill there was no rioting in town as in other places. After the Bill was finally passed in June 1832 Maidstone celebrated with cannon fire and the ringing of bells. The 1832 Reform Act gave the vote to all men occupying property in the town worth £10. The freemen retained their votes for life provided they lived within seven miles of the town, but non-residents were disenfranchised. However, the increase in the number of resident voters was at first fairly insignificant, rising from 716 in 1831 to 945 in 1832 and 1,232 in 1835, out of a total population of about 16,000. Paradoxically, once reform had been achieved, the town's reformist zeal faded and the Tories rapidly recovered support. Corrupt practices continued, and there were disputes over the rating of property for franchise purposes.

Parliamentary reform was followed by municipal reform. When the town was visited by the municipal reform commissioners in December 1833, the Tory majority on the corporation ill-advisedly voted not to cooperate with them, and the visitors went to the Whigs for information. Not surprisingly, the commissioners' report was highly critical. They found that the Tories monopolised the bench of jurats, excluding Whig candidates 'equal in wealth and respectability' and ensuring that all mayors were Tory. There was concern that two of the senior jurats were brewers and thus in a position as licensing justices to favour their own public houses. There was also criticism of the bribery and corruption surrounding elections to the common council and of the exclusion of many large ratepayers from participation in town government, while poorer freemen had a prominent role. The commissioners concluded: 'the present [civic] constitution has not worked well'.[9]

In September 1834, the Whig interest hosted a large public dinner in the town in support of municipal reform. During the proceedings the Rogues March, a tune traditionally played by the military when a man was brought out to be flogged, was played to great cheers. The following year, despite a petition to Parliament signed by 400 freemen, the old civic regime came to an end. The Municipal Corporations Act of 1835 reduced the corporation from 53 members to 18, with a mayor, 5 aldermen, and 12 common councillors; these were to be elected by all the male ratepayers in four newly-designated wards of the town. Aldermen held office for six years, common councillors for three, and there were now to be annual elections.

Public improvement

In Hanoverian England civic oligarchy and corruption did not necessarily mean urban neglect and lethargy and this was certainly the case at Maidstone. The period saw important civic improvements in the town with town administration increasingly decentralised. A number of the town's long-established courts – the old manorial court leet, court of pleas, market court and town sessions – faded into unimportance during the early eighteenth century. Even the activity of the Burghmote seemed to be sporadic before its suspension in 1742–7. On the other hand, the work of the corporation was increasingly supplemented by other bodies, including private companies (involved in the Medway navigation) and the later trustees of the poor and pavement commissioners. Efforts to improve the town's market facilities and the river navigation have already been described, but improvements were also made to civic amenities, water supplies and sanitation.

One the earliest projects after the Restoration was the opening of a tree-lined and railed public walk in the Fair Meadow beside the Medway to entertain the growing numbers of landowners coming to town. This was one of the first public walks on the London model in any provincial town. The path was laid and the first trees planted in 1699, but work continued for several years, and the walk was repaired and relaid in 1766 and 1814. By the later Stuart period a good water supply was also increasingly regarded as a necessary amenity for a fashionable town. In the 1660s the conduits and pipes which had brought water to the town from Rocky Hill since the sixteenth century were in a ruinous state, and required extensive work. In 1715 a plumber was contracted to maintain the pipes and conduits for a yearly sum. Most inhabitants still drew their water from the three fountain houses constructed in the 16th century, but the better off probably had by-pipes to their houses from the main supply. Though the main conduit in the High Street was extensively repaired in 1783, the growing population and extent of the urban area led to the town being 'very badly supplied with water'. Residents more and more often made their own arrangement; in 1805, for instance, a number of houses in the area of St Faith's Street received piped water from a source owned by the Earl of Aylesford and Heathorn's brewery. Not until the 1820s was there a concerted attempt to improve public provision.

Although there were minor improvements to the town streets in the earlier period, the rising population and volume of traffic by the late eighteenth century caused mounting problems. We hear in 1791 that the streets 'are not properly paved and cleansed, and are not lighted . . . and several of them are very narrow, incommodious and dangerous'. Legislation that year appointed a pavement commission comprising the town MPs, members of the corporation, freeholders and substantial ratepayers, with power to levy rates and raise loans to finance civic improvements. Action was taken to pave and light the streets the following year, while scavengers were employed to clean the town and collect household refuse. Other nuisances, such as the butchering of animals in the street, were banned. In 1796 a second Act of Parliament authorised the raising of further rates and in 1808 the medieval bridge, frequently condemned as out of date and obstructed, was substantially widened and improved. Eleven years later the third Maidstone Paving Act sanctioned extensive town improvements, including the building of a town wharf, further repaving and street widening. In addition, drains were laid, and the water supply was greatly enhanced with the installation of iron pipes carrying 30,000 gallons a day to seventeen public conduits. In 1822 the pavement commissioners made an agreement with John Gosling, whose company later became the Maidstone Gas Light and Coke Company, to introduce gas lighting to the town, with 196 lamps installed in public areas. In 1834, one writer claimed that 'it would be difficult to find a country town more brilliantly lighted than this.'

There were also improvements to public buildings. In 1764 the corporation carried out the demolition of the Lower Court House, and the construction of the present classical-style town hall; the cost was largely met by donations, and by the West Kent justices who used it for assizes and county business. As we saw in Chapter Four, new market buildings were erected in the 1820s and 1830s. There was also a proliferation of new chapels and commercial public premises which provided an expanding arena for the town's changing cultural activities.

The Church and dissent after the Restoration

Religion remained an important force in Maidstone's cultural life after the Restoration, influencing all aspects of the community. But by the early eighteenth century the town was also the focus of a growing range of new style social and cultural activities, heavily modelled on those of the metropolis, and these played an important part in consolidating the town's position as a fashionable county centre in the Georgian era. Urban sociability was also linked with the growth of educational provision. By the end of the eighteenth century there was an upsurge of nonconformist churches, along with a proliferation of philanthropic organisations as the town's burgeoning middle class began to create their own sense of social identity. These major developments will be discussed in detail in the rest of this chapter.

After the Restoration the Church of England was restored and clergy required to conform under the 1662 Act of Uniformity. The Presbyterian minister of All Saints, John Crump, chose to leave the church, and many of the congregation are said to have gone with him. The Conventicle Act of 1664 made nonconformist meetings of more than five persons illegal, and the Presbyterians led a clandestine and persecuted existence for a number of years, probably meeting in a private house, as did the small congregation of Arminian Baptists which had existed in the town since the Revolution. Some of the Baptists had been imprisoned in 1660 for refusing to take the Oath of Allegiance. Joseph Wright, a prominent member of the congregation, was one of two men who presented a Baptist petition with 20,000 signatures to the king in 1661; he was subsequently imprisoned in Maidstone for some twenty years on various charges, before becoming James II's choice as mayor in 1687. In 1672 Charles II's Declaration of Indulgence enabled the licensing of dissenters' meeting houses and the Presbyterians obtained a licence for St Faith's chapel, while the Baptists had meeting rooms in Maidstone and Tovil. The revocation of the king's declaration saw a new campaign of harrassment against the town's dissenters. In the 1680s a number of Quakers suffered heavy fines for preaching in the town. The Compton Religious Census of 1676 estimated there were 310 Protestant dissenters at Maidstone; ten were said to be Baptists and Quakers, the remainder Presbyterians who also attended some Church services. The figures are suspiciously round, and almost certainly underestimate the scale of nonconformity in the town, although the great majority of the population probably remained within the established Church.

After the Toleration Act of 1689 we hear of a strong Presbyterian congregation in the town with some 700 attending services in 1690.[10] By 1736 the meeting had built a new chapel in Mitre Yard, Market Buildings, known as the Earl Street chapel. This contained seats for 400, which suggests that, if the 1690 figure is correct, there had been some decline in numbers. In 1745 differences over doctrine led to the secession of part of the congregation who called themselves Independents and met in a house on St Faith's Green, soon after building a chapel in Week Street.

At the same time, the Anglican parish church, All Saints, retained an important role in the social and cultural life of the town. Into the late eighteenth century the minister and parishioners delineated the parish boundaries and confirmed the church's area of authority by going in beribboned procession to beat the bounds. The church gave religious sanction to civic ceremonies such as the mayoral election and sessions of the county assizes. It was also associated with the new cultural activities in the town during the eighteenth century. There were sermons to voluntary societies and the church bells were augmented (six bells in 1667, eight by 1741, ten in 1784) to cater for the new fashionable practice of change ringing. As we noted above, religious divisions between Anglicans and dissenters may well have inflamed political divisions in the town in the later Stuart period, particularly after James II's attempt to pack the corporation with nonconformists sympathetic to religious toleration. But in the early Georgian town religious differences may have been increasingly muted by a growing commitment of the respectable classes to public sociability.

The rise of public sociability

By 1700 the town's cultural activity was increasingly fashioned by genteel and metropolitan values. As we saw in Chapter Four, there was a growing influx of gentry visitors to town and they encouraged the development of a constellation of new social entertainments. Residence in the countryside was regarded as unfashionable and intolerable. For those gentry and rural well-to-do unable to afford to spend all their time in the capital, county towns offered the next best thing in cultural style. The image of the town as a smart urbane centre was increasingly promoted in print. Although early town newspapers in 1725 and 1737 proved unsuccessful (probably due to the proximity of London and its many publications), from 1786 the *Maidstone Journal*, edited by John Blake, presented a steady stream of news, notices and advertisements publicising the social, cultural as well as commercial activities of the town in mid- and West Kent. After 1815 there was also the more radical *Maidstone Gazette*. Valuable civic promotion was likewise provided by William Newton's *History and Antiquities of Maidstone* in 1741 with its handsome, rather idealised panorama of the town at the front and its depiction of Maidstone as the county town of Kent. There was another history by Walter Rowles in 1809 and various other town guides and descriptions.

Fashionable socialising began early in the town. By the 1720s Maidstone already had assemblies for cards and dancing. According to Defoe, scandalous behaviour by 'some loose persons' led to the withdrawal of respectable company, but this was doubtless no more than a temporary social hiccough and by mid-century the town had its own assembly room, probably linked to one of the great inns. In 1786 assemblies were held monthly at the Asssembly Rooms on St Faith's Green; the next decade they took place at the Star Inn, where they remained until 1819, when new County Assembly Rooms were built near the barracks by public subscription. At the opening of the new rooms between three and four hundred 'fashionables' attended, the ladies in dresses descibed as 'very superb'. The assemblies continued into Victoria's reign and were attended by the 'nobility and gentry of the county'. Public music-making was another important social entertainment for the better off. In 1750 there was a concert at the Assembly Room and next year a benefit concert at the grammar school with a London violinist as soloist. Unlike Canterbury Maidstone does not seem to have had an early music society, but by the 1790s a concert society met every Wednesday night at the Bull, with another music society gathering at the Star listening to performances of works by Correlli and Stamitz.

The first reference to the theatre after the Civil War was in 1730 when Mr Dymer's travelling company visited the town. Two years later he erected a theatre booth in the yard of the Star and enjoyed enormous success, drawing it was said 'the greatest audiences that ever were known, the country gentry coming in from all parts'. In the middle decades of the eighteenth century a Canterbury manager staged plays in the town, sometimes with the backing of town societies, and by 1770 a New Theatre had been opened at the bottom of the High Street. This in turn was superceded by another further up the street managed by Mrs Sarah Baker which was extensively rebuilt and refurbished in 1798; the auditorium was still relatively small – measuring 85 ft by 23 ft, but with a pit, boxes, and gallery catering for ordinary townsmen as well as the better off. Mrs Baker went in for spectacular performances; for instance, in 1815 the play 'The Miller and his Men' concluded with the explosion of the mill, staged by Signor Hengler, the fireworks expert at the Vauxhall gardens in London. In 1832 the theatre was elaborately refitted with a new proscenium arch, Italianate curtain, and five gas chandeliers. One reviewer declared a few years later that 'there are few provincial theatres which can boast of a more talented company'.

Sporting activities were likewise an important urban entertainment, often associated with heavy drinking, feasting and gambling. In 1730 the gentlemen of Maidstone organised a cock-fight at the Royal Cockpit at the Ship against the gentlemen of Sandhurst in Sussex with high stakes of two guineas for each battle between the cocks. In the 1780s the East and West Kent gentry held regular cock-fights in the town. Horse-racing seems to have been less important than elsewhere, partly because of the strong competition from Canterbury races. There were five race meetings at Maidstone in 1735 and four more in the period up to 1770. In the 1780s there were a number of races at Coxheath but these were probably run by army officers at the military camp there. Cricket had a greater impact. As early as 1646 we find townspeople betting on a match at Coxheath between two teams of gentlemen and by 1786 a club was in existence at Penenden Heath, with gentlemen playing matches against other local teams; this remained active until 1819. By 1830 an Artichoke cricket club was in existence, based at the public house of that name, which appears to have been more middle class in composition, and typically played opponents for a sovereign a man. In 1834 a club described as Leeds (Maidstone) played the MCC at Lords and won; the team consisted of six gentlemen and five players, possibly professionals. At a return match at Leeds, there were estimated to be between eight and ten thousand spectators. About the same time a new team was formed in Maidstone by 'a party of young gentlemen'.

Not all sociability was genteel or fashionable. There was a good deal of more traditional street entertainment, supported by the lower orders but with some elite patronage as well. Bare knuckle fighting and foot races were sponsored by publicans with heavy drinking and large-scale gambling. Wagers were made on almost every kind of feat. In 1790, for instance, a Maidstone bricklayer bet that the elderly horse which drew his cart could travel to London Bridge and back twice in twenty-four hours which it duly did. There was heavy gambling too in 1814 when a soldier at the barracks undertook to walk sixty miles in twenty-four hours and finished the distance in seventeen. Other popular socialising was associated with the town fairs and 5 November with large bonfires in the streets. Whitsuntide was marked in the town by games and sports on Penenden Heath including donkey, women's foot and wheelbarrow races watched by large crowds. By the 1820s, however, traditional outdoor entertainments like this seem to have been on the wane, partly because of civic and street improvement and partly due to increasing upper- and middle-class concern at what they saw as public and moral disorder. No less important, moreover, was the growing competition, particularly after 1800, of new leisure, educational and religious activities attracting the support of respectable townspeople.

By the later Georgian period a great deal of public sociability not just in Maidstone but many other British towns was organised by clubs and societies. As one writer declared in the eighteenth century 'we are of all nations the most forward to run into clubs, parties and societies' – indeed one could claim that the British invented the modern style of voluntary association in this period. Of the various town societies in George III's reign, the most prestigious was the Maidstone Society for Promoting Useful Knowledge which in 1786 assumed a county role. The founder was William Shipley, who with Lord Romney had been largely responsible for the creation of the London-based Society of Arts (now the Royal Society of Arts) in the 1750s. Shipley retired from the capital about 1768 and may have set up the Maidstone Society – modelled on the London one – soon after. Among the corresponding members of the Maidstone body were Benjamin Franklin, the American patriot and scientist, and Arthur Young, the leading agricultural reformer. The society was active in promoting improvement and innovation in agriculture, household economy, the mechanic arts, and other branches of useful knowledge. Thus it publicised resuscitation techniques pioneered by the Humane Society for victims of drowning and suffocation, exhibited early ventilators, used telescopes to view the planets, and supported educational reform. In 1784 it sought to control the fever which broke out in Maidstone gaol and nine years later it opened an experimental garden for cultivating new species of plants.[11]

Shipley was also involved in the Masonic Lodge of Fortitude which met at the Bell Inn and which had twenty-two members by 1783, including a wide swathe of leading townsmen, among them a grocer, linen draper, wine merchant, paper-maker, shipowner, surgeons, and a schoolmaster. The lodge master was Clement Taylor the town's Whig MP, and the lodge was prominent in publicising the work of the Humane Society and other advances. One writer claimed that the lodge was 'a school of universal utility and a worthy example to other lodges'. Masonry seems to have come fairly late to Maidstone but from 1785 the Bell on Week Street was the venue for meetings of the Provincial Grand Lodge for Kent.[12] One possible explanation for the limited success of Masonry in Maidstone may have been party divisions (the Masons were mainly Whig); another factor perhaps was the variety of other types of associations competing for membership and public attention.

As well as the improvement and music societies already mentioned, by the close of the century the town had a wealth of clubs and similar bodies – an agricultural society, benefit societies, book club, bachelors' society, cricket club, card society, Gibraltar society (probably a dining club meeting at the Gibraltar pub), running club, trapball society, plus, as we have seen, a number of Tory and Whig political clubs. Though the genteel classes played an important role in the more fashionable associations such as Shipley's improvement society or the agricultural society, what is evident by the end of the eighteenth century is that there was growing support from middle-rank inhabitants and to a lesser extent skilled workers. Benefit or friendly societies proliferated in bigger cities from the early eighteenth century to provide a means of mutual support, savings and conviviality for artisans. As in most other southern country towns, lower-class clubs of this type came late, but by the early nineteenth century, as we saw in Chapter Four, Maidstone had a number of societies whose processions on Whit Monday attracted large crowds to hear the bands and to see the members marching with banners and decorated hats and their wives carrying nosegays of flowers. Maidstone's social affluence in the Georgian period was not a monopoly of the rich. In some measure, it percolated down the social order and embraced the middle and artisan classes.

Education

Fundamental to the growth of middle-class and artisan sociability was the improvement in educational standards over the period, though this was selective and uneven. The town's Tudor grammar school in Earl Street continued to be controlled by the corporation. One's impression is that during most of this period it was a small, sleepy institution providing old-fashioned classical instruction to the sons of town respectability. The appointment of John Law as master in 1664 proved a long-lasting mistake. In 1689 we hear the school under Law was 'wholly neglected and most of the scholars are gone and taken away'. Despite being convicted of manslaughter, Law clung to his post and was only prised out after protracted legal action. Law's successors were more worthy but failed to raise the school's educational profile, apart from one or two famous pupils such as Christopher Smart, the Georgian poet, who became insane. Only under John Cherry (master 1777–95) was there any significant expansion of the school with the taking of boarders from the countryside. But in 1818 the master Edward Allfree counted no more than twenty-eight boys including fifteen boarders; there was no usher or second master. One of the problems was the small endowment to pay the master's wages, but as Allfree remarked another difficulty was the competition from other schools.

In addition to the rival attractions of well known schools in London, Tonbridge and elsewhere, competition came from various private establishments in the Hanoverian town. In the early nineteenth century an important rival for the grammar school was a subscription academy established in 1827; this was also an Anglican establishment but exclusive, with fees of eleven or twelve guineas a year, and pupils nominated by shareholders. There were numerous other private schools in Maidstone during our period; in the decade after the Restoration four or five teachers were licensed in the town and the number of establishments almost certainly multiplied in the eighteenth century. Some offered a more progressive curriculum, including mathematics, languages and commercial subjects, but others, particularly those for young ladies, provided more basic domestic education. One or two schools aimed at those of modest means, such as the girls' school advertised by a struggling widow in 1813, which promised to pay particular attention to needlework, and charged thirteen shillings a quarter.

However, for the great majority of Maidstone's lower-class children the only formal schooling was offered by charity schools. The first charity school, the Bluecoat school, was established in the town in 1711, endowed by Josiah Woodward, the well known moral reformer and minister of All Saints. It subsequently benefited from other bequests and donations, and from an annual charity sermon. By the early nineteenth century it was providing instruction for 53 boys and 43 girls whose Anglican parents were 'of sober and industrious habits'. Pupils attended for three years; the boys were taught reading, writing and arithmetic, and the girls reading, knitting and sewing. A second Anglican charity school was established about 1792 (under the will of Sir Charles Booth), at which up to 55 boys were similarly taught basic literacy and 30 girls received instruction in reading and some writing. The first Sunday school, which also taught spinning to poor girls, was started by the Church in 1787, with the view that 'industry is the best foundation on which to build piety'. It may also have sought to reduce the poor rates by training the needy in a useful trade. Other Sunday schools were probably begun by the town's nonconformist churches shortly afterwards. By the first years of the nineteenth century there were two small dissenting charity schools, known as the Greencoat and Browncoat schools. Although these were established and broadly financed by the chapels, they were also 'generously supported' by Anglicans as well. In the 1830s the Greencoat school clothed and educated twelve boys and twelve girls, while the Browncoat school provided for twice that number.

After 1800 the provision of schooling was increasingly inadequate for the needs of an expanding urban population. There was mounting concern both in the town and at the national level that educational failure would lead to idleness, social disorder and crime. Two national voluntary organisations had branches at Maidstone: the British and Foreign School Society founded a school in 1807, which had the support of Anglicans and nonconformists but was more influenced by the latter; and the National Society founded another in 1811 which was exclusively Anglican. Both societies were concerned that working-class children should not be trained above their station in life, but taught industriousness and deference. A British school for 200 boys was opened in Wheeler Street, Maidstone in 1812, under the supervision of a committee of representatives from the various chapels. The boys were 'taught to reverence the scriptures, respect their parents and instructors . . . to be inoffensive in their deportment, [and] honest, sober and useful in society.' They were also taught to read the bible, and some learnt writing and arithmetic; they paid a penny a week. Concern was soon expressed that girls were being neglected and not taught to 'understand their duty and obligations as moral, social and accountable creatures'. It was estimated there were 700 poor girls in the town without any education. In 1814 a British school for girls was established on St Faith's Green and the Anglicans' Sunday and spinning schools were transformed into a National school, 'for educating the children of the poor in the principles of the established church'; this had accommodation for 240 boys and 100 girls. In 1823 a new building was erected for the British schools, funded by loans from various local tradesmen and manufacturers. It was agreed that 'no peculiar religious creed or articles of faith be taught at the said school . . .'. By 1832 the British boys' school had taught well over 1,900 pupils, while over 3,400 children had received instruction at the National school by the end of the decade.[13] It is likely that the majority of town children still did not attend a day school in the 1830s, but some of them may have obtained a basic level of literacy at Sunday school. In 1834 the Sunday schools of all denominations could accommodate 2,000 children.

If schooling remained rudimentary for the lower orders, educational opportunities for the better off markedly improved during the eighteenth and early nineteenth centuries. Book ownership was already quite common at this social level before the Civil War and private purchases multiplied from the late seventeenth century with a growing range of works supplied and advertised by town booksellers and printers. Library facilities also advanced. Though Maidstone may have had a small collection of books at All Saints church by the 1650s, the important parish library was set up after legislation in 1709 encouraging this kind of establishment. County gentry donated books and by 1730 the library probably had over a hundred volumes. Soon after, the town purchased by public subscription books from the library of Thomas Bray, the founder of the SPCK. Unfortunately the library of nearly 600 works was not a success. The books were mainly religious and historical works, many of them in Latin; borrowers were comparatively few, and the collection was neglected. It did not appeal to the smart literary tastes of genteel society which were better served by commercial libraries such as the circulating library attached to Blake's bookshop in the 1780s. A number of these commercial libraries serviced the town by 1800. During the early nineteenth century, however, there was growing demand for a public library. In January 1831 letters to the *Maidstone Gazette* pointed out that Canterbury, Rochester and Chatham already had public libraries, and called for one in Maidstone. The result was not a public library but a Literary Institution, established on a subscription basis, which effectively excluded all but the prosperous. The Institution opened in September 1831, with the Earl of Romney as president, and by 1834 there were 148 members and nearly 2,000 'well selected volumes'.

Yet growing artisan and lower-class demand for public facilities was not completely neglected. In 1834 several hundred men met at the Fountain public house to establish a mechanics reading room and library. There was a complaint that the 'higher classes monopolised all the learning and left them [the lower-classes] the monopoly of labour.' It was hoped that a body of this kind would provide an alternative to the drunken appeal of the public house and promote artisan improvement. Over a hundred men enrolled immediately, others joined afterwards, and the reading room opened later that year, with premises in Union Street, which quickly proved too small for the number of readers. The subscription was a penny a week, newspapers and periodicals were provided, and useful and improving books were bought as soon as funds permitted. Many of the members were unable to read, but other members promised to read to them, and in some instances to teach them.

There were other avenues for educational improvement as well. By the early nineteenth century, if not before, 'philosophical' lectures on astronomy, electricity and other branches of physics were given in the town by itinerant lecturers. These lectures were sometimes under the patronage of the mayor, and were restricted by price to the middle classes and gentry. Although they were advertised as educational, they were also evidently a fashionable social entertainment. More serious, in the winter of 1833/4 the Maidstone Philosophical and Literary Society organised a course of lectures, and in September 1834 a permanent Philosophical Society was established to continue their work. It was agreed to be 'extremely desirable that the working classes should be admitted to the lectures' for 6d each, and that special accommodation be provided for them. But in the event the cheapest admission price was 1s 6d.

The growth of religious pluralism

Yet despite the growth of secular cultural and social activities, for many middle-class and artisan inhabitants before and after 1800 the centre of much of their social and cultural life remained focused on church and chapel meetings, with their prayer meetings, breakfasts, tea-parties and organised walks. The growth of nonconformity in the late eighteenth century was striking, though not all congregations prospered. In 1782 there were said to be 209 Presbyterians and 42 Independents in the town, which indicates a decline from their earlier heyday. The Baptists had moved to a meeting house in Rose Yard in the 1740s and this had just over 40 members by the 1780s. In 1796 the congregation united with the Presbyterians at the Earl Street chapel, and after 1813 described themselves as Unitarians. The Rose Yard meeting-house was taken over the following year by a group of Particular or Calvinistic Baptists, an offshoot of a congregation at Chatham. This group had 33 members in 1806 and 59 by 1818. In 1820 a number of members withdrew to form the Providence Baptist church in Mote Road. Despite this, the Rose Yard chapel was reportedly 'too small' in 1822 with services attended by many who were not actually members. A new chapel was built in King Street with seating for 650, at a cost of £2,049, raised by loans and a £1,000 mortgage. In 1831 a dispute over the admission of non-members to communion led to a further loss of members by secession, and the formation of the Zion chapel in Brewer Street. But this too was soon in crisis, for in 1833 the pastor and 73 members seceded, opening their own Bethel chapel in Union Street the following year. The Brewer Street chapel continued to be used by Baptists for a few years afterwards, but was no longer really viable.

Methodism was probably established in Maidstone in 1774, although until 1792 the congregation seems to have relied on the services of travelling preachers. In 1782 there were estimated to be over 130 Methodists in the town. They at first met in a building on Saint Faith's Green, but in 1805 a chapel was opened in Tyler's Lane, later Union Street. A few years later there were 120 members, and in 1814 the chapel became the head of its own circuit of preachers. By 1823 when the membership had grown to 319, with many more non-members attending services, the chapel was demolished and an attractive lancet-style building was erected, with seating for 1,200. Maidstone's Methodists were at this time all Wesleyans, and Primitive Methodists and other separate groups were not represented in the town. The Society of Friends or Quakers had ceased to exist in Maidstone in the late seventeenth century, but they continued to be active in the county. They were re-established in the town in 1805; the next year a room was officially licensed for meetings. In 1810 land was bought for a meeting-house and the costs of this and the subsequent building were met by a county-wide subscription. By 1822 some of the Society's county meetings were held in Maidstone, although the congregation remained small.

The Church of England made less progress than the nonconformist congregations. All Saints remained the only Anglican church until the consecration of Holy Trinity in 1828, though this did not become a separate parish until 1841. While there were some philanthropic, educational and other associations linked to the Anglicans, the church itself was slow to respond to the new social and cultural needs of an expanding town. By 1835 when the town's population was around

17,000, nonconformist chapels could seat 4,350 people, and the Anglican churches about 3,000. In 1809 Walter Rowles reckoned that nearly half the population were nonconformists, and this may have been true of those attending religious worship. By 1835, however, there were nearly ten thousand people who could not be accommodated at any one time in either church or chapel. Many people were probably occasional attenders, and the population figure of course includes infants and those who were too aged or infirm to go to church. But there were undoubtedly thousands who took no part in organised religion at all, most of them probably poor people. None the less, for the respectable middle- and artisan classes the town's chapels and churches, together with associated societies, played an important role in creating a network of social contact and relationships, fuelling growing middle-class consciousness, so influential in the making of the Victorian town.

In conclusion, Maidstone by the early decades of the nineteenth century had established itself as the leading town in the county, overtaking Canterbury in population size by 1831. Its economy, as we have seen, was strongly diversified with growing commercial links with the metropolis and there was a sizeable and affluent middle-class living alongside much larger numbers of poor. Despite recurrent political instability the town had seen important advances in civic amenities, and Maidstone's county importance was underpinned by a wide range of religious, associational and other cultural activities. By 1835 the town was growing well beyond its Tudor and Stuart limits, with the appearance of fine middle-class villas across the river in the West Borough and artisan terraces on the north and south sides of town. Along with this upsurge of private housing, discussed in Chapter Six, Maidstone's main streets boasted a growing number of large, often classical-style public, ecclesiastical and commercial buildings. The modern town had visibly arrived.

Notes

1. Cf W.A. Speck, *Tory and Whigs: The Struggle in the Constituencies 1701–1715* (London, 1970); N. Rogers, *Whigs and Cities: Popular Politics in the Age of Walpole* (Oxford, 1989); J. Evans, *17th Century Norwich: Politics, Religion and Government 1620–1690* (Oxford, 1979).
2. For the charters discussed here and later see W.R. James, *The Charters and Other Documents relating to the King's Town and Parish* (London, 1825).
3. K.S. Martin, ed., *Records of Maidstone* (Maidstone, 1926), pp. 162–7.
4. B. Henning, *The House of Commons 1660–1690* (London, 1983), p. 278; R. Sedgwick, *The House of Commons 1715–45* (London, 1970), esp. p. 266; for corruption by Bliss: [anon.], *A Relation of the Proceedings at the Election of Burgesses for Maidstone* (London, 1701).
5. James, *Charters*, p. 170 ff.
6. James, *Charters*, p. 16 ff; J.A. Phillips, 'From Municipal Matters to Parliamentary Principles: Eighteenth Century Borough Politics in Maidstone', *Journal of British Studies*, vol. 27 (1988), pp. 327–51.
7. Phillips, ibid; L. Namier and J. Brooke, *The House of Commons 1754–90* (London, 1964), p. 313; R. Thorne, *The House of Commons 1790–1820* (London, 1986), pp. 217–18; Centre for Kentish Studies [Kent Archives Office], Maidstone Borough quarter sessions 1793, Md/JQr4.
8. John Gale Jones, *Sketch of a Political Tour . . .* (London, 1796); *Parliamentary History*, vol. 34 (1799), pp. 579–655.
9. *British Parliamentary Papers: Appendix [Part II] to the First Report of the Commissioners on the Municipal Corporations of England and Wales 1835* (Irish University Press ed., Dublin, 1969), vol. 3, esp. pp. 760–1.

10.   G.F. Nuttall, 'Dissenting Churches in Kent before 1700', *Journal of Ecclesiastical History*, vol. 14 (1963), pp. 175–89.

11.   D.G.C. Allan, *William Shipley, Founder of the Royal Society of Arts* (London, 1979); for the Maidstone society see various items in the Leicestershire Record Office, Gainsborough Papers, DE 3214/364/38–42; also for the county society *Transactions of the Kentish Society for Promoting Every Branch of Useful Knowledge throughout the County of Kent* (Maidstone, 1793).

12.   Freemasons' Hall, London, Library, MS. SN 967 (moderns); *Freemasons' Lodge of Fortitude No. 422* (Maidstone, 1782); G. Smith, *The Use and Abuse of Free-Masonry* (London, 1783), p. 389 ff. There may have been earlier military lodges associated with regiments based in the town.

13.   For the schools discussed in the above paragraphs see F. Streatfield, *The History of Maidstone Grammar School* (London, 1915), p. 50 ff; *Parliamentary Papers*, 1819, XA, *Report from Commissioners: Charities in England for the Education of the Poor*, pp. 127–30.

Bibliographical Note

The primary sources for this chapter overlap with those listed for Chapter Four. The Maidstone Borough Burghmote minute books (Centre for Kentish Studies [Kent Archives Office], Md/ACm1/16, ACp1–17, have valuable information on town politics. Also important for politics, public sociability and religion are the local newspapers – the *Maidstone Journal* (1786–) and the *Maidstone Gazette* (1815–). An important source is the collection of ephemera of the printer John Blake, which illuminates the great variety of social activity in the town; this collection is at Maidstone Museum. W.R. James, *The Charters and Other Documents relating to the King's Town and Parish* (London, 1825) is excellent for urban politics and abuse before the 1832 Reform Act. *Counties, Cities and Boroughs, Kent* (*c.* 1807) reprints various documents concerning Maidstone politics. For *Parliamentary Papers* used in this chapter see footnotes.

For religion as well as the article by Nuttall (footnote 10) on the earlier period, there are various denominational histories: G.L. Knighton, *Three Hundred Years of Religious Freedom, 1662–1962. The Unitarian Church Maidstone* (Maidstone, 1962); Karl Showler, *A Review of the History of the Society of Friends in Kent, 1655–1966* (Canterbury, 1970); A.W. Smith, *Wesleyan Methodist Church. A Short History of the Maidstone Circuit, 1814–1914, and of the Union Street Chapel, 1823–1923*, (Maidstone, no date).

Chapter Six

THE VICTORIAN AND EDWARDIAN TOWN: URBAN GROWTH, THE ECONOMY AND SOCIETY 1835–1914

Victorian Britain saw an accelerating pace of urban growth so that by 1851 the majority of the population lived in cities and towns, and at the outbreak of the First World War the figure was as high as 80 per cent. The most rapidly expanding centres were the rising industrial cities and factory towns of the Midlands and the North, the great ports like Liverpool and Glasgow, and of course London, which was now not only the national metropolis but an imperial capital. The older provincial towns, including county towns like Maidstone, also had an important part to play in the urban transformation of Britain. Although the rate of growth in these towns was generally more modest, and they escaped the more disruptive consequences of rapid industrialisation, they undoubtedly experienced important economic and social changes. As their physical and spatial configuration evolved, and as local trade and industries adapted to increasing competition, they sought to create and shape a new urban image and identity.

In the case of Maidstone this image still incorporated elements that derived from its ancient role as a market town, although its Georgian heyday as a county town and genteel social centre was now largely over. Maidstone continued to have trading relationships with other Medway towns and the metropolis; and there were differing views as to whether the coming of the railways enhanced or undermined its position in these respects. As a market town, it was still dependent to some extent on the fortunes of the surrounding agricultural area, while the demands and resources of the rural economy continued to underpin the production of agricultural machinery and the output of the town's breweries. However, the town's industrial base was considerably strengthened by the consolidation of older industries serving national markets, as, for instance, in paper manufacturing, where the greater use of steam power, and the mechanisation of manufacturing processes, allowed the owners to concentrate production in fewer, more conveniently located mills. In addition, new manufacturing concerns were established in the engineering trades and food production, and these helped to diversify the industrial character of the town. Urban growth also created employment opportunities and encouraged the expansion of the commercial and professional classes as well as affecting the layout and appearance of the town with the spread of suburban development on the outskirts. This strong Victorian phase of urban development shaped the middle- and working-class character of the community, but it was largely over by the 1880s. In the last years of the nineteenth century the town became more vulnerable to changing economic conditions and the momentum of growth slackened.

Population growth

The pace of change was set by the increase in the town's population which grew from 15,790 inhabitants in 1831 to 35,475 inhabitants in 1911. As Table 1 shows this represented a steady increase of around two to three thousand people a decade from 1841 to 1881.[1] The rate of growth was lower than in the early decades of the century and – at an average of 12.4 per cent per decade – just under the average for the whole of England and Wales. The overall doubling of the population had a major impact on the town, but there were other county towns in the south and west of England which experienced considerably higher rates of increase over the nineteenth century as a whole. The contrast with other county towns was particularly marked between 1881 and 1911 when Maidstone's rate of growth, at an average of 5.8 per cent a decade, was only half the decennial averages for the whole of England and Wales. In this period, the contrast with Reading, Chelmsford and Bedford, other county towns within the metropolitan orbit (with rates of growth of between 27 and 34 per cent), is particularly striking. Later in this chapter we will try and explore the reasons for this waning growth.

A small proportion of Maidstone's population increase came from the rise in numbers in the county gaol and County Asylum at Oakwood (after 1833) whose inmates amounted to 5.9 per cent of the recorded population in 1911. Otherwise much of the population growth continued to stem (as in the decades after the 1780s) from natural increase, as births consistently outnumbered deaths; but in most decades except the 1880s urban numbers were also swelled by migrants. As in the eighteenth century, there was no great flood of long-distance migrants into the town. The birthplaces of the inhabitants, as recorded in the census of 1851 and again in 1871, show that the greater proportion of residents had been born locally, either in the town itself or neighbouring towns and villages in Kent. The details for 1851 are set out in Table 2 which shows the predominance of shorter-distance migration to the town; the most important sources of migrants after Kent were London and the neighbouring counties. Devon and Hampshire supplied the largest numbers from elsewhere, perhaps because they had paper industries, and there were small contingents from Ireland and other overseas countries. In 1871 78.1 per cent of the 26,196 inhabitants had been born in Kent (including Maidstone), a proportion only slightly lower than in 1851 when the figure was 81.3 per cent.

The town's birth rate was the key factor in determining the rate of population growth but the most noticeable aspect of this was the decline after mid-century. The decennial average birth rate fell from a peak of 32.8 in 1861–70 to 30.8 in 1881–90, 23.2 in 1901–10 to a low of 20.6 in 1911, figures which were consistently lower than the national average. All towns in Kent experienced a falling birth rate in the years immediately before the First World War, but the average in Maidstone was consistently below that in Kent's urban districts as a whole. The decline in the birth rate in the later decades of the century may have been linked to migration out of the town. Migrants were typically young, and the net outflow from the town between 1881 and 1891 probably consisted of people in their late teens and twenties, going to seek better prospects and raise their families elsewhere; significant numbers probably went to London.

The relatively low birth rate in Maidstone may also have been connected with a slightly larger proportion of females to males in the 20 to 45 age-group. This was higher than the average for urban districts, possibly due to the demand for domestic servants in the town, and may have led to more women remaining single. Figures for marriage rates for the town are not available, but in 1851 the Maidstone registration district (which also included several rural parishes) was close to the national average for the proportion of its inhabitants over the age of twenty who were married or widowed. Later in the century figures for the registration district reveal a growing tendency for people to delay marriage or stay single which was more marked than in the country as a whole. A drop in the number of married women in the 20–25 age-group by 1891 (from 33.3 per cent in 1871 to 25.6 per cent twenty years later) is particularly significant, and goes some way towards explaining the low birth rate, as the number of illegitimate births was small. In 1911 information on the marital status of women aged between 15 and 45 reveals a continuing trend of late or non-marriage. In Maidstone 53.1 per cent of women in this age-group were single, whereas in England and Wales the rate was 50.4 per cent; figures for the county of Kent were a little below the national average, but higher than in Maidstone.

At the same time, the decline in the birth rate in the late Victorian period was offset in part by mortality trends. The average crude death rate for Maidstone remained steady at about 24 between 1841 and 1880 (though there were sharp annual fluctuations). During the 1880s, however, it fell to 20.2, as improvements in the town's sanitary condition began to have an effect on the health of the inhabitants (discussed in Chapter Seven). There was a slight rise during the 1890s to 21.6, partly due to the 1897 typhoid epidemic, although excluding that year's figure the nine-year average was still 21.1. But the first decade of the twentieth century saw renewed improvement with an average of 18.5, and during the four years ending in 1914 the average was 13.8. By then epidemic diseases were no longer a major cause of death, and among adults the largest numbers died from heart disease, cancer, tuberculosis and chest diseases such as pneumonia and bronchitis. Particularly striking in this period was the decline in the infant mortality rate which is discussed in Chapter Seven (see p. 157).

Physical growth of the town

As the population increased, the area between the main streets became more densely packed with dwellings, and new additions were made to the built-up area as the town expanded up to its boundaries. Developments visible at the start of the nineteenth century now accelerated. Small courts and yards tucked away behind the town's main streets became home to many of the working class. By the mid-nineteenth century these had become more numerous and more closely crowded. Bonny's Yard, for example, which was entered by an alley on the south side of King Street, contained in 1821 some half dozen cottages; by 1848 there were over fifty small houses in the yard and courts adjoining it, many of them crowded back to back. A few were of the standard pattern of three rooms built one above the other, but the majority had four small rooms, two of which were without windows and relied on 'borrowed light' from the room in front. Other courts were smaller, but no less closely packed. Usually unpaved, they were generally furnished with one or more shared earth 'privies', and sometimes with a well, but many residents were obliged to fetch water from one of the town conduits.

During the first half of the century the town also expanded to cover the area between King Street and the county gaol with housing. The land between King Street and Union Street, owned by Lord Romney and mostly gardens and meadowland in 1821, was largely built over by 1848 with dwellings for the respectable classes. Some houses were relatively modest, but others were intended for a more affluent class of occupant. Albion Place, which subsequently became part of the Sittingbourne Road, formed a new street of imposing villas for the town's more wealthy citizens, while Clarendon Place, at the end of King Street, acquired more fine houses, as did the adjacent part of the Ashford Road. Marsham Street also contained comfortable middle-class dwellings. However the area between Union Street, Wheeler Street and the prison walls had by the same date been largely filled with terraces of small tenements for the lower classes. Brewer Street, newly constructed around 1830, consisted mainly of respectable but modest houses. Beyond the gaol, further working-class terraces were built in the area near the barracks bordering Sandling Road. On the south side of town, there was new building of a similar type to the east and west of Stone Street. Many of these terraced houses were two up, two down dwellings, although a number of them had gardens, some of them quite long. Terraced houses for a slightly higher income group were a little larger, with extensions, probably sculleries and possibly a third bedroom above it, at the rear.

The upsurge of residential development in the West Borough during the 1830s and 1840s created further social differentiation in the community as the town's wealthier classes began to move away from their shops and businesses in the centre of town, preferring to live in this new suburban area upwind of the town's growing industrial pollution and coal smoke, and well away from the fetid courts of the poor. In 1834 Lord Romney had Rocky Hill Terrace erected as a row of six 'superior class' houses, in 'a good and commanding situation' near a supply of spring water, between the London and Tonbridge roads. Soon afterwards a local builder, William Clever, constructed a row of large villas in Bower Place, off the Tonbridge Road. There was also building for middle-class occupancy on the Tonbridge Road at Surrey Place, and by 1848 at Bower Terrace, which boasted a row of comfortable semi-detached houses. Further from town Summerfield Terrace was built amidst fields on the London Road. On the other hand, some older middle-class residential streets were suffering a decline in status by mid century. Knightrider Street became increasingly the domain of the working class and of gentlefolk in reduced circumstances, while Lower Stone Street acquired a very mixed ambience, some wealthy remaining among residents of every other class.

During the later nineteenth century the town continued to fan out in northerly and southerly directions; many small streets were laid out near the gaol. There was also building for working-class occupancy between Stone Street and the River Len, but it was the West Borough that registered the greatest rate of population increase, as this district was transformed by industrial developments as well as new house building. Formed initially as a middle-class suburb, streets continued to be laid out for middle-class occupancy along the London Road, and also on the Buckland Road. From the 1870s the area fronting Rocky Hill on the Earl of Romney's land was further developed for superior housing. The estate was developed in two phases between 1874 and 1887 with the plans stipulating the construction of houses valued at no less than £800 (£1,500 the pair), with lawns, carriage drives and stables. Business development was prohibited. The Westree building estate followed in 1887 with 14 acres divided into 260 housing plots, raising £13–14,000 when sold.

But the West Borough never became an exclusively middle-class district. After the opening of the first South Eastern Railway station to the south of Tonbridge Road in the 1840s, the west side of the river also developed as an industrial and commercial district (the gas works had already been built in St Peter Street in 1819). The station was moved to the site of the present West Station in 1856 when an additional line was built, attracting warehouses, new workshops and manufacturing establishments to the area by the river. With rising employment prospects in the district, the West Borough in the late nineteenth century saw a rash of houses built for respectable working-class and lower-middle-class occupancy. There were working-class houses on the Upper Fant Road by 1884 and also on Bower Lane and Prospect Place, while towards the end of the century working-class terraces were developed between Tonbridge Road and the railway line. The opening of the Barracks Station in 1874 no doubt gave an impetus to residential building in the Buckland area, but the construction of the East Station the same year and opening of the Ashford line in 1882–3 initially had a negative effect on the borough's housing stock, as working-class houses at the north end of Week Street had to be demolished to make way for the station and track. But in the long term it may well have boosted lower-class development on the north side of town.

One effect of the more intensive development of the West Borough was to increase traffic on the medieval bridge over the Medway, which in 1874 was found to be in need of extensive repair. Deemed too narrow and unsatisfactory for the traffic passing over it, as well as too low and inconvenient for river barges, it was decided to replace rather than repair it. The new bridge, designed by Sir Joseph Bazalgette, a well known London engineer, was built alongside the old bridge between 1877–9. The cost was £32,000, half of which was met by the Rochester Bridge wardens, the important North Kent charitable trust, and the remainder by a mortgage of the town rates.

As in Victorian Britain generally, working-class terraces were erected by small speculative builders and rented out by them or by other small tradesmen who bought the property for investment purposes. In 1862 the Cottage Improvement Company embarked on a programme of letting sound working-class housing as a commercial enterprise. Although motivated in part at least by philanthropy, and taking as its motto, 'at the root of half our social difficulties lies the question of the homes of the poor', the company was profitable from the start, paying an initial dividend of 4.5 per cent which soon rose to 5 per cent. Directors and shareholders were local business and professional men, and the company bought up working-class houses, and repaired and rented them out, acquiring 130 during the first ten years. There was little problem with rent arrears, which suggests the careful selection of tenants; but the ideal of providing good quality working-class housing proved more difficult to attain and on occasions the Medical Officer of Health had to intervene to order improvements to company houses. Overall, however, it seems probable that this 'five per cent philanthropy' provided above average accommodation in the one twentieth of the town's housing stock owned by the company in the late nineteenth century.[2]

The building of working-class housing may have been given some impetus by the so called Starr-Bowkett building societies which began to operate in Maidstone during the 1870s. These societies initially had a hundred subscribing members, who contributed a small weekly sum, and entered a ballot for an advance of £200, with which to buy a house. The advance was then gradually repaid, and as the society's funds increased, ballots and advances became more frequent, until all contributors had bought a house. In theory, a society was wound up when all the money had been repaid, in the case of the Maidstone societies twelve-and-a-half years after the last advance. In practise many societies got into difficulties, as members were unable to maintain their subscriptions and repayments, or lost interest when they failed to win the ballot. In some instances the society increasingly became a form of lottery with cash prizes.[3] How far the Maidstone societies operated as intended is unclear, but it seems likely that they did enable some poorer townspeople to own their own houses. Three societies had been started by 1882, and a further four before 1894, when the Building Societies Act made balloting illegal, and so brought such bodies to an end.

In 1841 there were 3,221 houses in the borough, occupied by an average of 5.59 persons per house. During the next thirty years building more or less kept pace with population growth, and in 1871 there were 4,685 houses, occupied by an average of 5.6 persons. Subsequently the number of new houses outpaced the population increase and the average occupational density declined from 5.53 persons per house in 1881 to 4.86 persons per house in 1911. However, these figures may have reflected improved housing for the middle classes and skilled workers, masking persistent overcrowding in poorer areas of the town, which worsened in the early twentieth century. At the same time, Maidstone was somewhat better in this respect than the county's urban districts as a whole with 3.1 per cent overcrowded in 1911 compared to an average of 3.5 per cent. By that date the terraced house, built to cater for a range of income levels, had become the most important component of Maidstone's housing stock whether in the narrow working-class streets near the county gaol or in the respectable Edwardian terraces towards Tovil. As such it was one of the most visible and enduring features of Maidstone's urban growth in the century before the outbreak of the First World War.

The changing pattern of employment

The growth in Maidstone's working-class population as reflected in the physical transformation of the town was a consequence of the increase of employment opportunities as the local economy expanded and diversified. Table 3 shows the changes in the number of male workers employed in different sectors in 1851 and 1911, so far as these can be calculated from the published census returns. Two features stand out. One is the way that urban growth brought new jobs in building, transport and service industries as well as further underpinning the commercial sector of the town's economy. The second is the growth in manufacturing employment with the advent of new breweries and mills, workshops and factories in the town.

As the town grew the building industry expanded substantially, with a proliferation of small construction firms, while the numbers of men employed in quarrying and related trades also increased. Transport was another major area of rising employment with a more than threefold increase of male workers by 1911. Of these, 524 worked in road transport and 361 on the railways. Sixty years earlier, when the town was smaller and the volume of trade less, the numbers were 82 and 40 respectively. At that time, the town was served by only one branch railway line. By 1911 there were not only additional lines and three stations in the town, but a borough tram system, and bus services between Maidstone and other towns, while steam haulage and the first petrol lorries increased the carriage of goods by road. On the other hand, employment in river and maritime transport declined by almost half over the same period as shipping on the Medway suffered from road and rail competition.

The most notable development in the pattern of employment in the town was the rise in jobs in the service sector: the professions, financial services and other 'white collar' occupations, together with central and local government. This was also a growing sector of employment for women as the percentage of women employed rose from 4 to 12 per cent. The increase in the professional and subordinate service category, more than doubling between 1851 and 1911, was due mainly to the growing ranks of subsidiary workers, such as solicitors' clerks, since professional practitioners as a group advanced only modestly in number, if at all, during the nineteenth century. The sole female professions were teaching and nursing. The numbers of female teachers rose from 118 in 1851 to 201 in 1911, while nurses and midwives, who were hardly considered a professional group in 1851, had achieved that status by 1911, their numbers increasing from 33 to 104, as local hospital provision improved. Another component of the service sector was banking, insurance, finance and accountancy where the total employed (male and female) rose from 97 to 293; here the insurance industry was the major employer, with a slower increase of banking employment.

The increase in the number of commercial clerks, rising twentyfold during the sixty years up to 1911, was the most striking change in male employment; women also began to be employed in this capacity. Clerks were mainly employed by the town's burgeoning manufacturing and trading sector. The wholesale grocer, Charles Arkcoll, for instance, employed fourteen clerks in 1892. By then office work was increasingly regarded as socially acceptable employment for respectable young women, partly as a result of the spread of the typewriter. The number of employees in local and national government, including civil servants, the Post Office, the police and officers at the prison and other institutions, also multiplied. The number of male employees nearly quadrupled (to 380), and the number of females jumped from 8 to 196. This increase in government employment reflected Maidstone's continuing role as a county town with a range of administrative agencies. In 1851 the category embraced court officials, prison officers, the borough police force and a small number of council and allied officials, as well as employees of the Post Office and the small tax, customs and excise offices in the town (the main excise office for the area was at Rochester). As the century progressed, the town police force was enlarged, and the County Constabulary, founded in the 1850s, located its headquarters on Stone Street at Wren's Cross.[4] As we shall see, there was an important growth of borough and county council officials (with the establishment of the county council in 1889) and postal workers.

Yet despite these changes, there was much continuity in the pattern of urban employment with substantial numbers of workers remaining in the commercial and industrial sectors. The figures for these sectors in Table 3 must be regarded simply as indicative; there was no manufacturing category as such in the census returns and in compiling these figures assumptions have been made about the allocation of different occupational groups, particularly those trades which combined manufacturing and trading functions. The figures for the commercial sector need to be inflated somewhat to take this into account. In 1911 only a grouped return was printed, and some male manufacturing and commercial employees were counted together, while 7 per cent of the male and 4 per cent of the female workforce were unclassified. The most accurate figures that can be calculated indicate that the wholesale and retail trading sector had 15 per cent of the male workforce and 10 per cent of the female workforce in 1851. In 1911 it still employed 15 per cent of males but only 8 per cent of females, although in both cases the actual numbers rose as the workforce was much larger. In terms of the number of businesses the trading sector seems to have been fully developed in size by 1851, although its nature and organisation continued to evolve as the next section will describe. The best estimate we can make of the contribution of manufacturing to the town's employment is that in 1851 24 per cent of the male working population and 32 per cent of the female workforce belonged to this sector, whereas in 1911 the figures were 23 per cent and 33 per cent respectively. Behind such relatively stable percentages, however, lay important shifts in the nature of manufacturing employment.

In contrast to these growth sectors, the numbers engaged in agriculture fell, as one might expect. The expansion of Maidstone's residential area reduced the extent of agricultural land within or close to its boundaries, while the conversion of arable fields to pasture during the 1880s and 1890s curtailed the amount of labour required. Nevertheless, much of the land in the vicinity was used for the cultivation of hops and fruit, which were labour intensive crops little affected by the general agricultural depression from the 1870s. Agriculture thus remained a significant employer, and seasonal work, especially hop-picking, continued as a vital source of income for poorer families in the town. The hop growers were also important customers for the town's tradesmen, and it was claimed in 1881 that 'the difference between a good and a bad hop season, in the amount of money circulated in the town, is not less than £200,000.' Included in the figures for agricultural employment were those working in market gardening; in 1881 the town's most noted grower and fruit expert Thomas Bunyard had between forty and fifty employees.[5]

Maidstone's labour force as a whole was still predominantly male, with the proportion of women and girls in employment actually declining as a proportion of all females (aged ten or over) from 36 per cent in 1851 to 34 per cent in 1901, and 32 per cent in 1911. This fall probably reflected a contraction in the employment of young girls, which during the Edwardian period was offset by a small increase in the numbers of married women working outside the home. In 1911 750 out of 6,611 married women and 446 of the 1,509 widows in the town were in employment. Opportunities for women were increasing, at a time when male unemployment was probably driving more married women to enter the labour-market (see Table 5). Domestic service was the largest employer of (mainly unmarried) women and girls, with 1,177 in this category in 1851 and 1,360 in 1911, but in the early years of the twentieth century factory work was increasingly available. In the retail trade there were female shopkeepers, and female assistants in the women's clothing trade, but shop assistants were predominantly male until the early twentieth century when female assistants became more numerous.

Distribution and services

As an important regional centre of trade and commerce, the coming of the railways generated mixed feelings. When the Kent lines, one through Maidstone and the other to the south, were first proposed in 1834–6 there was strong opposition to a line through the town. Though the mayor at a public meeting warned that if the line were laid to the south, 'Maidstone would be ruined as a commercial town', Lord Marsham and a majority of the town council persisted in opposing it and, in the event, the South Eastern Railway track was built through the Weald, passing no nearer to Maidstone than Paddock Wood. Within a decade, however, there was a growing recognition in the corporation that 'we have taken a false step and we fear lost much of our trade'. Strong pressure for a railway line to Maidstone developed, and something close to panic occurred when alternative proposals envisaged opening up other parts of the town's trading hinterland to rail traffic. The Paddock Wood to Maidstone branch line was finally built in 1844, giving Maidstone a slow indirect rail link with both Ashford and London. The journey time between Maidstone and the capital was similar to that from Ashford to London, while rail travel from the town to Ashford was actually longer than by road. A second line, from Maidstone to Strood, was completed in 1856, giving the town access to London via the canal tunnel and the South Eastern Railway North Kent line. In 1874 the town was linked to the London Chatham and Dover Railway at Swanley, and finally in 1884 this route was extended to give direct communication to Ashford, Canterbury and the coast. Even after this, rail communications with East Kent continued to be unsatisfactory, as the services of the two companies involved did not connect, and there was no through service for goods or parcels beyond Ashford. Between 1889 and 1894 the town council was involved in a lengthy and expensive battle to rectify the situation, and afterwards they continued to press for further improvements, particularly in passenger services. In 1898 they succeeded in getting cheap Saturday market trains from all stations within ten miles of Maidstone.

The effect of the railways on Maidstone's wholesale trade in the area is difficult to determine. Contemporaries considered that it had been adversely affected, but there was no decline in the numbers of wharfingers or coal or corn merchants in town. Provided they could still compete with London suppliers on price, there was no real reason why merchants of this sort should have lost custom, and the town's own steady growth doubtless helped them to remain viable. The wholesale grocery, drapery and other shop trades may have been more vulnerable to competition from London wholesalers, though their position was quite strong, sustained by an extensive network of local carriers. In 1842 before Maidstone was linked to the railway, it was claimed that 'the wholesale trade of Maidstone consists of supplies to smaller shopkeepers and rural tradesmen, generally at a credit of twelve or eighteen months. The London merchants (even if they were likely to risk a trade so peculiarly local) cannot undersell the Maidstone merchants.'[6]

Directories do not distinguish wholesale and retail traders until late in the century, and so the possible effect of the railway on numbers cannot be discerned. Later in the century developments such as brand-naming, pre-packing and advertising were changing the nature of wholesale trade, and direct dealing between manufacturer and retailer was increasing. In 1872 there were six wholesale grocers in Maidstone, whereas in 1898 there were only three. However, two of the latter, Arkcolls and Laurences, were very large concerns, and able to compete with London warehouses both on price and on the variety of goods offered, in a way smaller wholesalers could not. The Arkcoll family had been grocers in Lower Stone Street since the 1820s, and by 1872 they had built up a very considerable wholesale only business. In 1892 they were said to be 'one of the largest mercantile firms to be found in the provinces', and the largest importer of Dutch cheeses in the country. Vast quantities of other goods were also sold, and the business at that time employed between sixty and seventy people. There was a warehouse in London, and the firm made extensive use of river transport, the proprietor being a director of the Lower Medway Company. William Laurence's business was founded at about the same time as Arkcolls, and rapidly developed a very large wholesale as well as a retail trade. Like Arkcolls the company was a major importer of cheese and other groceries, cured bacon on a massive scale, and employed some sixty people in 1892. In the years before the First World War, a shopkeeper at Ickham in East Kent attributed his reputation as a high quality provision merchant to cheese and butter supplied by Laurence's. A traveller called to take the order, the goods were sent by rail to the nearest station, collected by local carrier and delivered to the shop. This probably formed the pattern of much of Laurence's business. The Ickham shopkeeper also bought drapery from Marchant and Tubb, a very large Maidstone firm of wholesale drapers and clothiers, the order again being placed with a commercial traveller.

During the first half of Victoria's reign, Maidstone's markets continued to play both a wholesale and a retail role in the supply of food to the town, but their importance to retail customers steadily decreased as provisions dealers preferred to trade from shops. The wholesale trade in fruit and filberts by-passed the market, as we saw in Chapter Four when selling crops on the tree became the norm in the early part of the nineteenth century, but other markets continued. The monthly cattle market experienced mixed fortunes. During the late 1840s and early 1850s the amount of tolls – now collected directly by the council – indicate a steady level of trade, and in 1855 a second monthly market was established. By 1864, however, Maidstone was suffering strong competition from markets in Ashford and other towns, and there were complaints about the state of the Fair Meadow which was consequently resurfaced. As competition intensified, the number of animals passing through the market declined from an average of 32,000 animals a year during the 1870s to an average of just over 26,000 a year during the following decade. As we have noted, this was a difficult period for agriculture in general, and many local farmers only survived by combining livestock with fruit or hops, in which the market trade remained buoyant. The market nevertheless held out against the competition, and from 1889 it was held weekly with stock sales periodically boosting tolls. In the early twentieth century the market was flourishing again, and in the period December 1912 to November 1913 almost 32,000 animals were sold at the regular markets, and over 9,000 at the stock sales. In addition, animals continued to be traded at the four annual fairs, although by the late nineteenth century, the most important of these by far was the October fair. Over 20,000 animals, the great majority of them sheep, were bought at the fairs in 1907, some 13,000 of them in October. From 1879 stock sales at the fairs had been moved from the Fair Meadow to Lock Meadow in the West Borough, as building encroachment had made the Fair Meadow no longer large enough, while Lock Meadow had the additional advantage of being closer to the railway line. Lock Meadow was bought by the council from Lord Romney in 1891, and in 1914 an agricultural hall was built there for fatstock shows and exhibitions.

The trade of the town's weekly corn and hop markets was also subject to fluctuating activity but again remained steady in the long term, despite a sharp fall in corn production in the county. In 1865 the council bought up the lease of the old Corn Exchange, now badly in need of improvement, and two years later the exchange and the general provisions market underneath were rebuilt. The new exchange was planned for additional use as a concert hall while the provisions market was completely redesigned with what were virtually small shops opening on to an outside arcade. In the long term some of these market shops proved unsuccessful and were later converted into the town's fire station.

As we saw in Chapter Four, the number of retail shops in the town was already rising sharply by the early decades of the nineteenth century with as many as 435 tradesmen listed in a directory for 1839. The figure had risen to 475 by the time of another directory in 1851 and this may actually understate the true position as another, locally produced, directory for 1872 lists approximately 700 retailers. Other evidence from the 1851 census suggests that the main upsurge in retailing had taken place by mid-century. By then a recognisable 'shopping centre' had appeared in the central streets, especially Week Street, High Street and Gabriel's Hill, where large stores and fashionable and specialist shops were clustered.

By the 1830s shopkeepers in the main streets were beginning to move away from credit trading and the previously common practice of haggling with customers over the price of goods. Fixed prices led to enhanced price competition between traders, and shop advertisements emphasised the cheapness and excellent value of their stock. In 1839, for instance, Frederick Bean, a haberdasher and hosier, newly arrived in Maidstone from London, was selling his goods 'at the lowest possible price for ready money'. More and more the price of goods was stated in advertisements. By mid-century the trade skills of food retailers, especially grocers, were becoming less vital, as factory-produced goods became more widely available. Whereas previously the grocer had blended tea, cleaned and stoned dried fruit and generally prepared items for sale, he increasingly sold goods which were prepared, blended, and in some cases pre-packed and weighed by the manufacturer or wholesaler who supplied them. Already in 1839 one Week Street grocer, though still advertising his own blends of tea, was offering sauces, pickles and curry powder prepared by a London supplier. Manufacturers began to give their products brand names, which could be promoted in the press to stimulate customer demand, and these formed a growing proportion of the grocer's stock-in-trade. Fry's chocolate, Lea and Perrins sauce and Horniman's tea were advertised in the *Maidstone Journal* in 1867, for instance. By the 1880s the retailing of tinned goods was also commonplace. Edward Sharp, prior to setting up as a manufacturer in the town, retailed tinned meat of various sorts, salmon, sardines and Swiss milk at his 'cash stores', as well as other branded products such as Cadbury's cocoa.

Goods of this sort also made it increasingly easy for any unskilled person to set up as a grocer, and in the second half of the nineteenth century we find mounting numbers of small general stores and corner shops particularly in working-class residential areas. A significant number of these shopkeepers were women – wives, trying to supplement family income, and widows and spinsters endeavouring to eke out a livelihood. Shopkeepers of this class generally found it necessary to give extended credit as a way of obtaining and retaining their working-class customers. In consequence their business position was often precarious, and between 1872 and 1882 there was a rapid turnover in the names listed in directories. By the end of the century, however, the trade of small shopkeeper appears to have become rather more stable, with lower turnover rates. This was in part due to improved living standards for many working-class customers, but also to the ever widening range of branded goods which were available, allowing back street shops to offer products identical to those sold in the town centre. As we shall see, some of the established, skilled grocers responded to changed conditions by using their expertise to become manufacturers themselves, and the products of local firms took their place in Maidstone's shops alongside those of other nationally known names.[7]

Another development which changed the pattern of shopping in Maidstone in the late nineteenth century was the start of co-operative retailing. Although the first co-operative society was established in the town as early as 1829, this was short-lived, and it was not until 1887 that a second society was founded with 87 members subscribing for 51 £1 shares. It commenced retailing on a small scale in a shop on the Kingsley estate in the south of the town, but subsequently moved to premises in Knightrider Street. By 1892 the annual turnover was £3,771, and there were 254 members.[8] Dealing strictly in cash, and paying a dividend to members as a share of profits, its customers were mainly the respectable working class – not the poor – and it competed more with the town centre shops than with those in the back streets.

Competition on another front came from a new phenomenon in retailing, the multiple trader or chain store. Some of these were the branch shops of large retailers in London or elsewhere, while others were the retail outlets of manufacturers. Both kinds of shop mushroomed in Maidstone after the 1870s. Thus George Mence Smith, a London paint and varnish trader, expanded his activities rapidly in south east England, and had a shop in High Street by 1872. The same year the newsagents W H Smith had a stall at the railway station, the shoe manufacturers Pocock Bros of London were trading in High Street, and Upsons, who later became Dolcis, owned a shop in Week Street. By 1898 Freeman Hardy and Willis had amalgamated with Pococks, and were trading from their High Street shop; five years later they also had an outlet in Week Street. George Leavey, the London merchant tailor, and the grocery chains Home and Colonial, Liptons and International Tea all had shops in the town before the end of the century, and within a few years they had been joined by Boots Cash Chemists and Maypole Dairy. These stores provided serious competition for the lower-class custom of Maidstone's established retailers, especially the provisions dealers, because they bought in huge quantities, and were able to undercut the traditional grocers on staple items. The town's shoemakers were likewise affected, although the impact of the multiples is difficult to quantify, since factory-made shoes were also sold by other retailers. This may have been started in the 1830s by the innovative Frederick Bean, whose haberdashers shop had a footwear department where 'shoes of the very best London manufacture' were on sale. Other retailers followed his example after mid-century when the introduction of sewing and riveting machines enabled factory production to dominate the trade. The numbers of shoemakers listed in directories fell from sixty-six in 1872 to fifty-four in 1903, many of them by the latter date trading wholly or partly in ready-made footwear. Ready-made clothing also became more widely available from the 1850s when Singer sewing machines came into general use, and by 1872 there were ten outfitters shops in Maidstone. Other tailors and drapers increasingly stocked ready to wear clothing, but bespoke tailoring remained an important trade. Much women's clothing continued to be made by dressmakers, due to the nature of Victorian and Edwardian fashions.

The number of shops listed in the 1903 trade directory had fallen slightly to 643, but if this figure is accurate the fall was only temporary, as the 1911 census return indicates the existence of 695 shops. This stability in numbers disguises the overall expansion of the retail sector, with businesses increasing in size, and many boasting long frontages, occupying two or three adjacent premises. Some had grown into virtual department stores. One of these was Frank King and Sons, whose Stone Street business occupied three adjacent shops and had six departments selling clothing, tailoring, hosiery, millinery, dressmaking and footwear; grocery and provisions were sold from separate premises on Gabriel's Hill, and the business had between thirty and forty employees. Denniss Payne and Co, listed as drapers and outfitters at two adjacent High Street shops in 1885, took over two further shops during the following decade, and dealt in shoes as well as clothing and drapery of all kinds. They also operated as ironmongers, plumbers and gas-fitters from a shop further down the street, but by 1898 had disposed of a hatters and hosiery shop higher up the street.

The period also saw a proliferation of food and drink retailers. The rise and subsequent reduction of public houses and beershops is discussed in Chapter Eight. But although these remained important suppliers of drink and meals to the lower classes, with the larger inns-cum-hotels like the Star on High Street and the Bell on Week Street catering for the better off, other outlets multiplied. By the end of the nineteenth century the town had a number of respectable restaurants and cafés, particularly in Week Street and on Gabriel's Hill. Cheaper establishments including fish and chip shops also doubtless spread in artisan and working-class districts, though our information here is sparse.

Along with markets and retailing, the service sector continued to develop as a major pillar of the urban economy up to the First World War. On the professional side, the number of legal practices in the town declined from 22 firms in 1839 (24 partners) to 15 in 1898 (20 partners). Likewise, the number of physicians and surgeons does not seem to have expanded greatly despite the growth of the West Kent Hospital (discussed in Chapter Seven). On the other hand, there can be no doubt that these established professional groups remained powerful economic forces in the town, partly through their strong links with county society, partly because of their heavy involvement in civic affairs, both voluntary and official, and partly because of their growing volume of business – reflected by the rising numbers of dependent staff. Other professions also achieved major importance in the expanding town, for example, architects. The Whichcord family, John Whichcord senior and his son John junior (Whichcord and Ashpitel), was notable for designing many of the major buildings in Victorian Maidstone including churches (for instance, Holy Trinity, St Philip's), public buildings (Oakwood Hospital, West Kent General, municipal baths) and commercial premises in the Victorian town (Blake's, Kent Fire Insurance in High Street), as well as some housing developments (Rocky Hill terrace). But they were also active outside the town – John Whichcord senior, as well as serving as mayor, was the county surveyor in the 1820s and 1830s and had a national reputation as an architect. The teaching profession also expanded (see Chapter Seven), as did newer professions such as estate agents and accountants.

As we noted earlier there was also some advance in financial services, particularly insurance. One company, the Kent Fire Insurance and United Kent Life Assurance, founded at the start of the nineteenth century, had its head office in Maidstone, but as the century progressed many other companies acquired offices or agents in the town (the number of firms increased from eleven in 1839 to thirty-seven in 1898). Banking expanded more slowly, and it was not until the end of the century that the Kentish and London and County banks, both long established in Maidstone, were joined by Lloyds. By 1914 the arrival of a branch of the London and Provincial Bank had brought the total to four.

Administrative services also continued to grow, linked with the town's established position as the county town. Not only were the assizes and West Kent quarter sessions still there, but after 1814 the Court of General Session met in Maidstone dealing with a growing amount of administrative business (prisons, police, vagrancy, finance, lunatics) for the whole county. In 1889 the Kent County Council took over the work of General Sessions. Initially, it started with a small number of officials, often drawn from the town (thus two bankers from the Kentish Bank served as county treasurers). But after 1903 there was a great increase of activity with new departments established including those of the County Surveyor, County Medical Officer of Health and Kent Education Committee. The Education Department employed an increasing number of staff, though its offices did not finally move to Maidstone from London until 1913. By then the council probably employed about 200 staff in the newly enlarged offices at the Sessions House. The council also had a growing staff at the County Asylum at Barming (which was extended in 1906 and 1912), the county gaol, and in the teaching profession. As already noted, the County Constabulary was established in 1857 and had its headquarters on Stone Street. County expenditure on salaries and services undoubtedly had a significant impact on Maidstone's economy particularly after the end of the century. As we shall see in Chapter Seven, there was also a considerable increase in the activity of the borough council – from policing to parks, from museums to trams – and this again probably provided some boost to local employment and demand. The Maidstone Rural District Council established after 1894 was less important, though it had its offices in the town on King Street.

In the case of government agencies, the Post Office expanded as an employer with the rising volume of mail, while the institution of the Post Office Savings Bank in 1861, the absorption of the telegraph system in 1868, and the telephone system during the early twentieth century, further increased the number of staff and the general business for the town. We know least about the most important government employer in the town – the army. The barracks on the Sandling Road, established at the end of the eighteenth century, served as the official home of the West Kent regiment and as a cavalry base, but other regiments used it en route for the colonies. In the 1860s 600 men were said to be stationed there, though the numbers probably fluctuated greatly with the barracks empty at certain times. Even so, the general economic impact on the town was probably considerable, with local contractors supplying the barracks with food and other goods and services, while soldiers flocked to spend their meagre pay in the pubs and brothels at the northern end of town. More select officers and their families frequented the fashionable sociable events at the County Assembly Rooms and elsewhere.

Industrial development

The manufacturing sector saw both important continuity and change. The paper mills remained important employers in the Victorian town. Brewing expanded, as did the manufacture of mineral waters, while engineering and food processing developed to be major local industries. Oilseed processing and the manufacture of animal feeds, tanning and rope and sacking manufacture continued to feature in the local economy. As in any town there were also numerous small- or larger-scale workshops manufacturing clothing and other everyday necessities. Table 4 outlines the numbers employed in Maidstone's principal industries in 1851 and 1911 to suggest the individual contribution which they made to the growth of the manufacturing sector.

A major trend in the economic history of the nineteenth-century town was the consolidation of firms within the older industries. In the paper industry manufacturers concentrated operations into fewer, larger mills and increasingly specialised in particular classes of paper. In the 1840s the industry as a whole mechanised rapidly, prices tumbled, and many smaller mills ceased to be viable concerns. Particularly hard hit were those mills which lacked a suitable water supply for the manufacture of high quality white paper, and consequently produced browns and other cheaper sorts.[9] By 1848 five mills on the Sandling, Pratling and Aylesford streams had shut down, and a sixth, Pratling Mill, had been taken over by a maker of millboard. Some white paper mills also closed. Padsole Mill, in the centre of the town, changed hands frequently during its relatively brief career as a paper mill due to successive bankruptcies, and ceased to operate altogether in 1846.

The process of rationalisation is best exemplified by the district's largest producers of high quality paper, Hollingworth brothers, who were operating seven mills in 1830, but gradually concentrated production on two mills, so that Otham and Turkey were the only ones still in operation in 1865. Both had been mechanised, but the Otham mill was subsequently reduced to pulping rags for use at Turkey, and it had stopped working by the end of the century. Allnutt and Sons also took the decision to mechanise, and they installed machines at Great Ivy and Lower Tovil mills to produce coloured and fancy papers. After the 1870s their mills passed into the hands of the Green family who closed Great Ivy about 1884 in order to concentrate machine production at Lower Tovil, where they made a variety of specialist papers. This family also produced high quality paper by hand at the Hayle Mill nearby. Great Ivy Mill was reopened in 1890 by the Ivy Millboard Company making that product from wood-pulp. Another of the local mills, Upper Tovil, had converted to machine production by 1860 when it was making newsprint from esparto grass and straw. In 1880 it was being operated by the Tovil Paper Company, but in 1896, following a fire, the mill was bought and rebuilt by A.E. Reed and Co. Within four years it was producing 250 tons of newsprint a week for *The Times* and other London newspapers, largely from wood-pulp. An additional mill, Bridge Mill, was opened by Reeds on an adjacent site during the 1890s, also for the machine production of printing paper. Medway Mill was another relatively late newcomer to the scene, being built in about 1860 to produce wrapping papers. A machine mill, it was originally owned by Macey and Elves, who had interests in shipping, but was sold to Monckton and Co. by 1872, and then again to the Medway Paper Mills Company who ran it during the 1880s and 1890s. At this time the company made specialised products such as fly-papers, as well as cartridge and wrapping papers – a significant proportion of their output being exported to the colonies. About 1905 Balstons, who owned the nearby Springfield Mill, brought an action against the Medway Company for smoke nuisance and the mill was closed. It was subsequently bought by Balstons, who installed vats for the manufacture of white paper. The Balston family's Springfield Mill continued to operate as a steam-powered vat mill producing fine white paper, the number of vats being increased from ten to eighteen by the end of the nineteenth century. As a result of all these changes, in the years before the First World War there were only eight mills remaining in or near the town. Five of them, Turkey, Lower Tovil, Hayle, Springfield and Medway were making top quality white and specialist papers (the last three producing it by hand); Upper Tovil and Bridge mills made large amounts of printing paper by machine, and Ivy Mill produced millboard.

Despite this period of reorganisation, overall employment in paper manufacture held up well. The census returns underestimate the total numbers working in the Maidstone industry, because of the location of some of the mills and their workers just outside the town. In 1865, for instance, government inspectors recorded 728 female employees in seven paper mills in or near the town, almost twice as many as those recorded in the 1861 census. Even centrally located mills may have been hiring women coming in to work from the country districts, possibly due to a shortage of female labour in Maidstone itself.

It is likely that mechanisation had an adverse effect on employment for those with traditional skills. During the 1840s and 1850s, when machines were installed in some of the Maidstone mills, numbers of local journeymen became entirely reliant on 'the tramp' for their livelihood. A lengthy itinerary took them from Kent across southern England to Exeter, then north to Lancashire and Newcastle, and finally south again to Maidstone. They walked a stage each day receiving lodging and a small payment at each mill. In the long run, however, expanding production may have increased overall employment opportunities. An estimate of the numbers employed in each mill in 1881 suggests a small increase in the total number of employees since 1865. At the same time, the composition of the workforce began to change. Census figures for 1901 and 1911 point to a reduction in the female workforce probably as a result of the more widespread use of raw materials such as straw rather than rags; the operation of chaff cutting machines was men's work. Legislation restricting night work by women may also have had an effect.

Later nineteenth-century Maidstone was also home to related paper-processing industries. Two notable manufacturers of stationery, H.C. Pearson and Co. and Hobbs and Sons, developed in the town in this period; by 1880 the former had moved to extensive new premises on the Broadway in the West Borough, where notepaper and business stationery were cut and printed. Another important part of their business was the manufacture of paper bags, with additional premises opening for this work about 1890, but the firm also found it convenient to give 'an immense quantity of work' to female outworkers. Hobbs and Sons were in business in Stone Street by 1872, and within a decade they had some 200 employees. They too produced paper bags, many of them printed, together with colour lithographs of oil paintings – their staff included a number of artists. Other businesses were founded after the turn of the century: the printer W.P. Dickinson had begun to manufacture stationery by 1903 and a firm of London printers, Alabaster Passmore and Co., opened a factory at Tovil in 1907.

As we know, brewing had been important in the town since the seventeenth century, but during the Victorian period it enjoyed a new phase of prosperity with a rising number of employees in this and related trades. During the 1830s a number of new breweries opened in Maidstone, probably hoping to supply the many beerhouses which appeared after the passage of the Beer Act in 1830, but only one of these firms, Martin's Brewery in Havock Lane, survived more than a decade or two. Two of the town's older breweries, Heathorn's and Fish's in Earl Street, also closed, but the Lower and Medway breweries continued to prosper.

The Lower Brewery was a Brenchley and Stacey family business until 1870, when the last surviving partner, Courtney Stacey, formed a new partnership and the business became Isherwood, Foster and Stacey. In 1881 the business was turned into a limited company, with capital of £150,000. The brewery had a considerable number of tied houses in Maidstone, although the number remained fairly static between 1833 and 1890 when the brewery controlled 40 public houses – just under 30 per cent of the town's 139 licensed premises. The Medway Brewery expanded markedly after struggling in its early years. The original proprietor, William Baldwin took a succession of partners, the last, in 1860, being A.F. Style, and in 1882 the business passed entirely into Style's hands, although Tyrwhitt-Drake later became a partner. The brewery developed a large trade with London, and branch stores were established there and also at Hastings. In 1890 Style and Co. owned 36 licensed houses in Maidstone, as well as a number in the lower Medway area. In the 1890s the brewery was destroyed by fire, and rebuilt on a much enlarged scale, and in 1899 it amalgamated with the Chatham brewers E. Winch and Sons, all production subsequently being carried on in Maidstone. The new company had more than 350 tied houses, and in 1907 it was listed in the *Financial Times* as the second most profitable provincial brewery in the country. Up to the First World War the company continued to grow, and other breweries were bought, including Charles Arkcoll's Lion Brewery at Chatham.

In addition to these older firms, two other successful breweries were established in Victorian Maidstone. Mason's Waterside Brewery may date from the 1840s, but the family had certainly commenced brewing by 1860. The business flourished, winning prizes for its beer, and by 1892 it had acquired thirteen tied houses in Maidstone, though it remained a small family business. Fremlin's Brewery, which was begun by Ralph Fremlin in 1861 in the derelict Heathorn Brewery in Earl Street, quickly turned into a large concern. Fremlin ran the business almost single-handedly at first, establishing a niche for himself in the market by aiming to supply private houses with beer in bottles and small casks. He was apparently motivated by his support for the temperance movement, with its dislike of public house culture, and no tied houses were acquired. Fremlin's main product was pale ale, for which there was increasing demand as public taste shifted away from porter and heavier beers, and by 1881 the firm had stores in London, Brighton and Rochester. By then the Maidstone workforce stood at something over a hundred including eight coopers. New, up to date premises were built in 1883, and a few years later Fremlins began to supply pale ale to Courage's brewery in London, becoming one of the largest brewers of pale ale in the country. From the 1890s the firm was also brewing lager in response to public demand, and this proved an immense success. The firm always retained their interest in temperance, and in 1906 they advertised in the local press their National Temperance Ale, a non-alcoholic brew, but by 1908 they had changed policy and begun to acquire tied houses.

Because of their earlier policy against tied houses, Fremlins were less directly affected by the decline in public house numbers after the 1870s than other breweries with their closer ties to the retail sector. But it was the public houses which suffered most from licensing restrictions, temperance campaigners, and general shifts in the pattern of leisure. After legislation in 1869 local magistrates used new powers to de-license low-class premises. In 1874 there was one public house to every 138 persons in the town. Seventeen houses closed between 1876 and 1888 mainly because of competitive pressures as some landlords enlarged their premises. But during the 1890s the magistrates began to respond to public concern about the drink trade and to pressure from temperance organisations. The latter constituted a strong interest group in late nineteenth-century Maidstone, as in other British towns, seeking to influence the decisions of the bench over new or extended licences. Legislation in 1904 gave magistrates further powers to close 'redundant' public houses and institute procedures for compensation. The town's licensing justices took firm action, and, despite strenuous resistance, twenty-four of Maidstone's public houses had been closed by 1914, leaving 106 licensed premises or one to 238 persons.

As in the eighteenth century, other branches of the drink industry were located in the town. The earlier distilling industry was re-established in Maidstone in 1853, when Grant's Cherry Brandy distillery moved to the town from Dover. A very successful business was built up operating from Hart Street, adjacent to the railway station in the West Borough. In addition to cherry brandy – an expensive product with supposed medicinal properties – the company distilled hollands gin and imported foreign wines and spirits. By 1892 Grants had an orchard of 20,000 cherry trees at Lenham, where for a time they also had a second distillery; but even this orchard was not sufficient to supply all their needs, and cherries were bought in from local growers. In the latter part of the century the company was exporting on an extensive scale.

The manufacture of mineral waters was another expanding industry in the late Victorian town, when alcohol was a live political issue and temperance organisations were in their heyday. Methods of bottling aerated drinks were improved and there were factories in most Kentish towns. At Maidstone the 1872 directory listed nine ginger beer and soda water manufacturers including one – Spencer Bow Swinfen – which had been in business since the 1830s, after mid-century combining ginger beer production with brewing. The largest manufacturer in the late Victorian period appears to have been Daniel Lyle, in business in Church Street by 1882, and in King Street by 1898, who had depots in several other towns in the county; his advertised specialities were soda water and ginger ale. Two more flourishing businesses were those of J.W. Maskell, established in St Peter Street by 1872, and

Walter Hayward, in operation in Milton Street by the 1890s, both of which, like Lyle's, were still in business in the 1960s.

Among new developments the most significant was the expansion of the engineering industry during the second half of the nineteenth century, although the extent of this is not fully indicated in Table 4 since the peak of employment probably came in the 1890s. The 1839 directory for the town lists five iron or brass foundries, two braziers, and one engineer. All except two of the foundries had ceased trading by 1872. One of these, Joseph Brown and Sons, was also an engine and pump maker, and the other, Garrett, Balls and Co., was a manufacturer of agricultural machinery. Members of the Brown family remained in business at least until 1882, while Garrett and Co. became one of six major engineering companies operating in Maidstone in the late nineteenth century. Four of the six, Garrett and Co., William Weeks, Jesse Ellis, and Drake and Muirhead, were engaged in the production of agricultural machinery, while the other two, Richard Dann and Gardner and Co., worked principally in brass.

With the exception of Garrett and Co., all the firms were established during the mid-Victorian period, and they all grew and prospered until the last years of the century, when some of them ran into difficulties. Garrett and Co., subsequently Garrett, Saveall and Co., who moved to Maidstone from Leiston in Suffolk, concentrated on agricultural machinery until the 1890s when, perhaps because of American competition, they began to diversify. By 1898 they were also millwrights, and the last record we have of the firm in a directory for 1903 shows them also producing paper-making and printing machinery. William Weeks and Son, in business as iron founders and engineers in High Street by 1872, also diversified, expanding into the Perseverance Iron Works in Waterside, where they operated as millwrights and general and agricultural engineers. This company became increasingly unprofitable during the 1890s, and continued to operate under financial difficulties after the turn of the century. However, the firm survived, wiped out its losses between 1910–11, and remained profitable thereafter. The business of Jesse Ellis was not so fortunate despite a promising start in 1869 as an agricultural and haulage contractor, with financial backing from Aveling and Porter, the Rochester traction engine manufacturers, for whom Ellis had previously worked. The firm expanded vigorously and by 1882 they were also boilermakers and manufacturers of agricultural machinery. Three years later the business moved to extensive works in St Peter Street in the West Borough, with a railway siding, and a wharf with a steam crane for unloading heavy raw materials from barges. In addition, the company acted as agents for the agricultural engineers Ransomes of Ipswich, who produced specialised implements for hop cultivation for which Ellis held the patent. They were also contractors for the repair of roads for Kent County Council, but in 1904 this contract was lost, the company found itself overstretched, and was declared insolvent three years later. The St Peter Street works was given up, but Ellis continued to do some contracting work, and manufactured agricultural machinery at Allington forge, until the business finally closed in 1910; soon after, the premises in St Peter Street were taken over by Sharp's.[10] The remaining firm of Drake and Muirhead, later to be Drake and Fletcher, began operations in Maidstone during the 1870s, and by 1882 they were established at the Kentish Engineering Works in the West Borough as mechanical engineers, agricultural implement manufacturers, millwrights and brass founders. By the early 1890s their major specialisms were machinery for spraying hops and fruit trees against pests, plant for sewage works, and gas and oil engines, and the business was evidently a sizeable concern.

Diversification was also important to the success of the two firms principally engaged in brasswork, Richard Dann and Gardner and Co., both established by 1872. Dann's enterprise developed out his family's High Street ironmongers and braziers business, and his main products were brewers' plant and beer engines, and hot water, gas and sanitary engineering. By the 1890s he had also diversified into electrical engineering. His Invicta works was said to have supplied 'copper and steam pipe fittings' to 'all the mills in the neighbourhood', as well as electricity to several large local businesses. In 1898 the company was occupying Jesse Ellis's original premises in Union Street, and it was still listed at that address in 1903, but by 1910 it had gone. Gardner and Co., at the Medway Brass Works on Waterside, were listed simply as brass founders in the 1872 directory, but were also described as engineers in 1882; by 1898, when they were located in Brewer Street, they were producing beer engines. They remained in business into the inter-war years.

Electrical engineering was a new, expanding industry in the late nineteenth century. A firm of mechanical and electrical engineers, Stevens and Barker, was in business in St Peter Street by 1898. In 1905 W.A. Stevens experimented with converting a motor car to electric power, and the following year began to collaborate with the Tilling bus company in London, which led in 1908 to an electric drive bus. The chassis and engines for these were made at the Maidstone works, which grew rapidly to be a major employer after the First World War. A less enduring engineering venture was bicycle manufacture. Richard Dann had made a further diversification into this field by 1898, and that year Beckett and Co. were likewise listed as engineers and cycle manufacturers, although neither business continued for more than a few years.

The manufacture of food products was yet another area of factory employment in the later nineteenth century as the processing of food was increasingly taken out of the hands of the ordinary retailer, and factories were established to produce patent, ready-prepared products – the convenience foods of the Victorian housewife. In Maidstone a number of food retailers and others attempted to diversify into manufacturing. For example, the High Street confectioner Ebenezer Steer was manufacturing 1,500 tons of jam by 1881 from extensive premises in Pudding Lane; large quantities were sold to local wholesalers and to 'the mining districts'. Another jam factory was opened in 1891 on a two-acre site in Hart Street by Charles Chambers, a local fruit grower. The large, electrically powered factory employed about 150 people, the majority of them women, though it had closed by 1895.

Confectionery was produced by one of Maidstone's major manufacturing companies, Edward Sharp. Sharp's business developed out of the Week Street grocery shop which he had started in 1876, and where the sweets were first made by his wife. The recipes came from another local confectionery business, that of Jackson and Smith, with whom Mrs Sharp had a family connection. Output expanded after 1889 when Sharp employed a sugar boiler, and during the 1890s production included items such as jellies, custard powder and lemonade powder. Between 1897 and 1913 the increasingly large-scale manufacture of sweets was carried out in a disused skating rink on Sandling Road. The highly successful 'Kreemy Toffee' was introduced in 1911, and two years later a new factory covering half an acre was opened in St Peter Street, the workforce numbering nearly 300. The business continued to increase in scale, and in January the next year the *Kent Messenger* carried an advertisement for a further 100 young female workers. Sharp's offered to pay railway fares from the surrounding villages, and it is possible that they were experiencing difficulty in recruiting sufficient staff. A male employee at the factory said that in 1914–15 most of the girls travelled to work from nearby villages.

The other highly successful venture into food manufacturing was launched by George Foster Clark who started his business producing baking powder, self-raising flour and lemonade powder for sale in his grocery shop. In 1891, encouraged by the success of his products, he began full-time manufacture in a small building in Mote Road. Foster Clark well understood the value of advertising as illustrated by his adoption of the Eiffel Tower – a well known contemporary symbol – as the trademark for his lemonade powder. In 1895 the firm moved to the Chambers jam factory premises in Hart Street, which became the Eiffel Tower works. Expansion made Foster Clark's a nationally known brand name in the years before the First World War, producing a range of convenience foods which included custard powder, jellies, dessicated soups and canned goods, as well as lemonade powder. The company's employees were mainly women, many of whom travelled to work from the local villages.

Finally, brief reference should be made to the town's old established and long declining thread industry which in 1839 was represented by a twine maker and two rope makers, James Clifford and George Gilbert. Twine had ceased to be made in the town by 1872, and Gilbert's business closed shortly after that date, but Clifford managed to develop a sizeable concern using convict labour in Maidstone gaol and Canterbury prison to make hop-pockets from Dundee jute. Clifford's also made a wide range of other items, including sails, tarpaulin and coconut matting as well as rope, and the business flourished into the late twentieth century.

The labour force: working conditions and industrial relations

We know most about the conditions of workers in the paper mills since, as employers of women and children, these were twice subject to inspection by factory commissioners during the nineteenth century. Maidstone's economy offered relatively few opportunities for juvenile employment except in the paper mills where some child labour survived up to the 1860s. In 1865 commissioners found boys of ten and occasionally less at work, but there were no longer any girls younger than thirteen years old, perhaps due to the general influence of the factory reform campaign (at this time there was no legislation controlling employment in paper mills).

For both adults and children conditions in paper mills were poor. Visiting commissioners in both 1841 and 1865[11] reported problems with dust in the rag rooms, which adversely affected the health of some women, and excessive heat in the sizing and drying rooms, which made workers susceptible to chills. Employees complained of headaches from noise, sore eyes from bleach fumes, and of numb and permanently swollen hands from picking discolouring material from cold pulp in winter. Some said they had no proper meal breaks and had to eat as they worked.

In 1841 hours at all the local mills were broadly similar, the average working day for adults and juveniles being 12–14 hours, although some of the women on piece-work worked only nine or ten. Many of the men worked 24-hour shifts, however, normally doing three a week, and the apprentices and other boys who assisted them did likewise. On overtime, dayworkers might often work for 16 hours, while the 24-hour shifts sometimes extended to 36. By 1865 there had been some reduction in hours in most mills, although excesses remained. At Turkey Mill, for instance, the hours of both men and boys apparently increased, the usual shift being 15 hours, but this sometimes extended to 19 hours or all night, while engineers worked 24-hour or even 36-hour shifts. At Springfield Mill, however, where vatmen retained a degree of independence by operating a kind of piece-work, long shifts might be worked in order to catch up for the traditional one or two days' holiday ('St Monday') still sometimes enjoyed at the start of the week.

Improvements in working conditions followed legislation in 1867 which extended existing controls on factory employment to paper mills. Factory inspectors were given the power to demand that fans be installed in dusty areas, and meal breaks and annual holidays were laid down. Some improvements were evidently carried out; in 1892 we hear that an 'air propeller' had been fitted in the machine room at Lower Tovil Mill – 'a very necessary appliance where the heat is so great'. The hours worked by women and children were gradually reduced by this and subsequent legislation though 24-hour shifts were still permissible for men. Long working hours were a fact of life in Victorian England, but information for other Maidstone industries is scant. In 1872 building trade employees were working a 58.5 hour week, and pressing for this to be reduced to 54. In 1911 Sharp's factory operated 12-hour shifts, day and night, even though much of the workforce was female and prohibited from working nights by the Factory Act; night work had ceased here by the First World War, when a 7 a.m. to 6 p.m. shift was worked. Shop work also involved very long hours, 8 a.m. to 8 p.m. being quite usual, and on Saturday night many shops did not close until 10 or 11 p.m. The first moves in the town towards early closing one day a week were made about 1861, when a public meeting decided to recommend closure at 5 p.m. on Wednesdays during July and August. By the early twentieth century the Wednesday half holiday had become the norm in the town.

As for industrial relations, our best evidence again is for the paper industry where employers and the Original Society of Papermakers had reached a truce by the 1840s. The Original Society continued to operate a closed shop at Hollingworth's Turkey Mill, and restricted apprentices to one per machine, just as in hand mills there was one per vat. By 1874 only six of the 350 or so machine mills operating in the country employed Society men at union rates; these six were all in Kent and included Turkey Mill. The proprietors of the 'carded' mills tried to present a united front in negotiations with their men but at some point Balstons broke ranks and agreed their own wage rates with their employees, with whom they had a good if paternalistic relationship. Because of the conservatism of the Hollingworths and the continued operation of vat mills, Maidstone was a stronghold of the dwindling Original Society into the second half of the nineteenth century. In 1854 the United Brotherhood of Papermakers was founded as a craft union for machine mill workers, mainly on the initiative of members of the Original Society. It later became the Amalgamated Society of Papermakers, and by 1898 had a number of members at Upper Tovil Mill. The union for unskilled paper workers, the National Union of Paper Mill Workers had no members in the town until 1913, when it began to grow rapidly.

Very little is known about trade unionism in other Maidstone industries, although an increasing number of workers were probably organised during the second half of the century, as first the skilled and then the unskilled formed unions. A trade union directory for 1861 lists Maidstone branches of the paper-makers and three other unions, the Boot and Shoemakers, the Compositors and Printers, and the Stonemasons. Building craftsmen of all kinds are known to have been unionised by 1872 and that year the Kent and Sussex Agricultural Labourers Union was founded and organised from the town.[12] Most brewery workers, however, were unskilled and unlikely to have been organised before the 1890s. In the service sector a branch of the shop assistants union was formed in 1896. A Trades Council had been formed in the town by the late 1880s, but this fell into abeyance during the early years of this century. In May 1914 it was revived, and the first meeting was attended by union delegates from the railwaymen, railway clerks, telegraph clerks, postmen, printers, papermakers, bricklayers, agricultural labourers and other unions.

There was a wide divergence between the wages of unskilled and skilled men. Some unskilled workers in paper mills were paid as little as £1 a week in the later nineteenth century, compared with the £2 16s 6d of skilled paper workers and an average wage of £1 15s 8d for all employees, including boys, paid at Garrett and Co.'s foundry in 1881. Foremen at Turkey Mill received between £3 and £4 10s and the principal foreman as much as £8 a week plus house, coals, and light. Wages for the town's skilled men remained high throughout the period to 1914, and falling prices further increased their real value. This enabled skilled workers to adopt a respectable life style which contributed to the stability in social relationships that was such a feature of the town throughout the mid- and late Victorian period.

It is also notable that the relationship of many Maidstone employers with their employees was marked by an increasingly explicit paternalism during the second half of the century. In 1872 the Hollingworth brothers took their entire workforce at Turkey and Otham mills on a trip to Ramsgate, and the workers subsequently assembled en masse to present their employers with an illuminated address expressing their thanks and good wishes, and assuring them that 'the bond of union . . . between employers and employed is more firmly secured than ever'. John Hollingworth responded by saying that on the day of the trip he 'was excessively proud of them when they walked through the town of Maidstone; but he was still more proud when they reached Ramsgate . . . . on being highly congratulated on having so numerous, so well-conducted and so respectable a family.' By the 1880s the Hollingworths were paying pensions to retired employees and widows, as well as giving Christmas gifts and bonuses to their workers and to the poor of the town. Before 1871 Fremlins' employees had been provided with a reading room, where books could be borrowed, and which was used for musical entertainments. Workers were also given a bible on joining the firm, a book every New Year's Day and a monthly periodical, presumably of an improving nature. To encourage thrift, Fremlins paid interest on sums deposited in a savings bank, and they also supported a sick benefit club, which in 1887 had a reserve of £500.

The social order and civic leadership

Maidstone in the Victorian and Edwardian era had an increasingly complex social order. Alongside the paper mill workers, traditionally well paid and conscious of their social position, there was, as we have seen, a larger body of respectable, relatively well-off skilled workers belonging to new industries such as engineering. No less important in shaping the social pattern of the late nineteenth-century community was a small but growing body of clerks working in council and government offices as well for the railway, insurance and other service companies. Below them in an increasingly regimented social pecking order were the numerous shop assistants (still largely male) and the many unskilled or semi-skilled workers in older industries such as brewing, as well as the new food factories (increasingly dominated by women). The town's many domestic servants, predominantly female and largely single, also stood in serried rank towards the bottom of the social order, though with nuanced gradations according to servant rank and size of household. Outside this established order remained considerable numbers of poor, probably constituting up to a fifth of the town's population. As we shall see in Chapter Seven, poverty remained a constant social presence throughout the period with the local indigent – labourers, casual workers, the sick, elderly and orphaned – regularly replenished by inflows of poor families from the countryside. Poor relief, far from helping them to escape the social category of pauperism, tended to imprison them

View of the nineteenth-century town from the West Borough.
Photograph: Kent Messenger Group Newspapers.

Middle-class villas, Somerfield Terrace, London Road, built in the 1840s.
Photograph: Maidstone Museum.

Draycott House, Tonbridge Road; home of the Bentliff family. Middle-class seclusion behind ornate gates.
Photograph: Maidstone Museum.

The construction of Maidstone East Station in 1874. Note the middle-class villas on the skyline.
Photograph: Centre for Kentish Studies.

The Sessions House prior to the building of County Hall in 1915.
Photograph: Kent Messenger Group Newspapers.

The gateway to the barracks during the Edwardian era.
Photograph: Kent Messenger Group Newspapers.

Maidstone fair in Lock Meadow.
Photograph: Maidstone Museum.

George Mence Smith's shop, 19 High Street, open by 1872.
Photograph: Maidstone Museum.

Honnor's, corn and coal merchants, 108 Week Street.
Photograph: Maidstone Museum.

32 TUMBLERS FOR **4½d**
32 TUMBLERS FOR **4½d**
32 TUMBLERS FOR **4½d**

32 Tumblers of Delicious Home-
made Lemonade can be made from a

4½d. BOTTLE
OF
EIFFEL TOWER
CONCENTRATED
LEMONADE

Ask your Grocer for it or send 6
stamps to G. FOSTER, CLARK
and CO., 2, Eiffel Tower Factory,
Maidstone, when a bottle will be
sent by return, post free.

EIFFEL TOWER CONCENTRATED LEMONADE.
EIFFEL TOWER CONCENTRATED LEMONADE.
EIFFEL TOWER CONCENTRATED LEMONADE.

Advertisement for Foster Clark's lemonade.
Photograph: Kent Messenger Group
Newspapers.

Charles Arkcoll's extensive wholesale grocery premises in Lower Stone Street in the 1890s.

A timber wharf by the old bridge, 1860s.
Photograph: Maidstone Museum.

Women at work in Springfield Mill.
Photograph: Maidstone Museum.

in a separate under-class of deprivation. This under-class was blurred at the edges, and included poor working women with families and others eking out an existence at the margins of society, with the aid of soup kitchens and charity.

As well as the employed and under-employed there was a large group of self-employed. Some, backstreet shopkeepers and beerhouse keepers, who employed no-one else, and whose businesses frequently failed, struggled to keep themselves out of the under-class of poor. Above them was the second rank of shopkeepers, small masters, builders, respectable publicans, and lesser professional men. Many of these had only a few employees and sailed close to the wind financially. Insolvency was a recurrent threat exposing the contrast between social expectation and pretension and economic reality. But there can be little doubt that this middling and lesser bourgeoisie, however broadly defined, played a vital role in the emerging social, civic and cultural world of Victorian and Edwardian Maidstone.

Social distinctions between different social groups were manifested in a growing variety of ways: through differences in wage rates, for example, and more and more through variegated permutations in life-style. Not only did the better off increasingly live in the more respectable outer areas of town, particularly in the West Borough, but house façades, size or existence of a front garden, railings, ornamentation and the like, physically demarcated the different social ranks even within a single street. Inside homes a profusion of heavy furnishings visibly manifested the social superiority of the middle classes. Among other features defining the many ranks of the social order was the presence and number of servants, membership of church congregations and of the multiplying number of temperance, philanthropic and other organisations, and party affiliations.

In all these ways then, Victorian Maidstone was an increasingly stratified and segregated society – certainly more than in the eighteenth century. But it was not an openly divided community compared to some of the big metropolitan cities and factory towns. This was partly because of its still relatively small geographical size, with people able to walk easily from one side of the town to the other, with wealthier districts close by poorer ones. It was also probably because of the absence (or only tardy emergence) of any clear consciousness of conventional class demarcations. And this in turn was linked to another major factor: the rise of a new local elite which sought through its social and public leadership to create a redefined sense of urban identity.

Maidstone's early Victorian elite showed some continuities with the past. But the steady expansion of the economy added considerably to the numbers of the leading commercial, manufacturing and professional classes. From the perspective of local directories the most important social distinction was that between gentry and tradesmen, as these were listed separately. In the 1839 directory the gentry included five groups: first, the two aristocratic families resident in the town, and seventeen members of the old county gentry living in the big houses in the environs plus a number of lesser country gentry; secondly, members of the genteel professions – clergymen, doctors, solicitors; thirdly, the military, whose officers were always counted as gentry; fourthly a numerous group of people without an occupation – mostly rentiers and the retired but including single women and widows; and, fifthly, a few of the wealthier merchants and industrialists. Among the latter, the Balstons and Hollingworths, both paper-makers, were gentlemanly industrialists, who remained committed to the town, and were staunch supporters of Tory and Anglican interests. Along with the former paper-making family the Whatmans, who lived at Vinters, they were amongst the richest families by the mid-nineteenth century, and the leading figures in a new emerging middle-class elite. However, most of the town's manufacturers at this time were not included in the gentry section and were listed as tradesmen without private residences.

Lord Romney of the Mote was the main aristocratic figure in the community. Romney was Lord of the Manor and owned much of the land adjacent to the town, amounting to over 16,000 acres in 1843. A patron of the West Kent Infirmary, he also sponsored other societies in the town. Another member of his family living in the town, Viscount Marsham (Boxley House) was President of the Horticultural Society, a visiting magistrate at the prison, deputy governor of the Kent Fire Insurance and president of the West Kent Infirmary. The Ladies Marsham supported various charitable causes and became involved in running a savings bank or penny club. However, as the century progressed the town's institutions did not depend upon aristocratic patronage, and increasingly the only involvement of the neighbouring county gentry was as patrons, presidents and vice-presidents of the Horticultural Society and the hospitals. By the 1840s and 1850s Maidstone was no longer important as a leading social centre for the county gentry. Some of the old functions were kept up in the mid-Victorian years, such as the county balls, which still attracted landed support. But in other respects, Maidstone's social role in the county was in decline as access to London improved, and the country gentry devoted more time to improving their country residences.

Although deference was still shown to the gentry, and, as we shall see in Chapter Eight, few local people ever represented the constituency in Parliament after 1832, the town was no longer dependent (as it had been earlier) on aristocratic and gentry custom for part of its prosperity. As the urban economy diversified and developed, a new distinctly local middle class established its ascendancy in the late nineteenth-century community, able to assert its social autonomy with its own leaders. Among these, as we have already noted, were representatives of some of the old industrial and commercial families – a tightly knit group, some of whom had inter-married. Long important professional groups, increasingly town focused, also had a role to play in this new social environment: thus solicitors like J. Whatman and the Monckton family (James Monckton was town clerk for many years), were prominent in town affairs, along with William Day, the auctioneer and estate agent, and Dr Plomley, a town physician and leading philanthropist. But the ranks of the urban establishment were now extended to include those who successfully exploited widening economic opportunities in the mid- and late Victorian period. A new essentially monied elite was formed, drawn from mill owners, brewers, food manufacturers, merchants (including timber and wine merchants), and wholesale grocers. From mid-century these successful parvenus were living in new town houses in the more select streets. Some of them invested in town lands and were listed as directors of the gas and water companies and the Lower Medway Navigation Company. Most were public spirited, acting as committee members of a wide range of cultural and charitable organisations. As early as 1839 the trustees for the management of the town charities included a paper manufacturer, a linen draper, two ironmongers and a timber merchant; while the trustees of the Benevolent Society were recruited even more broadly and included three industrialists, six tradesmen, three professional men and one gentleman. In the second half of the century a few wealthy individuals – the wholesale grocers Arkcolls and Laurences for example – were particularly prominent in this activity as well as on the town council.

However, it was not just the new rich who were active in civic affairs. Institutional involvement was one of the ways in which the social elite were able to give a lead to Maidstone's respectable tradesmen, the middle-rank bourgeoisie, who were increasingly well represented on the town council as well as among the trustees of the poor and other agencies of local government. The first reformed council after 1835 contained a cross section of the town's wealthy and employing classes. Eleven were tradesmen, but there were five builders, another prominent group in a fast growing town, two brewers, and two paper manufacturers, as well as two bankers, an auctioneer and a gentleman of independent means. The composition of the council was not much changed in 1872 except for a slightly higher proportion of tradesmen, and only two builders and two manufacturers. There were also two gentlemen, two solicitors, an insurance agent, and the proprietor of the *Maidstone Gazette*. A decade later four councillors were described as gentlemen, (probably retired businessmen) and there were four professional men, four manufacturers and again two builders and a newspaper proprietor, this time the owner of the Conservative *Maidstone Journal*. One councillor was a fruit grower, and there were seven tradesmen. Of the latter, four were connected with the retail drink trade. The only working-class councillor on the nineteenth-century council was John Potter, a journeyman paper-maker and trade union official, elected in 1880. In 1903 the composition of the council was much as it had been in 1872, the majority being tradesmen, and the remainder builders, professionals, gentlemen and a single manufacturer. The same classes provided representatives for the county council from 1889, and some members served on both councils simultaneously. There was considerable continuity of council membership and some Maidstone families – Day, Stacey, Argles, Ellis, Franklyn, Laurence – repeatedly held office as councillors, aldermen, mayors and justices of the peace over the century.

The only notable change came after the 1870s when the brewers and major industrialists no longer played so much of a role in the town, although the School Board formed in 1872 continued to draw support from established nonconformist ranks. Increasingly by the turn of the century we find the town's wealthiest inhabitants moving out of the town. By 1903 some industrialists – the Styles and the Fremlins for example – were listed as residents of neighbouring villages along with professional people and the manager of Turkey Mill, Colonel T.H. Pitt JP. In some measure they took the place of the old titled gentry, most of whom had now gone from the area. The death of the third Earl of Romney in 1874 led to large sales of town holdings in order to pay off debts: 240 acres of undeveloped land in the West Borough were sold in 1884 and the remainder of the Mote estate (2,468 acres) in 1895. No members of this once powerful family lived at the Mote from the 1880s and the area around the Archbishop's Palace had ceased to have its old social cachet. Even some of the town's business dynasties had come to an end – the Hollingworths had no successors, nor apparently the Garretts. They were replaced by a new generation of successful businessmen, such as George Foster Clark who was active in town affairs and local politics in the early twentieth century. Nevertheless, there was considerable social and public continuity up to the First World War. Some of the old manufacturing and merchant families – the Cliffords and Laurences for example – still had representatives on the town council after 1900 as did that important professional family the Days – William Day senior was mayor in 1903, while his son, William junior, held the office for the first time in 1906, and was chairman of the education committee.

There was no sharp division between old and new wealth in the history of Maidstone's social and civic elite up to the First World War. Throughout the nineteenth century its members had cooperated with local tradesmen in taking control over the town's public and voluntary institutions. Virtually unchallenged until the rise of labour as a new industrial and political force after 1918, this local oligarchy shaped the destinies of Maidstone during a period when urban growth and industrial development were bringing new and demanding challenges to the quality and viability of town life. Members of this elite identified strongly with the town, seeing in its institutional and governmental development a way, not merely of providing for necessary services, but of shaping the tone and character of the new society that was coming into being.

Notes

1. All Tables are found in the Appendix.
2. Kentstone Properties Plc, *Report and Accounts 1987*.
3. See H. Ashworth, *The Building Society Story* (London, 1980), pp. 40–1; E.J. Cleary, *The Building Society Movement* (London, 1965), pp. 105, 114.
4. [Anon.], *Kent Police, 1857–1957* (n p, 1957), p. 21.
5. For hop-growers and the trade of the town see [anon], *Industries of Maidstone* (Maidstone, 1881), p17; for Bunyards, ibid, p. 33.
6. *Maidstone Gazette*, 22 November 1842.
7. M. Winstanley, *The Shopkeeper's World* (Manchester, 1983), p. 209.
8. W.H. Brown, *The Co-operative Story of Kent* (Manchester, nd), pp. 16, 24.
9. P.W. Lewis, 'Changing factors of location in the papermaking industry as illustrated by the Maidstone area', *Geography*, vol. 52 (1967), pp. 280–93.
10. R.A. Whitehead, *Jesse Ellis and the Maidstone Wagons* (Tonbridge, 1992), p. 33.
11. *Parliamentary Papers*: 1843, XIV, *Children's Employment Commission. Report on Employment of*

Children . . . in Paper Mills; 1865, XX, *Report of Commissioners on the Employment of Children and Young Persons in Trades and Manufactures.*
12.   R. Groves, *Sharpen the Sickle* (London, 1981), p. 54.

Bibliographical Note

For general urban developments in the Victorian and Edwardian period see P.J. Waller, *Town, City and Nation* (Oxford, 1983), and R.J. Morris and R. Rodger, eds., *The Victorian City 1820–1914* (London, 1993). In this chapter much use has been made of local newspapers. There were a number of newspapers published in the town during the period. The *Maidstone Journal*, the first regular publication, founded in 1786, continued until December 1911 when it was absorbed into the *South Eastern Gazette*. By the 1830s it had abandoned its avowedly neutral political stance and become Conservative in tone. The *Maidstone* or *South Eastern Gazette* [the main title varied at different periods] was founded in 1815 as a radical Liberal organ but later in the century became more conservative. It ceased publication during the 1970s. The *Kent Messenger* commenced publication in 1859, and still continues. The *Maidstone and Kent County Standard* was published between 1874 and 1912. Files of all these newspapers are held on microfilm at Maidstone Reference Library, with the exception of the *Maidstone and Kent County Standard*, which is held at the British Museum Newspaper Library at Colindale.

In addition, there is valuable material in trade and street directories; the minutes of the Borough Council in the Centre for Kentish Studies [Kent Archives Office], Md/AC 3; and the printed census returns. Two late nineteenth-century publications, a collection of articles from the *Maidstone and Kent County Standard*, reprinted anonymously as *Industries of Maidstone* (Maidstone, 1881), and E.P. Edwards, *Maidstone in 1892* (Brighton, 1892) provide important information.

The section on population draws on the Registrar General's annual reports. The account of the town's growth is based on maps, the borough medical officer of health's printed reports (Maidstone Reference Library, MAI 628), and the papers of town landowners, notably Lord Romney, in the Centre for Kentish Studies, U1515. For railway development the principal published source is Edwin Course, *The Railways of Southern England: the Main Lines* (London, 1973) and *The Railways of Southern England: the Branch Lines* (London, 1974). The section on shops was influenced by J.B. Jefferys, *Retail Trading in Britain, 1850–1950* (Cambridge, 1954), and D. Alexander, *Retailing in England* (London, 1970). Much material on the paper industry was drawn from the various articles by A.H. Shorter, all of which have now been reprinted in R.L. Hills, ed., *Studies on the History of Papermaking in Britain* (Aldershot, 1993) and also from A.H. Shorter *Paper Making in the British Isles* (Newton Abbot, 1971). D.C. Coleman, *The British Paper Industry, 1495–1860* (Oxford, 1958), A.D. Spicer, *The Paper Trade* (London, 1907), and C.J. Bundock, *The Story of the National Union of Printing, Bookbinding and Paperworkers* (Oxford, 1959) are also useful for the study of this industry. The Hollingworth family papers in the Centre for Kentish Studies (U1999) were also consulted. *Parliamentary Papers*, 1843, XIV, *Children's Employment Commission. Report on the Employment of Children*; and 1865, XX, *Report of Commissioners on the Employment of Children and Young Persons in Trades and Manufactures*, supplied much information on working conditions in paper mills. The discussion of the breweries was aided by the unpublished work of the Maidstone Industrial Archaeology Group. Statistics on public houses are taken from the various returns on licensing in the *Parliamentary Papers* from 1868–9 onwards. On food manufacturers we consulted H.V.R. Geary's unpublished work on Sharp's in Maidstone Reference Library; Irene Hales, 'The Sharp's Kreemy Toffee story', Part one, *Bygone Kent*, vol. 7, 250–7, and also her article in the same journal, 'George Foster Clark and the Eiffel Tower Works', vol. 10, pp. 250–6. The census enumerators' books for 1861 (Maidstone Reference Library, microfilm) were examined for the section on the town's social structure.

Chapter Seven

THE VICTORIAN AND EDWARDIAN TOWN:
THE RISE OF PUBLIC SERVICES

The unprecedented growth of urban populations in the nineteenth century posed challenging public problems for town authorities, particularly during the period from the 1830s and 1860s when existing amenities and services came under most pressure. Environmental deterioration due to inadequate sanitation and water supply, increasing air and water pollution, pressure on housing, and loss of communal and recreational space, affected all townspeople to an extent and bore especially hard on lower-class inhabitants and the poor. Living standards may have benefited from an increase in industrial employment but the urban labour force was also affected by the instability of the industrial economy due to seasonal factors and periodic trade depressions.

The political response to deteriorating urban conditions was slow to develop but from the 1850s new central departments of government were being established with powers of inspection and regulation, while successive Acts of Parliament gave local authorities new powers and responsibilities. Since much of this legislation was permissive, there was considerable variation between towns and cities in the timing and nature of local provision mirroring in part the scale of environmental and social pressures in such communities. Though environmental conditions worsened in Maidstone in the first half of the nineteenth century, the town's problems were not as acute as in the faster growing towns of the northern industrial districts. Life expectancy in the 1850s, although lower than in the rural districts, was higher than in the big cities with populations of over 100,000. On the other hand, the response of Maidstone's civic authorities to emerging problems had distinct financial and social limits and the town lagged behind in areas of provision that required substantial capital expenditure. This reflected the reluctance of the property owners, tradesmen and shopkeepers represented on the council and other agencies of local government to support measures that would increase rating assessments. But during the mid- and late Victorian period the council was also slow to exploit the borrowing powers provided by central government for new sewerage construction or the acquisition of utilities such as gas and water.

This picture of Maidstone as a town whose municipal affairs were dominated by a tight-fisted corporation does less than justice, however, to the ambitions of more progressive councillors and the paternalistic attitudes of its social leaders. We also need to take into account the custom in the town of sounding out wider opinion by holding public meetings of ratepayers, a procedure that helped foster the image of a town in charge of its own affairs. No less important, municipal provision was only part of the story. In Maidstone as elsewhere there was considerable voluntary effort behind philanthropic and educational provision in which the town's ruling elite had a leading part – exemplifying their role and status in the community. As we shall see, the overall growth of public services owed much to a complex, shifting interaction of official, voluntary and commercial activity.

Policing the town

Public order was the first major issue addressed by the reformed council after 1835. The small borough police force established under the 1819 Improvement Act was increasingly ineffectual, and by the 1830s crime had become a major source of anxiety in the town. There was frequently fighting and disorder at the fairs, and by the beginning of 1836 burglaries had reached the unprecedented level of five a week; it was said that 'a feeling of insecurity generally prevailed'. According to the mayor, there were in the town, 'a great number of bad characters who . . . had no other mode of getting a living than that of plunder'. There was he said, 'no one thing in Maidstone wanted more than an efficient police'.[1]

It was calculated that an efficient police force, carrying out day and night duty, and consisting of a superintendent, two sergeants and eight constables, could be established for £600 a year. A borough constabulary, modelled on the metropolitan police was set up, under the control of the council's watch committee. There were subsequent claims that 'a great change for the better has taken place in the streets; prostitutes and other disorderly and bad characters are deterred from pursuing their former annoying and disgusting conduct.' The town's public houses and beershops were placed under vigilant inspection, so the 'government of the town is greatly improved'. However, the town's thieves may have turned their attentions to nearby rural areas, not protected by a police force until 1857.

The police initially operated from the town hall, but in 1841 a police station was opened on King Street. At first only an area within three-quarters of a mile of the town hall was patrolled, with the inhabitants paying an additional rate for the privilege. As the town grew the patrolled area was extended, and the size of the force increased – rising to 23 in 1869, and 47 in 1905. In addition to crime prevention, from 1864 onwards the police increasingly took on a number of administrative functions, such as the inspection of lodging houses and weights and measures. From 1869 the constabulary was subject to annual government inspection, and was always pronounced efficient. Such figures as we have for the numbers of crimes reported show some fluctuation from year to year, but the levels seem relatively low, despite growing social problems, and many offenders were apparently apprehended. Cases in the town magistrates' court 1902–10 show a predominant and predictable mixture of larceny, drunkenness and felony cases, with a small number of offences linked with the barracks. At the same time, the success of municipal policing may also reflect advances in other areas of urban provision.

Town improvements: the pavement commissioners

Although local government in early Victorian Maidstone was fragmented between different bodies, there was much overlapping membership which prevented these bodies becoming strongholds of different political factions as we find in other towns. Until 1866 the pavement commissioners, largely composed of members of the town council, continued to have responsibility for paving, lighting and water supply. During the 1840s and 1850s they struggled to keep up with the rapid growth of the town and came under pressure from local councillors and doctors concerned about the health of the inhabitants. As we saw in Chapter Six, from 1841 to 1881 the trend in the crude death rate showed little sign of declining and rose quite sharply in some years. During the 1850s, for example, the annual crude death rate fluctuated between about 22 and 28 per 1,000 live persons. It was not until after 1881 that the adult mortality rate began to fall noticeably.

Even so, the town was fortunate to avoid the mass fatalities from cholera epidemics that occurred in other places and especially London. In 1849, for instance, Maidstone, almost alone among southern towns, virtually escaped attacks, although epidemic outbreaks were experienced in neighbouring districts. The main threat came from localised outbreaks among the London hop-pickers at East Farleigh. In a report in 1849, Dr Plomley, the Medical Officer for the Maidstone Poor Law Union, attributed the spread of the disease to the appalling conditions in which hop-pickers lived – in barns, sheds and one room cottages. This localised outbreak caused 98 deaths, and there was a recurrence in 1854 with a further 88 deaths. Twelve years later the town itself was infected, the disease being introduced not by the hop-pickers, however, as was always feared, but carried up the river by barge from Chatham. The outbreak took hold mainly in the poor courts of the town. But overall mortality in the Maidstone Registration District (which included East Farleigh) was no worse than in earlier cholera epidemics – with 83 deaths and 250 cases reported.[2]

Despite the relatively low incidence of cholera in Maidstone, the fear of an epidemic was a powerful influence helping to focus public attention on medical and hospital provision for the poor as well as their living conditions. Cholera was one of a group of diseases known as the zymotic or fever diseases which were beginning to be thought preventable in this period by means of sanitary improvements and associated advances in water supply. Among such diseases were typhus and typhoid and other enteric diseases including infant diarrhoea. All were endemic and periodically epidemic in Maidstone as in other towns. Yet environmental improvements were not easily achieved. Improvement of the water supply was particularly difficult because the town was still dependent on public conduit water supplemented by about seventy-five private wells and handpumps. The pavement commissioners had attempted to improve supplies in 1819 with a second reservoir and the construction of new iron pipes, but it was still necessary to fetch water from the public conduits in pails and in summer the conduits and pumps were liable to run dry.

During the 1840s campaigning organisations such as the Health of Towns Association which originated in Liverpool had succeeded in making the sanitary conditions of British towns and cities an issue of wide public concern. In Maidstone there are indications of increased activity in nuisance removal during this decade and the council acted to try and curb the pollution of the River Len at the back of the High Street. More important, the reappearance of cholera in the area together with impending legislation on public health gave an opportunity for sanitary reformers in the town to press their case. In 1847 the mayor, John Whichcord, the prominent architect and county surveyor for many years, was active in this campaign. He called on the council to investigate 'what the real state of the back parts of the town was' and to consider 'whether any steps were necessary to be taken for their improvement'. The plan was for councillors to inspect their own localities. This was carried out, but the subsequent report of a council committee highlighting the problems of the poorer streets, was overtaken by a wide-ranging condemnation of the sanitary condition of Maidstone by Dr Francis Plomley and a colleague David Walker. Their private survey was made public in a series of letters to the mayor published in the *Maidstone Gazette* in February and March 1848.

The chief concern of the letters was the relation between dirt and disease in the poorest streets and in the town as a whole. The authors were critical of the builders of poor quality cottage property and complained about the virtual absence of building controls. Much was made of the hardships of the poor in damp and dilapidated properties and the difficulty of keeping themselves and their houses clean when water was supplied intermittently and had to be fetched from the conduit. These poor courts and streets were the fever streets of the town:

> either without water or an inadequate supply, without paving and without sewage [sic], surrounded by open drains and cesspools, pig styes and slaughter-houses, with myriads of disgusting nuisances emitting loathsome smells, and volatile poisons, not only producing disease in their immediate locality but vitiating the whole atmosphere of the town, and affecting the whole mass of the population.'

It was not only the poorest courts but many other streets, 'consisting of hundreds of houses', that exhibited sanitary defects. Inspired by the contemporary belief that the fever diseases were caught from the poisonous exhalations emanating from accumulations of decomposing animal and vegetable matter, the letters argued for wide-ranging measures to cleanse the town of all impurities. Scavenging, drains, sewers and water were all linked together in a broad agenda of sanitary improvement. Adequate supplies of water, along with better paving and refuse disposal, were necessary to keep the town streets clean and the drains flowing. The River Len was picked out for particular condemnation as a 'sluggish, dirty river, which receives a great deal of the filth of the town', but again this was linked to a more general criticism of drainage and sewers. It was alleged that drains were frequently blocked up and smelly because of open gratings and the sewers old or non-existent. Maidstone, they wrote, 'is one complete series of cesspools', and in the oldest and most densely occupied parts of the town overflowing privies and cesspools were common, permeating the soil and polluting local well water. With a zeal reminiscent of the national public health campaigner Edwin Chadwick, they argued that the cost of a proper sewage and refuse system could be offset by disposing of town wastes to farmers as manure.

In 1848 a public meeting supported the proposal of John Whichcord and other reformist Liberals that a government inspector be asked to undertake an enquiry into the health of the town under the provisions of the 1848 Health Act, and the *Maidstone Gazette* carried a notice that the provisions of the Act were to be enforced in the town. In the event, however, a Local Board of Health was not established under the Act, although the council did appoint an Inspector of Nuisances. In addition, a plan was agreed in 1850 to build public baths and wash-houses on the Fair Meadow with a loan of £5,000 from the Public Works Loan Board. The baths were intended more as a measure to promote public health than as a recreational amenity, but a swimming bath was built in addition to the private baths. Whereas the swimming pool became a cheap popular amenity (2d Monday to Friday, 1d at weekends), the wash-houses were little used and closed in 1858.

Another concern at this time was the state of common lodging houses which provided a home for single men and poor families without permanent accommodation. After discussion by the Watch Committee, the Lodging House Act of 1851 was adopted. This empowered councils to keep a register, specify the number of lodgers permitted and make by-laws concerning cleanliness, ventilation and separate accommodation for the sexes. Of the thirty-five premises approved by the council, fifteen were public houses, the majority of them centrally located and apparently respectable premises. However, despite registration and the additional control exercised by licensing magistrates, the town's lodging houses remained a cause of concern until well into the twentieth century.

By mid-century the improvement of water supply and sanitation was clearly on the council's agenda, but progress was held up by competing schemes and vested interests. In particular there was an unwillingness on the part of the inhabitants of the wealthier districts to bear the cost of improvements in poorer areas of town. In the case of water supply the early 1850s saw the first plans to pump water from the Medway and investigations made into the possibility of deep-boring river water. A special committee set up to consider the question produced reports in 1852 (by the surveyors Whichcord and Bulmer) and again in 1855 – reviewing plans for a new waterworks by the eminent engineer, T. Hawksley. Public health was not the only issue. The lack of a plentiful supply of water hampered fire-fighting, with the result that a serious fire in 1855 caused £4,000 worth of damage in the Earl Street area.

The 1855 committee urged that improving the water supply should be undertaken by the pavement commissioners 'as a great sanitary measure' rather than handed over to a water company. But the councillors failed to win over the ratepayers to this idea: a first scheme was voted down by a public meeting in 1855 and a second proposal by a large majority in 1858. The situation was finally resolved by private enterprise in the form of the Maidstone Waterworks Company, incorporated by Act of Parliament in 1860. Cooperation with the pavement commissioners was ensured by an agreement which required the company to fill up the town reservoirs, make water available for street cleaning, and place fire hydrants by the new water mains. The incorporation of the water company raised the question of the location of new supplies. The company eventually decided to use spring water, which was intercepted from the ragstone along the railway line to Paddock Wood, and piped to a new pumping station at Farleigh and thence to a reservoir at Barming from where it supplied the town by gravity.

The pace of sanitary improvement was also protracted. Various schemes for improving drainage and sewerage were put forward, only to be abandoned because of the expense. In 1857, for example, a proposal for a new main sewer in the northern district of the town, in anticipation of a likely increase in building and population there, was defeated on financial grounds. The following year an accumulation of stinking mud forced the state of the River Len on the attention of the commissioners again. A sewer from Turkey Mill (identified as a source of pollution) to the River Medway was recommended, although some of the commissioners had reservations about increasing the amount of sewage flowing into the river. As early as 1851 the effluence of the gas works was being monitored. The 1855 report on the water supply drew attention to deposits of refuse from paper manufactories and oil mills, and in the early 1860s the appearance of dead fish in the river was attributed to the filth flowing from the mills around Tovil Brook. The town sewage was also thought to be a pollutant and at one point Aylesford sued the Maidstone authorities for contamination of the river upstream. A committee was set up in 1864 to investigate the position; their report criticised the extent of industrial pollution but side-stepped the issue of the town's sewage, arguing that for the time being the river had a sufficient flow to make the sewage harmless.

In the early 1860s the pavement commissioners were again under pressure over the continued inadequacy of sewage arrangements in the town. An enquiry in 1860 revealed that 887 houses or nearly a quarter of the houses within the commission boundary had no sewers and of these, 682 were in streets which the commissioners had not paved or lit. A spate of sewer construction followed. By 1864 the Len sewer was complete, a deep main sewer laid in the High Street and new connections made in Tonbridge Road and Canning Street. It was not until 1866, however, with the formation of a Local Board of Health that a comprehensive scheme of drains and sewers was planned. Even then implementation was much delayed because the Local Government Board initially turned down an application to raise money from a mortgage of the rates on the grounds that the scheme failed to make provision for an outfall sewer below Allington Lock.

Public health after 1866: the Local Board and Urban Sanitary Committee

Despite the tardiness of the sewer building programme, the formation of the Local Board of Health and the appointment of a part-time medical officer in 1866 opened a new chapter in the history of public health in Maidstone which began with a series of measures intended to stop further deterioration in the condition of the town. The Local Board framed by-laws regulating building standards for new houses, and the worst features of early nineteenth-century building were outlawed. Back to back houses were prohibited, and minimum standards laid down for structure, height of rooms, size of windows, and density of buildings. All new houses had to be certified fit for occupation by the medical officer of health, who was also empowered to certify buildings unfit for habitation. New responsibilities were taken on by extending the term 'nuisance' to cover overcrowded houses (the first time this concept had been officially recognised), and industrial premises including unclean and improperly ventilated factories and workshops, and, perhaps most important, fireplaces and furnaces that were polluting the atmosphere. The latter provision resulted in action against smoke nuisance affecting seven mills, the gas works, engineering works, lime and cement works and all the bakeries and blacksmiths.

Public health activity was further extended by the Public Health Act of 1875 and the appointment of a new full-time medical officer, Mr M.A. Adams. His annual reports monitored progress in improving the health of the town, drew attention to outstanding problems, and the important priorities. The arterial drainage system was at last completed in 1879 and a small sewage works constructed at Allington. However, several recently built districts in the outskirts of the town such as Wheeler Street, Fant and Tovil – centres of a severe diphtheria outbreak in 1888–9 – still exhibited old problems of unpaved pathways, animal husbandry (especially pig keeping), and poor house drainage. The condition of house drains was thought to be a problem in other parts of the town too, along with continuing pollution of the subsoil, and the escape of sewer gas. The medical officer also proved a determined critic of the old hand flushed pan closets favoured by the Local Board and advocated a radical reform of the system of rubbish disposal. These preoccupations – common to other medical officers in this period – influenced the actions of the Local Board of Health in overhauling domestic sanitation, including the repair and replacement of house drains and the filling in of cesspools – actions that helped combat disease by improving domestic hygiene.

After the Local Government Act of 1888, responsibility for public health was taken over by the sanitary committee of the Urban District Council (comprised of borough councillors). There were several outstanding problems. Even in the 1890s wells were still in use (polluted wells were discovered in Paradise Lane, off Padsole Lane, in 1893), and many houses were said to have closets with no means of flushing. There was also the continuing problem of the condition of the old courts. In 1893 the medical officer was instructed to prepare reports on School Court, Bonny's Yard and other similar places. The reports presented a bleak picture of overcrowded and dilapidated slums. As the medical officer remarked of houses in School Court: they were 'contemptibly mean dwellings and that is all I can say about them'. Some property was condemned before 1914 but the council put off demolishing them. Nor was the Urban District Council able to make any headway in supplying cheap housing in the town although they were permitted to do so by the Housing of the Working Classes Act in 1894. In 1914 the council estimated that an additional 200 working-class houses were needed in the borough, and set up a Cottage Building Committee to supervise the building of new houses, but costs proved problematic.

Towards the end of the century the work of the health authorities was increasingly of a routine nature: testing wells, taking action against overcrowding and insanitary conditions, paving and lighting, and exercising other new powers of regulation and inspection such as the analysis of foodstuffs and milk. But from time to time, councillors and officials were faced with sudden emergencies. In 1892 the threat of a cholera outbreak was taken very seriously and caused the medical officer to mobilise officials and police, and issue handbills and posters. A more devastating emergency arose in 1897 with a sudden outbreak of typhoid fever which spread rapidly after September and in a few months 1,847 cases were notified, with 132 deaths. During this period there were daily meetings of the sanitary committee; emergency hospitals were improvised in schools and missions; teams of nurses brought in; relief stations set up for the poor; and a charitable relief fund started.

The medical officer had been warning for ten years that part of the Farleigh supply was surface water and liable to contamination, but nothing had been done. He now traced the outbreak to the contamination of one of the Farleigh springs from the primitive sanitary arrangements of a hop-pickers' camp. The local government inspector confirmed the Farleigh works as the source and this supply was shut down and remained cut off until 1933. There were considerable recriminations at council meetings following these revelations and a lively correspondence in the *Kent Messenger* was directed against councillors who were shareholders in the water company, especially Alderman Ellis (a director of the company) and other councillors who owned cottage property. The outbreak also revived the issue of private versus council ownership. On several earlier occasions in the past a group of councillors had expressed disapproval of the operations of the gas and water companies in the town. An attempt to take over the gas company in the 1880s failed although the council did insist on closer regulation. In 1896 a move to take over the water company by a compulsory purchase order was defeated at a ratepayers' meeting. After the typhoid outbreak this had stronger support and negotiations were begun to purchase the company, but once again no agreement was reached and the company remained in private hands.

The 1897 epidemic was a traumatic but exceptional occurrence since typhoid had appeared only as an occasional and minor autumnal visitation in the last third of the century. A more prolonged anxiety was the incidence of respiratory diseases which were acutely endemic. Tuberculosis, for example, was responsible for 37 per cent of all deaths in the age group 15–35 and 27 per cent in the age group 35–45 during the 1880s. This was a debilitating disease for which little public treatment was available. Beds were set aside for tuberculosis cases at the Maidstone Union Infirmary at Coxheath but it was difficult to persuade people to undergo treatment there, and the great majority of chronic cases relied on the outpatient's department of the West Kent General Hospital. Influenza was also coming into the purview of the medical officer as a killer disease in the later 1880s: 'a widespread epidemic disorder to all intents and purposes new to the present generation of medical men'.

The diseases which most dominated the annual reports of the borough medical officer were those affecting the young. These were bound to have a disproportionate impact on the disease statistics because of the age composition of the population. In 1881 and 1891 just under two-thirds of Maidstone's population was under thirty-five years old and just over one third under the age of fifteen. Among the infectious diseases, measles consistently claimed the highest number of deaths, followed by whooping cough; the statistics for measles cases probably underestimated the extent of the disease since it was not notifiable officially before 1900 and tended to be lightly treated by parents – 'more as a domestic incident than a serious malady'. Scarlet fever and diphtheria were also killers in this period and responsible for a series of epidemics in the 1890s. The borough medical officer, M.A. Adams, was in the advance guard of medical opinion in ascribing causation to microbes but he still retained some older ideas. Among the causal factors he supported were atmospheric conditions – the frequency of stagnant fogs aggravated by flooding in the lower part of the town – and exhalations of sewer gas. At the same time Adams supported contagionist views about the spread of disease and instituted new preventive policies. These included isolating infected patients, disinfecting clothes and fumigating houses. A Borough Infectious Hospital was opened at Fant in 1884 and a disinfecting station and laundry in 1887. In the 1890s the medical officer also sought the cooperation of school managers to close schools at times of epidemic. In a period when the anti-toxins available were ineffectual, these were the only methods which could be used for curbing the spread of infectious diseases. Ironically, smallpox, the one disease that might have been stamped out because of the availability of vaccination, continued to recur. The medical officer knew that Maidstone was vulnerable because of the presence of the barracks and neighbouring mills – both sources of infection for the outbreak of 1881. But he was frustrated by the low rate of vaccination in the town. There was no concerted opposition to vaccination; rather the medical officer thought the public were indifferent and he criticised the vaccination officer for lax enforcement.

Nevertheless, the transformation in Maidstone's life expectancy was maintained throughout the third quarter of the nineteenth century – illustrated as we saw in Chapter Six by the fall in the adult death rate. The decline in the average rate of infant mortality was even more impressive. The average for the 1870s was 157.4 per 1,000 live births. This rate fell steadily decade by decade to an average of 113 in 1900–11. Of course such averages obscure short-term rises, mainly due to the varying incidence of summer diarrhoea, but overall the rates were much better than in most industrial towns. In the country as a whole infant mortality remained high in the last two decades of the nineteenth century and actually increased in many cities. Improvements in Maidstone's mortality rates were in part a result of the slow down in the rate of population growth, but they also reflected the activity of local bodies in promoting public health. Maidstone was behind other towns in acquiring a comprehensive drainage and sewerage system, but the public health policies of the later nineteenth century seem to have paid off in terms of life expectancy. The decline in infant mortality was quite exceptional. This may have been linked to the low birth rate, although better housing and improvements in the sanitary condition of older houses would have contributed by raising standards of domestic hygiene. How great a contribution the local hospitals made to the general improvement in public health in the town is unclear. The West Kent General Hospital, an early nineteenth-century voluntary hospital, was steadily extended towards the end of the century with additional wards, but its services remained limited. The Ophthalmic Hospital was established in 1847 on an adjacent site but even after expansion was treating only forty-two patients in its wards in 1891.

The late 1870s were evidently a watershed for life expectancy in Maidstone. As the medical officer of health wrote in the 1890s, Maidstone after the Public Health Act of 1875 improved its ranking in the league tables of the Registrar General significantly, moving from 'the position of an unhealthy town district to that of a comparatively healthy country district'. Comparing the census figures of 1881 and 1891 he showed that Maidstone had a lower death rate at all age groups than the national average; from 1889 the rate was lower than in any of the large and great towns, leading the council to boast that it was 'the healthiest town in England'. That protracted battle against disease mortality which had so overshadowed the community and its development in preceding generations was now at last being won.

The treatment of the poor

As we saw in previous chapters, the plight of the poor had likewise been a long-standing concern in Maidstone as in other British towns – spurring both public action and private benefaction. A mounting crisis in the relief of the poor evident by the 1830s, and the longer-term problems of periodic unemployment in the industrialising towns, generated new tensions and ambiguities in contemporary attitudes. Looked at from the perspective of the Poor Law Reform Act of 1834 with its emphasis on the deterrence of pauperism, and the abolition of outdoor relief in favour of concentrating provision on the workhouse, nineteenth-century attitudes seem to be more punitive than those in the eighteenth century. But official policy was not necessarily translated into local action, despite the existence after 1834 of a government department with poor law inspectors. Workhouse conditions were influenced by local practices and a more general softening in attitudes during the later decades of the century. Moreover, as the history of poor relief in Maidstone illustrates, it is misleading to focus only on workhouse provision: as in the past the relief of distress was accepted as a communal responsibility, as a proper object of voluntary funds and organisation and one that eventually after the 1890s involved the town council in providing relief work for the unemployed. This communal response to social distress may have contributed greatly to maintaining the stability of social relationships in the town especially during the later nineteenth and early twentieth centuries.

There was considerable resistance to the administrative innovations of the Poor Law Amendment Act of 1834, particularly in the fiercely independent industrial towns of the North. In Maidstone, also, the Trustees of the Poor objected to the changes from the start and petitioned Parliament against the Bill before it became law. It was not so much the policy of deterrence that was at issue as the question of local control. Under the New Poor Law individual parishes were to be grouped together into unions, managed by Boards of Guardians who would administer a national system of relief, overseen by a central Poor Law Commission. The town's trustees were opposed to the idea of centralised control, and to authority being transferred to persons without local knowledge. Reorganisation of the parishes in the Maidstone area did not take place until 1836, when the town reacted with dismay to its incorporation with those rural parishes which already formed Coxheath Union. The trustees protested to the Poor Law Commissioners that 'a trading town could not work efficiently in concert with agricultural parishes', and that Maidstone's population was greater than that of all the other parishes put together, and could not be properly represented by two guardians on the board like any other parish. The commissioners were not swayed, and Maidstone was attached to Coxheath Union, which was renamed Maidstone Union; but such was the strength of feeling in the town that no one came forward to serve as a guardian until 1842. That year Maidstone appointed four guardians, subsequently increased to eight in 1878 on the grounds of urban growth; in the long term at least, the town's voice was clearly heard in policy-making.

After union the inmates of Maidstone workhouse were moved to Coxheath, and the Knightrider Street premises sold. The trustees continued to collect the town's poor rate, however, and to authorise the payment of outdoor relief. This remained important, despite the new law, since the numbers of applicants for relief were too numerous to be accommodated in the workhouse. Nevertheless, Maidstone's expenditure on poor relief fell sharply, and by 1843 expenditure was only just over half the average of the three years immediately before union. Throughout the second half of the century between 1 and 1.5 per cent of the population of the town were living in the workhouse. In the six months to Lady Day 1858 the number of inmates belonging to Maidstone parish was 333, a figure that was little changed in the same six-month period twenty years later. Numbers rose towards the end of the century, however, peaking at 490 in 1897, albeit fluctuating from year to year, according to the severity of winters and prevalence of illness. As for out-relief, the percentage of the population claiming support for themselves and their families varied from 1 to 2.5 per cent – a notably high level.

Details of the inmates – which first become available in 1885 – show a pattern common to Victorian workhouses and point to the inappropriateness of a policy aimed primarily at deterring able-bodied males from becoming long-term paupers. Thirty-eight per cent of inmates were the old – the most important group – and 26 per cent comprised children aged thirteen or under. The remaining inmates included mothers of the children, and women, probably mainly single, who entered the workhouse infirmary for confinements. Others were chronically sick or disabled, including mentally handicapped persons and epileptics, for whom there was no other provision, but not the mentally ill, who were removed to the County and other asylums. Only twenty-two inmates, less than 6 per cent of the total, were males aged between eighteen and thirty-five.

The trustees of the poor deviated from official policy in continuing to accept some responsibility for tramps and casuals in the town, and after the closure of the old workhouse they made regular payments to the proprietor of a 'trampers lodging house'. By 1848 they were renting the whole lodging house, and apparently administered it as part of the Poor Law system. Tramps were only permitted to stay one night before moving on, and the lodgings were harsh, straw being provided for them to sleep on only in winter. In 1854 the police were given a key to the lodging house to admit vagrants found on the street late at night. The lodging house was closed in 1862 on the grounds of expense, but large numbers of casuals were given temporary accommodation at the workhouse, especially during the summer, when numbers were swelled by hop-pickers. In the six months ending in September 1870, for instance, nearly 16,000 casuals passed through the workhouse. Maidstone also had to face the problem of accommodating hoppers, who increasingly arrived by train and alighted in the town in large numbers. The Local Board erected tents on the Fair Meadow, and in 1876 over two thousand hop-pickers were sheltered there. During the 1880s they were lodged in one of the market buildings. Hoppers were still apparently using the workhouse casual wards at the end of the century, but the harsh treatment they received made many prefer to sleep in the town's streets or market-place.[3]

In some other respects the Maidstone Union adhered quite strictly to the principles of workhouse relief embodied in the 1834 Act. Within the workhouse, for example, different categories of pauper lived separately – children divided from their parents, men and women in separate wards, and the elderly further segregated (although by 1906 elderly married couples were given a room together). Uniforms were worn, and men were required to work at oakum picking, stone breaking and gardening. Women were engaged in nursing, cleaning and washing, and the girls also worked at washing and making straw bonnets. Boys under sixteen were taught shoemaking and tailoring, with the intention probably of clothing the inmates. Other boys worked on the land.

Another principle of the 1834 Act was that workhouse inmates should enjoy a standard of living slightly lower than that of the lowest-paid worker. This principle determined the workhouse diet and in Maidstone Union, as in most of the south and east of the country, the inmates ate mainly gruel and bread with a little cheese. Meat was eaten once a week, but there were no fresh vegetables – those grown in the workhouse garden were sold. Quantities of food were adequate, but the diet was monotonous and unpalatable. During the later part of the century, however, workhouse diets began to improve with greater knowledge of nutrition and softening attitudes towards the poor. After 1900 the food became more varied and the children's rations of meat and milk approached those recommended by the newly-published workhouse dietaries, though able-bodied adults still ate gruel for supper four times a week. Even so, the average cost of feeding a person in the workhouse for a week in 1878 was 3s 8d, a sum which cannot have been equalled in many poor families. In 1900 the revised diets increased the cost to 5s 7d a head, a sum well in excess of the rate calculated as a minimum for the urban poor by the social investigator Seebohm Rowntree. Women and children may often have fared better nutritionally in the workhouse than in low income families where the breadwinner took the lion's share of the limited amount of food.[4]

There was, nevertheless, a stigma associated with being in the workhouse. Inmates lived apart from the rest of the population, and were allowed out only with special permission. On such occasions they were easily recognised by their uniforms as paupers. Institutionalisation was intended as part of the deterrent to those who were not genuinely destitute, and it applied also to the workhouse children, who were educated in the workhouse school, and expected to have a proper understanding of their lowly station in life. Towards the end of the century, the general softening of attitudes led to some unease about institutionalising children and labelling them as paupers, and there was a gradual shift in policy towards boarding children out with families, where they could attend ordinary schools. By 1899 fifty-four children had been boarded out and two boys sent to the 'Training Ship Exmouth', the first workhouse children to be placed in training institutions. Others followed and in the early years of the twentieth century numbers of children were placed in training homes or charitable orphanages, where the union paid for their maintenance. By 1906 the workhouse school had been closed. Those children not boarded out in the early twentieth century for the most part stayed in the union only for short periods of time. Many of them belonged to a class called by the guardians the 'ins and outs', whose families lived a hand to mouth existence, having recourse to the workhouse when they were temporarily defeated by distress. It was said of these children that 'the workhouse is the best place they know, and they cry when they have to leave it'. Official policy from 1912, however, was that unions should remove all children other than the sick and infants from workhouses; at Maidstone Union this process was not completed until 1915. By then deterrence had largely ceased to be a factor in the treatment of the resident poor, and only vagrants and those travelling in search of work still faced a harsh regime when they took shelter in the workhouse.[5]

As already noted the Maidstone Trustees of the Poor continued to pay outdoor relief, with the recipients, according to a return of 1878, almost all either ill, infirm, or women with families to support. A number of orphans living with relatives received payments, clothing was given in a couple of cases and some funeral expenses were met. There were no unemployed recipients, but at the end of the century people with small or irregular earnings were being relieved. Recipients of payments included hawkers, agricultural casual workers, seamstresses and charwomen, a very similar group to those at the poorest margin of society who had sought and been given out-relief a century earlier. Typically, they received a small sum of money and a quantity of bread or flour each week. In the early 1890s the government instructed boards of guardians not to deny relief to people with small savings or receiving friendly society benefits, and the Maidstone guardians evidently complied with this. The rigid distinction between those labelled paupers and the rest of the working class was becoming blurred in Maidstone as elsewhere.

Throughout the nineteenth and early twentieth centuries the town's many charities enabled numbers of inhabitants to avoid recourse to the union. In the late nineteenth century there were thirty-eight almshouses belonging to different charities. Gill's, Wright's and Fisher's charities provided small annual sums to poor householders and widows, while Edmett's charity offered more substantial weekly sums to the elderly and infirm, and Cutbush's charity paid weekly pensions to poor women. Edmett's charity also supplied clothes, bedding, fuel, medical aid and food to the sick. Various charities provided for the distribution of bread, and these benefactions were administered collectively by the trustees of the poor.[6]

The unemployed and other needy also benefited from less formal charity. Widespread unemployment due to severe weather frequently led to the establishment of a subscription relief fund, as for instance in 1842, 1847, 1861 and 1864. During the hard winter of 1866–7 massive snowfalls and severe frost brought all outdoor work to a halt and at a public meeting called by the mayor, a subscription appeal was launched which attracted contributions from wealthy townspeople and employers, as well as those lucky enough to be still in work, such as the employees of Springfield Mill. It was a very positive community response far removed from the harsh principles which governed official relief under the Poor Law. The money was distributed by the churches, in the shape of tickets for bread, meat, groceries and coal, and within a week 1,800 families were assisted. A soup kitchen was instituted and a local doctor urged that a store of old clothing for distribution be set up. He reported 'whole families of little children . . . sleeping without the smallest particle of bed clothing'. The soup kitchen – opened in the town every winter between 1887 and 1914 – was maintained by donations, with handsome contributions from the town's MP and other local notables, but also many small sums from ordinary working people. It was used by the unemployed and many poor families struggling on low wages. Arrangements varied slightly from year to year, but in the 1890s tickets were usually sold for a penny, the majority being bought in books for distribution by charitable persons; by 1914 all tickets were being distributed free by the church volunteers. Another charitable endeavour during the 1890s was the Christmas dinner at the Corn Exchange for the town's poor children, again funded by public subscription with upwards of 600 children being entertained. Subsequently the event became a tea, known as the Robin Tea, with fund-raising organised by the *Kent Messenger*. Many children also received boots from the fund.[7]

Providing relief work for the unemployed became official policy in the late nineteenth century, thereby reinstating a type of local support abolished by the changes of 1834. Circulars in 1886 and 1893 issued by the Local Government Board encouraged local authorities to provide work for the unemployed, and Maidstone responded by organising winter work clearing snow and repairing roads. In the early months of 1895, during another exceptionally severe winter, about 50 men were employed in a quarry, 100 in laying out a recreation ground, and between 200–300 in clearing snow from the streets. Preference was given to married men with families. The provision was small-scale but Maidstone was said to be the only municipal authority in the area which had started relief work. The same year the urban district council set up a labour bureau, where the town unemployed could register for work. By the end of the year 86 men had registered, 71 of them labourers. The following decade saw unemployment increase both locally and nationally and in August 1908 the guardians of the poor asked the town council to set up a labour exchange and a distress committee under the provisions of the Unemployed Workmen Act of 1905; 1,180 men applied for work at the labour exchange during the first three months and 963 were registered; between December 1909 and February 1910 a further 1,136 men registered, most of whom were provided with relief work. Unemployment continued at a high level throughout 1910. During the two years January 1909–December 1910, only 391 of those registered were found work with private employers, 1,377 men were employed on public relief work in the town, while 1,162 were found temporary work as hop-pickers and 35 worked on the Christmas post. By then, however, unemployment and its relief were increasingly seen as concerns of central rather than local government, and in 1911 the labour exchange was taken over by the Board of Trade.

The introduction in 1908 of state old age pensions for those over the age of seventy had little immediate effect on the numbers of elderly being supported by the Union, as those who had at any time claimed poor relief were ineligible for a pension. In December 1909 the town council, which now acted as the local Old Age Pensions Committee, reported that during the first year 542 people had been granted pensions up to the full 5s, with 66 declared ineligible. The pension was not sufficient for maintenance, but helped those with a small income or other means of support to remain independent. One of the first recipients, was an eighty-year-old widow resident in one of the town's almshouses; on drawing her first pension she declared that she would 'no longer have to stint myself of light or firing'. Many of those drawing their pension for the first time were said to be so overcome with emotion that they were scarcely able to sign their names.[8]

The provision of elementary schools

In all British towns and cities the Victorian period was notable for a spate of school building testifying to the growing concern with educational provision. In Maidstone the main voluntary effort was directed towards providing day and Sunday schooling for working-class children. The Anglicans were particularly active, encouraged by the Canterbury Diocesan Board, and the town saw a number of new church day schools erected between the 1840s and 1870s. This expansion in school provision was doubtless an important factor in diminishing illiteracy levels in the population as a whole (measured by the numbers of those unable to sign the marriage registers). Along with other Kentish towns, Maidstone had lower levels of illiteracy than the national average (Kent as a whole was one of the least illiterate counties for brides and grooms). In 1856 only 28 per cent of grooms in Maidstone were still signing with a cross, and this was reduced to 15 per cent by 1871.[9]

The education census of 1851 listed thirty schools in Maidstone categorised as public day schools (with 3,603 pupils). They included eight schools founded by endowments – mainly the charity schools but also including the town grammar school, and the workhouse school. Nineteen day schools had been established by religious organisations with money raised from public subscriptions. Of these, only two were nonconformist schools – the British and Foreign Society school which celebrated its 30th anniversary in 1842, and the Wesleyan mixed day school, rehoused in new premises in 1858 to accommodate 272 pupils. A Catholic school (St Francis) was added in 1863. The remaining seventeen day schools were all Church of England schools, of which twelve were affiliated to the National Society. With a total of 2,652 children on the books, they had nearly three-quarters of those attending day schools. On the other hand, in 1851 the nonconformists had an equal share of the twenty Sunday schools and a larger number of pupils – 1,455 as against 932 in church Sunday schools. Most of the nonconformist denominations in the town had Sunday schools (Independents 4, Baptists 3, Wesleyans 2, and Unitarians 1).

There was also a proliferation of private schools for working-class children as well as for the commercial section of the population. In 1851 Maidstone had a total of 80 recognised private schools (as against the 29 private schools recorded in 1839), but they were mostly very small and with 1,764 pupils catered for only about a third of the town's school population. Indeed Maidstone had a relatively higher proportion of pupils in public day schools (67 per cent) than any other town in Kent.

Moreover, money continued to be raised by the Anglican community for new school building to meet the needs of growing districts; as parishes in the town were divided new schools were built. From the 1840s there was pressure for single sex schools and separate infant schools so that during the Victorian period most of the Anglican parishes in the town supported three or more national schools. Only St John's built in 1861 and the Barming Heath school opened in 1863 were mixed schools. All Saints built a new school with three distinct departments in 1866 but other parishes had separate schools. St Paul's day schools opened in 1859 with 330 children on the register just prior to the formation of St Paul's as a new parish separate from Holy Trinity. All Saints parish had expanded accommodation in its national school as early as 1839 and by 1873 was supporting seven schools – two for boys, two for girls, and three for infants. There was also new provision for girls and infants by St Philip's (1866) and St Faith's (1871).

The chief purpose of this surge of voluntary school building was to ensure religious and moral instruction for the children of the working classes. None the less the town had only limited provision of free schooling, mainly provided by the eighteenth-century charitable foundations. Of these Sir William Booth's charity and the Bluecoat school – an institution that 'always appeared to excite the interest and secure the approbation of parishioners' – were the most important. After the Bluecoat school moved to new premises (the old workhouse building) in 1843, it offered free schooling for around twenty selected children 'teaching them what may be useful in their manhood'. After leaving, the boys were said to obtain situations as clerks, shop assistants, and footpages, although the girls mostly went into service. During the mid-Victorian years demand was strong and applications exceeded the number of places.

All the church schools charged a weekly 1d or 2d fee prior to the 1870s. The tone of the school, the number of poor children on the roll and attendance levels tended to reflect the social composition of catchment areas. For example, the Padsole boys' and infants' schools which were run jointly by All Saints and St Philip's served a very poor neighbourhood. Average attendance was recorded at only 50 per cent in 1873 compared with up to 80 per cent in some other schools in the area. St Paul's was another parish that sought to bring some schooling to the poorest. St Paul's day schools had 330 children on the books in 1861 with an average attendance of 70 per cent. It also had three Sunday schools associated with it, one for girls, one for boys attending the day school, and a third for working boys – described in 1862 as apprentices and errand boys. This new parish also supported a ragged school and a dame school in Bedford Row [later James Street]. In 1858 a parochial report had drawn attention to the lack of schooling of children of parents in casual trades – described as the 'broomdasher and matseller class'. The problem was confirmed by a house to house visitation of the parish in 1860 which revealed that 'a certain number of children of the broomdasher class, or children of negligent parents, would be unfit or unwilling to attend National Schools'. The ragged and dame schools along with a mothers' meeting and adult classes and a reading room were all part of an attempt to influence the behaviour of the poorest by means of educational contact plus a measure of welfare provision. The ragged school was open three evenings a week and on Sundays, with thirty-three boys enrolled and six volunteer teachers from the Literary Institute and Adult Bible Class. A basin of soup or porridge was given to each boy every night. Originally housed in a rented room, the school was moved to new premises in 1862. It closed ten years later and the children transferred to day schools.

The role of Anglican parishes in promoting working-class literacy was not limited to day and Sunday schools. The growth of parochial library facilities for children and adults was another important service. Intended as a way of maintaining the moral influence of the Church, these libraries gradually extended their stock to offer a range of reading – St Michael's parochial library, for example, included books on history, topography, science, travel and adventure. St Paul's parochial library had over a thousand volumes when it opened in 1858 and 225 subscribers two years later. Books were given out at the reading room twice a week at 12.00 a.m. and on Saturday night at 7.00 p.m. This parish also boasted a separate Literary Institute and Reading Room with its own library of more than a thousand volumes. The library charged 1d a month – raised to 2d in 1863 because of the damage done to books by children. However, a free library was started in Bedford Row to provide books for home reading to 'chimney sweeps, inhabitants of lodging houses, and children attending the ragged school'. This library was supported by the parish 'as a counteraction to the pernicious cheap literature of the day.'

The importance of keeping in touch with older children who had left the elementary school was recognised by the provision of Youth Institutes from the 1860s which combined educational provision of an elementary kind with recreational opportunities, and these will be described in a later chapter. By the 1870s the Sunday schools were also catering for older children. At the Wesleyan Sunday school more than half the pupils in 1850 did not attend day schools, and by the 1870s, if not earlier, this school had nine classes graded according to age. An attendance register shows that most of the pupils at this school had parents who belonged to the skilled working class or trade categories or who were clerks. However, absentees often came from poorer backgrounds and there was a special class held for what were called refractory boys aged ten to thirteen. All the Sunday schools provided an elementary education, and some were organised on monitorial lines like the national schools. Their success in maintaining and expanding numbers, albeit with erratic attendance levels (rarely much above 50 per cent on average for those schools with published figures), was testimony to the way these schools, with their classes, treats and outings, became an accepted part of the life of the community in the Victorian period.

The strength of voluntary educational provision in day and Sunday schools in Maidstone meant that the Education Act of 1870, which was passed to 'fill the gaps' in voluntary provision with the building of school board schools, was redundant in Maidstone since the town always had more school places than pupils according to official criteria. During the passage of the 1870 Act and immediately afterwards the local Anglicans mounted a vigorous campaign to raise funds to improve voluntary provision. They were unable to prevent the Liberal-dominated town council passing an order to establish a school board, but through electoral manoeuvring the Anglican party won seven of the nine seats on the board and remained in effective control until it was abolished under the 1902 Education Act. As a result, in Maidstone the school board functioned only as an attendance committee to enforce compulsory education.

The slow down in population growth in the last decades of the century alleviated pressure on school provision, although two new schools were established in this period: St James' school in 1877 and St Peter's infant school in 1895. All the voluntary schools received grants from the government under the 1870 Act and were subject to inspection. The district inspector reported favourably in the 1870s and 1880s on the extent of school provision and the standard of accommodation. In a report in 1878 he wrote that the four principal schools in the town, all Anglican, had some of the best buildings in the district: 'I doubt, indeed whether there is another town of its size in England where the elementary schools are on the whole more exceptionally commodious and well built'.[10] In the longer term, however, the age and location of these schools created problems. The schools were situated either in the older parts of the town or, in the case of St Michael's (Barming Heath) and St Stephen's, close to the borough boundary before it was extended in 1934. For the most part the schools were located on roadside sites that were too small to permit modernisation, and as traffic grew in the twentieth century they became increasingly unsuitable.

Another problem was that the Maidstone schools seem to have had exceptional difficulty in securing regular attendance. A special factor was the length of the harvest and hop-picking holidays which meant that schools were virtually closed for the greater part of August, September and October. Low attendance affected other months too, and in the poorer districts especially, periodic bouts of infectious diseases – mainly scarlet fever and measles – disrupted schooling for weeks. Though quick to blame parents, few of the government inspectors seem to have recognised the financial burdens that schooling imposed on the poor, not only in finding school pence but also (as the Maidstone District Trades Council pointed out in 1911) in the continual pressure put on poor children to bring money for charitable collections. Yet the district inspector believed the problem of irregular attendance was one of attitude rather than money. The situation was made worse, he claimed, by the continued activities of private schools which 'aided the game of hide and seek between parents and children on the one hand and the school authorities on the other'. All of which may explain why the Maidstone School Board was especially vigorous in trying to enforce attendance. In its last year 664 summonses were taken out against parents involving 725 children of which 242 were successfully prosecuted.

If schooling was irregular, it was also short. Few ordinary townspeople in late Victorian Maidstone were able or willing to keep children at school longer than they were legally compelled to do. In 1898 out of a public school population of around

5,000, only 530 children were in standards 6 or 7, which offered a more advanced curriculum for twelve- to thirteen-year-olds. This was probably due in part to a lack of facilities. Despite the growth of state aid, the parochial authorities found that increasing expenditure on schooling was causing financial strain. After 1891 there were real difficulties in supplying free places and Maidstone was one of the last authorities in the county to abolish school fees. Well before then several schools had begun to increase fees to finance better facilities. But in the provision of advanced classes, Maidstone lagged behind towns with active school boards, although a centre for training selected children as teacher assistants (pupil teachers) was in operation by the 1890s. In general, the history of lower-class elementary education in Maidstone demonstrates the problems of the voluntary sector in developing educational opportunities for older pupils. By the close of the nineteenth century, the resources available were no longer equal to meeting the changing concept of elementary education and the higher standards of provision required by central government.

Middle-class schooling and adult education

In Maidstone, as elsewhere in Victorian Britain, educational institutions both reflected and reinforced the growing status and class divisions of urban society. The expansion of private classical and commercial schools was an important agency in this process, both marking out a separate sphere of middle-class education but also serving to differentiate between the social groups which comprised the middle class. As we saw in Chapter Five, in the early nineteenth century private classical schools had proliferated in Maidstone to cater for genteel wealth, but by 1871 the *South Eastern Gazette* was commenting on the lack of provision for middle-class schooling in the town, particularly for its wealthier inhabitants. It may be that competition from fashionable private classical or public schools in London, Canterbury and elsewhere in the county was creaming off many better-off pupils. The few schools of this type in the town by the late nineteenth century were quite small and boarding rather than day schools. The town grammar school had only 46 day scholars (along with 8 boarders) in 1868. In that year the Schools Inquiry Commission gave a very unfavourable account of the school on Earl Street, surrounded by factories. Though the school finally moved to a new Gothic style building on Tonbridge Road in 1871 and new scholarships were provided, progress remained slow, and at the end of the 1880s, there were still only 64 pupils, the majority of them boarders. However, the school began to expand rapidly after the appointment of the Rev. Watson in 1890 who set about modernising the curriculum and raising the school's status.

But for much of this period the most flourishing sector of private day school provision was aimed mainly at tradesmen, and was frankly vocational in purpose. Earlier experiments with schools combining the classical and the commercial seem to have been shortlived and later schools were simply described as commercial or modern schools. There was also a group of schools offering a private education for middle-class girls. In the 1860s these included several very small genteel establishments – one-teacher schools – in Albion and Marsham Place, occupying private houses adapted to the purpose. One also finds some larger establishments taking boarders as well as day girls. Of these the most successful was the Ladies Boarding and Day School in County Place, whose headmistress until 1848 had formerly run a commercial and classical seminary in Upper Church Street. In 1867 a new girls' school with a preparatory section was opened which subsequently became known as Miss Leaver's High School for Girls. However, the most important development in this sector was not the product of market forces but of a decision by the Charity Commissioners to enable surplus funds from the Rochester Bridge charity to be used for the establishment of a grammar school for girls in 1884. The school was built in Albion Place for £4,500.

For much of this period the voluntary sector also played a key part in supplementing middle- and working-class school education through the provision of classes for adults, thereby helping to compensate for the lack of publicly funded support for post-elementary (advanced) classes for children. Victorian Maidstone had a legacy of early nineteenth-century cultural institutions including the Literary and Mechanics institutes (amalgamated in 1852), and these offered broadly educational lectures for mainly middle-class audiences. From the 1860s more regular but basic night classes for adults were organised by some of the churches, but the most important of the Anglican initiatives in this regard was the educational work of the Maidstone Church Institute (founded in 1854). By the 1880s this was offering a range of classes in modern subjects: French, science subjects, and commerce. In addition, the Institute was a centre for University extension lectures and in 1895 the Institute's Hollingworth Hall was placed at the disposal of the University Extension movement. This main Church Institute was essentially a middle-class body, but, as we shall see in Chapter Eight, other institutes and improvement societies catered for those lower down the social scale.

Technical and art education owed its beginnings in Maidstone to the Anglican church as well. Canon Henry Collins, Vicar of St Luke's Church, helped found the School of Art in 1867 which subsequently took advantage of government subsidies to diversify its courses. Private benefaction and voluntary contributions also supported the Howard de Walden Institute for cookery, opened in Marsham Street in 1891. Thus various elements in an emergent system of adult education were in place by the 1880s, by when the initiative in further educational provision was passing from the Anglican Church and local philanthropists to the town council.

The expanding role of local government in the late Victorian and Edwardian era

From the mid-nineteenth century a series of Acts of Parliament enabled and encouraged town councils to provide new recreational and educational amenities and services of various kinds. These legislative opportunities were eventually taken up with more or less enthusiasm by most town councils, so that by the 1880s we see the development of a more dynamic municipal regime. The first of these measures was concerned to counteract the loss of public recreational facilities caused by large-scale urban development. The provision of parks and allotments was inspired by a belief common from the mid-Victorian period that councillors, as well as philanthropists, should be concerned with the moral health of townspeople, not just their physical health. The provision of a town museum and library was intended to go further in encouraging a rational use of leisure and as such the council was careful to regulate the way in which facilities were used. Some projects originated in the private benefactions of leading townspeople, but others were started after consultation with the ratepayers at a public meeting, and supported by public funds. Education was another key area of growing municipal intervention, though after 1889 responsibility in the town was increasingly shared with the county council.

Parks and allotments

In the 1860s Maidstone's relatively small size meant that open space for recreation could easily be reached on foot, even though much land had been enclosed early in the century. Rapid expansion in the later decades of the nineteenth century created a more densely packed urban environment, as the Fair Meadow was lost to the baths and to hard surfacing for the market, and small areas of open land were built over. Space for recreation became less easy to reach, especially for children, while demand for proper playing areas with level surfaces increased as modern forms of football and other sports became popular. The town's cricket club secured the use of the Mote park after 1857, but other sports clubs were less fortunate. The demand for recreational space, and a nationwide movement towards the provision of public parks and gardens influenced both Maidstone's benefactors and the town council, and together they responded to the public need.

Maidstone's first public park was the Brenchley gardens, adjoining Chillington House, laid out and given to the town by Julius Brenchley, a member of a local brewing family, at the same time as his benefaction to the museum in 1870. The gardens of the Archbishop's Palace were also opened to the public after the Palace was bought for the town by subscription, in commemoration of Queen Victoria's Golden Jubilee in 1887. Both gardens were managed by the council, and in the early years of the twentieth century they arranged for brass bands to play there during the summer months. The need for sports grounds was first addressed by the council in 1878, after receiving requests from the town's working men's club and other organisations that part of Penenden Heath, which had long been used informally as a public open space, should be made into a formal recreation ground for the town. Lord Romney sold the council the necessary land, which was fenced and laid out as sports pitches. Further facilities for the playing of sport were provided on four acres of land on Barming Heath which was cleared, levelled and laid out as a recreation ground in 1883–5, with the help of public subscription. Another example of private and municipal co-operation was the Cornwallis playground opened a decade later.

Named in honour of the town's MP, the land on Tonbridge Road was given to the town by Herbert Monckton, the town clerk, because 'the want of free playgrounds within the borough and near to those requiring them is more and more apparent every day, as many desirable spots are built over, leaving the street as the only available place where children can congregate after school, unless they go to distant grounds outside the town.' The acre-and-a-half of land was levelled and planted by the town's unemployed. In 1897, the urban district council rented land from the London Chatham and Dover Railway for two playgrounds and in 1913 a further playground was provided in Stone Street. The council also hired out the Lock Meadow in the early 1890s for more formal sports and athletics meetings, but after 1896 this function was largely taken over by the private athletic grounds on a ten acre site on London Road.

Another pressing demand for land within the borough was for allotments. By the 1880s a number were provided on Barming Heath and on land rented from the council in Scrubbs Lane by the trustees of the poor. Non-payment of rent became a problem, indicative perhaps of the way allotments were used to encourage self-help among the very poor. An Act of Parliament in 1887 made it a duty of sanitary authorities to rent or purchase land for allotments if representations were made by six ratepayers. The following year seventy allotments were let on council land at Rocky Hill, and on land rented from Lord Romney on Hastings Road. Additional land was subsequently acquired, and by 1912, the council had allotments at nine locations in and around the town.[11]

Museum and library

The development of new civic institutions marked another step forward for the council. The earliest of these derived from the Museums and Libraries acts, passed in 1845 and 1850, which permitted such institutions to be rate financed. In 1853 the Maidstone physician Dr Plomley offered his collection of stuffed birds to the town, as the nucleus of a museum collection, but a public meeting voted against adopting the legislation and setting up a museum. Two years later, however, when Thomas Charles of Chillington House bequeathed his library and collection of art and antiquities to the town, another public meeting voted, almost unanimously, to implement the Acts. The mayor justified municipal expenditure on the museum by declaring that it would be 'a means of uniting together the man of letters and the man of business – the artisan as well as the employer – in one great effort for the intellectual improvement and instruction of the whole community.' Our town, he added, claims 'to be the great emporium of business in Kent, let us make it also the headquarters of science and art and all other intellectual attainments.'

The museum at Chillington Manor opened to the public in January 1858. Although the museum was rate supported, the rapid growth of the collections mainly derived from the donations of local gentlemen. Further accommodation was soon required, and the two wings of the house were added in 1868 and 1870, with the help of local benefactors – Julius Brenchley, Alexander Randall, the councillor, and Samuel Mercer, a local banker. Brenchley gave his collection of artefacts at the same time, and his art collection passed to the museum on his death in 1873. That year the Tudor south wing of East Farleigh Court Lodge was rebuilt adjacent to the museum, and in 1889–90 a four-room extension was erected at the expense of Samuel Bentliff, a Maidstone leather merchant. It is clear that the museum was a great focus for civic pride. It was also very popular with the public who visited it in large numbers. An experiment with Sunday opening in 1878 proved highly successful, and, despite petitions against it from clergymen, Sunday school teachers and others, the council decided that the museum should remain open.

The library attracted much less interest from the town's worthies, and developed comparatively slowly. A reading room was opened in 1858, at the same time as the museum, and in 1867, under the terms of Randall's bequest, this was moved to the east wing of the museum, where books and periodicals were available for reference. In the 1870s there were about 8,000 books, including those of the old parochial library. A bequest from the Brenchley Trustees in 1890 was used to establish a borough lending library, initially with 1,500 volumes, of which 400 were fiction and 'light literature'. Books were not on open access but had to be selected from a purchased catalogue, while borrowers needed to be ratepayers or to be guaranteed by ratepayers – in 1893 they numbered only 687. The head curator lamented that 'the general public of Maidstone do not use the library more', but it was evidently a fairly exclusive club. In 1897, it was thought 'not fitting to the requirements of a county town' and in honour of Queen Victoria's diamond jubilee, the Victoria Free Library was erected adjacent to the museum. Public subscriptions again financed part of the building, but this time much of the cost was met by the council. Thus by the end of the century, Maidstone had a public library which it considered worthy of the town, comprising a reference collection, lending library and newsroom; a juvenile library was added in 1906. As in virtually all libraries, borrowers preferred to read fiction, and between 1901 and 1908 this accounted for around 78 per cent of all books borrowed. The curator criticised this 'mental dissipation at the expense of the ratepayer', and decided to curb the purchases of works of fiction, but this had little effect on public taste. He also deplored the use of the newsroom by the unemployed, who, he thought, used it as 'a place of idle resort', when they should have been seeking work. Numbers using the newsroom almost doubled between 1901 and 1908, over two thirds visiting during the daytime. It was clearly a vital social resource for those with time on their hands and little money in their pockets.

The municipality and education

The most notable example of the new spirit of municipal enterprise, in the eyes of many local councillors, was the founding of the Technical Institute, an educational establishment that in many late Victorian industrial towns and cities symbolised local aspirations to develop a modern educational service. National legislation in 1889 and 1890 enabled borough and county councils to become involved in technical education and Maidstone council (in conjunction with Kent County Council) used this measure both to support existing institutions and to acquire its own municipal technical school. Initially the council agreed to support the privately run Maidstone School of Science and Art; but in 1891 they approached the County Council for a share of the funds available under the 1890 Act in order to build a technical school close to the museum. The new municipal school, erected at a cost of £11,000 and opened in 1894, enrolled about 500 students in the first year. Thereafter modest growth came from diversifying courses, adding to the range of science and art classes with languages and women's subjects – shorthand and typing, scientific dressmaking and a cookery school. Prior to the late 1890s the council had also supported the Howard de Walden Institute with financial aid for cookery classes for girls recruited from the public elementary schools, but after various disputes support was withdrawn in 1901.

The council also clashed with the Charity Commissioners in the 1890s over the new scheme for the eighteenth-century Bluecoat school made necessary by a decline in pupil numbers. The new scheme sought to establish a school of science for boys to give a 'useful and practical education at a cheap rate and of a more extended character than that previously given in the National schools'. Part of the endowment was to be used to promote the education of girls either through exhibitions or, in a later proposal, by the provision of evening continuation classes. However, the scheme was strongly opposed by the borough council who wanted all the money from the endowment to be used for providing exhibitions and scholarships to the grammar schools and the municipal technical school.[12] Although the boys' grammar school was administered by the Charity Commissioners by the 1880s and council members were a minority of the governing body, the council maintained a grammar school committee and provided small grants to the boys' and girls' schools in the 1890s to help them appoint specialist staff. It seemed sensible therefore to use the funds of the Bluecoat school to improve the flow of elementary pupils going to the grammar schools. But this plan was thwarted by the conversion of the Bluecoat school into the Woodward school, a secondary school for boys, in 1903.

Ironically, by the Education Act of 1902, the council lost control over the educational institutions which it had done most to support in the later nineteenth century. As a non-county borough Maidstone became a Part III authority with responsibility for elementary education alone. Education in Maidstone was divided between two elected bodies, the borough council and the Kent County Council with the latter now responsible for the grammar schools and technical institute. On the other hand, the new status of the borough as an education authority offered a belated opportunity for leading nonconformists in the town to influence educational policy at the elementary level, through representation on the new education committee. This committee soon gave a vigorous lead to educational development in the town at the elementary level. This was largely due to the partnership which

*The public baths and wash-houses, built on the Fair Meadow in 1851.
Photograph: Maidstone Museum.*

The West Kent Hospital, Marsham Street, built in 1832, and extensively altered in 1862.
Photograph: Maidstone Museum.

Medical staff and young patients in a temporary hospital during the typhoid epidemic, 1897.
Photograph: Maidstone Museum.

The Bluecoat school and pupils, Knightrider Street.
Photograph: Maidstone Museum.

New · Mission · Room · for · the · Parish · of · St Paul · Maidstone ·

The new mission room, subsequently St Luke's school, built in St Paul's parish, 1887.
Photograph: Maidstone Museum.

The boys' grammar school, Tonbridge Road, built in 1871.
Photograph: Maidstone Museum.

Tonbridge Road council school. One of the town's first council schools, opened in the early 1900s.
Photograph: Kent Messenger Group Newspapers.

*Laying the foundation stone of the Technical Institute, opened in 1894.
Photograph: Kent Messenger Group Newspapers.*

The Loose tram at the terminus.
Photograph: Kent Messenger Group Newspapers.

developed between councillors Day and Laurence, two prominent nonconformist businessmen, both strongly committed to educational progress, and the new superintendent of schools, E.W. Abbott, a former headmaster and product of Westminster Training College.

One of the first priorities of the education committee was to phase out the pupil teachers in schools and to increase teaching staff. The number of fee-paying schools was reduced to two and an incentive scheme introduced to improve school attendance which succeeded in raising average attendance levels to 90 per cent by 1906. A special effort was made to promote music in the curriculum and in the 1890s Maidstone had a flourishing schools orchestra.[13] However, the task of modernising schools proved more difficult and controversial, because of the expense of building new schools and the need to close some old ones to defray part of the cost. Although the total supply of school places still exceeded numbers on roll, schools near the borough boundaries were under pressure from rising numbers since they attracted children who lived outside the borough. New schools, Abbott argued, needed to be larger and more economical of staff and with better facilities. Hence Tonbridge Road and Union Street, the earliest of the council schools, were much larger than the old church schools, with Tonbridge Road having 540 pupils compared to the 296 at Heath Road which it replaced. The improvement of school accommodation and the requirements of the government elementary school codes of 1904 and 1907, enabled Abbott to deflect criticism and to blame rising expenditure on the Board of Education in London. Another factor promoting school improvement was the criticism of Maidstone schools in the reports of a new, more zealous government inspector. It was not only the Church of England schools that were censured. In 1908 the Wesleyan day school was threatened with censure as an 'inefficient' school and despite the protestations of the school managers, the school was finally closed in 1910. Defenders of the school claimed that the Board of Education was in collusion with the borough education committee, given council plans to build a new public elementary school for 1,000 children in Union Street.

The churches in Maidstone were proud of their schools, and Abbott was careful to recognise their contribution, but the legacy of outmoded school buildings was a constraint on the ambitions of the education committee to develop more advanced school provision, while a scheme to develop junior technical classes in the technical school was frustrated by the Board of Education in London. However, the committee were able to institute other measures, underlining the growing role and importance of the local education committees prior to 1914. Thus they set up a careers advice and juvenile employment bureau and an advisory care committee. Thanks to Councillor Laurence, a great advocate of medical provision, a school medical service was started in 1901, a year ahead of national legislation. In the period up to 1914 the borough education committee succeeded in keeping Maidstone abreast of other towns in the field of elementary schooling, but plans to extend educational opportunities for working-class children were not implemented until after the First World War.[14]

Municipal enterprise: electricity and trams

In the country as a whole there was a surge of activity in the capital expenditure of local authorities around the turn of the twentieth century not only because of the building of schools and libraries, but also because of the municipalisation of new public utilities. Not all municipal authorities were affected to the same extent. Earlier in the nineteenth century, as we have seen, Maidstone council had allowed gas and water to be supplied by private companies but developments in the supply of electricity from the later nineteenth century offered new opportunities for intervention. The question of an electricity supply to Maidstone first arose in 1882, when the Local Board considered applying to the government for authority to build an electricity works. Before a decision was made, various private companies applied for parliamentary authority to do the same, but in the event nothing was done. When in 1892 the council finally sought and obtained approval for a works it was still undecided how best to act and spent several years in consulting electrical engineers and approaching commercial companies. It was not until 1899 that the Urban District Council decided to carry out the work themselves. The works were designed by the borough surveyor and the consulting electrical engineer was W.A. Stevens, later of Tilling-Stevens. Built on the Fair Meadow, adjacent to the baths, to have the benefit of a riverside wharf for coal supplies, the works opened in 1901, and generating capacity increased steadily, to meet growing demand from industry and domestic consumers. Output increased from something over 300,000 units in 1902 to over 3,000,000 units in 1914, even though gas lighting still remained widespread in the town.

While the electricity works was in course of construction, the council decided to apply for authority to run electric trams in the borough. Horse-drawn trams had been considered some twenty years earlier, but a public meeting had concluded that trams were not necessary in a town the size of Maidstone, and the council decided not to proceed. By 1900, the steady outward spread of the town, and the fact that 'houses are badly needed for artisans on the outskirts of the borough', made a tram service desirable.[15] By then there was ample evidence that trams in other boroughs ran profitably. The council applied to London for authority to proceed with the undertaking, but this was at first refused, and it was not until 1903 that permission was granted for a single line as far as the borough boundary on the Barming Road. The line, which was powered by the borough electricity works, opened the following year, and proved a considerable success. Further lines, to Loose and Tovil, were inaugurated in 1907 and 1909, but a proposed line to Penenden Heath was shelved, and the network was not extended further. In 1912 plans were drawn up for a motor bus service for areas not served by trams, but these ideas were abandoned, and Maidstone did not acquire a bus service until after the First World War. Nevertheless, the municipal tramway system of the Edwardian period was a notable undertaking, and in 1913–14 Maidstone was one of 409 local authorities with municipal tramways, as against the 877 tramways operated by the private sector.

Moreover both electricity works and tramway operations appear to have been profitable trading concerns.

The municipal history of Maidstone illustrates the *ad hoc* way that councils in medium-sized county towns acquired new responsibilities in the nineteenth century. In this community late-Victorian pride in municipal achievement was relatively low key, compared with some of the larger cities in the country, but there is evidence of a growing sense of civic ambition as manifested in the work of new committees, particularly in the educational field. The expansion in the role of local government came about partly because of the limited ability of the voluntary and private sector, so important earlier, to deal with the increasingly complex and large-scale urban problems of the late Victorian period; but also because corporate life began to acquire an administrative momentum of its own. It was carried along by a small group of long-serving councillors with increasingly clear perceptions of the public good, working closely with a core of energetic and professional town officers. As the next chapter shows, Maidstone council was not strongly politicised, nor was it subject to the political demands for a progressive municipal programme that occurred in county towns such as Northampton with its influential radical traditions. Yet Maidstone's municipal record was not very different from that of more politically 'advanced' towns and its decision to undertake the management of some public utilities provides an example of municipal capitalism and civic policy unfettered by doctrinaire considerations. By the start of the twentieth century, there can be no doubt the growing municipal provision of public services was an important force in shaping a new sense of urban consciousness in the community.

Notes

1. *Maidstone Gazette*, 8 March 1836.
2. There is a more detailed account in a cholera file in Maidstone Reference Library (MAI 614.69). See also *Parliamentary Papers*, 1850, XXI, *Epidemic Cholera. Report of the General Board of Health*, Appendix B.
3. Minutes of the Trustees of the Poor, Centre for Kentish Studies [Kent Archives Office], P241/8/8; Expenditure of Maidstone Union, P241/19/17; Maidstone Union Accounts (Maidstone Reference Library, MAI 362.5); Maidstone Union Letters, box 2, (Maidstone Reference Library); Maidstone Local Board minutes, Centre for Kentish Studies, Md/ACm6/1.
4. *Parliamentary Papers*, 1872, LI, *Return of Industrial Employment of Indoor Paupers*; M.A. Crowther, *The Workhouse System* (London, 1983), p. 217; Maidstone Union Accounts, 1901 (Maidstone Reference Library, MAI 362.5); Rowntree's figures quoted in E.J. Hobsbawm, *Industry and Empire* (London, 1969), p. 161.
5. Children in the Workhouse Committee, Centre for Kentish Studies, G/Ma/AZ14; *Kent Messenger*, 17 February 1906.
6. Minutes of Trustees of the Poor, Centre for Kentish Studies, P241/8/8; Maidstone Charity Accounts, 1853–69, P241/25/13.
7. *Maidstone Journal*, 21 January 1867, 28 January 1867, 12 January 1892; *Kent Times*, 7 January 1892; *Kent Messenger*, 11 January 1902, 7 January 1905, 3 January 1914, 17 January 1914; *Parliamentary Papers*, 1895, VIII, *Second Report of Select Committee on Distress from Want of Employment*, Appendices 4, 5.
8. Centre for Kentish Studies, Maidstone Borough Council Minutes, Md/ACm3/11–14; *Kent Messenger*, 2 January 1909.
9. Literacy and illiteracy rates for Kentish towns and registration districts at various dates are noted in W.B. Stephens, *Education, Literacy and Society 1830–1870: The Geography of Diversity* (Manchester, 1987).

10. *Parliamentary Papers*, 1878–9 [C-2342-1] *Committee of Council on Education. Report on Mid Kent and Maidstone District by Mr Carrington Ley*, pp. 614–28.
11. Centre for Kentish Studies: Borough Council Minutes, Md/ACm3/4,15; Urban District Council Minutes, Md/ACm6/6; *Maidstone Journal*, 2 April 1892; *Parliamentary Papers*: 1898, LXXVIII, and 1903, LIX, *Returns of numbers of allotments*.
12. Centre for Kentish Studies, Council Minutes Md/ACm3. Details of the Charity Commissioner's reorganisation scheme are available at Centre for Kentish Studies [CH52].
13. D. Russell, *Popular Music in England, 1840–1914. A Social History* (Manchester, 1987), p. 47.
14. For a fuller account and an assessment of the work of the education committee see the thesis of K. V.C.Williams, 'Elementary Education in Maidstone 1903–1932' (unpublished MA thesis, University of London, 1978).
15. Centre for Kentish Studies, Council Minutes, Md/ACm3/4, 6; Urban District Council Minutes, Md/ACm6/5–8; *Souvenir of the Opening of the Electricity Works, 1901* (Maidstone Reference Library MAI 621.31); A.S.Lamprey, ed., *A Guide to the Borough of Maidstone* (Maidstone, 1914), p. 69.

Bibliographical Note

As in Chapter Six, extensive use has been made of the local newspaper press, and the minutes of Maidstone Borough Council (Md/ACm3) and the Urban District Council (Md/ACm6) at the Centre for Kentish Studies [Kent Archives Office]. These minutes contain summary reports of the various committees.

The main sources for information on public health are the Annual Reports of the Borough Medical Officer of Health at the Centre for Kentish Studies (Md/ HM A2); also see material in Md/ HM and HP. Maidstone Reference Library holds a file of materials relating to the 1897 typhoid epidemic, MAI 614.49T, and there is further information in appendix B of a *Report of the General Board of Health on Epidemic Cholera* in the *Parliamentary Papers*, 1850, XXI. John Whichcord's views on public health are in his pamphlet *Observations on the Sanitary Condition of Maidstone with a view to the introduction of an Act for promoting Public Health*, (1849). There is also useful information in articles by Irene Hales in *Bygone Kent*, vol. 4, pp. 639–46 on 'Maidstone's water supply', and in the same journal, vol. 5, pp. 217–23, on 'Maidstone's typhoid epidemic'. For poor relief the most important documentation is in Centre for Kentish Studies, P241; Maidstone Reference Library has published Poor Law accounts, and a box of correspondence at MAI 362. For the police see *Parliamentary Papers*, 1870, XXXVI, and annually thereafter, for reports of Inspectors of Constabulary. The Centre for Kentish Studies also holds material at Md/Ca3.

For education in the town, the Centre for Kentish Studies has much important material in the Maidstone parochial records (P241), including an extensive collection of school log books. Also deposited there are the minutes of the grammar school governors and of the Wesleyan day school, and a single surviving annual report from the School Board. For published accounts of the grammar school in this period see F. Streatfield *An Account of the Grammar School in the Kings Town and Parish of Maidstone* (Oxford, 1915) and H.J. Cope, *Maidstone Grammar School, 1549–1949. A Record* (Maidstone, 1949). See also K.V.C. Williams, 'Elementary Education in Maidstone 1903–1932' (unpublished MA thesis, University of London, 1978).

Chapter Eight

THE VICTORIAN AND EDWARDIAN TOWN: POLITICS, RELIGION AND CULTURAL LIFE

In Victorian England the public life of towns and cities was largely dominated by the ambitions and attitudes of the urban bourgeoisie. The Reform Act of 1832 gave them a voice in national politics, while the Municipal Corporations Act of 1835 consolidated the role of bourgeois elites in the political life of incorporated towns. As with many aspects of nineteenth-century urban life, however, there were variations between towns and cities with regard to the composition of the urban middle class and its social and political views and influence. The industrial towns and cities of the North and Midlands were the forcing ground for the formation of a clearly defined and politically assertive middle class in the nineteenth century as well as being the strongholds of nonconformity and liberalism. In contrast, there were many smaller country towns still embedded in the political and social structures of rural England, with a relatively small and fragmented middle class characterised by deferential attitudes towards the landed gentry and aristocracy. Occupying the middle ground between these two models of urban society were county towns such as Maidstone, where the formation of a strong middle-class presence was shaped by the persistence of traditional elements in the town's political and social life, as reflected in the continuing strength of Conservative politics and the influence of the Church of England, despite the growth of nonconformity in the late eighteenth and early nineteenth centuries.

In Victorian Maidstone party and sectarian loyalties served to structure and integrate middle-class activities. The ethos of a broadly based and expanding middle class, led by a local elite recruited from both traditional and new rising economic groups, permeated the religious, political and cultural life of the town. Middle-class people with a variety of church loyalties financed and organised the activities of a growing multitude of associated religious organisations, and in this and other ways, they succeeded in promoting a vibrant and diversified associational life in the nineteenth-century community. Such a world incorporated growing numbers of respectable artisan and skilled mill and factory workers and their families who also maintained links and loyalties to their own more popular associations. At the same time, the rise of incomes and greater availability of leisure in the later nineteenth and early twentieth centuries began to create a wide range of new opportunities for working-class families in sport and entertainment, while, in the political arena, organised labour started to challenge the political hegemony of the middle class at the local level. These themes and issues are the main concern of this chapter.

Politics

Nineteenth-century Maidstone was a very complex town politically, and it is difficult to establish precisely the inter-relationships between class, sect and party in voting patterns. The old reformist Whigs, now called the Liberals, seem to have had a relatively small following among the members of the town elite, and their main body of support was probably drawn from nonconformist tradesmen and some of the skilled workers. The Liberals had the first working-class councillor in the town in 1880 – John Potter of the Original Society of Papermakers. Conservatism, on the other hand, owed much of its strength and support to the wealthiest members of the town elite and to its connections with the Anglican church, although towards the end of the nineteenth century Anglican temperance interests gave some support to the Liberal cause. Despite the general lack of elite support, the Liberals were a considerable force in town politics. They succeeded in controlling the council in 1835–7 and 1858–73, and they held the parliamentary seats between 1852 and 1857, 1859 and 1880, and 1900 and 1906. But this Liberal ascendancy of the mid-Victorian years has to be set against the strong resilience of the Conservative interest in the town which eventually came to dominate.

After municipal reform in 1835 all ratepayers were entitled to vote for the town council and the borough was divided into four and later six wards for electoral purposes. The Tory *Maidstone Journal* predicted that scenes of 'riot and turbulence, animosity and ill-feeling' such as had distinguished Maidstone elections in the past, would become annual occurrences, and the first few elections were hard fought, with 'animosity and ill-feeling', if not rioting, much in evidence. There was an initial Liberal landslide with the election of twelve Liberal and six Tory councillors, who went on to elect a Liberal mayor and six Liberal aldermen. But this predominance was short-lived, and in 1837 the Tories regained control, retaining it for the next twenty years. Liberal support reached its lowest point in 1853, when the party held only two of the twenty-four seats, although it soon began to revive, and, as we have noted, the Liberals held control for fifteen years from 1858; thereafter the balance again shifted towards the Conservatives. By the mid-Victorian years municipal politics were more subdued and sober compared with the faction-ridden corporation politicking of the 1810s and 1820s. Many prospective councillors were returned unopposed, and elections became relatively infrequent. Municipal politics became more contentious again with the short-lived upturn in the Liberals' prospects after the turn of the century.

As we saw in Chapter Five, parliamentary reform in 1832 had only a limited effect on parliamentary elections and representation in Maidstone. More crucial for opening up the parliamentary electorate was the second Reform Act in 1867, which gave the vote to all male householders and certain categories of lodgers and almost doubled the number of voters in Maidstone to 3,420, or approximately one in two townsmen. The Reform Act of 1884 affected county rather than borough constituencies, and the proportion of the male population entitled to vote at Maidstone's first single member election in 1885 was virtually unaltered from that in 1867. There was no further extension of the franchise until 1918, although the percentage of men registered to vote increased to approximately 60 per cent by 1910, a figure in line with that for the country as a whole. Surprisingly, however, this growth in the size of the electorate did not fundamentally alter the party complexion of the town.

Although party contest died down in local elections, parliamentary elections continued to be hard fought with allegations of bribery and corruption recurrent throughout the entire period. According to critics, the Conservative party's electoral success depended heavily on corruption, including the bribing of electors. Not only poor freemen were susceptible to *douceurs* as in the past. In the view of the Liberal MP Robarts in 1835 the reformed electorate was in this respect 'if possible worse than the old'.[1] Corrupt practices ensured one of the seats went Conservative in 1835, and two years later the young Benjamin Disraeli incurred such heavy debts in fighting and winning a seat that at the next election he was forced to find a cheaper parliamentary berth elsewhere. In 1838, following a by-election contest, charges of corruption against the victorious Conservative candidate led to the result being overturned.

Local Liberals attempted to put corruption behind them. In 1835 they formed the Maidstone Society for the Promotion of Purity of Election, which had as its aims the eradication of bribery and coercion, the election of candidates pledged to oppose such activities, and the unseating of any member returned by illegal means.[2] Liberals seem to have refrained from abuses at the 1835 election, when they held one seat, and (so far as one can judge) in other elections before 1859. Their policy was motivated not just by altruism: the Liberal party had difficulty enough finding candidates with deep enough pockets to afford legitimate election campaigns, even less corrupt ones, a situation that may have contributed to the decline of the Liberal cause in the town during the late 1830s and 1840s.

The Liberal *Maidstone Gazette* published a catalogue of complaints about Conservative electoral practices. In 1838 it reported how Conservatives had refused to trade with those voting against them. It also printed a lengthy analysis of elections in the town since the granting of the charter of 1747, and estimated the total cost of those elections at £146,000; despite all this expenditure the two parties had ended up sharing the town's representation more or less equally. This showed, the newspaper claimed, that neither party could expect to hold Maidstone permanently and that:

after fighting and quarrelling for ninety years with a forty-Kilkenny-cat power of party feeling; after ruining each other in trade; after incurring a degree of odium which few other boroughs can equal; each party has secured in the aggregate, no more than its fair share of representation, and that fair share being precisely what they might have secured, had they understood each other, without the illegal expenditure of a single farthing, or a single act of coercion, or a single expression of ill-will.[3]

However, this appeal for the sharing of the constituency fell on deaf ears, and the 1841 election was again contested, unsuccessfully, by the Liberals. Although roughly a third of the electorate voted for the Liberal candidate without financial reward, a hundred Liberals apparently did not bother to vote, believing they could not win against concerted Conservative corruption. In 1847 the Conservative candidates, G. Dodd and A.J.B. Hope, were returned unopposed, and subsequently numerous supporters received anonymous New Year's gifts of £5 in the post. In response, the Liberals turned their attention to parliamentary reform, trusting in an extension of the electorate as the best tactic for combatting Conservative political fraud.

There had long been a radical group within Maidstone's Liberal party, and a West Kent Reform Association was established in the town in early 1838. But radical activity was fairly limited in the town in the decade or so after the first Reform Act. In 1848, however, Chartists turned up in force at a public meeting called by the Liberals to discuss the question of further parliamentary reform. The meeting declined to support the six far-reaching reforms of the Chartist movement, and gave its support to a resolution in favour of householder suffrage and triennial parliaments, rather than the universal male suffrage and annual parliaments of the Chartists. But a number of Chartists spoke, and they agreed that the resolution in favour of reform, although falling short of radical demands, was worthy of positive support. One speaker, who was met with both cheers and laughter from the audience, saw the proposed reform as a step towards a general enfranchisement which would eventually include women and educated eighteen-year-olds. The Rev. Dobney, the well known nonconformist minister active in promoting social causes in the town, declared himself a Chartist and called on the middle classes to reconsider their opposition to the extension of the franchise to all men. Despite, or perhaps because of, the revolutionary climate which was gripping Europe in 1848, all the speakers stressed their belief in the importance of using moral rather than physical force in the pursuit of their demands. The reformist resolution passed by the meeting was published in the press, and circulated to reform societies in other towns.[4] Maidstone seems to have lacked the class antagonism of the kind that occurred in some of the northern factory towns and there is no evidence that the 1840s were a crisis decade in social relations.

After 1848 Chartism faded away and the Maidstone Liberals ceased to put their faith in parliamentary reform, which disappeared from the immediate political agenda. A move to share the constituency at the 1852 election was frustrated by a faction within the Liberal party, who put up their own candidate at the hustings (and subsequent by-election), an episode which ended any prospect of future electoral pacts. At the next election both seats were retaken by the Conservatives, after the rejection of a petition alleging corruption. Thereafter the Liberals reverted to the use of bribery. They took both seats at the 1859 election, weathering a petition against them alleging corruption, and held the constituency for twenty years. The extension of the franchise in 1867 did nothing to alter the pattern of voting, and the two Liberals, W. Lee and the local man James Whatman, were elected in both 1865 and 1868. After 1870 Sir John Lubbock (whose Act led to the introduction of bank holidays in 1871) held one of the seats for the party, but the Liberals' marginal lead over their opponents was lost in 1880, when, to apparent surprise on all sides, the Conservatives recovered both seats. The constituency was reduced to one member at the 1885 election, following the redistribution of seats, and this was held by the Conservatives until the end of the century.

Electoral corruption was by no means confined to Maidstone. In 1873 Parliament replaced the open system of voting with a secret ballot and in 1883 the Corrupt Practices Act curtailed the amount of money which could be spent on elections, but bribery persisted. In 1900 the Liberal who won the seat from the Conservatives was found guilty of wholesale bribery, the election was declared void, and he was barred from standing for Maidstone for seven years. There were further allegations of bribery against the successful Conservative candidate at the 1906 election though this time they were rejected. In October 1910 when the local Conservative Association discussed its preparations for the second election that year, it referred to 'the necessity of avoiding anything in the nature of corrupt practices', implying that their use was not altogether a dead issue.[5]

Corruption was not the only or necessarily the most effective means of obtaining political allegiance, particularly later in the century when there was a secret ballot. Both party organisations were active, and the Conservative victory in 1880 was attributed to the greater energy and organisation which they had displayed. There were Liberal and Conservative registration offices in the town by 1867, and these did their utmost to get the names of supporters added to the register of electors, and those of their opponents removed. Both parties also maintained their clubs and associations, as in the eighteenth century, and these provided social events and entertainments, as well as instructing and influencing members politically. A Working Men's Constitutional Society had been formed in Maidstone by 1872 as an adjunct to the Conservative party, and a Kent County Working Men's Liberal Association was established in 1880, though this was aimed more at county voters. By 1882 we find Conservative and Liberal social clubs in the town, and four years later the Conservatives had male and female branches of the Primrose League, which gave fashionable entertainments and summer fêtes, but may also have attracted lower-class members.

By the latter part of the nineteenth century, interest groups other than political parties were concerned to influence the outcome of elections. Two important groups, in open opposition to one another, were the drink and temperance lobbies. As in the past Maidstone's prosperity depended in part on the brewing and distilling trades, and the town also had an active Licensed Victuallers Defence Association. Opposing them was a strong temperance movement centred on the churches. Widespread concern about drunkenness made the drink question a live political issue at the 1892 and 1898 elections; both lobbies posed a list of questions to the candidates, and public meetings decided from their answers which candidates to support. Not surprisingly, in both elections the Maidstone drink interest welcomed the answers of the Conservative candidate and voted unanimously to support his campaign. The temperance lobby, on the other hand, while preferring the Liberal's position, was unable to offer him unanimous support at either election. This was because of divisions within their ranks over other aspects of the Liberal platform, notably Irish Home Rule and the disestablishment of the Church in Ireland and Wales. Anglicans opposed such measures, and at both these elections Unionist Liberals voted for the Conservative candidate.

Another group of townspeople who were seeking to influence politics nationally were women, but there is no evidence of any suffragette activity in Maidstone until January 1914, when a branch of the National Union of Women's Suffrage Society was formed. This described itself as non-militant and non-political, and drew women from both sides of Maidstone's political divide in a quietly conducted campaign. The women were at pains to stress that they had no wish to intrude on male territory, and wanted the vote primarily to have a say in matters concerning women and children. Women by the late nineteenth century were active as party workers for both the Conservatives and the Liberals, and a growing number were involved in Labour politics.

The emergence of Labour as a pressure group was the most important development in the later nineteenth century affecting town politics both parliamentary and local. A branch of the National Labour Electoral Association (NLEA) was formed in Maidstone in 1889 by Arthur Field, an official of the Dockers' Union, and some seventy members were present at a meeting in November that year. The NLEA was closely linked to Maidstone Trades Council and most members appear to have been trade unionists, including paper-makers, engineers and tailors. The NLEA's primary concern was to obtain an 8-hour working day, and, at an open air meeting in December 1890, Field urged his audience to try to 'tilt elections towards Labour'. The 8-hour day was made a test question for parliamentary candidates, and Field threatened 'a warm corner in Maidstone for the candidate who refuses to adopt it', although there is no evidence that Labour had any strong influence on this election.

Field founded the Kentish Independent Labour Party (ILP) in 1893, and thereafter the Labour cause in Maidstone grew in strength, a Fabian Society being formed in 1895. At the 1898 election the Liberals held an open air meeting in the Fair Meadow with a largely working-class audience, and promised support for the eight hours movement. One of the speakers, the working class Lib/Lab MP for Stepney, W.C. Steadman, commended the Liberal candidate, J. Barker, to the audience as a Labour candidate, who had sprung from themselves, and the meeting resolved unanimously to support him. Unfortunately, Barker was unseated for corruption in 1900 and he was replaced by the rather more gentlemanly Liberal Sir F.H. Evans. Labour were not able to put forward candidates of their own before the First World War.

From the end of the 1880s, the control of local politics by the two major parties was increasingly affected by the development of Labour organisations in the town. At the municipal elections in 1889, candidates in the two wards contested were asked by the NLEA to support demands concerning the employment of casual workers and the holding of council meetings. In King Street ward the Liberal candidate accepted these demands, and was endorsed by the NLEA, but in Stone Street ward the demands were rejected, and Labour support denied to the Liberal candidate. As a result, the Conservative majority in King Street was overturned, but in Stone Street, the unsupported Liberal lost his seat to his Conservative rival. On the other hand, attempts to elect Labour members to the council were less successful. In 1894 the Stone Street Working Men's Radical Club nominated Arthur Field as candidate for that ward, but Field garnered only seven votes and the Liberal candidate took the seat. After the turn of the century the newly-formed Maidstone Labour Representation Committee put forward candidates to municipal elections, without success. Though Labour failed to gain any power in late Victorian and Edwardian Maidstone, its arrival served to generate a more active phase in urban politics after the relatively quiescent mid-Victorian years, to some extent reviving the town's earlier reputation for political controversy.

Religion and church activities

Throughout the nineteenth century, party politics was influenced and animated by religious division. However, religion was also a vehicle through which middle-class people sought to improve the quality of life in the town – not only spiritually but morally and socially – through voluntary causes and activities, some of which were aimed at changing the attitudes and outlook of the poor. In this way church and chapel-based activities drawing on middle-class support made a significant contribution to the organisational and associational life of all Victorian towns and cities. There were differences between communities, of course, in the strength of the various denominations and what was achieved by them. In Maidstone all denominations were involved but, as in many county towns, the Anglican church was to the fore, shaking off its somnolence at the start of the century. It took a leading role in developing an elementary school system, supporting institutions concerned with the welfare of the poor, and contributing increasingly to the wider social life of the community.

The religious census taken on 30 March 1851 recorded at Maidstone a total of 12,618 attendances at religious services of all kinds, including Sunday schools. Making adjustments for multiple attendances we can estimate the number of people going to church that day at 8,816, or 42 per cent of the population – a figure a little below the national average, but not untypical for an urban district. When we make allowance for an estimated 30 per cent of the population who were infants, infirm or at work on Sunday, it is likely that 61 per cent of those able to attend a religious service actually did so.[6] These figures seem high by modern standards, but they were greeted with some dismay at the time. The lack of adequate church accommodation was considered partly to blame; Maidstone could seat only half its total population in all its churches and chapels, though these were rarely full. Contemporaries also recognised that many of the poor were not church-goers, since attendance was very much a part of the respectable lifestyle of the middle and skilled working classes.

Accommodation for worshippers in the Church of England was expanded by the building of the classical-style Holy Trinity church in 1826–8, and the restoration of the ancient St Peter's chapel in the West Borough in 1836, but Maidstone remained a single parish, greatly in need of reorganisation. In the years following 1836, the newly-established national Ecclesiastical Commission reallocated money to create new parishes in areas affected by population growth. Consequently, in 1839 the ecclesiastical parish was divided for the first time, when Tovil parish was formed and St Stephen's church built by John Whichcord senior. St Peter's and Holy Trinity parishes were separated from All Saints in 1840 and 1841. As the town continued to expand, additional churches became necessary, and in the late 1850s St Philip's and St Paul's churches were built. These two, together with St John's (erected on land given by Lord Romney in Mote Park) became separate parishes in 1861. St Faith's parish was carved out of Holy Trinity in 1871, and at about the same time St James' chapel was built as a mission of St Paul's to serve the poor area behind the gaol. By now the growth of the West Borough had made St Peter's church inadequate, and St Michael's church (designed by Sir Arthur Blomfield) was constructed in Tonbridge Road, a parish being assigned to it in 1877. All the seats in this church were free, as this was a predominantly working-class parish. For some years after that, further expansion took the form of missions in working-class areas, with seats free for anyone who wished to attend. In 1896 one of these missions, St Luke's, was made a parish, and a new church, built in ragstone and ashlar in the Art Nouveau style, was consecrated the following year.

A further census of the Anglican congregations in 1880 gives some indication of the impact of this church expansion on attendance.[7] In 1851 the town, together with Tovil, had six Anglican places of worship, including the chapel at the workhouse and another at the County Asylum. One of these failed to make a return but the recorded attendance at the other five churches and their Sunday schools was 3,738 (morning service), 2,944 (afternoon), and 1,243 (evening). Altogether attendance probably approached nearly 40 per cent of the potential congregation. By 1880 the town's Anglican churches could accommodate just over 7,000 people. No count was made at the small St John's church, or at St James' mission, but at all the other churches there were only 1,714 in attendance at the morning services and 2,662 in the evening; Sunday school attendances, which boosted the figures in 1851, were not counted. The highest attendance figures were at Holy Trinity, which was the church attended by the military from the barracks. The figures are too imprecise to be conclusive, but they suggest that despite the efforts of the Church to expand and improve its ministry, the proportion of the population going to Anglican services was probably falling during the period, although subsequently missions may have reached more of the working class.

Attendance at Maidstone's nonconformist churches in 1851 was a little over half that for the Anglicans. The census recorded total attendance at 2,326 in the morning, 462 in the afternoon, and 1,905 in the evening, or 22 per cent of potential church-goers. The three congregations described as Particular Baptists (Calvinist) had the largest overall attendance (7.4 per cent of the available population), followed by the Wesleyans (4.8 per cent), and Lady Huntingdon's Connection (4.5 per cent). Other denominations with much smaller congregations included the Independents, Unitarians, Primitive Methodists, and the Society of Friends.

The nonconformist churches were in a state of flux in the mid- and late nineteenth century. Lady Huntingdon's Connection, a Calvinistic Methodist sect which had only arrived in the town in 1838, had disappeared by 1872, when the Brewer Street chapel it had used was occupied by a congregation described as Presbyterian; this too had gone by 1882. The Week Street congregation returned as Independent in 1851 subsequently became Congregational, and as such opened a second chapel in the West Borough in 1874. Similarly, the members of King Street Baptist church were by 1840 seeking to move beyond their exclusive Baptist beliefs. After appointing as minister the Rev. H.H. Dobney, a non-sectarian, who 'regarded all Christians as brothers', they gradually evolved into a non-denominational church. The Baptist chapels in Union Street and Mote Road continued, but Union Street had become General (Arminian) rather than Particular (Calvinist) in character by the 1890s. That chapel survived financial difficulties and a threatened foreclosure on the chapel mortgage in 1857, and by 1892 membership had increased to such an extent that all seats in the chapel were let and fund-raising was begun for a new chapel on the site of the Bluecoat school. This was finally built in 1907. A third Baptist chapel was opened in Priory Road at about the turn of the century.

Other nonconformist churches also maintained a presence in Maidstone and some expanded their congregations, although not in line with the population increase. The Unitarians in Week Street retained steady support until late in the century, adding a Sunday school in 1874; but on two occasions in the 1890s the congregation was unable to support its minister. Finances improved after the turn of the century, however, and in 1908, with a membership of 109, attendance at services was so great that the Week Street chapel was overcrowded. The Wesleyans also consolidated their position in the town, meeting at their impressive building in Union Street, and after 1868 in the West Borough as well. At first a house in Upper Fant Road was used for services and as a Sunday school, but in 1871 a building in Bower Lane was bought and converted into a chapel, and eleven years later this was replaced by a newly-built chapel on Tonbridge Road.

The Primitive Methodists, however, had a more difficult time. They were a new, primarily lower-class denomination, established in Maidstone as a mission of the Hull Circuit about 1839 with meetings in a building known as Salem chapel in Brewer Street, which by 1845 also housed a small Sunday school. It was also their practice to preach in the open air, and camp meetings were held annually. The congregation's initial expansion appears to have been slow and a loss of members led in 1845 to a rebuke from the missionary committee in London. Many of the sect's preachers were women, whose family commitments limited their ability to travel widely in the area, but despite this, congregations and membership in the Maidstone circuit increased steadily. Lacking wealthy members, the denomination struggled financially, and the rebuilding of the Brewer Street chapel in 1871 burdened it with debt for over twenty years; in 1892 the congregation was said to be 'at an exceeding low ebb'.

Lines of conflict and tension between and within religious groups were many and varied, but the most serious hostility was between the Church of England and dissent which spilled over into local and municipal politics. The Anglicans' control over day schooling was a major concern of the town's nonconformists as we have already seen. But the issue which strained relations most severely was the church rate, levied on all ratepayers for the upkeep of the Anglican churches in the town. Conflict over this reached major proportions in the 1840s when the church's decision to levy a rate for the three newly-opened churches, in addition to All Saints, caused the long-standing resistance of the town's Quakers to develop into a major battle, with regular seizures of nonconformist property. In 1848 a proposal by the non-denominational minister, the Rev. Dobney, for a voluntary rate was rejected. The distraint of property continued while a series of test cases not directly concerning Maidstone made their way through the courts to the House of Lords. Conflict did not finally end until 1853 when rates made by a minority in vestry were declared illegal.

There was conflict also between Protestants and Catholics, a denomination which at the time of the 1851 census had yet to establish a presence in the town. Anti-Catholic feeling was deep seated in Maidstone, and there had been a mass protest on Penenden Heath against Catholic emancipation in 1829. In 1851 local Catholics led by the recently converted Henry Wilberforce, the son of William Wilberforce the anti-slavery campaigner, and the former Anglican priest of East Farleigh, sought a meeting-place in Maidstone. Negotiations to buy a property caused an outcry and there was no further progress until 1858, when Wilberforce brought an Italian priest to the town. At first he gave mass at his own lodgings, and later that year began to offer Catholic instruction to children at the barracks, which seems to have been the home of most of his flock. An appeal for funds was made within the Catholic church, and Grove House in Week Street was bought in 1860 for use as a presbytery, school and chapel. Finances were precarious, and fluctuated with the number of Catholics at the barracks, but a church building fund was started in 1871. St Francis church, designed by C.G. Wray with flowing tracery, was finally opened in 1880. An 1882 directory names the priest as Rev. Major Duggan, which suggests that links between the church and the barracks remained strong. In 1900 Grove House became a convent of the Sisters of Providence.

Maidstone was also affected by the new religious movements of the later nineteenth century, notably the founding of the Salvation Army, a branch of which was started in Maidstone in 1882 by Dr Woods-Smythe, a house surgeon at the Ophthalmic Hospital, who had previously been involved in mission work. Its first premises were the disused skating rink at the Assembly Rooms on Sandling Road, which was transformed into a 'Salvation Rink'. A great deal of animosity was initially aroused, and there were riots – mainly involving youths – when the Salvationists tried to march around the town, but the Army enjoyed some success in making converts, and soon found acceptance. In the 1890s it had a citadel in Station Road, and in 1907 moved to the vacant Baptist chapel in Union Street.

The churches had long been aware of the need to offer more than just religious services if they were to win and retain members and influence public morality. But from the mid-nineteenth century they redoubled their efforts in philanthropic work of various kinds and began to involve themselves in recreational activities as well as social welfare and education. This was a national phenomenon, although the more prosperous county towns seem to have been particularly prominent as a forum for religious endeavour of this kind, guiding congregations along the path of virtue. Anglican policy had often been rather more tolerant towards worldly amusements than the nonconformists and it was the Church of England which led the way in providing leisure activities in Maidstone, although by the 1880s almost all denominations were involved to some degree. The aim was to provide a worthy and improving alternative to what were seen as commercial entertainments of limited value, if not dubious morality. On to their existing framework of Sunday schools, bible classes and choirs was grafted an efflorescence of literary, musical, gardening, sporting and other recreational societies. Some of the new facilities and activities, especially those of the Anglicans, were funded by members of the town's elite class, including the Balston, Hollingworth, Clifford and Stacey families. In this wider area the least active was the Roman Catholic church, whose societies were mainly of a devotional nature or concerned with fund-raising; though there were parties and entertainments at Christmas, and in 1883, an excursion to the Crystal Palace. The Anglicans and nonconformists also continued to have many societies for bible study and religious discussion, and these in the latter part of the nineteenth and early twentieth centuries were steadily integrated into national bodies such as the Church of England Men's Society, Christian Endeavour and the Wesley Guild. Both churches and chapels depended heavily for funds on groups of women and girls who met to sew articles for sales of work, and organised money-raising teas and suppers. However, there was a great deal more besides, with church socials, concerts and outings becoming regular occurrences, and, as we have noted, a proliferation of societies.

One of the most widespread and popular types of church society were the literary societies. The Anglicans were the pioneers in this field, and in 1864 Holy Trinity church organised a course of lectures on topics ranging from 'John Milton and his Times', and 'A Day in London 500 years ago' to 'The Sea and its Inhabitants'. Tickets cost 3s for the course, or 6d for an unreserved seat to a single lecture; the programme was clearly aimed at a middle-class audience. Ongoing societies were formed later, and there were both Literary and Parliamentary Debating societies attached to the Church Institute, which was opened in Union Street in 1882. In 1892 there was a lively debate on land nationalisation, and three years later topics included old age pensions, trade unions and voluntary schools. More systematic adult education classes were also held there, as noted in Chapter Seven.

The nonconformists were not to be outdone, and in 1883 King Street chapel began what was to become one of the most active and successful of these societies, the Young Men's Society for 'literary work and mutual improvement', restricted to single men over the age of sixteen. The following year it changed into a Literary Society, hearing lectures on a variety of subjects; the ban on married men was quietly dropped, and in 1892 women were invited to join the society. Politics increasingly came to the fore, and in the mid-1890s the active ILP member Jesse Hawkes was involved in the society. A similar society was formed at Week Street Congregational church in 1889.

The Church Institutes provided for a much wider range of leisure activities than the purely intellectual. The principal Church Institute was founded in 1854, and in 1882 it moved to large premises built by public subscription in Union Street. It contained a well stocked library, lecture, reading and recreation rooms, and a large concert hall known as the Hollingworth Hall after a benefaction from the well known local family. A gymnasium and numerous sports clubs enabled the cultivation of a healthy mind in a healthy body, in accord with prevailing ideas of 'muscular Christianity'. A distinctly middle-class organisation, in 1892 it had 688 members, of whom 62 subscribed a guinea and upwards and received 'special privileges'; 440 subscribed at the standard rate of 10s; and the rest were ladies paying 7s 6d but excluded from the reading rooms after 7 p.m. In contrast, the St Paul's Literary Institute was established in 1859 in a largely working-class parish with a subscription of only 2d a week. Meetings were held in the evenings in the schoolroom, where newspapers and periodicals were available. Although the institute aimed to give young men 'opportunities for improving their minds and of acquiring knowledge', and quickly secured a library of 1,000 books, it also offered a wider range of leisure provision, including bagatelle and chess. The institute was open to all denominations, but it is not clear how far it attracted members of other churches. In 1860 the institute acquired a cricket club and later a horticultural society and athletics club. When St James' mission chapel was built in the poorest area of St Paul's parish in 1868, a similar club was started there, which charged only a penny a month. St Philip's and All Saints parishes embarked on parallel ventures at around the same time. The only nonconformist effort on these lines was the Dobney Institute, which was built by King Street church in 1889–90, and named in memory of their influential and recently deceased minister.

A conscious effort to reach out to the working classes was made by the nonconformists through Sunday afternoon concerts known as Pleasant Sunday Afternoons, or the Brotherhood. These were part of a nonconformist but non-denominational national movement which had begun in West Bromwich in 1875.[8] Its motto was 'brief, bright and brotherly'. The programmes normally consisted of an hour of congregational hymn singing, music, recitations and uplifting addresses, with the aim of drawing in working men who normally did not go to religious services. Two PSAs operated in Maidstone, one at King Street church from 1895, and one at Union Street Wesleyan church, which appears to have begun after the turn of the century. Both these efforts were popular and successful for many years, and at King Street a number of related organisations grew up including a book club, coal club, and slate clubs, into which members paid small weekly sums.

Many Maidstone churches and chapels ran clubs of this type as a practical way of helping the poor in their parishes or congregations. The small weekly subscriptions enabled poorer inhabitants to obtain necessities such as coal, blankets and clothing which they could not otherwise afford. Thrift was also encouraged by the well supported penny banks organised in some Anglican parishes. All Saints, a parish containing extremes of wealth, was able to give charitable help from its alms fund, and maintained a list of pensioners. The alms fund also supported women's sewing meetings in Padsole, at which middle-class ladies taught poor women and girls how to sew children's clothes, providing the materials at reduced prices. In such poorer districts, there were regular visits to poor households by church visitors, particularly Anglican ladies, as well as by nonconformist visitors, and if a high proportion of the socially deprived were still not attending religious services, many of them had come within the church's sphere of influence by other means by the end of the nineteenth century.

The churches also involved themselves in the temperance movement whose political activity was noted earlier. The Maidstone temperance movement was not initiated by the churches, but individual churchgoers were active in the first temperance society which began in Maidstone in 1836. The society's meetings and festivals often took place in chapel premises, and nonconformists and Anglicans became increasingly influential in the work, which was also promoted by temperance friendly societies such as the Rechabites, active in the town by the 1840s, and the Good Templars, founded in 1871. Church temperance societies were established later in the century, at Week Street Congregational chapel, and in the Anglican parishes, where various branches of the Church of England Temperance Society (CETS) were successfully established. St Michael's parish was particularly pro-temperance, and in 1880 it took the unusual step of promoting a coffee tavern as a joint stock company, encouraging working men to buy shares. Situated on the Upper Fant Road, and called the Queen's Own West Borough Coffee Tavern, it had twelve beds for lodgers, together with reading and refreshment rooms. In 1914 a Temperance Institute was opened in Stone Street by the CETS, which functioned as a teetotal working men's club, with billiards, bagatelle and the like.

The nonconformist churches, which in many cases held temperance principles as an article of faith, had few formal societies for adults, but were heavily engaged in work with children through the Band of Hope, an organisation begun in Leeds in 1847. The first Band of Hope in Maidstone was started by the Week Street Congregational church in 1851. Others followed within a few years, and by 1898 all the town's nonconformist congregations, except it would seem the Unitarians, had one or more of these organisations. In addition, secular Bands of Hope were attached to the temperance friendly societies, and these joined with the nonconformists in the Maidstone Band of Hope Union, which by 1906 had seventeen groups affiliated to it. The Anglicans were organising Bands of Hope by the 1880s, but they did not affiliate to the union, preferring to act in concert with the CETS.

The Band of Hope tried to instil teetotal principles in children by recreational means. It was aimed at working-class children, who were regarded as especially vulnerable to the demon drink. Nonconformist societies were mixed, but the Anglicans, in line with their policy on educational and recreational provision, organised separate societies for boys and girls. The children watched magic lantern shows, sang, recited and put on plays and entertainments, and like the Sunday schools, the societies had teas and outings. These were enormously popular, and in the years prior to the First World War two to three thousand children and adults left the town on annual CETS and Band of Hope excursions to Margate.

Other organisations likewise aimed to give moral guidance and practical help to working-class youth. The Anglican Girls Friendly Society (GFS) was formed in 1874, and within a few years there were branches in St Michael's, All Saints and possibly other parishes in Maidstone. The GFS sought to bring working-class girls under the moral influence of their social superiors, and middle-class ladies were enrolled as associates to supervise groups of girls.[9] There were recreational activities at the meetings, annual fêtes and garden parties, but the Society's main aim was to teach womanly crafts and virtues in girls destined for domestic service. Girls found places through the GFS's register, and were given prizes for staying with employers for one or more years. The organisation quickly became popular and continued to operate successfully into the inter-war years. The Church tried to reach and influence the town's growing number of factory girls through the Young Women's Christian Association, which had been established in Mill Street by 1882. This was not connected to any particular church, and was specifically aimed at 'the class of young women engaged in mills and factories'. By 1898 it had moved to Earl Street where it had a reading and recreation room. The Church had also set up a Young Girls' Help Association in St Paul's parish by 1882 which admitted girls to a Church Deaconess Home before finding them places as domestic servants or funding their emigration. The first organisation for young men was the Young Men's Christian Association (YMCA), which had a branch in Maidstone from the late 1860s. For younger boys a Boys Brigade was operating in St Philip's parish by 1892. However, the most successful of the organised youth movements in the town was the Boy

Scouts, and there were already four troops by 1910, although the real expansion took place after the First World War. In this as in so many other areas, social and philanthropic bodies in the town were often offshoots of national voluntary organisations.

Cultural life and leisure

As we have seen already, Maidstone's upper- and middle-classes, and even some of the town's artisans, had enjoyed an increasingly diverse and sophisticated social life since the Georgian era. But after the mid-nineteenth century the general improvement in living standards, together with a modest reduction in hours for some workers, enabled many more people to enjoy an ever widening array of commercial entertainments, as leisure services became an expanding sector in Maidstone's economy. At the same time, all but the very poorest classes were able to participate in the proliferation of amateur organisations which formed a growing part of the social and cultural fabric of the community. Voluntary societies, already well established before 1800, now extended their role and scope to embrace large sections of the town's population. Maidstone may have lost the genteel glamour characteristic of its Georgian heyday as a fashionable county town but in the Victorian and Edwardian period it remained a vigorously sociable society with a remarkably flourishing associational life.

Clubs and societies

The most prestigious associations were the town's literary and scientific societies. The exclusive Literary Society (mentioned in Chapter Five) continued into the 1840s as an elite organisation, alongside the Mechanics Institute which was relaunched in 1836 under middle-class patronage as a body 'for the promulgation of useful knowledge amongst the working classes of Maidstone'. The latter organisation was no doubt influenced by widespread respectable concern over lower-class unrest in the country at large, and the belief that social order could be improved by guidance and education, and the provision of what were deemed rational recreations. Despite its name and objective, and various attempts to encourage working-class involvement, the Mechanics Institute soon became an organisation of and for the middle class, and in 1852 it amalgamated with the Literary Society. Two further associations of the educated middle class were formed after the mid-century, the Kent Archaeological Society in 1857, and the Maidstone and Mid-Kent Natural History and Philosophical Society by 1872, both of them holding meetings in Chillington House. All these societies promoted lectures on a variety of erudite topics and developed lending libraries. Though some of their members came from the town, others travelled to meetings from the wider county, confirming Maidstone's cultural importance in the region.

Gardening was another form of rational recreation increasingly popular in the town during Victoria's reign. There was considerable genteel interest from the seventeenth century in the introduction of exotic plants to Britain and after 1800 the increasing middle-class emphasis on domestic and family life and the growth of spacious villas with large gardens in the new suburbs naturally encouraged the spread of gardening as a pastime. The first Horticultural Society started in 1834 but appears to have been replaced in 1842 by two further societies, which quickly amalgamated and continued until the 1880s. By then there were several other similar clubs in the town. The Gardeners Mutual Improvement Society, after 1864, aimed at a broader cross-section of the population, but appears to have been basically middle class, with a coterie of genteel honorary members who dominated the exhibitions. In 1867, however, nearly 5,000 people visited one of the society's shows, while nearly 1,000 had to be turned away during the cheap admission time in the evening, suggesting widespread interest in horticulture at all social levels. This society was still operating in 1898, when it had an associated Chrysanthemum and Fruit Society. By the 1890s the town could also boast a Rose Club, whose members included 'most of the leading inhabitants of the neighbourhood'. For working-class gardeners, church organisations provided the main focus of activity until the 1890s, when cottage gardeners' and allotment holders' societies were organised by ordinary townspeople.

As we have seen already in our discussion of the churches, numerous other organisations in the town had charitable or moral aims, and it is clear that as the century went on, an increasing amount of time and effort, mainly middle class, was devoted to such causes. By the 1890s organisations as diverse as the Shipwrecked Mariners' Benevolent Society, the Kent Discharged Prisoners Aid Society and the RSPCA, were operating in the town as well as branches of many nationally organised religious and missionary societies. There were also local campaigning organisations such as the Maidstone Social Purity Society, which sought to rescue fallen women and 'to raise the tone of public opinion on these subjects'. On the medical front, a branch of the St John Ambulance brigade began in 1878.

Increasingly important from the late 19th century, for political and recreational reasons, was the volunteer force, the forerunner of the territorial army. The first company in the county, the First Kent Rifle Volunteers, was formed in Maidstone in 1859, the year of the movement's inception as a defence force against foreign invasion, and another three companies were in existence by the early twentieth century. This patriotic organisation was established with the intention of recruiting young middle-class men, and the First Kents were initially commanded by a member of the Hollingworth family, while other local worthies served as officers. However, it is likely that, as in other towns, an increasing proportion of the rank and file were working class. The Volunteers drilled and went on manoeuvres each Easter, organised rifle competitions against other Kent companies, and quickly acquired a band, which sometimes played in the High Street to an appreciative audience during summer evenings. There was also an annual fête in Vinters Park, with music, amusements and fireworks.

Alongside these newer developments were the older self help and mutual aid societies such as the Freemasons and friendly societies whose convivial activities were also vital in encouraging membership. The early lodges of Freemasons had lapsed or removed to other towns by 1828, but a new lodge was founded in 1844, and a second in 1877. By 1882 a Freemasons' Hall had been opened in the former Presbyterian chapel in Brewer Street, and two years later a third lodge was opened.[10] By 1898 the number of lodges had increased to six. The town's small local benefit clubs were gradually replaced (from the 1830s) by societies affiliated to better financed national organisations, although the last known independent local clubs – the Friendly Brothers and the Hand in Hand Benefit Society – were both still operating in the 1860s. The first of the affiliated societies in the town was the Ancient Order of Druids, founded in 1836, which met in the Ancient Druids public house, built at approximately the same time; the members were described in the press as tradesmen. By 1867 with a further two lodges in the town, the Druids' annual fête and sports had become a major social event and in 1880 this was held jointly with those other affiliated societies, the Oddfellows and Foresters. At the close of the century, with membership coming within the reach of a growing section of the working class, there were sixteen friendly society lodges in Maidstone, six of them branches of societies based on temperance principles. Dinners, sports and fêtes were typical of the anniversary celebrations of the affiliated societies, which also organised concerts and soirees during the winter months.

Music

Continuing the earlier tradition, there was always a ready audience for music in nineteenth-century Maidstone, and we find a growing variety of entertainment available. Many professional performers included a Maidstone concert in their tours, the usual venue being the Corn Exchange. In 1848, for instance, Henry Russell, the American composer of 'Woodman Spare that Tree' and other sentimental ballads, appeared there for one night with admission prices at 2s and 1s, indicating a middle-class and perhaps artisan audience. Concerts of light classical and operatic music were also targeted at a similar audience. Until the latter part of the century, gentry patronage was frequently used as a method of influencing the social composition of audiences, but as the commercial and monied classes came increasingly to the fore in the town, price alone was relied on to achieve the desired effect. When Sousa and his band performed at the Corn Exchange in 1905, the best seats cost 5s, even the gallery cost 2s, and 1s only bought standing room. As in the eighteenth century, the well to do promoted subscription concerts of classical music of a more serious character than that offered by professional promoters. These concerts were by their nature exclusive, although by 1892 non-subscribers were being admitted at prices between 5s and 1s. There was also a growing number of popular commercial concerts with cheaper seats available, notably those of the Christy and other black, or black-face, minstrel troupes, which attracted large audiences and normally had a sixpenny gallery. A number of amateur minstrel troupes were formed in the town after the 1860s, performing often for charity, and with middle-class and later working-class membership.

Amateur music-making had long been regarded as an essential sociable activity of the upper and middle classes, both in the home and outside. Though music societies had existed in the town in George III's reign, they tended to become larger and more formalised in the Victorian period. Pre-eminent among the early Victorian societies was the Sacred Harmonic Society, which was begun by a local 'professor of music'. By 1842 it was performing, with professional soloists, an extensive repertoire of oratorio and other sacred music at select subscription concerts in the County Assembly Rooms. One concert in March that year was said to have been attended by 'a numerous and respectable company, which included many of the gentry and some of the aristocracy of the town and neighbourhood'. Other nineteenth-century music societies included a Cecilian Society, a Catch Club, and various glee clubs. The Sacred Harmonic Society was still holding concerts in the 1870s, but from this time choral music generally became the preserve of church and chapel choirs, who performed a wide range of sacred and other music at prices which were generally accessible. An Amateur Orchestral Society was in existence after 1898. The first major secular choral society since the 1870s, Maidstone Choral Union was founded in 1902 as a middle-class organisation, with a 5s subscription. There were initially 124 members, two-thirds of them female. In 1905 a Kent Musical Festival was launched with the first event in Maidstone; the Choral Union was one of five competing choirs. An Amateur Operatic Society had also been formed in the town by 1914.

For ordinary townspeople amateur music-making, particularly singing, was traditionally centred in public houses. But in 1842 the organisers of the Mechanics Institute attempted to introduce choral music to the working classes, as an improving and civilising recreation, through classes in Wilhem and Hullah's Sol-fa, a simplified form of musical notation. Much interest was aroused, and other classes were organised by the town's music teachers. The system of Sol-fa, and the more flexible Tonic Sol-fa, devised by John Curwen, which was subsequently adopted, gave a great boost to general musical life in Maidstone, as it did in many towns. By 1869, a Maidstone Tonic Sol-fa Association was in existence, which was able to give a performance of Handel's Dettingen Te Deum, with a chorus of 250 voices.[11] Music was also encouraged in the town's elementary schools by the formation of school choirs and school orchestras after the turn of the century. By then commercial interests were making arrangements to facilitate violin classes and the hire of violins on what was known as the Maidstone system, which began at All Saints National School in 1898.

A further attempt to improve working-class standards and taste was the Penny Readings movement, which was briefly very successful in Maidstone during the 1860s. Penny Readings were programmes of music and reading by middle-class amateurs, with a minimal admission charge. During the winter of 1866/7 a series of twenty-three readings was given at the Corn Exchange, at which the average attendance was nearly 800. This might suggest that it was a lack of money rather than a lack of discernment which stopped many lower-class people attending other musical events.

Dancing remained another important aspect of the town's musical life. Until the later nineteenth century formal dancing was mainly a middle- and upper-class pastime. The county balls, in the Assembly Rooms, continued their seasons until about 1870. By then there were rival assemblies in Ashford, which were possibly more brilliant and fashionable, and certainly more expensive. In 1867, for instance, tickets at Maidstone cost 8s and those at Ashford 12s 6d. All the signs indicate that Maidstone was becoming less of a centre for upper-class society and in the latter part of the century the most glittering assemblies in the town were the West Kent Militia officers' balls. These took place in the Assembly Rooms which by 1880 had been partially converted into a roller skating rink to cater for a popular, if short-lived middle-class pastime. At about the same time a second skating rink was available in Church Street on Wednesday and Saturday afternoons, probably aiming at shop assistants and other lower-middle-class groups, with an admission price of 1s including the hire of skates. The whole of the Assembly Rooms were reconverted for roller skating in 1895, a special floor being brought from Chicago by one of the promoters, a champion fancy skater, but this venture was no more successful than the others, and by 1897 the Assembly Rooms, once the scene of elite dances, had become the premises of Edward Sharp, the sweet manufacturer.

The middle classes had a rather more enduring fascination for dancing quadrilles, which had become popular at fashionable society balls in the early years of the century, and subsequently found favour lower down the social scale. Quadrilles were set dances with complex figures, the best known being the Lancers. All the town's dancing teachers taught them, and specialist quadrille bands played at the quadrille assemblies which proliferated in the middle decades of the century. Quadrilles were still being danced at New Year balls in 1880, but soon afterwards their popularity began to wane. After the turn of the century, dancing became more of an all-class pastime, and regular Saturday night dances were held in the room of the Mechanics Institute at the Corn Exchange. Co-op dances were also organised there, with waltzes and tangos, then much in vogue, dominating the programmes.[12]

The theatre, music hall and cinema

The theatre enjoyed mixed fortunes in Maidstone during Victoria's reign. As in the early part of the century, the Theatre Royal continued to open for seasons under different management during the 1830s and 40s. In 1842 when it was under the control of Messrs Johnson and Lee of the Chatham theatre, conjurers and ventriloquists were on offer rather than plays, and later that decade the theatre's standards appear to have attracted criticism. In 1848 the new manager, Thornton, promised to conduct the theatre with 'strict regularity, respectability and propriety', and he arranged a programme of short dramas and farces. 'Box and Cox', and a musical farce 'The German Baron' were performed in February, but refinement was clearly at a discount; in May one Signor Plimmeri, 'the only perfect delineator of the monkey tribe' appeared in a piece entitled 'Jocko, the Brazilian Ape'. Prices ranged from 3s for a box to 6d for a seat in the gallery, but half-price admission was available for the second half of the programme, and if this applied to all seats, the gallery would have been accessible to almost anyone. The theatre nevertheless saw few subsequent performances, and it was demolished in 1851. In the second half of the century touring theatre companies played to respectable and appreciative audiences at the Corn Exchange. Touring pantomimes seem to have been the most regular and popular visitors. Otherwise the town was obliged to rely on amateur drama performances, such as those given in aid of charity during the 1860s by the middle-class Maidstone Amateur Dramatic Club. Touring circuses also visited the town periodically throughout the century apparently drawing good audiences, although ticket prices again restricted access to the middle classes.

By the time the Theatre Royal was demolished the town had acquired its first music hall at the Phoenix public house, near the barracks on Sandling Road. First listed in 1851 with a publican as proprietor, by 1872 the premises appear solely as a music hall, and the proprietor, Richard Farrant, as a musical agent. In 1867 another music hall was operating at the Castle Inn in Week Street. Other variety entertainment had to wait until the mid-1890s, when the Assembly Rooms skating rink in Sandling Road was briefly in use. In August 1900 Sylvester's Hippodrome opened for a short time in a booth in Lock Meadow, with a similar venture, Transfield's Hippodrome, two years later – to be replaced in turn by the New Hippodrome, on the same site, and again managed by Sylvester. This was 'quite a different building . . . run by other men on other lines than Maidstone has been used to in the past.' It was built of corrugated iron and wood, but possessed 'inner comfort, commodiousness and convenience', with a stage and galleries on the style of a London music hall, and seating for 1,500. A clearly respectable, although primarily working-class venture, it received favourable reviews in the press for its variety programmes, which included appearances by local amateur talent, as well as by touring professionals. The cost of admission to the gallery was 4d, although there were seats in the stalls at 1s 6d. The Hippodrome was burnt down in 1908, and the rather more plush Palace Theatre in Gabriel's Hill was opened, again with Sylvester as manager. Like its predecessor, this was a Palace of Varieties, offering twice nightly performances, but the audience may have included more middle-class people, as the variety theatre was by this time losing its earlier risqué reputation.

The travelling panoramic shows, which were in some ways forerunners of the cinema, appeared in Maidstone early in the period. The first exhibition of this sort was Gompertz' Panorama, which arrived with its views of the 'late war with the Sikhs' in 1848. Panoramas, also known as dioramas or myrioramas, were huge illuminated scrolls with a succession of scenes painted on them. Later on, photographs were sometimes used instead of paintings. By 1867 photographic illusion shows, such as Professor Pepper and Thomas Tobin's Ghost Illusion, and Young and Poole's Phantascope were visiting the town. The phantascope was said to be 'well adapted for introducing the illusions that belong to such stories as Faust and Margeurite, for not only are the spirits presented in the ordinary fashion of mortals, but they are made to dance in the air, and play all manner of tricks in a way to completely dazzle the senses.' The shows were aimed at a middle-class audience and the Corn Exchange was crowded every night. The first real films, 'animated pictures', were shown as part of the variety shows at the old Assembly Rooms in 1896, and Maidstone people may also have seen them in travelling booths at fairs around the same time. The early films were short, and many were on serious or educational topics, such as that 'illustrating the alien and emigration questions' which was shown at the Hippodrome in 1905, and 'the capture and carving up of a 75 ton whale' seen the following year. Subsequently, the Palace Theatre projected films as part of its variety programmes and a visiting cinema, described later as 'a very crude and flickering show with innumerable interruptions', played at the Corn Exchange in 1908. The first permanent cinema, the Empire Electric, was opened in a converted shop in Station Road, in 1910, by a local photographer named Dunk. The following year this was replaced by a purpose-built cinema, the New Empire Electric in Earl Street, and another disused skating rink in Pudding Lane was re-opened as the Popular Picture Palace, or PPP.[13] Cinema was a cheap entertainment, and rapidly became enormously popular with all social classes, attracting crowds of customers not only in the town but from adjoining villages.

Public houses and working men's clubs

Public houses remained central to many aspects of working-class leisure during Victoria's reign. As we know, the number of drinking houses expanded between 1830 and 1869, as many beerhouses were opened under the 1830 Act, and newly-built areas were provided with pubs, but subsequently the number of houses fell gradually until the end of the century, and rather more rapidly in the years before the First World War, as closures occurred under the 1904 Licensing Act. In the early part of the century opening hours were largely unrestricted, except for closure during the hours of divine service on Sundays. But Sunday opening was further curtailed by legislation in 1854 and 1855, and then in 1872 another Act brought late night drinking to an end, with the local magistrates deciding that 11 p.m. (10 p.m. on Sunday) would be the closing times in Maidstone. On the first night of early closing there was a near riot, as men went from house to house demanding to be served after 11 p.m. The next day was a Sunday, and at 10 p.m. a large mob, including a number of soldiers, congregated in the streets. A military picket eventually marched fifteen soldiers back to the barracks, and three other men were arrested. But if they closed earlier at night, public houses continued to be allowed to open from 5 a.m., for the convenience of workmen, especially those in lodgings.[14]

With the exception of higher-class inns and hotels, such as the Star in High Street serving the better off, the pubs mostly provided a gathering place for the lower classes, though we have only scraps of information about what went on behind their doors. As mentioned above, a few enterprising landlords began to offer music hall entertainment in the late nineteenth century, and evidence from before the First World War indicates that a significant minority of houses offered musical entertainment, sometimes, but not invariably, accompanied by rowdyism. It was said in 1906 that the back room of the Prince Albert on Sandling Road had been filled with soldiers and girls singing – until placed out of bounds to the military. Six years later the King's Head in High Street had a room with a piano, while the Queen Anne hosted regular performances by the well known local musicians, the Webb family.

Most public houses were patronised by a very well defined set of customers, carefully articulated according to social class. Even the residents of a single street might frequent different pubs. Some premises, like the Greyhound on Wheeler Street, had 'pleasure gardens' attached, but others, particularly the old beerhouses, were evidently very basic and often in a state of disrepair. A minority, as we have said, were better class, and these continued to have a mainly middle-class clientele, and to provide rooms for clubs and societies. The Mitre was said to be the resort of businessmen, and the Castle had a large club-room which was used by various friendly societies as well as the Dutch Rabbit Club. The Volunteers met at the Star, as subsequently did the cycling club and the football club. Publicans appear to have been much less active as sports promoters than in the early years of the century, but pub games such as billiards, skittles, darts and cards were much to the fore. Quoits also became increasingly popular, and by 1914 there was a public house and working men's club quoits league.

In the last quarter of the nineteenth century public houses faced a growing challenge from working men's clubs. The first was founded in 1867, possibly on the instigation of John Potter, the paper-maker and subsequent mayor of the town, at a meeting attended by that great proponent of working men's clubs the Rev. Henry Solly. The club had considerable middle- and upper-class backing, and was started with the aim of 'affording to the industrial classes the means of social intercourse. . . with mental and moral improvement; to provide refreshments; and to afford facilities for holding meetings of friendly and other working men's societies.' In short, it was intended as an unlicensed alternative to public houses, with some of the additional benefits of an organisation like the Church Institute. The club at first had premises in Earl Street, where science and other educational classes and concerts were held. An annual athletic sports meeting was arranged from 1878 at Preston Hall, Aylesford, the home of one of its patrons, H.A. Brassey, Esq. During the 1880s it moved to larger premises in Brewer Street, and in 1885 a second working men's club was opened in the West Borough. Other clubs were opened in Stone Street (1889) and in Whittington Street and at Tovil during the 1890s. By then the clubs had changed in character as working men took control of the organisations, and before 1900 they had all acquired drinks licences, which were not subject to the same restrictions on opening hours as public houses. Games such as skittles, quoits, billiards, whist and cribbage formed a major part of the activities, although athletics and other sports continued, and Brewer Street had a gardening society, as well as a pigeon and poultry fanciers' society attached to it. The Trades Council and a number of trade unions met at the Brewer Street club, and everywhere events such as ladies' concerts brought women on to the premises. In 1898 the clubs had nearly a thousand members in total, the Brewer Street and West Borough ones being the largest. The town also had two middle- and upper-class clubs, the Kent Club and the Maidstone Club, with a combined membership of 340, in addition to the Liberal and Conservative clubs, which had 400 and 350 members respectively.[15]

Sport

Sport was an aspect of Maidstone's social life which not only increased in importance during Victoria's reign but also changed in character, as codified games were introduced and amateur sport became a major pastime. Pedestrianism faded from the scene, and serious athletes increasingly competed for prize money at the athletic sports meetings organised by friendly societies and the town's working men's clubs; competitors came from as far away as London. Races were normally run according to a handicap system, which offered close finishes for the enjoyment of spectators, and prevented events being dominated by a few professional athletes. By the late nineteenth century athletic tournaments frequently included cycle races. A cyclists' touring club was meeting at the Star in Maidstone by 1879, at which date 'penny-farthings' would have been in use, but this had only a small number of members. By 1892 the competitive Invicta Cycling Club had been established and was using a track at Barming Heath recreation ground for races. The Church Institute cycling club was also in operation by that date. The price of bicycles meant that cycling at this time was an almost exclusively middle-class pastime, but it is clear from the proliferation of cycle dealers and repairers in the town from the 1890s that it was increasingly popular. Working-class people may have begun to buy second-hand machines.

Swimming was a sport which, thanks to the proximity of the river and the provision of the swimming baths, was open to rather more townspeople. Even after the opening of the baths in 1852, the river remained important for bathing. A swimming club was formed in 1844, with a shilling subscription, and members later described as 'consisting mainly of tradesmen and their sons'. The fifty or so members swam in the river at a spot known as the Elms Bathing Place, where a bathing house was built. The polluted state of the river ended the club's activities during the 1870s, but it was soon revived with games of water polo drawing many spectators. The new club was aimed at 'the better class of boys'; a second club, known as the Water Rats, began shortly afterwards and was open to boys under sixteen of any class. The clubs subsequently merged and became Maidstone Swimming Club, which began to use the public baths on a regular basis after the opening of a larger pool in 1895. Female members were now admitted, as the old pool was designated the ladies' bath, but bathing was still segregated until 1914, when mixed 'family' bathing was first introduced. By that date there was heavy use by schools and swimming clubs and during the months of July and August, on the eve of the First World War, there were well over 4,000 admissions at the municipal baths.

Among team games cricket was pre-eminent. The old-established Maidstone club found a permanent home at the Mote in 1857, and by the middle of Victoria's reign other local clubs were appearing, attached to churches, clubs and workplaces, and embracing virtually all social classes. By the end of the century there was scarcely a firm of any size in the town without a cricket team, and even the grocers, licensed victuallers and local press had formed their clubs. The general proliferation of teams in the county and beyond meant there was no shortage of fixtures. Lengthy match reports appeared in the press, indicating the high level of public interest. The Kent county team had fixtures at the Mote, and in 1892 special trains were laid on to bring spectators for a match against Yorkshire. Occasions such as this brought trade to the town, and that was probably one of the reasons why the town council, as in several other Kentish towns, organised annual cricket weeks in the years before the First World War.

Football arrived on the scene a little later, probably in 1868. It may have originated at the grammar school, since in 1869 a team called the Alligators, consisting of past and present grammar school boys, played the Maidstone team on a pitch at Rocky Hill. By the 1880s a fairly regular rugby fixture list was being played by the Maidstone club, though the problem of a suitable pitch was not solved until a move was made to the new Athletic Ground on London Road in 1895. Association football first appears during the 1880s, and support for the game grew rapidly during the next few years, exemplified by a flurry of requests to the council for pitches; but there were fewer workplace teams than with cricket. A Maidstone and District League was set up during the mid-1890s, and in 1896, one of the more successful local teams, Maidstone Invicta – formed it was said by a group of local businessmen – joined the East Kent League and turned semi-professional, changing their name to Maidstone United. They played first at Postley fields and after 1898 at the athletic ground, winning the Kent League Cup in 1898–9 and several subsequent years. The club was plagued at the start by low match attendances and finances were inadequate to cover expenses and buy players; concerts and other events had to be held for fund-raising purposes. But the level of support increased, and in 1912 the club made a profit for the first time, enabling it to increase the number of professional players from five to eight. Amateur football flourished alongside the professional team, and in 1914 local teams were playing in a number of amateur cup competitions.

Among other new sports in the town, the middle-class game of tennis was well established by 1892, when a mixed doubles tournament was played against a Sittingbourne team. By 1914 it was being played at the athletic ground and the

John Potter, the first working-class mayor of Maidstone, held office in 1908 and 1912. Photograph: Kent Messenger Group Newspapers.

Crowds welcoming the West Kent Yeomanry back from the Boer War in 1901.
Photograph: Kent Messenger Group Newspapers.

King Street non-denominational church.
Photograph: Maidstone Museum.

The Rev. H.H. Dobney, minister of King
Street church and social reformer.
Photograph: Maidstone Museum.

Enjoying the music at the bandstand in Brenchley Gardens.
Photograph: Maidstone Museum.

The Webb Family Band, notable Maidstone musicians, 1890s.
Photograph: Mrs I. Thomsett and A. R. Thomsett.

Edwardian Week Street, showing the Central Hotel, then a temperance establishment.
Photograph: Kent Messenger Group Newspapers.

The Royal Oak public house, King Street. A mid-Victorian photograph.
Photograph: Maidstone Museum.

MAIDSTONE CENTRALS F.C.
(LATE POST OFFICE PRINTING WORKS F.C.)

...AKER.   T. BARHAM.   A. J. SAGE.   J. STEVENS.   W. G. BEALE.   S. FEATHERSTONE   S. WOODWARD.   C. B. SMITH   G. MATTHEWS
                                                                      (Captain).   (Chairman).   (Trainer).

H. C. LEWIS   E. HALL.   W. LAKER.   C. PRICHARD.   F. STEVENS.   W. LANGRIDGE.   H. J. OUTTEN
(Hon. Sec.)   (Vice President).
        W. WEEDON.   E. WEEDON.   E. WOOD.
        (Sub Captain).

Winners Maidstone League 1st Division, Season 1911-12.
Winners Maidstone Hospitals Charity Competition, 1911-12.

Maidstone Centrals Football Club, 1911–12 (formerly the Post Office Printing Works team).
Photograph: Kent Messenger Group Newspapers.

A view of the Edwardian High Street, with the Star Inn on the left and the Georgian town hall on the right. Photograph: Kent Messenger Group Newspapers.

Priory tennis ground on Hayle Road, with an annual tournament held in July. By then the town also had a number of men's hockey teams, and a golf course was laid out at Oakwood Park in 1914.

High days and holidays

The leisure world of Maidstone's townspeople in the Victorian and Edwardian period showed considerable continuity with the past, but also an extraordinary variety of new entertainments, organised frequently by voluntary associations but also increasingly on a commercial basis. Two further developments are also visible. Firstly, the growing impact of external influences – metropolitan and national – in shaping the way people spent their free time. And secondly, the trend by the start of the twentieth century away from the more socially selective and segregated entertainments of the earlier period towards a greater measure of mass entertainment. These shifts are clearly visible when one looks at the changing pattern of the social year in Maidstone, how people spent their spare time at different seasons. Traditionally, there were recurrent breaks for leisure throughout the year. In the eighteenth century skilled workers often took time off from work on Mondays and Tuesdays; there were similar breaks at ecclesiastical feast times and at the town fairs; and for the upper classes a distinct 'season' of public socialising emerged – in Georgian Maidstone during the spring months. Though the elite 'season' probably disappeared in the early Victorian town as Maidstone's genteel reputation diminished, other festivities continued. As we saw in Chapter Six, St Monday survived in some firms until the 1860s, and the town's fairs retained at least some of their social and leisure significance, with side-shows and other entertainments. In 1868 'a large and influential number of the burgesses' demanded that the fairs be abolished, because of 'the evils arising' from them, and the council investigated 'the practicability of surrendering the charter for the . . . fairs without annulling the right to hold horse and cattle fairs'.[16] But this proved impracticable, and the fairs continued; as the century progressed there were fewer complaints about their social dangers and more acceptance of their role as a place for innocent largely commercial amusement. As for the traditional church feasts, in Maidstone as elsewhere one sees the rise of the Victorian Christmas as a family holiday, buttressed by the official recognition of Boxing Day as a bank holiday under national legislation in 1871 – proposed by the town's MP Sir John Lubbock. Most other feast times, however, faded in importance, except for Whitsuntide which had always been an important and widely observed holiday in the town, with processions, sports and festivities. This had its leisure significance consolidated with the bank holiday on Whit Monday.

Whit Monday and the August bank holiday became the occasions for holiday excursions. Initially these were not cheap: a South Eastern Railway excursion to Dover, Folkestone and a number of other resorts at Whitsun 1872 cost 3s return, third class; but skilled and a growing number of working-class people increasingly regarded them as an annual treat. Third-class railway tickets were certainly not aimed at middle-class excursionists. A favourite resort was Rosherville Gardens, Gravesend, which could be reached for 1s 6d third class in 1867. As well as attractive scenery, the gardens offered music, dioramas, ghost illusions and other amusements. There were also growing numbers of works' excursions to the Thanet coast.

By the early 1890s a Mr Baker was organising excursions from Maidstone and other towns on a regular basis, negotiating cheap fares with the railway companies. Many of the excursions were on Wednesdays, and most of his customers were middle-class inhabitants and perhaps shop-workers (taking advantage of early closing day). However, excursions were also sometimes sponsored by church youth groups, such as those from St Michael's mission, and Tonbridge Road Band of Hope, who travelled by train during the school holidays in August 1892. After the turn of the century charabanc outings became popular, often to the coast, and outing clubs were organised by public houses.

Nearer home, Maidstone's zoo was another popular attraction at holiday times immediately prior to the First World War. Originally the private collection of Sir Garrard Tyrwhitt Drake, a member of Maidstone town council, and mayor on several occasions, it was first opened to the public at his home Cobtree Manor in 1912. In 1914 the animals were moved to Tovil Court, which became the Maidstone Zoological and Pleasure Gardens, and proved a great attraction. Admission prices were a modest 6d, or 3d during the evening, and there were also refreshments at 'popular prices' and fairground amusements. On Whit Monday 1914 as many as 11,500 people paid for admittance, many no doubt coming from the wider area, but the outbreak of war caused the closure of the zoo the following year.

Taken as a whole, the public life of mid-Victorian Maidstone came under the growing sway of the middle classes. The landed classes steadily lost interest in most aspects of town life during the early nineteenth century except for their patronage of charities and hospitals; from mid-century few social gatherings in the town enjoyed gentry or aristocratic support. Already established in political power before parliamentary and municipal reform in the 1830s, the middle classes retained control throughout the period up to 1914. This was paralleled, as we have seen, by middle-class leadership in many aspects of the social and cultural life of the town for much of the period – in the churches, education, and leisure activities. Middle-class groups tried to dominate and supervise working-class life, not only through municipal and social policy, but through the operation and influence of church and cultural organisations.

Yet by the end of the nineteenth century we start to see lower- and working-class inhabitants take more control of their own lives. In employment and politics progress was slow, but in leisure activity the advance was more striking, abetted by commercial interests hoping to exploit a large potential market. The early Victorian working classes had their public houses, perhaps an occasional trip to the theatre, and holiday occasions such as the fairs, but long if erratic working hours, a general lack of education, and for many a rather precarious existence close to the breadline, prevented access to the more diverse leisure culture of their social superiors. Towards the end of Victoria's reign, however, shorter working hours, particularly the Saturday half holiday, the introduction of early closing on Wednesdays for shop-workers, and generally rising real wages, enabled the lower classes to develop their non-working lives to a much greater extent. The desire for self improvement was evident everywhere, as working people formed and joined church organisations, working men's clubs, and sporting, gardening and musical societies. The extension of the franchise to many working men in 1867 doubtless made the council more ready to provide facilities for working-class leisure, and their increased spending power gave impetus to the variety theatre, and eventually the cinema. By the early years of the twentieth century, a broad working- and lower-middle-class culture was asserting a powerful influence in the town, and was to become dominant during the inter-war years, marginalising older elite activities and institutions.

The major changes in the town's economic, social, governmental and cultural organisation during the reigns of Victoria and Edward VII which we have observed in Chapters Six to Eight had a powerful impact not only on the different social groups within the community, but on Maidstone's image and position in the wider region. Maidstone was already well established as the county town of Kent by 1800 and its ascendancy as an administrative centre was steadily enhanced by the acquisition of major county institutions and the County Council in 1889. But if the town's population growth remained head and shoulders above the lesser towns of the area, it was less notable seen in comparison with larger Midlands and northern cities and other county towns in the Home Counties, particularly during the later nineteenth century. Though the industrial sector, together with distribution and services, appear to have been reasonably buoyant for most of the period, those sectors dependent on the regional economy may have fared less well, with the Medway towns and metropolitan London increasingly powerful economic competitors.

Yet in other respects we see an urban community, with a more and more confident middle class, slowly but eventually modernising its civic administration and municipal and public services. We see a flowering of new social and cultural activities and institutions closely geared to the needs of the urban community and its diverse social groups, though with at least some societies and activities appealing to the better off of the neighbouring countryside. Above all, we see a townscape transformed by 1900 with a massive expansion of building – grand suburban villas west of the river, solid middle-class residences towards the Sittingbourne Road, small, cramped working-class terraces near the county gaol and off Stone Street, a number of major public buildings like the museum and library complex on Museum Street, the new grammar school on Tonbridge Road, the enlarged hospitals, and an extraordinary profusion of Gothic style and neo-classical churches and chapels, together with rather bombastic insurance offices and banks on High Street. Deprived of its high county fashionability, Maidstone none the less remained the natural focus of the regional economy and society, enjoying a strategic position which it would exploit with growing success in the inter-war period.

Notes

1. *Maidstone Journal*, 9 June 1835.
2. *Maidstone Gazette*, 13 January 1835; Maidstone Society for the Promotion of Purity of Election, resolutions, Clement Taylor Smythe Transcripts, Maidstone Museum.
3. *Maidstone Gazette*, 17 April 1838.
4. *Maidstone Gazette*, 23 May 1848.
5. *Report of Enquiry into Maidstone Election Petition, 1901* (Maidstone Reference Library); Minutes of Executive Committee of Conservative and Unionist Association, Centre for Kentish Studies [Kent Archives Office], U1634/A2/1/1.
6. *Parliamentary Papers*, 1852–3, LXXXIX, *1851 Religious Census*.
7. *Kent Messenger*, 15 May 1926, reprint of figures from earlier census.
8. A.H. Byles, *The PSA. What it is and how to start it* (London,1891).
9. M. Heath-Stubbs, *Friendship's Highway. Being the History of the Girls Friendly Society, 1875–1925* (London, 1926).
10. Personal communication; *Kelly's Directory of Kent 1882*.
11. D. Russell, *Popular Music in England* (Manchester, 1987), pp. 23–6.
12. *Graham's Illustrated Guide to Maidstone and Neighbourhood*, (Maidstone, 1884); H.V.R Geary, unpublished text in Maidstone Reference Library, 'Sharp's of Maidstone', p. 30.
13. Recollections of Mr P.G. Wallis, 1976 (Maidstone Reference Library, MAI 792.09); Copy letters to Mr K.A.E. Wells (ibid, MAI 792.09).
14. *Kent Messenger*, 24 August 1872; *Morning Advertiser*, 20 August 1872, quoted in Brian Harrison, *Drink and the Victorians* (London, 1971), p. 276; *Parliamentary Papers* 1874, LIV, *Reports from Borough Authorities*.
15. *Parliamentary Papers*, 1898, XXXVII, *Royal Commission on Licensing, Returns of licensed clubs*.
16. Maidstone Council Minutes, Centre for Kentish Studies, Md/ACm3/3.

Bibliographical Note

As in the other nineteenth-century chapters considerable use has been made of the local press in writing this chapter (see Bibliographical Note, Chapter Six). On the political background, N. Gash, *Politics in the Age of Peel* (London, 1953), J.A. Phillips, *The Great Reform Bill in the Boroughs* (Oxford, 1992), F.W.S. Craig, *British Parliamentary Election Results, 1832–1885* (London, 1977); F.W.S. Craig, *British Parliamentary Election Results 1885–1918*, (Aldershot, 1989); and H.J. Hanham, *Elections and Party Management* (Hassocks, Sussex, 1978) have all been consulted. Maidstone Pollbooks are available at the Reference Library and at the Centre for Kentish Studies [Kent Archives Office]. The Clement Taylor Smythe Transcripts in Maidstone Museum also contain some political material. The papers of the Maidstone Conservative and Unionist Association are at the Centre for Kentish Studies, U1634, and there is a 'Labour File' at Maidstone Reference Library (MAI 329).

The section on the churches draws on the 1851 Religious Census, and on the papers of the Anglican parishes and various nonconformist churches in the Centre for Kentish Studies and Maidstone Reference Library. A number of published denominational histories are available: D.A.H. Cleggett, *History of St Michaels and All Angels* (no date or place); R. Jeal, *Maidstone Baptist Church, 1834–1984* (no date or place); G.L. Knighton, *300 Years of Religious Freedom, 1662–1962* (Maidstone, 1962); A.W. Smith, *Wesleyan Methodist Church. A Short History of the Maidstone Circuit* (Maidstone, n.d.); Kathleen M. Topping, *The Church of St Francis Maidstone. A Narrative History 1880–1980* (Maidstone, n.d); (anon), *Maidstone Citadel Corps, The Salvation Army Centenary Brochure, 1882–92*, (np, 1992). Temperance material is held at Maidstone Reference Library (MAI 178), and among church papers.

For leisure and cultural life the local press was of overriding importance. There are also items of interest in the Clement Taylor Smythe transcripts. Maidstone Choral Union has a published history, *Fifty Years of Singing* (Maidstone, n.d.). For the cinema see the copy letters to Mr K.A.E. Wells, in the Maidstone Reference Library, and his article in *Memories of Maidstone* (West Malling, 1978); also Irene Hales, 'Maidstone's Theatres, Live and Electric', *Bygone Kent*, vol. 7. See also her article 'Maidstone's Zoo' in vol. 15 of the same journal. For swimming see Maidstone Swimming Club papers, (U1823) and the Town Council minutes (Md/ACm3/17), both at the Centre for Kentish Studies. For cricket see (anon), *Look to Your Mote, 1857–1957* (no date or place), and on football see *Memories of Maidstone*, as above, pp. 66–7; for pitches see the Local Board minutes (Md/ACm6/6–8), at the Centre for Kentish Studies. A.S. Lamprey's *Guide to the Borough of Maidstone* (Maidstone, 1914) has been generally useful, as has the oral testimony of Mr P.C. Webb.

Chapter Nine

THE FIRST WORLD WAR AND AFTER

There were dramatic shifts in the fortunes of British towns and cities in the decades before the Second World War. The urban centres of old industrial England, particularly in the North, which had specialised in the staple industries of coal, cotton, iron and steel and shipbuilding, were in decline, while those southern towns with new industries or more diversified economies like Maidstone, which also benefited from its proximity to London, became relatively dynamic centres of new growth. While not immune to the bouts of recession which affected the country, especially in the 1920s, the town's economy adapted to change, people flooded in and the tempo of activity quickened. Growing prosperity provided a rating base to finance expenditure on roads and transport, council houses and schools, just as the increased spending power of the lower middle class and working class had ramifications throughout the economy, underpinning changes in shopping and trade, recreational opportunities and leisure facilities. Although there were still many continuities, especially in politics, where the old families and interest groups were still prominent, the town became more open to external, modernising influences. One consequence was that Maidstone began to lose some of its distinctive characteristics and acquired buildings and styles of life that were increasingly common to the new urban England of the inter-war years. In all these respects the First World War might be regarded as a watershed in the town's history.

The First World War

Britain's involvement in the war directly affected Maidstone in a variety of ways, although only a few had lasting consequences. Firstly and most visibly, the town's lights were dimmed in 1915 and extinguished altogether the following year because of fears of attack by Zeppelins and other aircraft, a particular threat in Kent. In the event no bombs fell, but aerial fighting took place overhead. Secondly, Maidstone was turned into a kind of transit camp. People moved into town looking for war work, and as a military base many men passed through en route for other destinations: during the war period 2,343 officers and 70,848 other ranks were billeted in public buildings, schools and private houses, and accommodation was found for over 3,000 horses.[1] Hospitals were provided for the wounded at Hayle

Place and at the Howard de Walden Institute. In addition, by the beginning of 1918 the town had become a 'clearing house' for aliens under the National Service Scheme with some thousands passing through. These experiences may have helped to make the town more outward looking and after the war a connection was built up with Montauban, a small town on the Somme, which had been devastated, in part by the West Kent Regiment fighting there in 1916. Maidstone council formally 'adopted' the French town, which was sent farm machinery and fruit trees to help the community begin to cultivate their land again.

The more far-reaching consequences of wartime conditions came from the strains imposed on the local economy. The most immediate was the acute shortage of labour, due to enthusiastic voluntary enrolment followed by military conscription. During 1914 Maidstone men of all classes volunteered for service, much patriotic fervour was in evidence, and employers encouraged their men to enlist. The flow of recruits slowed during the spring of 1915, but in June a huge recruiting meeting re-awakened enthusiasm.[2] Workers in essential industries, such as quarrying and some sectors of engineering, were issued with badges so they were not pressured into enlisting, but some nevertheless did so. By the time conscription was introduced in 1916, the male workforce was greatly depleted, and employers were fighting to keep those men remaining. Some of Maidstone's industries, notably food and paper, had always relied heavily on female workers, but as the shortage of men became more serious, the 'dilution' of skilled male labour by women became more widespread, and even heavy labouring jobs were tackled by females.

The war also affected the town's industries in other ways. Supplies of imported raw materials were disrupted and exports to overseas markets became extremely difficult. Many factories went over, to a greater or lesser extent, to war production. Tilling-Stevens were engaged on munitions work, while Cliffords manufactured quantities of hop-screening cloth for use in the trenches as camouflage for gun emplacements. Drake and Fletcher's hop-spraying machines were adapted to War Office specifications for use against German gas, and Weeks and Son, engineers, took on other military contracts. In 1917, Sharp's factory was converted to carry out fruit pulping on a large scale in order to make jam for the army. For some employers the war offered important new opportunities: thus the Week Street tailor Armstrong won a contract for khaki uniforms and built a factory to manufacture them.

The industry most adversely affected by the war was brewing. Supplies of grain to brewers and distillers were curtailed to preserve food stocks, and in 1916 official restrictions were imposed on the strength and output of beer. Public house closures under the 1904 Act continued during the war. Further curbs on brewing early in 1917 reduced the output of the nation's breweries to little more than a quarter of the pre-war level; by this time shortages were occurring in local public houses even though steadily increasing levels of taxation had doubled the average price of a pint of beer, and public house opening hours had been greatly curtailed. Restrictions on brewing also had serious repercussions on the hop trade. Imports of foreign hops were banned in 1916, but the following spring, with much of the previous year's crop still unsold, there were fears that prices would collapse. The growers pressed for action, and after discussions with the trade, the government imposed a 50 per cent reduction in the acreage under hops, and set up a Hop Control Committee to buy all crops at an agreed price. Possibly because of the importance of the Maidstone market, George Foster Clark was appointed chairman of the committee, and acted as Hop Controller until 1925, after which trade was freed until 1931, when a further marketing scheme was introduced. Kent's hop acreage was reduced by more than a half, as many small growers gave up the crop completely, but a considerable acreage remained in the Maidstone area, and the annual influx of hop-pickers from London continued.[3]

With the exception of hops, Maidstone's markets and fairs were in a broadly flourishing condition during the war. The new Agricultural Hall in Lock Meadow, which opened in May 1915, became a venue for displays of farm machinery, and for fruit auctions, until the building was commandeered for use as a military slaughterhouse and subsequently for the accommodation of aliens during the last part of the war. Although the Corn Exchange was used throughout for billeting troops, the corn market continued to operate on a small scale. The war disrupted imports, and in May 1915 it was reported that wheat prices in the market, as elsewhere, had reached a level unknown since 1872 during the aftermath of the Franco-Prussian war. There were also shortages in the town's shops, especially of meat and margarine, although there was not an absolute shortage of food. Nevertheless, food prices soared, causing distress and contributing to industrial discontent.

Although wartime conditions enabled some workers, particularly women, to earn higher wages than ever before, certain sectors, notably the paper industry, continued to pay workers at pre-war levels. There was a rapid growth in trade union membership in the machine mills, especially at Tovil, during the first year of the war, and union officials were active in protesting about rising prices. Evidently fearing the permanent erosion of wages, they also demanded that women taking over male jobs be paid men's wages. In May 1915 the union demanded that A.E. Reed's at Tovil pay their employees a war bonus, that is, a temporary wage increase for the duration of the war. In the handmade paper mills the Original Society of Papermakers made three unsuccessful applications for a war bonus before calling a strike in April 1916. After three weeks the employers agreed to an increase of 1s a day for skilled men and 6d for others, and the men at Springfield and Hayle returned to work.

Probably as a response to food shortages, Maidstone council embarked on 'municipal farming' during 1915. The provision of allotments was also extended following a government order in 1916. The town council formed a Food Control Committee in 1917, as further government orders required local authorities to requisition various food supplies and distribute them for sale in local shops. The committee, which included representatives of labour and the food trades as well as councillors, also administered rationing when this was introduced. Shortages remained nevertheless and lengthy queues became an ever present feature of Maidstone life. During the winter of 1917/18 there was much criticism of the Food Control Committee by the town's Trades Council which complained, among other things, of butchers delivering to wealthy households while their shops were closed to other customers.

The distribution of coal was badly disrupted by war conditions, and there was a widespread shortage of domestic fuel. The government took control of the coal industry in 1917, setting up national and regional coal control committees, and Maidstone council then appointed a local committee to negotiate with the Southern Counties Coal Control Committee. In October 200 tons of coal were brought to Maidstone and stored in the Tithe Barn (the Archbishop's stables) for sale to the poor when the need arose. Another committee was appointed to negotiate and fix retail prices with local coal merchants.

Wartime conditions inhibited the plans which the council had been formulating to improve education and housing provision. Schooling was disrupted, classrooms being requisitioned for army use, most house building came to a halt, and development of the two small council-owned sites on the Tonbridge and Upper Fant Roads was deferred. All the council could do was press ahead with preparations for attacking the borough's housing shortage after the end of the war. An additional 15 acres of land adjacent to Tonbridge Road, the 'Cherry Orchard' site was bought for building, and in 1917 a Housing Committee, with a much wider remit than the old Cottage Building Committee, was set up. The committee held a competition to find the best plan for the Cherry Orchard site, which was to be a high quality estate with a density of no more than twelve houses to an acre; a plan for building 162 houses was eventually selected, to commence once the war ended. In the meantime, a plan of all possible building land in and near the borough was prepared to serve as the basis for future town planning.

One positive effect of the war was the heightened concern about the condition of the poor and the health of the population. A virulent influenza epidemic in 1918 devastated the town and, as a report in the *Kent Messenger* pointed out, those who suffered most severely were the poor 'living in the crowded, sordid courts and alleys which have long been a blackspot on the social aspect of the town'. Another well-publicised concern was the rate of infant mortality which had increased since 1914. Bolstered by national sentiment about the importance of preserving lives, and concern over the poor physical condition of many working-class recruits to the army, the attention of medical officers and philanthropic bodies alike was directed towards improving the child-rearing practices of working-class mothers. The first steps had been taken prior to the war with the registration and training of midwives, but a new initiative was the founding in 1916 of an infant welfare centre or 'school for mothers' as it became known, by Mrs Bellairs, wife of the Maidstone MP, with the assistance of the superintendent of the Kent midwifery service. This voluntary organisation was extended after the war (1919) into a maternity and child welfare centre supported by the council, with ante-natal clinics held in Padsole and Medway

Street. The council also appointed health visitors. As early as 1908 the medical officer had been urging the importance of providing better knowledge and training to mothers, since many children's diseases were due, he thought, to a 'want of maternal care and solicitude'. The war precipitated action on this issue.

Finally, the war helped to advance and strengthen the political claims of women and labour. This was not at first apparent in the case of women, as the initial rush of patriotic fervour caused the town's Women's Suffrage Society to abandon its campaign for the vote, and to channel its energies into the home front and support for war charities. But women also began to take an increased role in local administration by serving on committees, and this paved the way for greater female involvement in local politics during the inter-war years. By 1918 women's war work had made the case for their enfranchisement unanswerable, and women over thirty who were householders or wives of householders were given the vote in February that year.

As for labour, an organisation called the Maidstone Socialist Society became active during the early part of the war, and for a time held regular meetings at which a socialist critique of the war was discussed, and government intervention to control prices demanded. This organisation appears to have been shortlived, but as we have seen, the town's Trades Council began to be very active as a pressure group. Although the town council refused to accede to their demands and co-opt their nominees to fill council vacancies, the Trades Council was given a voice on council-appointed committees, and Labour's goal of elected representation on the council was achieved soon after the war. In addition, Frederick Burgess, a railway guard and a Maidstone man, was selected as the Labour parliamentary candidate for the borough in 1916, and following the reorganisation of the Maidstone constituency as a division of the county of Kent in 1917, the town's fledgeling Labour party began to prepare for the hustings. The extension of voting rights to all men in 1918 boosted their campaign. Large advertisements explaining Labour's aims and policies appeared regularly in the local press, and the tone of political debate in the town altered, as Labour challenged the Liberals as the main opposition to the Conservatives.

An expanding town

When the Armistice was announced, and the street and house lights came back on, it seemed to one observer that 'Maidstone was its old self again'.[4] In fact, the town was never to return to its pre-war self. One reason for this was that the late Victorian decline in the rate of population growth was arrested in the decade 1911–21, despite the number of war deaths, and in the next two decades demographic growth accelerated markedly. In the peak decade of 1921–31 the rate of growth was nearly three times the national average. Although this rate was not maintained subsequently, the population kept on increasing and Maidstone began to sprawl outside its old limits. Much of this growth was due to migration, and in small part reflected the national movement of population towards the more prosperous south

Fig. 4   Maidstone in 1932. (Kent Messenger Group Newspapers.)

east, and away from the depressed areas of the North and Wales. Between 1921 and 1931, migrants accounted for 60 per cent of the total population increase and a further 58 per cent between 1931 and 1951. The consequence was that by 1951, 33.1 per cent of the town's inhabitants had been born outside the county of Kent, compared with 21.9 per cent in 1871. However, a comparison of the distribution of birthplaces in 1951 with that for 1851 (Table 2) shows that the overall pattern of migration had changed only to a small extent over the hundred years. A rather larger section of the incoming population had been born in Scotland, Wales or the seven northern counties, but the town continued to draw heavily on those areas closer to home, the villages and small towns of mid-Kent, which had always supplied its migrants. The higher proportions of residents born in London and the neighbouring counties is suggestive, however. It appears that Maidstone was expanding not only because of thriving industries and commercial businesses which could absorb labour from depressed regions, but also because it was a desirable place to live and, increasingly, a convenient base for commuting.

The rapidly growing population had a marked visible impact on the topography of a town which even in the 1920s was expanding beyond its existing boundaries. The council, in line with contemporary thinking in the 1920s and 1930s, developed a ring of low density housing estates for rent to tenants on the periphery: at Cherry Orchard, Coombe Farm near Tovil, in the Upper Fant Road area, at Mangravet Wood on the Sutton Road, at Hastings Road, later known as the Foster Clark Estate, and finally at Ringlestone Farm. Some of these developments were made possible by sales from the Earl of Romney's estate to the corporation. The location of the Romney holdings, which included the Mote Park area but also land in Fant and Tovil and beyond the town boundaries towards Allington, was also a key factor in the development of middle-class housing, as it had been in the nineteenth century. In the 1930s Maidstone shared in the bonanza of private suburban house building that transformed much of the Greater London area. In a period of very low interest rates for mortgages and falling building costs, a new type of speculative builder emerged capable of exploiting the strong demand for private suburban housing by erecting large numbers of relatively cheap houses for owner-occupation and employing new techniques to sell them. In Maidstone new middle-class houses were built on all sides of the town in the 1930s, spilling over into neighbouring parishes such as Bearsted, but the major development, and a typical example of inter-war suburbia, was the Allington estate to the north west of the town. In 1931–2 the Romney trustees sold 15,625 acres for the relatively low price of £4,612 to the agent of the Maidstone builders, Messrs Cox. The latter laid out this large area on either side of the London Road with detached and semi-detached houses in a string of developments distinguished by suburban respectability and uniformity. The boundary extension of 1932 ensured that such estates as well as the new council estates would be incorporated within the town. Along with this spatial expansion of the town, stretching out well away from the old urban core, there was a widening circle of economic activity.

The developing economy and trends in employment

The vitality of Maidstone in the inter-war years was in part due to the success of the local economy in adapting to changing markets and carrying further that development of new and more specialised manufacturing production which had begun in the pre-war engineering trades. However, the most significant trend affecting the pattern of employment, as Table 6 shows, was the continuing growth in professional, white collar and commercial employment, which between 1921 and 1931 increased its share of total male manpower by over 5 per cent. These sectors very probably continued to expand in the 1930s and by the time of the next census in 1951 they employed 39 per cent of employed men. An important part of the increase came from the growth of local government, particularly the Kent County Council, but there was also a significant advance in the civil service – mostly during and after the Second World War. The 1951 figures also include administrative expansion under the post-war Labour government, with increasing numbers of white collar workers commuting to offices in London. In addition, there may have been a modest rise of jobs in legal, medical and financial services (discussed below).

Manufacturing employment showed a small but still significant increase during the 1920s, and given that the male workforce as a whole expanded by 19 per cent during that decade, considerable industrial growth is indicated. Although employment in manufacturing declined slightly in relative terms over the period 1931–51, the workforce continued to increase in size, absorbing much of the expanding population. In contrast, employment in agricultural and extractive industries declined in absolute as well as proportionate terms. However, the remaining sectors showed only a slight diminution in their share of male employment, and the building trades, along with transport and communication, continued to be important employers of male labour, absorbing a fifth of the workforce in 1931. This diversity of employment contributed to the resilience with which the town's economy came through the recessions of the inter-war years.

Trends in female employment show more marked changes, though the percentage of the adult female population in work remained constant at 32 per cent and there was no increase in the proportion of married women in the labour force, reversing the situation during the First World War. The decline in the share of female employment by the manufacturing sector is the most striking feature of the figures set out in Table 7, especially between 1911 and 1921. It may be that women bore the brunt of the temporarily depressed state of manufacturing in the two census years of 1921 and 1931, and there is some evidence to suggest that school leavers were replacing older women in industrial employment. But the most likely explanation is that more women were choosing to forsake the factories, because of the increasing availability of more congenial work as shop assistants, clerks and typists. Already in 1931 the percentage employed in this type of work exceeded the numbers in industrial employment by some 3 per cent. It should also be added that the professional category was swelled by increasing numbers of nurses and teachers as local hospital and school provision expanded. On the other hand, there was a significant decline in the numbers of domestic servants in the decade 1911–20, which continued, except for a brief rise during the depression in 1931, up to the Second World War and beyond. In 1951 only 470 women were in domestic service and the majority of these were non-resident. By then female service employment had been boosted by new opportunities in hotels and catering, although the sector was still slightly smaller than in 1931.

Shops and distribution

The most important trend during the inter-war years was the continuing invasion of national chain stores which by the 1930s clustered in prime sites in High Street and Week Street, squeezing out other, local traders. Despite this, the large drapery emporium of Blake and Sons continued in business in High Street well into the post-war years, but the old department store type businesses of Frank King and Sons and Denniss Paine and Co. had both been broken up by 1930. The first modern department store in Maidstone, Chiesmans, was established on the corner of High Street and Pudding Lane during the 1930s. The Maidstone Co-operative Society had expanded to three grocery shops by 1930, and four by 1938, but large-scale growth did not occur until after the Second World War.[5] While most customers of these stores belonged to the middle and lower classes, many families in working-class areas continued to patronise the multitude of corner shops, sometimes two or three to a street, making their purchases on 'tick'.

There were complementary developments in food and drink retailing. Public houses stagnated in number and became more respectable, while the number of ancient inns-cum-hotels declined (the Bell disappeared in the 1930s). At the same time, restaurants, cafés and tea-rooms increased their presence, notably in the High Street and other main streets. Already by the time of the First World War 'Ye Ancient Cafe' in Bank Street offered 'afternoon tea fancies in great variety', while the Carlton Café at the top of the High Street served lunch, afternoon teas, ices, and American iced drinks; lower down came the Middle Row Restaurant and Pocock's Restaurant near the bridge. By the 1930s there was strong competition from the extensive tea-rooms in Chiesman's department store on the High Street and the Granada cinema, as well as from smaller but respectable establishments in King Street and Week Street. If these places served mainly the better-off middle classes, including probably a growing number of women, poorer cafés in Stone Street and off High Street, together with fish and chip shops on Week Street, Stone Street and in working-class areas continued to feed the lower orders. Even here there were some advances by the 1930s, with the upgrading of cheap cafés and the arrival of ice-cream parlours and milk bars on Week Street and Lower Stone Street. By 1938 the national chain of J. Lyons had opened a café with waitress service near the town hall, attracting middle- and working-class customers from both town and countryside.

Maidstone in this period remained the shopping centre for a wide area of mid-Kent, and it was boosted in the inter-war period by improved transport from villages in the area. When the bankruptcy of a Staplehurst grocer was reported in the local press in 1930, it was attributed to the advent of motor buses to Maidstone, and competition from multiples. By that date the Maidstone and District Bus Company was operating an extensive network of services to and from the town; a new purpose-built bus station – one of the first in the country – had been opened near the Archbishop's Palace in 1922. There were also cheap day returns for Saturday shoppers on the railway (both the East and West Station lines to London were electrified in 1939). The increasing availability of private cars made shopping in Maidstone easier for the middle classes, though the shortage of parking places and congestion soon became serious problems. Alderman Foster Clark argued at a council meeting in 1926 that 'those towns which provided accommodation for motor cars would get the shopping customers in future', and the following year land in Palace Avenue was surfaced as a car park. However, in 1930 the council's proposal to buy and demolish houses in Faith Street and Havoc Lane for a car park was strongly opposed by the ratepayers' association.

In the wholesale trade sector Arkcolls and Laurences, the two major grocery firms, continued in business throughout the inter-war years and after, but they no longer dominated the trade of the area as in the past. The retail grocers, Ibberson and Wood, for instance, whose shop was opposite Arkcolls premises, did some trade with them, but they also dealt with wholesalers in Brighton and Battle, and obtained other products direct from manufacturers. A third wholesale grocery business Coombes Bros, was established in Boxley Road during the 1930s, while the long-established wholesale clothiers and dealers in household goods, Marchant and Tubb, remained a sizeable business into the post-war years.

The fortunes of the town's markets to some extent reflected the shifts and changes in mid-Kent agriculture during the 1920s and 30s, although they remained relatively buoyant. The corn market continued steadily, but the hop trade in Maidstone market was negligible during the 1920s when the industry was in difficulties and after 1931 all business was carried on direct with the brewers. In contrast, the town's cattle market suffered no diminution in size or importance, and large numbers of sheep and other animals continued to be traded at the fairs, especially in October and May. In 1920 the market was moved from the Fair Meadow to Lock Meadow, where the fairs were already held, and a number of improvements were made to the layout and facilities during the early 1930s. By 1936 a combination of sheep rearing and cherry growing had become typical of farming in the region, and the acreage of orchards in the county increased by 80 per cent over that of 1913. However, the acreage of soft fruit fell by nearly a half over the same period, indicating more intensive use of land and building development, and also growing competition from other counties. Even so a thrice-weekly produce market was started in the Agricultural Hall when it was released from military use in 1919, and this rapidly became a thriving concern, with more fruit traded through

Maidstone than in the past. During the 1920s Maidstone developed as a major poultry market, with several thousand birds sold each month. An egg packing station was opened adjacent to the West Station during the 1930s.

Industries

The manufacturing economy of Maidstone saw few changes in the relative importance of different industries during the inter-war years although each of them continued to evolve in various ways. The census returns of industrial occupations in 1921 and 1931 provide some guide to the relative importance of different sectors of manufacture, but are too imprecise for detailed analysis. In broad terms, trades comprising the engineering industry – which included not only engineering but metals and vehicle manufacture and the new electrical trades – formed the largest industrial sector in the town by 1939, followed by paper, food manufacture and brewing.

The principal engineering employers were Tilling-Stevens, the coach and commercial vehicle makers; Drake and Fletcher and William Weeks and Son, both agricultural and general engineering companies; and E.A. Gardner and Sons, who were brass founders and general and electrical engineers. There were also a number of other smaller electrical and mechanical engineering, sheet metal, brass founding and coppersmith businesses in the town. The rapid growth in motor vehicle ownership after 1918 boosted the establishment or expansion of motor engineering firms. Drake and Fletcher became agents for General Motors and other manufacturers, but the most notable motor engineers in Maidstone were Rootes, who during the 1920s became major motor wholesalers, and the country's largest motor retailers. During the mid-1920s they built charabancs on to a Tilling-Stevens chassis at their Len Engineering Works in Mill Street, but in 1928 they transferred their head office to London, and embarked on car manufacture elsewhere, confining the Maidstone operations to distribution and service.

All the main paper manufacturers operating in and near the town before the war continued in business after 1918. A.E. Reed's expanded their operations to a large new mill at Aylesford in 1920. The Ivy Millboard Co. had apparently ceased production, but a new paper company, Powell Lane Manufacturing, subsequently Medway Corrugated Paper, was operating at Tovil by 1930. The manufacturing stationers, William Hobbs and Son and W.P. Dickinson and Son, also remained in business, the latter also operating as printers. Alabaster Passmore and Co., the town's largest printing concern, employed increasing numbers at their works at Tovil, where they specialised in items such as coloured catalogues, and another growing printing business, Esgate Chamberlain and Co., on Sandling Road, expanded into box making in 1920.

Food manufacture and the long-established brewing industry remained important employment sectors. In confectionery, Sharp's continued to be the main employer, but two other nineteenth-century firms, Jackson and Smith, the makers of 'Bettina toffee' and Wallace V. Brett were still in business. Foster Clark's foods employed large numbers in canning fruit and vegetables and manufacturing custard powder, packet soup and other products. On the brewing front, the four firms in business in the pre-war period were all operating during the 1920s. Mason's Waterside Brewery expanded modestly as a family concern, but Fremlins, which began to buy or lease as many tied houses as possible from the mid-1920s, was floated as a public company in 1928; the following year it bought Isherwood, Foster and Stacey's Lower Brewery and all their tied houses, bringing the total number of houses under its control to over 350. Style and Winch at the Medway Brewery were also involved in further takeovers, but they themselves were bought up in 1929 by the London brewers Barclay Perkins. Style and Winch continued to brew in Maidstone under their own name, but Barclay Perkins took over the supply of beer to all their tied houses in London. This scramble for tied houses was partly a response to the further closures of licensed premises during the early 1920s, and the difficulty in obtaining licences for new houses. Mergers and declining outlets probably affected the level of employment in this industry, but the census figures are unclear. The 1921 census gives employment in the manufacture of drinks, but this included distilling and mineral waters: Grant's cherry brandy distillery and Hayward's, Maskell's and Lyle's mineral water manufactories all continued to operate throughout the inter-war years.

Among other occupational categories, the most significant in terms of employment were textiles and clothing and the making of wood products and furniture. The first category included the employees of two identifiable firms: James Clifford's old established rope, matting, sail and tarpaulin works, and Armstrong's clothing manufacturers, the latter continuing in business after their wartime contracts ended, producing in part for their own outfitters shop. In addition, there were numerous small tailoring and dressmaking businesses. In the second category we find two furniture manufacturers, S.P. Sanders, who had a factory on Boxley Road, and R.W. Robson who had a bedding, upholstery and cabinet making works in Union Street. Directories also list other firms of cabinet makers in the town and suburbs, whose employees added to the numbers recorded in the wood and furniture trades. This category also included thirty-six sawyers, some or all of whom may have worked for the town's three timber merchants. Another significant source of employment were the two Haywards brush factories.

The service sector

As we saw earlier, an important boost to employment in the inter-war town came from the growth of the service sector. In some long-established areas such as the legal profession there does not seem to have been any major upturn in the number of firms, though the size and volume of business may well have grown. Medical practitioners appear to have increased in number with the spread of general practices to some of the newer suburban areas and the expansion of medical facilities at the West Kent Hospital and the Barming Asylum. On the financial front, insurance firms remained a fairly stable group, though their overall business may have expanded; the number of banks, all national ones, rose to six; and the town saw the arrival in 1930 of the first branches of modern building societies (the Halifax and Woolwich Equitable), which had been joined by a branch of the National Building Society by 1938. The appearance of building societies doubtless reflects the rapid increase of the private housing market in the 1930s, which may also explain the growing incidence of estate agents in the town, rising from eleven in 1930 to nineteen in 1938.

One of the most influential developments in this sector, however, was the expansion of local government. Though there was a modest increase in borough council staff during this period, the county council experienced a major accession of buildings, functions and employees. In addition to the new county offices at the sessions house in 1913, the county acquired in 1921 the Springfield site, once the home of the Balstons; this housed the Education Department, County Library and, after 1931, County Supplies. At the sessions house new office wings were added in 1936 and 1939, when the complex was renamed County Hall. Other council offices proliferated in the town including the county surveyor's department in St Peter's Street and the dispensary on Knightrider Street established in 1919. During the inter-war years the council, despite attacks of financial stringency, enlarged its activities to embrace agriculture, library provision, medical services, unemployment and (after 1929) poor assistance and highways; the education service also continued to grow. Rising county expenditure – by 1938–9 reaching about £6 million – had a wide-ranging effect on the local urban economy. As well as the capital works already mentioned, the Barming Asylum was extended in the 1920s and 1930s and in 1927 a new nursing home opened there – leading to a substantial increase of staff. Housing for some council staff was built on the northern edge of the town and there was a considerable school building programme (discussed below). In 1939–40 the old county police headquarters at Wren's Cross was replaced by large new premises on Sutton Road. The ranks of county council employees in Maidstone expanded markedly. At headquarters at County Hall the number more than doubled from 230 in 1919 to over 550 in 1939 with a large number of others based at Springfield (County Supplies had 88 staff in 1933). The period also saw an increase of other council employees (including teachers) in the town. By 1939 the council was not only the biggest single employer in Maidstone but its economic impact on the property market, business supplies and general demand was undoubtedly powerful.

In contrast relatively little is known about the impact of the barracks along Sandling Road on the local economy. However, it probably continued to give employment to local civilian workers and to purchase supplies from town contractors, while soldiers crowded the public houses on the north side of town. During the inter-war period the barracks remained the base of the Royal West Kent regiment, though with other troops passing through, mainly for the colonies. Cut-backs as a result of government financial stringencies were probably offset in the late

1930s by preparations for war. Overall, the general growth of the service sector, along with the relative buoyancy of distribution and industry, confirmed the renewed strength and diversity of Maidstone's economy in the inter-war period. The variety of different labour markets not only mitigated the effects of periodic trade depressions, but also had implications for industrial relations.

Industrial relations, unemployment and the poor

In the years immediately after the First World War trade unionism grew, and the town's Trades Council was also very active. Unskilled and fragmented groups of workers began to be better organised, and in 1920 the National Union of Shop Assistants, Warehousemen and Clerks held well attended monthly meetings in the town, while the Workers Union recruited among the unskilled and semi-skilled in the paper mills. Nevertheless, many workers in the breweries and confectionery and food firms remained unorganised. It is probable that the long-standing union presence among skilled workers in the paper mills made it easier for them to recruit unskilled employees there than in industries which had no tradition of union membership.

Despite this growth in unionism, industrial relations between the wars were usually harmonious. Most businesses of any size provided welfare and leisure facilities, and there were outings and parties for employees' children. Hours remained very long by modern standards, and wages, particularly for women, were often low. In the immediate aftermath of the war the Trades Council lobbied for the removal of women workers, and the employment of ex-servicemen, especially the disabled. There was also a general negotiation of new wage agreements, in line with post-war prices, and this resulted in several strikes, including a major one at Springfield Mill in 1920. In 1926 the General Strike was joined mainly by printers, paper workers and railwaymen. There was also a limited response from bus and tram drivers, and from the unionised employees at the electricity works, while some builders – but not those working on council houses – likewise downed tools; but there were no stoppages in engineering, the breweries or at Sharp's. Foster Clark's was also largely unaffected, and workers at the Medway flour mill seceded from their union in order to remain at work. Employers' reactions varied. At A.E. Reed's mills, which were at a standstill, the company organised sports matches, transporting the men in lorries and giving them tea. At Turkey Mill, however, 'loyal' women employees were presented with watches when the strike was over, indicating rather different attitudes at that old established firm.[6]

As a manufacturing town Maidstone was inevitably affected by the instability of the British economy in the inter-war period, although even in the worst years of the Great Depression the level of unemployment never rose above 10 per cent of the workforce – a modest figure compared with the massive rates of unemployment in the severely depressed industrial areas of the North and Wales. Nevertheless, particular industries and groups of workers were vulnerable to the impact of economic recession.

Problems began to be experienced in 1920–1 after the post-war boom collapsed and in consequence numbers on the local register of unemployed began to rise, although they fluctuated seasonally and there were fewer out of work during the summer months. Labour organisations claimed that the official register understated the real number since some of the unemployed were not entitled to benefit. In 1921 a press report asserting that 1,633 were unemployed or on short time created much local concern since this was 9.7 per cent of the labour force. An appeal for donations to an unemployment relief fund, set up by the Trades Council and Labour party, claimed there were 'people in the town with half their home gone [half their furnishings pawned or sold] and their children hungry and shoeless'.[7] The majority out of work seem to have been engineering workers, but the unskilled also suffered. By the summer of 1923, however, the economic situation had improved to the extent that the council's proposed relief work schemes for the coming winter were all rejected by the Ministry of Health, on the grounds that 'the present state of unemployment in the area could not be regarded as abnormal'; but rising unemployment in the winter months made it necessary for relief work to be provided after all. During the following two years there was a gradual upturn in the situation, although according to oral evidence the labour market remained volatile, with lay-offs commonplace. Nevertheless, by 1926 engineering was said to have revived, there was 'an even tendency' in paper, and demand was reported in the building trade.

The onset of the Great Depression, and the collapse in world trade which followed the Wall Street crash in October 1929 and the banking crisis in Europe, had a rapid but not a devastating impact on Maidstone. In January 1930 the *Kent Messenger* printed a bullish report on the state of local industry headlined 'Prosperous Kent'. Paper-making in particular was proclaimed 'a bright spot in the Kent firmament', with every mill said to be fully occupied; but the newspaper admitted that the unemployment rate had increased, putting this at 8 per cent of the workforce, somewhat higher than the level of registered unemployed. The number on the register rose quickly and as a sign of growing distress in the town a deputation of unemployed men met the council at the end of January to ask for relief work. At a subsequent meeting in April, the men's spokesman claimed that the Communist Party was active among the unemployed. 'Some of the men', he said, 'had come to the limit of their tether, and they would as soon be in Maidstone gaol and their wives in the workhouse, with the ratepayers' money keeping them, as they would be walking about hungry.'[8] Although the situation improved during the summer, thanks mainly to seasonal fruit- and hop-picking, by the autumn economic activity was fading away: employees at Sharp's were on a three-day week, engineering was reported to be 'very slack', and the building trade had little work except for a few large contracts in the hands of major employers. The machine-made paper trade remained fairly good, but Balstons were about to shut down Springfield Mill for several weeks. Sixty men were labouring on relief schemes, and the council committee had to turn its attention to the provision of extra work for the coming winter. Unemployment continued to rise, and by November engineering was 'inactive', several paper mills were on short time, bricklayers were largely without work, and due to the generally depressed state of the local economy, distributive trade was reported to be 'very slack'. However, the total registered as unemployed in December 1930, 1,206, was still only 5.8 per cent of the workforce, although it would have been higher without civic relief work. Thereafter the situation deteriorated. By August 1931 it was reported that prospects in the paper industry were 'very poor' and there was no change for the better in the other industries. In October the unemployed total reached 1,771 and the following month 2,024 or 10 per cent of the workforce.

Relief work schemes on roads, sewers and other public works were still in operation until the latter part of 1932, and many repairs and improvements were brought forward. A public subscription fund – the Mayor's Employment Fund – was set up at the end of 1932, which provided some small-scale work, tidying up the parks and municipal cemetery, before being wound up a year later. The fund also helped support the Unemployed Social Centre which was started in the town early in 1933, although this was also financed by the work of its members. The centre had a canteen, a small library, and facilities for table tennis, dominoes and other games and there were also vocational training classes. Some men stayed as members of the centre for a considerable time suggesting the persistence of longer-term unemployment in the town. However, the centre was wound up in 1935 as the local economy revived and the number of unemployed fell to an insignificant figure. The later 1930s were a period of prosperity at Maidstone (as in other southern towns), possibly boosted by increased military activity prior to the outbreak of war.

During the depression years National Insurance and other state financed unemployment benefits introduced after the First World War, enabled most of those without work to avoid recourse to poor relief. But some families fell through the net, and for them the policy was to pay out-relief. Numbers of other families who needed assistance because of illness or other difficulty also received payments while remaining in their own homes. In Maidstone and the adjacent areas of the Poor Law Union around seventy families a week on average were assisted in this way during the 1920s, but some of them received only medicines or help with funeral expenses. A few families, usually large ones headed by widows, were forced to enter the workhouse, but after the introduction of widows' pensions in 1925, workhouse children were usually orphans or those with parents unable or unwilling to look after them. By the end of the First World War we find a small children's home attached to the Coxheath institution, but boys over eleven were sent to St Pancras schools in Watford and girls over eleven went to one of two training homes for domestic servants in Maidstone. Whenever possible, younger children were boarded out with families in the area, where they often remained until they left school.

During the 1920s the long-term inmates of the workhouse were all either old and infirm, chronic sick or mentally handicapped. Old age pensions enabled many of the aged poor to remain independent, but those without relatives to care for them often ended their days there. Some short-term sick also found their way to the workhouse infirmary, despite the continued expansion of the West Kent Hospital, and a number of women made use of the maternity unit. There was an annual influx of sick hoppers requiring treatment, but vagrants were not accommodated at Coxheath on a regular basis after 1917, when the casual wards were closed for the duration of the war and never reopened. By this time, attitudes towards workhouse inmates had become more humane, and the twelve guardians for Maidstone parish, four of them women, endeavoured to improve workhouse conditions as far as financial constraints allowed. There was also a Ladies Workhouse Visiting Committee, an outside voluntary body, who concerned themselves particularly with the comfort of elderly women. By 1925 the wards had been provided with gramophones; there was a small library; amateur concert parties made regular visits; outings were organised, and residents were permitted to spend holidays with relatives.

In 1929, the Local Government Act abolished Boards of Guardians, placing the administration of the Poor Law in the hands of county councils, and Coxheath institution passed under the control of Kent County Council's Public Assistance Committee [PAC], although the administration of out-relief was delegated to committees composed of former guardians with local knowledge. Maidstone had always resented losing control over its own affairs, and this was no exception. But despite claims that the old system administered by Maidstone 'was exceptional' in its provision, there seems little doubt that things changed for the better under the enlightened PAC Officer, John Moss, who set out to remove any lingering ideas of deterrence from Poor Law administration. The PAC modernised and improved the Coxheath building and installed central heating. Some elderly folk remained in residence, and for these the diet was raised to a high nutritional standard, but a policy of reducing the numbers of non-sick inmates was pursued. As a result of the payment of old age pensions being extended to those aged 65 in 1929, it was possible for many elderly people, with additional outdoor relief, to remain independent. By 1938 the small children's home had been closed, the children moved to County Homes, and part of the premises converted into accommodation for mentally-handicapped men. The Coxheath institution continued to operate until 1948, when the Poor Law was finally abolished and the buildings were transferred to the Ministry of Health for use as a hospital.

The increasing role played by central government in the relief of poverty and unemployment between the wars greatly lessened dependence on private charity in Maidstone. However, as we have seen, there was an unemployment relief fund, and some of the churches continued to give assistance where needed, and to foster self help by running penny banks and coal and clothing clubs. The town's almshouses, and the pensions paid by local charities continued to be a welcome resource for a minority of the elderly, and bread was still distributed by the town's bread charities during the early 1920s, but their importance was on the wane. In 1932 the Charity Commissioners diverted the proceeds of the bread charity funds to the general benefit of the town poor, and money was subsequently given for medical and educational purposes, or to help individuals in urgent need.[9] Yet many families continued to live on or near the breadline, and the annual *Kent Messenger* Christmas teas for poor children, and associated distribution of boots, continued even into the more affluent late 1930s. The boots fund continued to be supported by local employers and wealthy townspeople, and was also swelled by gifts from the numerous slate and tontine clubs in public houses and clubs.

Despite the economic problems of the inter-war years, and the periods of unemployment and short time working suffered by sections of the population, there were real gains in security and standards of living for working-class people. Trade unions were more and more able to secure improved wages and conditions for their members, even though the cost of living was falling for much of the period, and on the whole industrial relations were harmonious. Poverty was by no means eradicated, and the sick and old remained vulnerable, but state benefits and pensions, if not generous, increasingly reduced reliance on the Poor Law, and the stigma associated with relief began to recede. In addition working-class families benefited from the expansion of subsidised housing, and from the improvement in educational and health facilities provided by the municipality although, as we shall see, there were shortcomings in some of these services.

Municipal provision of public services

In all towns during the inter-war years, municipal activity increased as existing services were extended and new responsibilities acquired as a result of national legislation. As in the nineteenth century, the extent to which new policies were implemented varied considerably between towns according to local political and economic circumstances. Although the Maidstone council was dominated by Conservative councillors who tended to see themselves as the ratepayers' party and a party of economy, there was a broad consensus, nevertheless, on the need to improve housing and educational provision in the borough and to maintain a civic role in the town – despite the restrictions imposed by the financial policies of national governments. Continuity of council membership, especially among the chairmen of committees, helped to maintain the momentum, and some of the most active and committed of the councillors continued to be drawn from that relatively small group of established Maidstone families which had a long history of municipal service.

Council housing

The Maidstone council attempted to make full use of the powers and subsidies embodied in successive Acts of Parliament during the inter-war years. In 1925 the council participated in a Regional Town Planning Committee, to investigate conditions and resources in the region and to prepare an outline regional plan for urban expansion. The following year an outside consultant advised on a town extension scheme covering a total of 6,479 acres, much of it within the areas of Malling, Hollingbourne and Maidstone rural district councils. The borough boundaries were extended to incorporate these areas in 1932, although the transfer of some Hollingbourne land was brought forward to allow work to begin on the Ringlestone estate. A town planning scheme was also drafted during the early 1930s to ensure the zoning of the town into seven residential districts, but there was some opposition to the scheme. It was not adopted until 1936, by when new council house building was well advanced.

Even during the First World War, local councillors were conscious that an acute housing shortage was developing, but it was late in 1919 that building on council-owned sites went ahead, and even then a shortage of bricklayers continued to cause problems, and building plans had to be modified to allow for the use of concrete. Progress remained slow, and the first fourteen houses on the Cherry Orchard site were not completed and occupied until October 1920. At this stage housing policy was much influenced by the terms of the Housing Act of 1919 which provided for subsidised building, financed partly from the rates and partly by central government. In order to qualify for the subsidy, houses had to be built to generous minimum standards, particularly in terms of space. The Cherry Orchard houses, which had parlours and three or four bedrooms, cost more than £1,000 each to build, and exceeded the required building standards. But with rents of ten and twelve shillings plus rates, they were beyond the reach of those living in bad housing, as well as most ordinary working-class families. In the council's own words they were 'not for the people who must get out of slums'. They had in mind families living in eighty-three houses certified as unimprovable, whom the council was proposing to rehouse in wooden huts, following the example of a private developer in Bonny's Yard, where houses had been knocked down to make way for a cinema. The proposal was given up after strong protests from the Trades Council and an alternative project to provide concrete huts was also dropped because of difficulties in acquiring the land.

The growing working-class population in the town kept the issue of housing provision high on the council agenda throughout the 1920s, and estimates of the number of houses required to meet the shortfall and to rehouse families removed from slum dwellings were steadily revised upwards. As early as 1921 the figure was raised from an initial estimate of 358 houses to 534 houses, with the council expected to build 410. Meeting this target proved difficult. In 1921 there were 174 council houses under construction and a further 50 were erected during 1922 at the Coombe Farm site on the Old Tovil Road purchased from the Romney estate. However, a temporary halt was called to council building at the end of 1922 when the subsidies provided under the 1919 Act were withdrawn, although a grant by the Minister of Health enabled a further 30 houses to be completed on the Coombe Farm estate. To some extent the deficiency was made good by private builders who built working-class houses for rent, encouraged by a government subsidy under the 1923 Housing Act, which was topped up by the council to a total of £100 a house.

Two hundred of these subsidised private houses had been erected by the mid-1920s. It was not until after 1924 that renewed municipal house building began to make a significant difference to the town's housing stock. Council house subsidies were reintroduced by the Labour government in 1924, and these remained operative at different levels until 1933. For a town of Maidstone's size the record over these years was impressive, with building developments advancing at a rapid rate on five different sites. By 1929 1,000 council houses were occupied, and many more were under construction.

Both the 1923 and 1924 Acts set lower minimum standards for building; most of the homes built were smaller than those erected immediately after the war, and building costs and rents were consequently cheaper. To reduce rents to the minimum, some houses on the Coombe Farm estate were built without bathrooms, but this was outlawed in 1925. Many tenants, however, found the rents difficult to pay, despite a reduction of rents in 1928 to between 8s 9d and 12s 3d (including rates). Some tenants took in illicit lodgers to help make ends meet, and others rented houses which quickly became too small for their families. Thus council house overcrowding became a significant problem during the 1930s, although it was never as serious as in the private rented sector and was eventually remedied. The 1935 Housing Act enabled the council to build some extra large houses for big families on the Coombe Farm estate with more subsidised rents.

Slum clearance eventually started in Padsole and Upper Stone Street in 1933 under the 1930 Housing Act. Some of the displaced families were allocated houses, but flats were also built as the cheapest form of housing for those on low incomes, first at Ringlestone, and then, in 1936, in the Bonny's Yard area behind King Street. Those rehoused were obliged to have their furniture fumigated before moving into council property and many soon ran into rent arrears (the Ringlestone flats cost about 6s 4d a week). The council was not slow to evict them when this occurred. The King Street flats were quite large, some having four bedrooms, and the rents, although subsidised by 2s a week ranged from 7s 3d to 11s, equal to those of houses. The tenants came mainly from Waterloo Street, Sheals Place and yards on Upper Stone Street. There were problems from the start, both with vandalism by the tenants' children, and with the design and fabric of the buildings, which rapidly deteriorated.

Nevertheless, by the start of the Second World War when all house building schemes were halted, Maidstone councillors could claim to have largely eradicated the slums and 'to have broken the back of what was necessary to house the people of the borough'.[10] Although the rapid increase in the town's population meant that housing demand could not be fully satisfied, the 2,000th council house was completed in March 1940, with an additional 760 houses erected by then under the arrangements for subsidised private building. At the end of March 1939 only ten of the eighty-six local authorities in the south east of England had built more houses than Maidstone, and all of them had larger populations, in some cases considerably larger. Of those authorities outside the London area, only eight had a lower rate charge for housing than the 1.2d in Maidstone, and they had all built considerably fewer houses. Despite this, in only four towns in the region was the average council house rent lower than in Maidstone, and in all of these the rate charge was higher. As the council noted, the statistics were 'very satisfactory'.

No less significantly, the council had done what it could to encourage owner occupation of lower priced property. They used powers under the 1923 Housing Act to advance 90 per cent mortgages on houses valued at £600 or less – to be repaid over twenty years at 5 per cent interest. In 1934 the council built ninety non-subsidised houses which it offered for sale at cost price on twenty-year mortgages at 3.75 per cent interest. The average weekly repayment cost was 13s, a sum comparable to the rent of the largest council houses. By March 1940 a total of 650 loans had been granted to owner occupiers.

Roads and transport

As a consequence of urban expansion and the rapid increase in the use of motor vehicles the town began to suffer a growing traffic problem during the 1920s and 1930s. A census of the traffic passing over Maidstone bridge during the second week in August 1925 recorded 38,672 motor vehicles – 20,347 cars, 8,042 motorcycles and 10,283 lorries, which represented an increase of more than seven-and-a-half times on the volume of motor traffic recorded in 1913. Even though the number of horse-drawn vehicles had fallen during this period, the total volume of all traffic crossing the bridge increased over two-and-a-half times. At first, measures were taken to improve traffic flow by road widening and in 1926 the bridge was likewise improved at a cost of over £53,000 shared between the Ministry of Transport, the Rochester Bridge Wardens and the town council. During the later 1920s the speed of traffic in Week Street became a cause for concern, one-way systems were experimented with, and the first set of traffic lights was installed at the bottom of High Street. By 1929, however, pressure for a town by-pass was building up, and the town council argued the case to the Ministry of Transport and county council, who eventually conceded the need; but work had not begun in 1939, when the outbreak of war caused the project to be postponed.

Despite the great expansion in vehicle ownership, there was also a growing need for public transport as the town expanded and people moved to estates on the outskirts. The council's trams continued to run after the war, and there were also some private motor bus services, but whole areas of the town remained without public transport. After failing to attract private operators, in 1923 the council applied to Parliament for powers to operate its own bus services. A cross-town service was provided between Penenden Heath and London Road and a second service, between Park Avenue and Upper Fant Road, was started in 1926. The council also obtained authority to operate trolley buses, and it was decided to introduce these on the tram routes when the rails wore out. Trolley buses were calculated to be 2d a mile cheaper to run than petrol buses, and with their more rapid acceleration were quicker over short routes with frequent stops. There was also the further advantage that electricity would continue to be supplied by the council's own electricity works. The first trolley buses entered service during 1928, first on the Barming and then on the Loose route, but the Tovil trams were replaced by petrol buses, and there were no further trolley bus routes. Overall the services were well used, and slightly more than five million passengers were carried on corporation transport during 1930–1. Extra bus services were provided to the newly-built estates during the 1930s, and although some of these proved unviable, generally speaking council transport was a profitable undertaking before the Second World War.

Council schools

The expansion of the town also imposed new demands on the council's education committee with increasing pressure on school accommodation. The growth of housing estates required the building of new schools, but this problem was compounded by the inadequate distribution of existing schools. In addition, the education committee had to meet the challenge of a government requirement of 1918 that specialist teaching should be carried on in existing schools, not in separate centres. In the older church schools the curriculum for senior pupils was restricted by the lack of specialist teaching and equipment and cramped accommodation, and there were virtually no facilities for physical education and games. Not surprisingly, the ladder of opportunity, as it was known, was a narrow one in Maidstone, with few schools capable of preparing children for entry to higher courses and only a small number of scholarships available. In 1924 the Education Committee published a table which showed that only 71 out of 4,490 pupils in the town's elementary schools progressed to more advanced education.

On the positive side, the town's director of education until 1932, E.W. Abbott, was an acknowledged spokesman on educational affairs and frequently anticipated national thinking. He was supported by an education committee ready to exploit the new opportunities provided under the 1918 Education Act. The borough had already made a breakthrough in the provision of more specialist advanced teaching with the setting up of the Junior Technical school in the Technical Institute in 1918. In a speech that year the director looked forward to a wide range of educational and social improvements, including the provision of nursery schools, abolition of child employment, extra medical care and, above all, the introduction of new central and continuation schools for the town's senior pupils. The central school, with improved facilities and recruiting pupils from the borough as a whole, was seen by Abbott as crucial to upgrading the education of working-class children.

Yet in Maidstone, as elsewhere, the ambitions of the local council were thwarted by the government embargo on capital expenditure after the economic and financial crisis of 1921. This undermined the scope and activity of the new Maidstone and District Education Board established two years before under the chairmanship of William

Day, also chairman of the borough education committee, and with Abbott as district education officer. The intention was to promote greater uniformity and coordination in educational planning in Maidstone and the forty-two surrounding parishes. Without the support of central government, the board was wound up in 1923 and was replaced by a largely advisory body with Abbott as district secretary. An opportunity for comprehensive planning had been lost, though the new District Board performed some useful functions. It supervised grants made to ex senior school pupils attending the grammar schools, Technical Institute and School of Art; received reports on further education in the borough; and monitored the expansion of evening classes at the Technical Institute and at Union Street school. It also had responsibility for juvenile welfare including the juvenile employment bureau in the town.

The changing financial policies of the Board of Education in London also affected the borough's educational plans. In the period 1921–4 the Board of Education turned down Maidstone's proposals for building new schools and criticised what they regarded as the too liberal provision of medical care. At the same time, an attempt to turn Union Street into a central school by closing the junior department had to be abandoned because of an outcry by parents and lack of support from the town council. The Junior Technical School also made disappointing progress due to the reluctance of parents and employers to appreciate the opportunities the school provided. In 1921 it had only 84 pupils, compared to the School of Art with 125 full-time students.

After 1924 with restrictions on capital expenditure lifted, the education committee was able to push more strongly for the provision of central schools and to introduce selection procedures. Maidstone was one of a small group of authorities that anticipated the proposals of the Hadow Committee, a national advisory committee, seeking to establish central schools as modern secondary schools for working-class pupils – as an alternative to grammar schools. But reorganisation of the elementary school system faced many obstacles. In addition to financial constraints, the education committee had to overcome persistent suspicions that it was anti-Anglican and to win over church school managers for the conversion of old church schools into junior schools. Meanwhile, resources had to be found for junior school building, an immediate priority on new council estates.

The first reorganisation plan, presented to the council in 1924, recommended the building of a new junior school at Tonbridge Road and the establishment of central schools for boys and girls. The Loose Road project, as it became known, was to comprise a central school for boys with provision for specialist teaching, gymnasium, playing fields and a school health clinic. In line with current policy about ways of reducing the incidence of tuberculosis, there was to be an adjacent open-air school. The plan also envisaged a central school for girls on the site of the boys' grammar school which the county council wanted to move to new premises.

However, implementation was quickly overtaken by events. First, due to the rapid growth of the Mangravet estate, an emergency programme was put in hand to build a council junior school there. Opened in 1929, the school included a welfare clinic for mothers and children and the building was used for a variety of community purposes. Secondly, the town's reorganisation plan was amended to take account of a county council proposal to acquire a site for a new girls' grammar school. In view of this, the education committee decided to use the old boys' grammar school site to enlarge the facilities of the Junior Technical school as well as providing the central science school for girls as originally intended. The revised 1929 plan was especially significant in elaborating the idea of an alternative route to higher education, other than that of grammar school and university. It anticipated a set of central schools for boys and girls, feeding pupils to the Technical Institute and the Central School for Arts and Crafts, and thence to higher technological institutions.

In the event, the rising costs of the Loose Road project and further cut-backs in council expenditure imposed by central government in 1931 again curtailed the ambitions of the director and his education committee, and the project for a central science school was abandoned. At the same time, the procrastination of the county council delayed improvements to secondary education facilities: the new boys' grammar school was built in 1931 but the construction of the girls' grammar school was delayed until 1938, when it was erected on a 16-acre site at Little Buckland, near a largely middle-class area of town. Reorganisation plans were further modified to take account of schools wishing to opt out of the scheme, such as St Francis' Catholic school which remained a junior and senior mixed school. At Union Street, Abbott succeeded in converting the senior department to a central school, but at the price of restoring the junior school. Nevertheless, the director could report in 1931 that reorganisation into separate junior and senior schools 'was quietly and happily effected' in the southern and western districts of the borough. In addition, the major building achievement of this period – the Loose Road schools project – was completed in an amended form at a cost of £36,000. Although the projected open-air school was never built, the site was used for two central schools. Housed in a building constructed on an E plan, the Loose Road schools were widely regarded, in architectural terms, as the most advanced in the country.

When Abbott retired prematurely because of ill health in 1932, the town council took the opportunity to downgrade the education office, while maintaining continuity by appointing one of Abbot's lieutenants as clerk to the education committee. In that year Maidstone had five council schools, five Church of England and one Roman Catholic school with a total of 5,150 children on the roll. The Junior Technical school had 150 pupils enrolled and the two grammar schools about 400 pupils. By 1938 the Plains Avenue Infant school was built and the reorganisation of the town's elementary school system substantially completed. But by then new problems had arisen, with the continued spread of housing in the suburbs, the proposed raising of the school leaving age, and pressure to provide additional facilities for teaching handicapped and backward children. Government inspectors were critical of the lack of provision for physical education. But little more could be achieved before 1944 when the local education office became the divisional office of the Kent County Council.

Clinics and hospitals

In comparison with housing and education, the work of the health committee was more low-key. In large measure this was due to the early importance of voluntary and private provision, which continued up to the establishment of the National Health Service in 1948. By the 1920s the 'heroic' years of public health provision had passed and the reports of the public analyst and medical officer of health (MOH) dealt mainly with established and routine procedures: the analysis of water and foods, enforcing repair orders, grants of certificates and licences (for the sale of pasteurised milk, slaughter houses, and the like), granting contracts for refuse collection (until 1938 when the council turned to direct labour), issuing closure orders on 'unfit' houses. The MOH also kept the living conditions of hop-pickers under surveillance, and new by-laws introduced in the early 1930s sought to ensure decent accommodation for them.

Apart from these duties, three concerns figured prominently in the annual reports of the MOH. One of these was the care and treatment of infants and expectant mothers, a concern which came on to the public health agenda, as we saw above, during the First World War. In 1921 money was allocated, after much delay, for adapting part of the Old Palace as the main infant and maternity welfare clinic, with other clinics at the old St Faith's boys' school in Medway Street and at Barming. Ante-natal classes were held, doctors were in attendance, and regular visits made to expectant mothers and children under five. Despite the continuing reliance on voluntary workers, the Ministry of Health expressed satisfaction in 1926 at the way the clinic and its ancillary services were conducted. Health visitors were able to identify mothers and infants most at risk from disease – the 'problem families' of the 1920s – and when home conditions were thought unsatisfactory, those with severe illness were directed to the West Kent General Hospital through a voluntary agency. Unmarried mothers were looked after by another voluntary body, St Faith's Home. Most women gave birth to their children at home, but in 1927 a small maternity unit was opened at the West Kent Hospital, and ten years later this was replaced by a new eighteen-bed unit. Nine of the beds were financed by the council, and placed at the disposal of the Maternity and Infant Welfare Centre. Improvements were also made in standards of midwifery. A dramatic decline in infant mortality to 55 per 1,000 live births in 1931 was due more to improvements in nutrition, milk supply and environmental conditions than medical intervention. However, the health of older children benefited from the work of the school clinic, which offered treatment for minor ailments and dentistry. A pioneering clinic, it was always well supported and publicised.

A second main concern of the medical officer was the monitoring of infectious diseases, a duty which had been part of his routine work since the Notification of Diseases Act of 1889. Diseases most frequently notified were tuberculosis and the 'children's diseases' of scarlet fever and diphtheria. TB was a serious disease which was practically incurable in this period, although various treatments were attempted at the sanatorium, formerly the isolation hospital, on Fant Lane. There was also a county council tuberculosis dispensary for out-patients on Station Road, and in the later 1930s TB clinics were opened at Wren's Cross and Sheal's Crescent and there was a TB clinic and School Dental Unit at Foster Street. Turning to other infectious diseases, the numbers of reported diphtheria cases rose, possibly because of improved detection through bacteriological methods (swabbing). Patients were normally treated at home, and by the late 1920s the first of the anti-toxins used to combat the disease was distributed free at the police station and sanatorium. Smallpox was a lesser but persistent problem, and a new smallpox ward was built at the sanatorium; earlier resistance to vaccination had disappeared by this time.

The third and most frequent complaint in the annual reports was about the lack of hospital accommodation and the problems which poorer people suffered in paying for treatment. The West Kent Hospital, a voluntary hospital, was the main general provider of in-patient treatment. Several new wards were added, as a result of benefactions, during the 1920s and 1930s, and by 1938 the hospital had 135 beds. A radium clinic for cancer treatment opened in 1931. There was also specialist provision for complaints associated with ears, nose and throat at the Kent County Ophthalmic and Aural Hospital in Church Street. This Victorian voluntary hospital was extended and improved several times between the wars, and in 1938 it had 109 beds. A department for treating children with squints was opened in 1933. In the 1930s the town council began to assist poorer parents with children who had to attend the ophthalmic unit at the hospital, while a small number of people needing care at one of the hospitals were assisted by the town's Surgical Aid Society; but those who could afford to do so made private contributions to a Hospital Fund to cover the cost of treatment. In general, however, the range of public health provision in Maidstone was more limited than in larger cities and towns where clinics were established for diabetes, and venereal diseases. Despite the concern for children and mothers, we find little sign of concern for the wider aspects of environmental health and pollution, although the Medway still received discharges of mill and factory effluent. The office staff was tiny for the size of the town, with a MOH who doubled as school medical officer, a chief inspector and assistant sanitary inspector, a clerk and two health visitors, of whom only one was wholly supported by the council. In 1938 the number of health visitors was increased to four and the first woman officer appointed as assistant medical officer. The town council may have seen little need for more active support, given the decline in the death rate and the improving statistics of height and weight which promised an increasingly robust population. Maidstone, as we have seen, was not badly affected by the depression years and the buoyancy of the economy allowed for general improvements in living conditions as well as in nutrition during this period.

Urban society and politics

Maidstone society was evidently changing during the inter-war years as the numbers of working-class people grew, concentrated on the large council estates, and as new private housing developments fostered a greater sense of lower-middle-class identity among white collar workers and skilled manual workers, both as we have seen more numerous and better off than in the past. But strong traditional elements remained in the urban community with the old professional and commercial groups still dominating the town's powerful middle class. The middle class retained control over the town's public and private institutions, including the churches and voluntary organisations as well as political and administrative bodies, with a few leading families continuing to hold a mesh of key positions as officers of societies, chairmen of philanthropic and medical boards, and members of town and county council committees. Some leading public figures were listed in 1935 in the *Who's Who of Kent*. They included William Day JP, the surveyor and three times mayor, A.T. Epps JP, company director and chairman of the council's housing and higher education committees, and H.G. Tyrwhitt-Drake JP, six times mayor and four times deputy mayor 1915–32. The only woman listed was Mrs Grace Miles JP, a member of the Women Citizens Assocation, and of the Board of Guardians, and Secretary of the Maidstone branch of the Kent County Association for the Blind and to the North End Women's Adult school. Even here, however, there may have been growing shifts by the 1930s with the removal of the wealthier middle classes to houses in the adjoining countryside, facilitated by the motor car, and with the slow decline of church-going and the waning of some of the old pillars of voluntary organisation in the town, as we shall see later. In this new social environment middle-class influence over local politics became decisive.

Politically the trend toward Conservative dominance evident in the later nineteenth century was confirmed and the Maidstone parliamentary constituency remained a Conservative stronghold, with the seat held by the naval commander C.W. Bellairs from 1915 to 1931 followed by A.C. Bossom until 1959, after which it passed to J.J. Wells. The addition of a considerable rural area to the constituency in 1918 undoubtedly strengthened the already substantial Conservative vote, while the Liberal party nationally was in some disarray after 1918, and did not always contest the seat. The Labour party fought the seat long and hard but without any success. The closest contest was in 1922, in a three-way fight involving Bellairs, the sitting member, George Foster Clark, an eleventh hour Independent endorsed by the Liberals, and for Labour Hugh Dalton, the future Chancellor of the Exchequer. Foster Clark lost by only 33 votes and Dalton came in third place only 900 votes behind. Dalton did not contest the seat again, and he was replaced by Seymour Cocks in another three-way contest with Foster Clark and the victorious Bellairs the following year. After this second failure Foster Clark abandoned his political ambitions, and at the 1924 election a two-party contest between Cocks and Bellairs saw the latter take two-thirds of the votes. In 1929 another Labour candidate, J. Morgan, beat the Liberals into third place and the party did not contest the seat again until after the Second World War. Labour failed to capitalise on the situation, however. At the 1931 election the Labour vote also collapsed, largely because of divisions in the Labour party after Ramsay MacDonald formed the National Government with the Conservatives. Even in 1945 when there was a nationwide swing towards Labour, the Conservative A.E. Bossom was able to win the seat with a comfortable majority of 3,025 over Labour's O.L. Shaw.

Council elections excited little interest in Maidstone between the wars, and it was rare for more than half the electorate to vote, with a typical turnout of 40 per cent. As in parliamentary politics, the Conservative party grew in strength and dominated the council throughout the period. Labour contested almost every vacancy but found it difficult to make much headway during the 1920s because of an anti-Labour coalition by the other two parties. However, a breakthrough occurred in North ward in 1922 when the Labour candidate, Frederick Shrubsole, an official of the Transport and General Workers Union, was elected. Another seat was gained the following year, and North ward subsequently became a Labour stronghold. Although Labour councillors were increasingly accepted as part of the establishment and there were two Labour mayors, in 1935/6 and 1937/8, Labour representation on the council never rose above four before the Second World War while the Liberal representation declined from six members in 1936 to three in 1938. The only other change was an increase in the number of Independents elected in the 1930s, although half the six Independent councillors in 1938 enjoyed Conservative support. In 1920 the Women Citizens Association sought to sponsor an Independent candidate to represent the woman's point of view, but without success, and the only women to be elected as councillors – and then not until 1938 – were Gladys Strickland, an Independent with Conservative backing, and Dorothy Relf, a Conservative, both taking Labour-held seats. The only other feature of council politics to note was the conversion in 1940 of the Labour councillor, Cecil Hobday to membership of the Communist party. This caused much consternation among other councillors, who immediately passed a resolution banning Communists, and also Pacifists and Fascists, who had not been elected as such from sitting on council committees. The ban was not maintained for long, however, and within a couple of years Hobday was busy in committee work. He was re-elected as a Communist in 1945, but eventually lost his seat to a Conservative two years later, when all the Labour candidates were defeated and their stronghold of North ward fell to the Conservatives for the first time in twenty years. It was said that 'women voters largely decided the results'. In King Street ward they outnumbered male voters by as many as two to one. The growing Conservative ascendancy was doubtless associated with rising prosperity and the expansion of the town's lower middle class. Such developments also increasingly affected the social and cultural world of the community.

Cultural and social life

There can be little question that the community's cultural and social life was transformed in the inter-war period, especially in comparison with the mid-Victorian years. A crucial element in this was the decline of religious activity and church- and chapel-going. On 2 May 1926 the *Kent Messenger* carried out a survey of religious attendance at eleven Anglican churches (including the newly-built St Andrew's at Barming Heath) and thirteen other churches and chapels, to reveal a total attendance of 6,250, of which 2,689 attended in the morning and 3,561 in the evening. This was roughly half the figure recorded in 1851, when the town's population was much smaller, although the 1851 census was probably inflated by the inclusion of Sunday school attendance. These figures would suggest that by the 1920s only 15 per cent of the active population were church- or chapel-goers compared with 61 per cent seventy-five years before, although since attendance at services was becoming less regular between the wars the 1926 figure may under-estimate the total number of practising Christians in the town. In line with the broad national pattern, the majority of worshippers in all the Maidstone churches and chapels were women, about two-thirds on average, although in certain Anglican churches the figure was higher.

The Anglicans still had the largest number of worshippers, with 62 per cent of all recorded attendances (against 64 per cent in 1851). Nonconformist attendance, which had probably expanded in the later nineteenth century, had now declined to 38 per cent of the total. The town continued to support a range of denominational groupings, with the Congregationalists, Baptists and Wesleyans attracting the largest numbers, although Methodist unity in 1932 brought about the closure of the Primitive Methodist chapel. St Francis' Catholic church had a total attendance of 245 at its two services, just under 4 per cent of attendances – a little below the figures for the main nonconformist churches. Both the nonconformists and Anglicans sought to provide for the new council estates but found this an uphill task. A non-denominational place of worship, provided by the town council on the Mangravet estate in 1928 and administered by the Free Church Council, struggled to stay open due to funding problems and lack of support. The Congregationalists carried out most of the work there, and the church was eventually handed over to them in 1948. A new Anglican church, St Martin's, was opened in 1933 in a temporary building on Sutton Road adjacent to the new council housing, but this likewise had very limited support. Even the Salvation Army, which held meetings in the Mangravet area by the Second World War, met with a similar lack of success. If working-class apathy was increasingly widespread, this only aggravated a long-standing problem. More crucial for urban religion – and established perceptions of communal identity – was the growing defection of the respectable middle classes, due in large part to the continued growth of new-style leisure activities.

Rising incomes between the wars meant that there was more money available for leisure activities, while the widespread acquisition of cars, motorcycles and houses with gardens, created alternative ways of spending Sunday. Consequently, the social importance of attendance at religious services, particularly for the middle classes, declined. Some church organisations retained support and new bodies were formed, but there was nothing like the vitality of church life that characterised the late Victorian period. The most successful of the church organisations seem to have been those catering for children and young people. Most of the churches and chapels still provided Sunday schools. In 1921 King Street church had 186 children enrolled at its Sunday school, and there was an average attendance of 40 in the morning and 143 in the afternoon. Oral evidence suggests that attendance was very widespread during the 1920s, but that there may have been some decline during the 1930s. The Wesleyans' thriving Union Street Sunday school went into decline during the 1930s after the Wesleyans and Primitive Methodists amalgamated. Most other children's organisations were quite well attended: the Anglican Girls' Friendly Society, in particular, seems to have flourished, and there was a mushrooming of uniformed groups such as the Scouts, Guides and Life Brigades. But the Bands of Hope no longer enjoyed the spectacular popularity of the Edwardian years. The temperance movement in general had faded from importance by the 1930s, when intemperance was said to be 'rapidly curing itself', and in 1938, the St Paul's Band of Hope was renamed the Children's Guild, being thought 'more in accordance with the spirit of the times'. Women might still belong to a variety of fellowships and working societies, and for Anglican women there was the Mothers' Union, but such bodies played a less important role in women's leisure than before 1914. Men's organisations largely disappeared, although the Church Institute, with its seven acres of playing fields, remained an important social resource; the Institute amalgamated with the YMCA in 1935. Several other religious bodies had sporting facilities, including King Street Undenominational, which had a lawn tennis club; and all the churches held socials and outings, many of them well supported. But the days when two or three thousand people left the town on Church of England Temperance Society excursions were past. Church literary and debating societies likewise disappeared after the First World War, only the Society of Friends continuing with lectures and discussion groups on a more than occasional basis. It is probable that adult education classes organised by the local education authority and other secular bodies had taken their place.

A multiplicity of clubs and societies flourished in the town between the wars and these served as another alternative attraction to church organisations. A kaleidoscope of interests and hobbies were pursued, from politics of every shade, to stamp collecting, photography, gardening, music and amateur dramatics. An important innovation in women's leisure from 1918 was the formation of the West Kent Federation of Women's Institutes, with its base in Maidstone. In addition, an extremely successful branch of the League of Nations was active in the town, organising meetings with political speakers and claiming a local membership of 1,600 in 1926.

Of the town's civic institutions, the town library was the least successful. Re-organised in 1921 so as to give open access to the books, the library was not well used, many people preferring to take out books from the commercial library in Boots the chemists. During 1923–4 the town library had 2,250 registered borrowers, and by 1931–2 this had risen to 3,093, or only 7.3 per cent of the population, the lowest percentage recorded in a sample of fifteen Kentish towns. This may not be unconnected with the fact that spending on books and periodicals,

The League of Nations building, on the end of Middle Row in High Street, near the Cannon. A highly successful inter-war organisation.
Photograph: Maidstone Museum.

A food queue during the First World War.
Photograph: Kent Messenger Group Newspapers.

Maidstone Bus Station, opened in 1922 on the corner of Palace Avenue and Mill Street.
Photograph: Maidstone Museum.

Poor housing in an alley off Bank Street,
c. 1925.
Photograph: Maidstone Museum.

Children queuing for boots from the Kent Messenger *fund.*
Photograph: Kent Messenger Group Newspapers.

Allington Estate with Ringlestone in the background, 1930s.
Photograph: Maidstone Museum.

The Medway Brewery in St Peter Street. A late photograph, after the merger with Courage.
Photograph: Maidstone Museum.

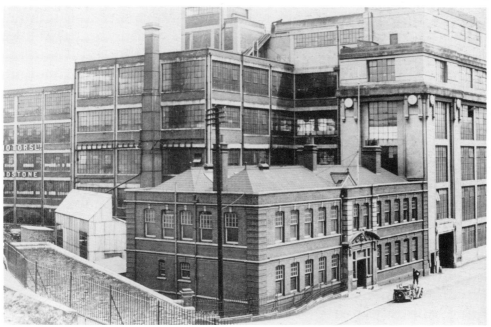

Tilling-Stevens' factory in St Peter Street.
Photograph: Maidstone Museum.

A National Farmers' Union luncheon. The town continued to maintain strong rural links.
Photograph: Centre for Kentish Studies.

A post-war photograph of the important poultry market which developed during the 1920s.
Photograph: Maidstone Museum.

The corn market.
Photograph: Kent Messenger Group Newspapers.

Widening Loose Road; relief work, c. 1922.
Photograph: Kent Messenger Group Newspapers.

although much higher than before the First World War, was low in comparison with other towns. The library was evidently not an important priority to the town council which spent less than £150 upon it annually in the late 1930s. It was not until the Workers Educational Association in 1944 asked the council for a new library with properly equipped lecture and reading rooms, and an increased book grant, that the council woke up to the fact that the existing library was 'not of the standard or order one would expect from a borough of the size and importance of Maidstone'; after the Second World War expenditure rose more than fourfold. As in the past, the museum and art gallery excited much more public interest and civic pride, and annual attendance jumped from 115,000 in 1921 to 167,000 ten years later, helped by the opening of the gallery's new Viscountess Bearsted wing in 1924.

The council was more active in promoting outdoor recreation, and the acreage of playing fields was considerably enlarged between the wars. The Clare Recreation Ground in Tonbridge Road was laid out on land given by Sir Edward Sharp in 1922, and in 1928 the council decided to buy Mote Park from Viscount Bearsted for £50,000. This was opened to the public in July the following year, and there were facilities for boating, fishing and tennis, as well as a large area of open fields, trees and a lake. To pay off the council's mortgage on the land, income was generated by the sale of deer, rabbits, wood and turves, and the letting of the gardens, greenhouses and grazing. South Park was laid out on Loose Road between 1928 and 1930, the council obtaining grants from the Carnegie Trust and the National Playing Fields Association towards the cost of the work which included a running track and golf course. In 1939 four acres of land off Poplar Grove in the West Borough were compulsorily purchased for use as a recreation ground, and an existing playing field off Upper Fant Road was extended. Other playing fields were provided with new or upgraded facilities, and the council continued to arrange for bands to entertain the public in the Brenchley Gardens and elsewhere during the summer.

Playing fields, both new and old, were greatly in demand. Numerous cricket and football teams hired pitches in the local parks, as did the schools. There were also facilities for tennis and golf probably aimed mainly at a growing middle- and lower-middle-class clientele with the charge of 1s 6d an hour for a tennis court in 1932. Another municipal service, the baths in the Fair Meadow, remained popular between the wars, but still lacked a filtration system; the water was merely changed twice a week, and the ticket price was highest on the days when the water was clean. Some people preferred to swim in the river, despite its polluted state. The usual swimming place was at the back of the old college, and the town swimming club continued to have springboards there, although they also used the baths.

The main spectator sports continued to be football and cricket. Professional football was disrupted by the First World War, but Maidstone United resumed play at the athletic ground in 1919. The team was a major force in the Kent League during the 1920s, when a number of professional players were added, but the 1930s brought them less success and professional football came to an end with the onset of the 1939–45 war. Maidstone had no particular reputation as a footballing town and faced competition for spectators from the Medway towns and metropolitan clubs. Cricket matches continued to draw crowds to Mote Park, however, and the town's rugby club retained a following.

Sport apart, the inter-war period saw the county town redefining its social importance in the mid-Kent area as a centre for mass entertainments. The two most popular leisure activities during the 1920s and 1930s were dancing and the cinema. Dances were held at the Corn Exchange, the Royal Star Hotel, previously the Star Inn, which acquired a second ballroom with a sprung floor during the 1930s, the Co-operative Hall, the Old Palace, Chiesman's and at many clubs and church halls. Some were clearly middle-class functions, such as the balls held at the Corn Exchange in 1920, with an entrance price of 7s 6d for a double ticket, and a few were gatherings of gentry, like the hunt ball held there in 1926, which was described as a 'brilliant function'. The majority, however, were advertised as 'select dances' with an admission charge of about 1s 6d. Dances at the Star are remembered as more select than most, with the women wearing long dresses and the men 'at least a dinner jacket if not tails'. 'That was the sort of thing you expected in those days', one of the regular patrons recalled. Some of the best dance orchestras of the day played there, as well as local bands, and the dances are said to have been very popular. There were also less formal tea dances. Jazz made an appearance at the Corn Exchange in 1920, but the more sedate dances were preferred. In addition to the public dances, many others were organised by employers for their workers. Tilling-Stevens had their own dance orchestra and concert party, and at Foster Clark's we hear of elaborate fancy dress carnival dances. There were also dances at the barracks for the military and their families, and these, like those at the Star, were usually formal occasions, with full dress uniform and white gloves the rule.

The two cinemas open before the First World War, the Empire Electric in Earl Street, and the Popular Picture Palace (PPP) in Pudding Lane, remained in business during the 1920s, and another, the Central, was built in King Street in 1920. The Empire, briefly used for live shows during the early 1920s, subsequently developed a reputation as a 'bug hutch' or flea-pit, and was avoided by the fastidious, but it nevertheless remained in business, renamed the Medina in 1936 and the Regal in 1939, finally closing in 1957. The PPP, which became known as the Pavilion, was a much larger cinema with a better reputation. The Central was a 'state of the art' building, with a restaurant, an organ and a seven-piece orchestra, and higher admission prices than the other two. However, this was bettered by the Granada which opened in Lower Stone Street in 1934, with its grandiose Corinthian portico (designed by Cecil Masey), spacious restaurant, air-conditioned auditorium and organ which ascended from the depths between films. The following year the Pudding Lane cinema was modernised to face the competition, provided with a new organ and renamed the Ritz – taking second place in the cinema hierarchy, until it was burned down in 1954.

The Palace Theatre, which played varieties twice nightly during the 1920s, was also in a generally flourishing state between the wars. Plush seats were provided for those paying higher prices in the circle and stalls, but even those seated on wooden forms in the 'gods', with their monkey nuts and pennyworths of 'speck fruit', were able to share in the general ambience of glamour. In 1930 the Palace (along with the Central and Pavilion cinemas) was bought by Messrs Overland and Benjamin, and run as part of a small repertory circuit, but by this time it was losing ground to the cinema, and to the Theatre Royal and Hippodrome in Chatham, which advertised in the Maidstone press and attracted many people from the town. Increasing numbers of people had their own transport, and there was a frequent and well-used bus service between Maidstone and the Medway towns running late in the evening.

Despite the growth of commercial entertainment, there was no shortage of amateur music or theatrical entertainment in inter-war Maidstone. The town had orchestral and dramatic societies, along with choirs, pierrots, and numerous concert parties, which were all the rage, especially during the 1920s. Concert parties were small groups of amateurs, whose shows included songs, music, recitations, sketches, and occasionally short plays, usually performed for charity in church halls and similar venues.

At the same time, public houses and licensed clubs remained an integral part of popular urban leisure in the inter-war years, if less important than in earlier generations. In Maidstone 1919 saw the last houses closed under the 1904 Act, which left 83 in business; the number rose to 89 when the borough boundaries were extended – a ratio of one public house to 504 persons. This was supplemented by twenty licensed clubs, ranging from the elite Maidstone Club and the political clubs, to the Oddfellows club in King Street and the working men's clubs. The public houses were cultivating a more respectable ambience, especially from the 1930s when a national debate took place among brewers over the concept of an 'improved public house'. Conscious that living standards and expectations were rising, the brewers began to improve facilities in order to compete with other sections of the leisure industry. In Maidstone much spit and sawdust remained, but modernised premises were increasingly common. The best remembered public house, known as the Gin Palace, and part of a wine merchant's premises on the corner of High Street and Week Street, had a balcony on the inside of the building, where a three-piece band played. It was a favourite Saturday night haunt for young people and courting couples and the house also boasted a ladies' room. Respectable women, particularly young ones, visited licensed premises to a growing extent, although normally escorted by men, and this trend became marked during the Second World War. In 1940, the Eagle, a beerhouse on Loose Road, was granted a wine licence, so that it could offer port and sherry to its growing number of female customers. Nevertheless, it was men, particularly from the working class, who continued to make up the great majority of public house customers.

Family outings now increasingly included holidays away from the town as workers benefited from employers like Tilling-Stevens giving them several days paid annual holiday. But for many people bank holidays remained the high points of the year, and the main opportunity for day trips and excursions to nearby resorts. In addition, as before the war, works outings took place in summertime from most local factories and mills. An employee at Turkey Mill during the 1920s, recalling annual outings to the seaside, said that all the workers were given a rose buttonhole to wear and half a crown spending money, before marching behind a brass band to the station for their train. Summer weekends and bank holidays also brought numerous fêtes and flower shows, many of the latter associated with workplaces, and there continued to be fun fairs at the May and October stock fairs. Another popular outing after 1933 was to the zoo, which Sir Garrard Tyrwhitt-Drake had reopened at Cobtree Manor, after a period organising annual circuses or menageries in the Agricultural Hall in aid of local hospitals. With low admission prices of 7d and 3d for children, the zoo, as before, proved very popular, with families travelling out from town on Maidstone and District buses or walking by the river.

These trends in Maidstone's cultural and social life had significance not only in terms of the way people spent their leisure time but in attitudes towards the town. In some respects the development of the cinema, dances and other entertainments in the town enhanced its regional importance in mid-Kent, drawing in crowds of younger people by bus, bicycle and car from the villages and market towns of the area. This went side by side with the town's continuing significance as a social centre for minor country landowners and wealthier farmers – evinced by the regular banquets and dinners in the town's hotels. If inter-war Maidstone had none of the fashionable county pretensions of the Georgian era, its cultural influence in the area remained considerable.

Within the community, however, a number of the social and cultural pillars of the Edwardian town were in the process of being displaced. The most important development here was the decline in church- and chapel-based activities discussed earlier. This was a consequence not only of a fall off in support for religion, but of the way that the scope for middle-class voluntary action was diminished as local and central government increasingly provided for education and wider forms of self improvement and played a growing role in social welfare. As a result, the wider role of the old middle-class families in the town diminished, although, as we noted earlier, the professional and commercial groups generally held on to their monopoly of council affairs. Some of the wealthiest families still acted as benefactors to the town in various ways. George Foster Clark, for instance, whose estate was worth just over half a million pounds when he died in 1932, was a leading philanthropist with gifts of land and money to the town. But overall the wealthy middle class no longer exerted that wide-ranging social leadership through religious and voluntary activity which had shaped the town's urban identity during the Victorian period.

As we have seen, rising levels of real income and the greater availability of time for leisure supported the upsurge of mass entertainments with purpose-built dance halls and cinemas supplementing a diverse network of amateur, club and work-based socialising and cultural activity. In Maidstone this new social world, more heavily influenced than ever before by external influences, not least the talkies of

Hollywood, increasingly involved and depended on the lower-middle classes and working-class population, which by the 1930s were often living, as we have seen already, on the outskirts of town. Here and in other respects – the trend towards new factories north of the town, the commercial and leisure competition from London and the Medway towns – we see pressures threatening to fragment the town's sense of community and identity. But this was more for the future. The growth of commercial entertainment, along with the changes in High Street shopping facilities helped to maintain the vitality of the town centre. Though the town retained much of its repertoire of large public and commercial buildings from the Victorian era, particularly on High Street, a number of major modern-style premises – including the Granada complex, the vast Rootes Showrooms on Mill Street, the multi-storeyed cement-faced Star House in Pudding Lane – asserted the town's renewed confidence. People may have become more interested in home centred activities, with better standards of accommodation and more space for gardens, but they still thronged the town's main streets, market, public gardens, and entertainments. The success of many of the town's firms, and advances in municipal services, also helped underpin the town's continuing urban coherence, its sense of collective purpose and civic pride. The expansion of the Kent County Council may have challenged the town's authority in a number of areas but there can be no doubt that in employment and financial terms it helped underwrite Maidstone's revived fortunes. In sum, despite all the changes of the period, Maidstone at the outbreak of the Second World War still had a recognisable identity not only as an urban community but as the prosperous and bustling county town of Kent.

Notes

1. Chief Constable's Report 1918, Maidstone Museum.
2. *Kent Messenger*, 5 June 1915; W.A. Armstrong, 'Kentish rural society during the First World War', in B. Holderness and M. Turner, eds, *Land, Labour and Agriculture, 1700–1920* (London, 1991), p. 112.
3. H.H. Parker, *The Hop Industry* (London, 1934), pp. 211–19; *Kent Messenger*, 16 January 1918, 26 January 1918, 7 September 1918.
4. *Kent Messenger*, 16 November 1918.
5. *Kelly's Directory of Kent*, 1930, 1938; *The Co-operative Directory* (Manchester, 1951), p. 236.
6. *Kent Messenger*, 15 May 1926; oral evidence.
7. *Kent Messenger*, 2 July 1921.
8. Centre for Kentish Studies [Kent Archives Office], G/Ma AM 57; Md/ACm 3/33; *Kent Messenger*, 1 March 1930.
9. Maidstone Bread Charities Scheme Confirmation Act, 1932.
10. *Kent Messenger*, 9 March 1940.

Bibliographical Note

Once again this chapter draws heavily on the local press, especially the *Kent Messenger*, on Kelly's Directories for the county, on the published census, and on the Borough Council minutes and other records in the Centre for Kentish Studies [Kent Archives Office]. Much information was also drawn from the recorded memories of townspeople. For an overview of the First World War years see Arthur Marwick, *The Deluge. British Society and the First World War* (London, 1991).

The discussion of housing development in the town used the Romney estate papers in the Centre for

Kentish Studies [Kent Archives Office], U1515, esp. T157 A–F. On local transport there are a number of monographs by enthusiasts: Maidstone and District and East Kent Bus Club, *Fleet History of Maidstone Corporation, 1904–1974* (Aylesford, 1975); D.J.S. Scotney, for the National Trolleybus Association, *The Maidstone Trolleybus 1928–67* (London, 1972); and a typescript by D. Kain and M. Coates, 'The Trolleybuses of Maidstone', in Maidstone Reference Library. On local industries the work of Irene Hales, in *Bygone Kent* has again been useful: 'George Foster Clark and the Eiffel Tower works, Maidstone', in vol. 10, no. 5; 'The Sharp's Kreemy Toffee story', vol. 7, no. 5; and 'Rootes of Maidstone' in vol. 7, numbers 10 and 11. On the latter company, use was also made of a report of a speech made to Maidstone Rotary Club by Reginald Rootes, in Maidstone Reference Library, MAI 338. The Centre for Kentish Studies has material on Foster Clark's at U1150. For the impact of the county council see E. Melling, *History of the Kent County Council* (Maidstone, 1975).

Material on the poor during this period is in the Centre for Kentish Studies, G/Ma, while the printed accounts of the Poor Law Union are in the Reference Library. For the years after 1929 John Moss, *Public Assistance in Kent, 1930–1948* (Maidstone, 1951) is useful. The discussion of education has drawn on the reports of the Maidstone and District Education Board in the Centre for Kentish Studies and the unpublished University of London MA thesis by K.V.C.Williams, 'Elementary Education in Maidstone 1903–1932', 1978. There are histories of the main educational institutions, for example H.J. Cope, *Maidstone Grammar School, 1549–1949. A Record* (Maidstone, 1949) and KCC Education Committee, *Maidstone Technical High School for Boys, 1918–1968* (Maidstone,1968). Information on public health has been taken mainly from the annual reports (1919–34) of the medical officer of health, Centre for Kentish Studies, Md/HM A2. Material relating to the various Anglican parishes [P241] and nonconformist churches [N series] is at the Centre for Kentish Studies.

Election results can be found in F.W.S. Craig, *British Parliamentary Election Results, 1918–49* (Chichester, 1983). For details of the social elite see the *Who's Who of Kent* (Worcester, 1935).

Chapter Ten

THE SECOND WORLD WAR AND AFTER

The preceding chapters have shown how Maidstone's appearance, and its economic and social character as a modern county town, was the product of a long process of evolution. The Second World War, despite its damage to the physical fabric of the town and the death and social disruption which afflicted townspeople, did not mark a fundamental break in Maidstone's development. In the immediate period after the war there continued to be certain continuities in the town's political and social life, despite the continuing erosion of its physical and collective identity by new housing developments, and the transfer of key municipal functions to external authorities. But from the late 1950s the pace of change quickened. Demographic, economic and social movements, already in evidence in the 1930s, accelerated markedly and by the early 1970s, at the time of local government reorganisation, Maidstone was becoming a very different place from the rather old fashioned town of 1945.

The Second World War

The outbreak of war was already being anticipated from 1936 when the town council set out to recruit and train air raid wardens, auxiliary firemen, ambulance drivers and first aid auxiliaries. However, the town was not on the government list of places supposedly exposed to attack, so Anderson shelters were not supplied. Maidstone was even considered, initially, to be a suitable place for the reception of evacuees from London, despite resistance from local residents to the idea, perhaps because of their experiences with the children of hop-pickers. In supplying the Ministry with figures of available accommodation, the town council warned of Maidstone's vulnerability to attack by air. Some evacuees arrived early in the war, but after 1940 the town, as predicted, was bombed. In August 1944 the danger from flying bombs was such that the town was declared an evacuation area, and 900 children left for the West Country, though returning two months later.[1] Maidstone did not suffer serious 'blitzing', but significant bomb damage occurred, especially in the autumn and winter of 1940, and during 1944 when there were flying bombs, and, on one occasion, long-range shells fired from France. The main town buildings such as the museum, West Kent Hospital, barracks, the boys' grammar school, and the East Station were all hit as well as factories, rows of shops (as in Mill Street), and numerous houses, including some in Hardy Street, destroyed when a Messerschmitt was shot down. Altogether 70 people were killed and 124 seriously injured by bombs during the course of the war. Where possible, people continued to live in the habitable parts of bombed houses, and it was not until 1944 that the County Council Public Assistance Committee set up a number of rest centres in the Maidstone area to provide temporary accommodation for 'bombed out' people.

As in the 1914–18 war, there was a large and frequently changing military presence in the neighbourhood, and in addition to the barracks an army encampment grew up in Mote Park, occupied by Canadians and Scots amongst others, plus some prisoners of war. Local industry suffered disruption, due to the attacks on merchant shipping, and there was a crisis in the paper trade because of the shortage of wood pulp. The food industries and breweries were subject to constraints as the government took charge of food supplies, and the breweries had on occasion to ration deliveries to public houses in the town. Tilling-Stevens went over to the manufacture of munitions, and during the first year of the war Rootes manufactured magnetos for aero engines; but this work was transferred elsewhere when it transpired that the town was vulnerable to attack, and the firm then carried out bodywork repairs for the military and manufactured mobile parachute units. Alabaster Passmore at Tovil took on much government printing, and in 1942 they printed the Beveridge Report, the blueprint for the post-war welfare state.

Again, as in the First World War, the male workforce was depleted as men volunteered or were conscripted into the forces, and their jobs taken over by women. In 1941 women were also conscripted, either into war work or the women's forces, and some girls and women were sent to work on munitions at Tilling-Stevens. The mothers of young children were exempt from conscription, but they were encouraged to work, and in 1941 the town council persuaded the Ministry of Health to provide day nurseries, the first of which opened that December in a house on London Road. This social facility was maintained by the council after the war, although the Ringlestone Day Nursery shut down in 1946, probably because the charges were too high for this working-class area; the other day nurseries were closed by the county council in the early 1950s. More generally, in the inter-war period Maidstone had built up a range of public health services and the Second World War fostered other developments in preventive medicine which included services for infants and expectant mothers, as well as day nurseries, advances in the treatment of tuberculosis and venereal disease, along with a more intensive approach to health education. However, after the implementation of the National Health Act in July 1948 the TB and VD clinics were taken over by the Mid-Kent Regional Hospital Board. The town's responsibility for public health was significantly reduced under this Act, and maternity and child welfare services, together with various aspects of preventive medicine, became the responsibility of the county council.

The war period also brought into being new governmental structures and services in other ways. Food supplies were controlled through local Food Control Committees which administered the orders of the Ministry. Maidstone set up its committee in June 1939. Strict control and rationing kept food prices low, but supplies were erratic and people were encouraged to grow vegetables. As much land as possible, including a great deal earmarked for building, was made available for allotments, and where necessary holders were assisted in breaking up the land. Seed was sold by the council at cost price. From 1940, in accordance with government regulations, allotment holders were permitted to keep poultry and pigs. The council used the greenhouses in public gardens to grow tomatoes and cucumbers for sale.[2] In addition, Maidstone responded to the requirement to provide communal eating facilities with a canteen serving 400 people in two sittings at the Corn Exchange, staffed by the WRVS. Some food not generally available on ration was channelled to these canteens, later known as British Restaurants, and nutritious meals were offered at a cost of 9d (5d for children), with cups of tea at 1d. The restaurant operated at full capacity for most of the war. The Kent Education Committee also began to provide meals for schoolchildren in 1941. Rationing and food shortages continued after the war, and although much allotment land was reclaimed for development, the British Restaurant remained open until 1950.

The Second World War had only a limited role in the process of economic transformation in Maidstone. There were hardly any long-term gains in terms of economic restructuring or new industries. But some improvement in social benefits occurred due to wartime conditions and these were carried over into the era of the welfare state. One also perceives the reinforcement of an older sense of community solidarity as the town struggled to pull through amidst the bombs, fears and rationing. However, the large street parties which celebrated VJ (Victory over Japan) Day in 1945 marked the close of an intense period of public patriotism.

Postwar: 1945–1974

The pace of change only gradually gained momentum after the end of the war. The population of the borough (which included the civil parishes of Boughton Monchelsea and Otham incorporated in 1954) increased modestly from 54,035 in 1951 to 59,790 in 1961, an annual growth rate of just over 1 per cent. Growth was mainly a consequence of migration since the rate of natural increase was very small. During the subsequent two decades, however, there was a much more rapid expansion with the addition of 11,197 people in the decade 1961–71 and a further 16,081 in the decade 1971–81, when the population total reached 87,068. Again much of this increase came from immigration which now included small but significant minorities from the Commonwealth countries and the European Community. Growth was accommodated by a further expansion of the town's housing area with much of the new house building taking place on the periphery, either in large municipal housing estates (notably Shepway), smaller private developments (towards Loose and at Allington), or ribbon development along the main roads. Housing needs were never so acute as to justify the high rise building solutions in vogue by the 1950s in the larger cities. Nor was the town faced with the development of large industrial plants, such as occurred in areas of high unemployment in the North. But the character and appearance of the central area was increasingly affected, as in other towns, by commercial redevelopment, office building, and the spread of car parks. On the north-east side of the town, an area of Victorian housing, villas were converted into offices and hotels, gardens converted into car-parks, and Albion Place became an office ghetto. Particularly obtrusive was the eleven-storey office block built by Bader and Miller in 1968 near the junction of High Street and King Street, towering over the upper town.

The town's growth was underpinned by the expansion of local employment opportunities as well as its attractions as a base for commuters. During the immediate post-war years there was already a 'sort of regular clientele going up and down to London by train' (aided by electrification in 1939). The increase in the numbers of residents commuting to work in London was more than balanced in the 1950s by the numbers travelling into Maidstone to work. The census of 1961 showed that just over 32,000 people worked in Maidstone, but the town's working population was a little under 27,000. At this time, the distributive trades were leading employers (over 5,000), followed by public administration and defence (around 4,700), professional services (around 4,200), the bulk of whom were teachers and nurses, and miscellaneous services (around 3,600), the majority employed in the garage trade. But there was still a large industrial workforce with about 8,000 employees (including over 800 women). Food and drink, paper and printing continued to be the largest industrial employers of both men and women, while metal manufacture and engineering, construction and transport all maintained a major economic presence in the town.

During the 1960s, however, the industrial economy came under growing competitive pressure and long-standing Maidstone firms began to go under or became subject to corporate takeovers as big national and multi-national businesses moved into the town. The paper industry in the town declined as activity moved increasingly down the Medway or elsewhere: Lower Tovil Mill closed in the early 1960s and Turkey Mill in 1976. Springfield ceased manufacturing artists' papers in 1962, in order to concentrate on industrial filters and similar products of which it became a major exporter. Much of Maidstone's food and drink industry ceased to prosper from around 1960 and the numbers employed fell significantly. Foster Clark's, badly affected by the arrival of frozen foods, was bought out by Oxo in 1965 after going into receivership. Sharp's enjoyed a brief boom when sweet rationing ended in 1954, but the firm ran into difficulties and merged with Robertson and Woodcock (Trebor). Grant's ceased to be a family business in 1960 and was subsequently taken over by a succession of companies. In brewing, Mason's Waterside brewery closed in 1960 after being taken over by Shepherd Neame of Faversham; the Medway brewery went the same way in 1964, following its earlier acquisition by Courage (who also acquired Maskell's mineral water manufactory);

Fremlins stopped brewing in 1972 having been bought out by Whitbread the previous decade. In the engineering industry, the electrical side remained buoyant, but elsewhere engineering survived mainly by concentrating on the motor trade. Rootes took over Tilling-Stevens in 1950, only to be taken over in turn by Chrysler in 1967. Drake and Fletcher expanded their business, acquired a Jaguar agency, and also remained in agricultural machinery until the Broadway site was sold in the 1970s. W. Weeks, however, closed their agricultural machinery business shortly after 1966. Other industries in decline included the pre-war furniture firms, all of which had shut down by 1960, although one new company, Len Ltd, employed significant numbers of workers at their Water Lane factory. Another exception was James Clifford and Son, the rope and sacking manufacturer, which diversified into floor coverings and travel goods.

However, rates of unemployment remained very low in the post-war town as in the region as a whole. The decline of industrial employment was more than offset by the expansion in wholesale and retail trading and the service sector. In 1960 Jackson and Smith, previously confectionery manufacturers, moved into the business of wholesale grocers, where the old firms of Laurences and Arkcolls still continued to thrive. On the retail side, the Co-op increased its number of stores and there was a continuing influx of chain stores (Sainsbury's opened a supermarket on Gabriel's Hill in the early 1960s, with a devastating effect on many of the small corner shops on the south side of town). The town's importance as a regional shopping centre was reinforced by the economic decline of the Medway towns, and by the 1960s Maidstone could boast as many as three department stores as well as a multitude of old-fashioned and new-style shops, large as well as small specialist establishments. This retailing importance was confirmed somewhat later by the building of the functional Stoneborough Centre (1974–6). Employment in the service sector benefited from the expansion of local government as Maidstone consolidated its position as the headquarters of the Kent County Council. After fairly limited growth in the post-war years the early 1960s saw the rapid growth of council departments, with some powers being taken from district councils. The planning, education and road departments in particular saw a major increase of staff and there were important extensions to council offices at Springfield in 1957 and 1961–5; in 1964 a large new County Library was opened there, replacing the maze of old huts previously used. Other county agencies maintained or enlarged facilities in and about the town including the Kent Fire Service (with its new headquarters at Tovil in 1950), and the Kent County Constabulary on Sutton Road, to mention two of the most important.

There was also a major expansion of office work available in government employment. The establishment of the National Health Service in 1948 and other elements of the welfare state led to the proliferation of local bodies such as the Kent and Canterbury Executive Council of the NHS. There was also additional work in the offices of the newly nationalised electricity and gas boards (the town's electricity works were taken over in 1947, the gas company in 1948). If the number of banks declined, building societies multiplied, particularly on the High Street, while insurance was a particularly dynamic sector with 48 branch offices and 11 brokers by 1960. In the longer term medical services were boosted by the arrival of the NHS, though in the 1950s expenditure on preventive medicine in Kent, as elsewhere, entered a period of decline.

Another factor offsetting the decline in industrial employment was the growth in opportunities for female employment. Most striking in this period was the growth in married women's employment, especially in part-time work: by 1971 66 per cent of the female labour force was married. If local employment in several sectors continued to expand, commuting became increasingly common. Nor was this simply a white collar exodus of office workers and civil servants going to London, since the men who travelled to work elsewhere included paper and other industrial workers. Many of those who came to swell the town's population in the 1960s may have been employed outside Maidstone.

The scale of growth was bound to put pressure on housing, although the housing shortage was more acute in the aftermath of the war than subsequently. The virtual cessation of house building during the war and the number of homeless or inadequately housed people, many of whom occupied the recently vacated army huts in Mote Park and on the Boxley Road, contributed to what seemed at the time a crisis in housing supply. The major council house building effort was concentrated on the Shepway estate, by far the largest of the new housing areas in post-war Maidstone. In February 1951 the one thousandth council house erected since the war was completed, a rate of house building not exceeded by any other district in the south east except Brighton. In the five post-war years 1945–50 the council erected 932 houses compared with 264 in the private sector. These included the pre-fabricated Easiform houses erected on the Shepway estate by Gough Cooper and Co. Ltd, as well as conventional two and three bedroom houses and some small-scale blocks of flats.

Despite the building effort, in September 1951 there were still 2,483 applicants on the housing list, plus 176 applicants for the planned old people's flats. During this period the council had to keep to government housing allocations which were well under the numbers calculated as necessary by the housing committee. The committee proposed 600 houses a year, a number based on the assumption that additional houses were needed for an expanding labour market as well as to replace older property and to accommodate the normal increase in population. Such thinking influenced the markedly expanded house building programme of the 1950s, which was also affected by the designation of slum clearance areas after the Housing Act of 1957. By May 1961 the Shepway estate numbered 2,409 houses, increasing the population of the Shepway ward to 15,337, almost double that of the second most populous area, North ward. In addition, a new development was started around the first of the trading estates at Park Wood, with the building of a further 408 houses. By this time private house building was making a bigger contribution, although applications to build beyond the borough boundaries were frequently turned down because of the provisions in the Kent Development Plan for maintaining a natural green belt around the town. In 1961 there were 17,834 dwellings in the town of which only 7,870 were owner-occupied, underlining the scale of council house building in the post-war period. This situation was reversed in the next decade with the surge of white collar and professional people in the town. The great private house building boom of the 1960s, mainly on the outskirts of the town (with a good number of smaller developments and infilling), came to eclipse the rented sector; by 1971 52 per cent of dwellings in the town were owner-occupied and only 29 per cent rented from the council with 19 per cent in the privately rented sector.

This large accession of new accommodation meant that overcrowding was never more than a minor problem in Maidstone and, no less significantly, it contributed to the improved quality of housing in the town. Between 1961 and 1971, for example, the number of households lacking hot water on tap fell from 30 per cent to 8 per cent, and those without a fixed bath or shower declined from 21 to 9 per cent. In 1971 only forty houses were still without a WC, although 12 per cent of houses were still reliant on outside toilets. The highest overall standards were in council houses and the majority of defective houses were concentrated in the privately rented sector.

Though new housing, mainly on the outskirts, contributed to an enhanced life-style for many inhabitants, it also aggravated the traffic problems of the town, already noticeable by 1940, with growing congestion in the centre. Council motor bus services were expanded after the war and from 1958 to 1967 a trolley bus service was in operation to the Shepway estate. Motor bus services subsequently took over but increasingly people preferred to travel to work by car: 38.9 per cent of the employed population did this in 1971, while another 1.7 per cent used motor-cycles. Only 22.4 per cent used buses and 6.2 per cent travelled by train, probably those who commuted to London. As car use grew, road building and improvement became a council priority along with traffic circulation and car parking. The long-delayed Maidstone by-pass was finally opened in 1963 to keep coastal traffic out of the town and a ring road scheme also emerged that decade, but this was held up by prolonged disputes with the Ministry of Transport which had its own plans for redirecting traffic. The building of the first multi-storey car park in Medway Street was undertaken in the early 1960s setting a precedent which eventually had a disruptive impact on the townscape.

Town expansion also created further pressure for church and school building. In the former case the widening of the borough boundaries and the provision of churches on new estates brought the number of Anglican churches to fourteen with a further church, Christ Church opened in Wallis Avenue by 1966. In addition, the town had nineteen nonconformist churches, including some new denominations. The long-term decline in church and chapel attendance eventually led to the closure of a number of churches but this did not occur until the 1970s. The provision of new schools (especially at the primary level), along with other welfare services, were a high priority during the post-war years, although these were now the responsibility of Kent County Council rather than the borough. The largest of the new schools were the Shepway County Infant and Junior schools built in 1950–1 for over a thousand children. Another major new school complex was envisaged after 1944 with the purchase of Oakwood Park, a site of 120 acres intended for primary and secondary schools and a county college. In 1950 the new Maidstone Technical Institute was opened there. Elsewhere in the town, several of the old council schools were upgraded into county secondary schools, one for each part of the borough. But the county council was resistant to the developing pressure for comprehensive education at the secondary level, in part because of its long-standing emphasis on technical education exemplified by the Maidstone County Technical schools, with the girls' school in Albion Place and the boys' school on Tonbridge Road. Even when comprehensive education was introduced after the 1964 government circular the grammar schools were not affected.

The political and social life of the town was also changing rapidly in the 1960s. At the parliamentary level, the constituency remained loyally Conservative, with large majorities returned for successive Conservative MPs (Sir Alfred Bossom took Maidstone with a comfortable majority even during the Labour party landslide of 1945). This penchant for Conservatism was underpinned by the large rural electorate and continuing prosperity in the town. A similar pattern obtained in local elections with the Conservatives maintaining control of the council, with the growth of the Liberals in the 1960s being mainly at the expense of Labour. On the other hand, local social and political leadership was affected by the passing of the old family firms and elite families. There was still scope for individual gestures on the part of the wealthier inhabitants, however, as evidenced by the donations of land by the Moncktons and the offer of Boughton Mount for use as a special school by Mrs Foster Clark. Sir Garrard Tyrwhitt-Drake was another notable benefactor, opening his private collection of carriages to the public in 1946, and on his death in 1964 leaving Cobtree Manor to the public – the zoo had been closed in 1959, and the manor was eventually converted by the council into a Museum of Kent Life. But increasingly the well to do not only preferred to live outside the town but tended to pursue their social and political ambitions elsewhere. On the council itself, there was remarkable continuity in council membership up to the mid-1950s. In 1951–2, for example, the mayor, C. Gordon Larking, an accountant, and all the aldermen, including William Day junior of the long-standing firm of surveyors, had all sat on the 1938 council; but in 1961 this no longer applied, and the aldermen and most of the councillors of 1951 had been replaced. Party politics pervaded council elections and debates more and more. This continued after local government reorganisation in 1974 when the borough council was reconstituted with the merger with the rural district council. In some respects 1974 saw the most important structural changes in the corporation since the royal charter of 1549. The spatial jurisdiction of the town was massively extended to include a good part of its economic hinterland and the non-elected aldermen, descendants of the Tudor bench of jurats, finally

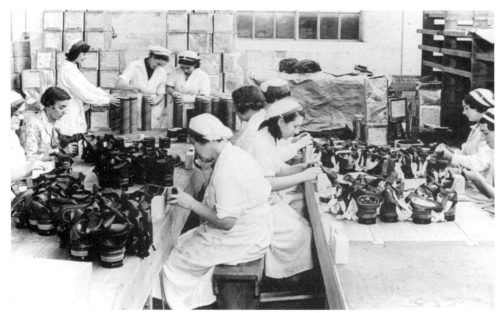

Women assembling gas masks and munitions at Tilling-Stevens during the Second World War.
Photograph: Kent Messenger Group Newspapers.

Reading the casualty list during the Second World War.
Photograph: Kent Messenger Group Newspapers.

The mayor and corporation returning from All Saints through bomb-devastated Mill Street, November 1940.
Photograph: Kent Messenger Group Newspapers.

A street party to celebrate VJ Day.
Photograph: Maidstone Museum.

Aerial view of industrial Maidstone, c. 1960.
Photograph: Kent Messenger Group Newspapers.

Aerial view of the Shepway Estate, c. 1960.
Photograph: Kent Messenger Group Newspapers.

The Regal cinema after its closure in 1957.
Photograph: Kent Messenger Group Newspapers.

disappeared. However, there was considerable continuity in regard to the division of administrative functions with the county council, the new borough council continuing to exercise responsibility for a range of local services, notably housing and local planning. In terms of administrative functions, the most important changes had occurred during and after the Second World War with the borough losing its police powers in 1943, educational responsibilities in 1944, fire service in 1948, and its medical officer of health and other medical and welfare functions the same year.

Some of the old traditions persisted in the social life of the town, and concerts and other musical performances were organised by bodies like the Maidstone Choral Society. The Corn Exchange concert hall became the municipal theatre (subsequently called the Hazlitt) in 1955. Nevertheless, the social world of the town, including its public entertainments, was affected by the general migration of leisure activity from the public and commercial arena into the home – a phenomenon taking place across Britain during this period. The advent of television depressed cinema audiences in Maidstone as elsewhere, and by 1961 only two cinemas remained of the five open in 1945. Old-style dance-halls also suffered eclipse.

Maidstone's post-war history deserves detailed research and study in its own right and can only be sketched in this chapter. But the watershed decade for the town seems to have been the 1960s, which was decisive both in terms of changes in its social makeup and in the remodelling of its central area. The most important feature of this decade, however, was the pressure on the local industrial economy; though unlike towns and cities which relied predominantly on industrial employment, this situation did not affect Maidstone's prosperity. Indeed the 1960s and 1970s were characterised by the paradox of an exceptional rate of population growth even though the industrial base of the local economy was in decline. This was a consequence of the way that Maidstone had become increasingly a satellite of London, while maintaining and consolidating its administrative and service role as a county town and expanding its economic position as a regional shopping and trading centre.

Maidstone in perspective

This book has told the story of how Maidstone became the county town of Kent and as such one of the most successful towns in the county. Though the status of county town was in part self-promotional rhetoric, the town's recognition as the county town attracted growing fashionable and lucrative gentry patronage in the seventeenth and eighteenth centuries, underpinning its regional status, while the arrival of the Kent Council Council in the 1890s ensured a powerful boost to the urban economy. At the same time, as we have seen, Maidstone's development as the county town was by no means inevitable. Maidstone was a relative late-comer in medieval Kent, emerging in the twelfth century after many of the other important towns were established. Even in the fourteenth and fifteenth centuries this small archiepiscopal market town had a countrified air, with much of the parish given over to agriculture and a limited range of trades and urban institutions; only the large ecclesiastical complex focused around All Saints distinguished the town. But its strategic trading position on the Medway was to prove increasingly important from the close of the Middle Ages as the West Kent and Wealden economies expanded and regional commerce developed, while the securing of the royal charter in 1549 proved decisive in ensuring the town's municipal institutions and civic leadership. As we have seen, Maidstone's later achievements owe much to the imaginative work of the town's Elizabethan and Jacobean rulers in gaining the support of county landowners and consolidating the town's position as a major administrative centre for the shire. Without a long ingrained tradition of civic autonomy, Maidstone may have found it easier to accommodate the demands and conceits of prickly and pretentious county gentry than other ancient boroughs in the shire; though even here relations with local gentry were tense during the 1620s. After the Restoration, though, good relations with county landowners helped underpin the town's growing reputation as the county town which was also boosted by marketing and the distinctive development of specialist consumer industries. In the eighteenth century Maidstone seemed to be in the mainstream of English urbanisation, one of the most prosperous provincial towns not only in Kent but in southern England.

The Victorian era, however, steadily revealed the limits of the town's importance as a county town. The town's rate of growth though significant in historic terms lagged behind that of more specialist industrial towns and cities in the Midlands and the North. Thus Leicester which had 46,000 inhabitants in 1831 – two-and-a-half times Maidstone's figure – had 212,000 in 1901 – more than six times that of the Kentish town. Other towns in those regions had even more spectacular rates of growth. Urbanisation by itself is no prescription for collective happiness and, as we argued in Chapter Seven, Maidstone's slow rate of growth may have helped it escape some of the worst environmental, social and class problems of the bigger cities, but by the later nineteenth century sluggish growth may have hampered attempts to modernise the town's image and amenities. Some of the local reasons for Maidstone's slow advance in this period have been identified. But it is important also to see this from a regional perspective. In 1901 no inland town in the south east of England (outside the metropolitan area) had populations of more than 100,000 people and only three in the South East as a whole (Southampton, Portsmouth and Brighton) exceeded that figure; this compares with thirty-two urban centres across Britain. Though fierce industrial competition from other regions and the heavy reliance of the South East on an uncertain agrarian economy played their part, another factor no doubt was the powerful impact of the metropolis. Metropolitan growth in the eighteenth and nineteenth centuries continued to rely heavily on immigration from the Home Counties, while London commerce and industry provided tough competition for smaller urban centres in the region. As we have seen repeatedly in this study, London from the sixteenth century onwards afforded a variety of economic opportunities for Maidstone but it also set the parameters of expansion.

Among the middle-rank towns of the south east, however, there was no uniform pattern of urbanisation in the early modern and modern period. A number of ancient centres such as Colchester, Winchester and of course Canterbury, were unable to maintain their earlier importance, in part at least due to urban competition, with Buckingham affected by the rise of Aylesbury, Winchester by Portsmouth and Canterbury by Maidstone. County towns such as Aylesbury and Chelmsford, though enjoying considerable rates of growth in the nineteenth and twentieth centuries, failed to achieve the population levels of other major county towns, possibly due to their lack of incorporation in the earlier period. A limited number of middle-rank towns in the Home Counties benefited from the success of specialist industries – thus Reading (a biscuit town), Oxford (from the 1920s motor cars) and Maidstone (with brewing, paper and later food manufacture and engineering). In the struggle against urban rivals, early incorporation, county town status and a diversified economy including specialist industries all helped, though civic policy and other local circumstances were also influential. Despite its Georgian affluence, Maidstone's growth rate in the nineteenth century was only towards the middle of the spectrum for county towns in the region. During the inter-war years, however, as we noted in Chapter Nine, Maidstone with its thriving industries, shops, services and county council offices moved into the top flight of expanding towns in the South East.

Growth rates provide a necessary but not a sufficient explanation of urban development. More significant and interesting perhaps is the way that towns managed their economic progress or decline and sought to create and reshape their communal identity accordingly. In late medieval Maidstone, and many other smaller provincial towns, wealthier inhabitants sought to establish their own urban identity apart from the ecclesiastical authorities through communal religious and social institutions such as guilds and fraternities. After the Reformation the new communal emphasis in Maidstone was on a Protestant commonwealth associated with the grammar school, moral reformation, and a Puritan magistracy; here there were affinities with other larger godly cities like Gloucester or Coventry. But Maidstone as we know always maintained better relations with its local landowners than many other English cities and in the century after the Glorious Revolution of 1688 this relationship fructified in Maidstone's cultural renaissance as a genteel county town, where gentry, professional men, local merchants and manufacturers might celebrate their prosperity with a cocktail of metropolitan-style social and leisure entertainments. This new image of urbanity was always somewhat artificial, however, failing to embrace the large majority of lower-class inhabitants and dependent in part at least on county patronage, which increasingly subsided after 1800. In the Victorian era one sees the emergence of a more distinctly urban bourgeois culture and identity more heavily associated with religion, philanthropy and voluntary action. But the new vision in turn had only limited success in incorporating the lower classes into a sense of urban community. By the late nineteenth century it was increasingly influenced and fragmented by a new raft of commercial leisure entertainments, inspired by national and international fashion and appealing in particular to the working classes with their rising living standards.

In the early twentieth century the pressures of accelerating changes in the townscape and greater economic growth created new problems of urban identity. But up to the Second World War many of the established features of town life survived – some indeed reinforced by the war: a sense of communal solidarity, the stability of old family firms, the continuity of middle-class social leadership, the ancient urban palimpsest of private and public buildings in the heart of the town (not badly affected by bombing), and an active town council. As we suggested above, the post-war period marked a turning point in the town's communal history: as the urban economy (especially in the 1960s) moved away from established industries towards a greater dependence on services and commuting; as outside agencies (central government, the county council) intruded on the autonomy and activity of the town council; and as rapid housing development along with the massive environmental problems spawned by the motor car began to disrupt the old physical coherence of the town (here British towns seem to have been more vulnerable than most continental cities). These and other challenges have continued unabated in the last quarter of the twentieth century. As in the past they require a strong communal response – to proclaim a strong sense of civic consciousness and historical awareness of a community with nearly eight hundred years of continuous urban history, which is manifested still (despite the damaging work of developers) by the handsome array of public and commercial buildings in the upper High Street, the dusty line of seventeenth- and eighteenth-century houses in Lower Stone Street, and the ragstone splendour of the Archbishop's Palace, the old college, and All Saints. One hopes that this book, like Russell's work a hundred years ago, will serve to explain why an understanding of Maidstone's history is important to its townspeople – and also to the wider world.

Notes

1. Public Record Office, HLG 7/60, P.P. Cooper to Roundell, 7 October 1938 (we are indebted to Dr John Welshman for this reference); Maidstone Borough Council minutes, 1939 (Centre for Kentish Studies [Kent Archives Office], Md/ACm3/42); *Kent Messenger*, 11 May 1945.
2. Maidstone Borough Council minutes, 1939–43 (Centre for Kentish Studies, Md/ACm3/42–46).

Bibliographical Note

As already noted, this chapter is intended to give only an outline of developments in the town after 1939. The *Kent Messenger* has been used extensively, though it was greatly reduced in size and local coverage during the war years. Trade and street directories have been used, along with Maidstone borough council minutes, official government publications and oral testimonies. Elizabeth Melling's *History of Kent County Council* (Maidstone, 1975) was valuable.

APPENDIX

Tables

Source for Tables 1–7: Published Census Returns

TABLE 1

Overall Population Trends

	Births	**Deaths**	**Excess of births over deaths**	**Population growth**	**Net increase/ decrease by migration**
1841–50	6,369	4,695	1,674	2,719	+1,045
1851–60	6,776	5,240	1,536	2,276	+ 740
1861–70	8,079	5,957	2,122	3,180	+1,058
1871–80	9,003	6,482	2,521	3,427	+ 906
1881–90	9,503	6,197	3,306	2,522	− 784
1891–1900	8,199	7,042	1,157	1,370	+ 213
1901–10	7,998	6,354	1,644	1,959	+ 315

TABLE 2

Birthplace of Inhabitants 1851 and 1951

Birthplace	1851	1951
	%	%
Kent	81.0	67.0
London	5.0	6.0
Adjacent Home Counties[1]	4.0	6.0
Northern Counties[2]	1.0	4.0
Other English Counties	6.0	7.0
Ireland, Scotland, Wales, Islands	2.0	3.0
Overseas	0.5	7.0[3]

1. Surrey, Sussex, Middlesex, Essex.
2. Northumberland, Durham, Cumberland, Westmorland, Lancashire, Yorkshire, Cheshire.
3. Of these 2,478 (64 per cent) were British Nationals.

TABLE 3

Male Employment by Sectors 1851 and 1911

Occupations	1851	1911
Building, Quarrying, etc.	467	1,261
Agriculture	770	592
Transport	426	1,349
Services	393	1,410
Wholesale/Retail Trade[1]	1,674	2,346
Food Manufacturing/Tobacco/Drink/Lodging[2]	–	1,571
Manufacturing	443	2,269
General/Factory Labourers	–	437
Other Occupations	–	764

1. Figures inflated by inclusion of food workers. The 1851 figure also includes craftsmen-retailers.
2. Figure for 1851 underestimated because of the inclusion of craftsmen-retailers and small manufacturers in wholesale/retail trades.

TABLE 4

Main Service and Industrial Employments (Males) 1851 and 1911

Service Employments	1851	1911
Professional and Subordinate	173	393
Banking/Insurance/Accountants	97	293
Clerks	17	344
Local/Central Government	106	380

Industrial Employments

Paper	257	497
Stationery/Printing/Lithography	70	300
Brewing/Mineral Water/Distilling[1]	63	172
Food Processing[2]	–	351
Metals/Engineering/Vehicles	142	574
Engineering/Millwrights	47	364
Iron/Brass/Foundry	39	–
Miscellaneous Metal	56	45
Electrical Apparatus	–	56
Vehicle Manufacture	–	109

1.   Understated: some employees listed elsewhere.
2.   No category in 1851.

TABLE 5

Main Employments (Occupied Females) 1851 and 1911

Industrial Employments	**1851**	**1911**
Paper	389	425
Stationery/Printing	1	144
Food Processing[1]	–	357
Total Industrial	389	866
Service Industries[2]	159	606
Domestic Service/Charwomen/Laundry	1,387	1,850
Wholesale/Retail Trade	629	1,629

1.   No category in 1851.
2.   Includes teachers and nurses.

TABLE 6

Male Employment By Sectors 1911–51
(Estimated Percentage Of Employed Workforce[1])

	1911 %	1921 %	1931 %	1951 %
Manufacturing	30.0[2]	31.7	36.0	34.7
Service Industries/Commerce	27.0	25.0	30.1	35.1
Transport Communications	12.3	12.2	11.9	8.8
Building	11.5	5.2[3]	9.1	11.0
Agriculture /Extractive	8.5	7.0	5.7	2.4
Personal Service	4.1	2.9	3.1	1.0
Labourers	–	8.5	–	–

1. The percentage of the total workforce represented by these figures was: 93.0 per cent 1911, 91.6 per cent 1921, 99.6 per cent 1931, 93.0 per cent 1951.
2. Estimated: the census did not differentiate between manufacture and commerce in the food and drink trades.
3. Understated: some of the category of labourers should be included with this.

TABLE 7

Female Employment By Sectors 1911–51
(Estimated Percentages Of Employed Workforce)

	1911 %	1921 %	1931 %	1951 %
Manufacturing	32.7	25.4	22.2	24.2
Service Industries/Commerce'	22.1	39.4	40.2	62.4
Personal Service	40.6	28.3	34.5	7.5

1. Includes professional, white collar workers, clerks, etc.

Index